Applying
the Humanities

THE HASTINGS CENTER SERIES IN ETHICS

A Continuation Order Plan is available for this series. A continuation order will bring delivery of each new volume immediately upon publication. Volumes are billed only upon actual shipment. For further information please contact the publisher.

Applying the Humanities

Edited by
DANIEL CALLAHAN
ARTHUR L. CAPLAN
and
BRUCE JENNINGS

The Hastings Center
Institute of Society, Ethics and the Life Sciences
Hastings-on-Hudson, New York

PLENUM PRESS • NEW YORK AND LONDON

Library of Congress Cataloging in Publication Data

Main entry under title:

Applying the humanities.

   (The Hastings Center series in ethics)
   Bibliography: p.
   Includes index.
   1. Humanities—Moral and ethical aspects—Addresses, essays, lectures. 2.
Ethics—Addresses, essays, lectures. I. Callahan, Daniel, 1930–   . II. Caplan, Arthur
L. III. Jennings, Bruce, 1949–   . IV. Series.
AZ103.A42 1985   001.3   85-9479
ISBN 0-306-41968-8

© 1985 The Hastings Center
Institute of Society, Ethics and the Life Sciences
360 Broadway
Hastings-on-Hudson, New York 10706

Plenum Press is a division of
Plenum Publishing Corporation
233 Spring Street, New York, N.Y. 10013

Printed in the United States of America

Contributors

Robert L. Belknap is Professor of Russian at Columbia University, where he has served as Acting Dean of the College and Director of the Russian Institute. A Dostoevsky scholar, he has also published numerous articles on literary theory and undergraduate general education.

Robert N. Bellah is Ford Professor of Sociology and Comparative Studies and Vice Chairman of the Center for Japanese Studies at the University of California, Berkeley. His publications include *Varieties of Civil Religion, The New Religious Consciousness,* and a collaborative study of American values entitled *Habits of the Heart.*

Daniel Callahan, a philosopher by training, is Director of The Hastings Center. His recent books include *Ethics in Hard Times* and *Abortion: Understanding Differences.* A cofounder of the Hastings Center, he is also an elected member of the Institute of Medicine, National Academy of Science.

Arthur L. Caplan, a philosopher by training, is Associate Director of The Hastings Center. His publications include *The Sociobiology Debate, Concepts of Health and Disease, Ethics in Hard Times,* and numerous articles on applied ethics and the philosophy of science.

Eric J. Cassell is Clinical Professor of Public Health and Director of the Program for the Study of Ethics and Values in Medicine at Cornell University Medical College. His publications include *The Healer's Art, Talking with Patients,* and numerous articles on medical ethics and the theory of clinical medicine.

Otis L. Graham, Jr. is Distinguished University Professor of History at the University of North Carolina, Chapel Hill. His most recent book is *Toward a Planned Society: From Roosevelt to Nixon.*

Kathryn Montgomery Hunter, a literary critic by training, is Assistant Professor of Humanities in Medicine at the University of Rochester. She has written widely on English literature, the graphic arts, and the role of literary studies in medical education.

Bruce Jennings, a political theorist by training, is Associate for Policy Studies at The Hastings Center. His publications include *Ethics, the Social Sciences, and Policy Analysis*, and *Darwin, Marx and Freud: Their Influence on Moral Theory*.

Bruce Kuklick is Professor of History at the University of Pennsylvania. His books include *The Rise of American Philosophy* and *Churchmen and Philosophers: From Jonathan Edwards to John Dewey, 1746–1934*.

Edwin T. Layton, Jr. is Professor of the History of Science and Technology at the University of Minnesota. His publications include *Revolt of the Engineers: Social Responsibility and the American Engineering Profession*, *The Dynamics of Science and Technology*, and numerous articles on the history of technology.

David Little is Professor of Religious Studies at the University of Virginia. His books include *Religion, Order, and Law* and *Comparative Religious Ethics*.

Ruth Macklin, a philosopher by training, is Associate Professor of Community Health and a bioethics consultant at Albert Einstein College of Medicine. Her publications include *Man, Mind, and Morality: The Ethics of Behavior Control* and *Moral Problems in Medicine*.

Mark Crispin Miller directs the Film Study Program in the Department of Writing Seminars at the Johns Hopkins University. His publications include articles on literature and cultural criticism, and he writes on television programming and advertising for *The New Republic*.

Fred Nicklason is Assistant Professor of History at the University of Maryland, College Park. As a public historian and consultant, he has written numerous expert witness reports for court cases involving American Indian tribes.

Martha C. Nussbaum is Associate Professor of Philosophy and Classics at Brown University. Her publications include *Aristotle's De Motu Animalium*, *The Fragility of Goodness: Luck and Ethics in Greek Tragedy and Philosophy*, and numerous articles on philosophy, ethics, and literature.

Bruce L. Payne is Director of the Program in the Humanities, Policy, and the Arts at the Institute of Policy Sciences and Public Affairs, Duke University. His publications include *Ethical Dilemmas and the Education of Policymakers* and several articles on ethics and public policy.

Kenneth Prewitt, a political scientist, is President of the Social Science Research Council and has taught at Stanford University, Columbia University, and the University of Chicago. His books include *The Recruitment of Political Leaders, Labyrinths of Democracy,* and *Introduction to American Government.*

J. B. Schneewind is Professor and Chairman of the Philosophy Department at the Johns Hopkins University. His most recent book is *Sedgwick's Ethics and Victorian Moral Philosophy.*

Peter N. Stearns is Heinz Professor of History and Co-Director of the Program of Applied History at Carnegie-Mellon University. His applied historical work has focused on problems of old age and retirement, including social security policy. He is author of *Old Age in European Society* and *European Society in Upheaval.*

Conflict in the Humanities:

① Food for the Soul

or

② Application in the Marketplace

Contents

ix

Introduction

For well over a decade now, a large number of those trained in the humanities have sought to take their learning and their perspectives out of the academy and into the market place. Some have done this by shifting the focus of their scholarship from technical issues characteristic of their discipline to matters of general public and social concern. Some have left the academy altogether and work as humanists in settings as diverse as hospitals, legislatures, and corporations. Whichever course they may take, however, their choice of a vocational direction poses some distinct challenges to modern American notions of the proper scope and role of the humanities.

Is there a place for the humanities outside of the university or classroom? If so, what might it be? Are questions of medical ethics, or the making of welfare or criminal justice policy, or the logic of nuclear deterrence, appropriate topics for someone with training in the humanities? If the humanities do have a contribution to make to such issues, how does it differ from that of other fields? What is the distinctive contribution of the humanities to such issues?

This book is a collection of essays that tries systematically to explore such questions. The papers commissioned for this book grew out of a project organized by The Hastings Center and supported by a grant from the National Endowment for the Humanities (NEH). Over the years The Hastings Center has worked back and forth between the sciences and the humanities in addressing and analyzing ethical questions in the biomedical sciences and the professions. A persistent issue has been the legitimacy of humanists' exploring areas once left to scientific researchers and clinical practitioners. If those from the sciences have often asked skeptical questions in that respect, many of those from the humanities have found some of their humanistic colleagues no less doubtful. For its part, the NEH has been a central actor in the American humanities since the mid-1960s. It has had to define the nature of the humanities in order to do its work and it has thus been caught up in many of the same debates and controversies as the field itself.

The project addressed two related issues. Does it make sense to speak of an "applied" humanities? What ought to be the role of the humanities in issues of public and social policy? The point of asking the first question—and being thus forced to use the less than felicitous term *applied*—was to see to what extent and in what way the methods and perspectives of the humanities could be brought to bear on practical as distinguished from theoretical problems. And the practical problems we had in mind were essentially those that can be called social or policy issues. Over the course of the project we noted quick, almost instinctive responses to both questions. On the one hand, there was a snap assertion that of course the humanities could be applied; indeed, they were of their nature meant for application and thus it was simply redundant to talk of an applied humanities. On the other hand, there was an equally ready assertion that the humanities were not meant for direct application to practical problems and that they most decidedly do not belong in the rough-and-tumble arena of politics and policy. It is not that they have nothing to say in such matters; it is only that their task is to probe those deeper human issues and to frame those larger questions that ultimately underlie and shape the more immediate pragmatic and policy dilemmas.

If many came to our project with ready responses of that kind, they more often than not went away chastened. Both the history of the humanities and the conceptual problems posed by the notion of application in the humanities made it increasingly difficult to see any straight path through the thicket of issues we encountered. The organizational plan of the book represents the way in which we tried to understand the range of problems posed by the idea of applying the humanities.

We had to understand, first of all, the history of the humanities. That history made clear that the questions we raised about the humanities—questions that had seemed to us at first to be utterly new—were as old as the Greek roots of the humanities in Western culture. Martha Nussbaum's paper explores those roots and shows that the question of the public and social role of the humanities was there from the very beginning. David Little takes up the story in the Renaissance and Reformation, tracing the modern lines of our present struggle. Bruce Kuklick concentrates his attention on the way in which the contemporary humanities became professionalized, that is, organized along tight disciplinary lines and for the most part restricted to the confines of the university. That recent history, he believes, helps to explain some of the wariness that is often the spontaneous reaction within the academy to the idea of taking the humanities beyond its borders.

One historically important item that quickly caught our eye was the fact that the great intellectual and cultural power of the sciences stems in part from the happy marriage of theoretical and practical interests. Although basic research has always occupied a most prestigious place in the sciences, there has nevertheless always been a high regard for those engineers and other technologists who apply theory to the needs of society. Is there something that the humanities can learn from that experience? That is the question Edwin T. Layton tries to answer. Jerome B. Schneewind, reflecting on the unhappily scant sociological knowledge about the humanities and those who work within them, looks at the recent outburst of work in "applied ethics" as a case study in the possible function of application in one important field of philosophy.

The next section of the book takes up more directly the possible role of the humanities in public policy. Daniel Callahan explores the various meanings of public policy and, borrowing from recent work in the social sciences, proposes a set of possible models of the public policy–humanities relationship. Robert N. Bellah's paper focuses on the possible role of the humanities as a source of social vision. He is concerned, moreover, with the place of tradition in our public life and the ambivalence of much contemporary work in the humanities toward the idea of tradition. Bellah's paper provides a pertinent backdrop to the contribution of Bruce Jennings and Kenneth Prewitt. They argue that a new rapprochement between the humanities and the social sciences offers the possibility of combining the ingredients necessary for a fresh public philosophy. Mark Miller's essay, no less sensitive to the need for a public philosophy, concentrates on the humanities and the media; for better or worse, the latter have now become a principal means by which common cultural ideas and images (or the lack thereof) are transmitted to the general public.

The papers by Eric Cassell and Bruce Payne examine the way in which the humanities can make a contribution to two important fields, the biomedical sciences and the policy sciences. Both fields, they note, have a recent history and tradition that often works against a role for the humanities. But both fields, for that very same reason, have a pressing need to integrate the humanities if they are to carry out their own work properly. Not only can the humanities be applied in those fields, they *must* be so applied if each field is to achieve its own fundamental aims.

The next section of the book considers a critical problem that must be confronted by those who would press for an applied humanities. What ought to be the proper academic and intellectual standards for such an enterprise? Peter Stearns, Fred Nicklason, and Otis L. Graham, Jr., consider that question within the field of history. Ruth Macklin, in turn, responds within the context of philosophy, and Kathryn Montgomery Hunter does the same for literature. Finally, to conclude the volume Robert L. Belknap reflects upon the project and issues as a whole and provides some general insights on the task that occupied us.

As a group, the authors worked together for a period of two years, taking part in some six extended meetings. They commented upon each other's papers and worked long and hard to bring coherence to a subject fraught with incoherence, misunderstanding, and confusion. This book is a companion volume to a previously published report from The Hastings Center, *On the Uses of the Humanities: Vision and Application* (Hastings-on-Hudson, New York: The Hastings Center, 1984).

This book was made possible by a grant from the National Endowment for the Humanities. We would like to thank the Endowment and in particular Arnita Jones, the NEH program officer who worked closely with us on this project for their support and encouragement. Special thanks are also due to Ellen McAvoy, Mary Gualandi, and Eva Mannheimer for their skillful and good-humored editorial and typing assistance.

DANIEL CALLAHAN
ARTHUR L. CAPLAN
BRUCE JENNINGS

PART I

The Changing Shape of the Humanities

CHAPTER 1

Historical Conceptions of the Humanities and Their Relationship to Society

MARTHA C. NUSSBAUM

I begin with two contrasting stories told by Greek philosophers about the role of the philosopher and philosophical study in their society. Both stories are told about Thales, a legendary figure around whose name gathered all sorts of stories pertaining to current conceptions of "the wise man" or of intellectual activity generally. The first is told by Plato:

> While Thales was observing the stars, o Theodorus, and gazing upwards, it is said that he fell into a well; and a witty and attractive Thracian servant girl made fun of him, saying that he was eager to know the things in the sky, but that what was behind him and just by his feet escaped his notice.[1]

The second is told by Aristotle, also about Thales:

> For when they reproached him because of his poverty, saying that philosophy was of no use, they say that, having observed through his study of the heavenly bodies that there would be a large olive-crop, he raised a little capital while it was still winter, and paid deposits on all the olive presses in Miletus and Chios, hiring them cheaply because no one bid against him. When the appropriate time came there was a sudden rush of requests for the presses. He then hired them out on his own terms and so made a large profit, thus demonstrating that it is easy for philosophers to be rich, if they wish, but that it is not this that they care about.[2]

These stories will serve to set the stage for my project, which will be to examine some ancient Greek conceptions of the relationship between

---

[1]*Theaetetus* 174A.
[2]*Politics* 1259a6 ff, trans. G. Kirk.

MARTHA C. NUSSBAUM ● Departments of Philosophy and Classics, Brown University, Providence, Rhode Island 02912.

certain sorts of intellectual activity and the practical life of the city, asking what light these views shed on our contemporary questions. And we can begin to orient ourselves within this culture's debates about the proper role of the intellectual vis-à-vis the city if we notice two interesting facts about the pair of anecdotes. They are, in a sense, contrasting stories. The first one depicts the intellectual as a figure whose lofty pursuits have made him incompetent to deal with simple practical matters; the second shows us that he can be very competent when he wants to be— indeed, that he can be all the more competent in practical matters because of his intellectual pursuits. If he neglects the practical, then, it is a matter of choice. But the two stories have, as well, certain shared features. First, they both assume that there is a problem in the intellectual's relationship to practical affairs: he is vulnerable to the charge of being too cut off from the practical. It is a serious and a legitimate charge against him that his pursuits are of no practical use. The first story takes the charge to be justified, and the philosopher, therefore, to be a silly character. The second story shows the philosopher going to a great deal of trouble to refute the charge and triumphantly succeeding. In neither case does anyone suggest that the charge is in some way misconceived or illegitimate. Second, however, the two stories both show us that the philosopher finds in his intellectual pursuits some sort of value other than a strictly instrumental value. In the first, he seems to care for what he is doing in a way that makes no reference to its usefulness; the second tells us that, although he can turn his studies to a useful purpose, he cares about something else.

In my discussion of the period of Greek thought between Thales and Epicurus, I shall be pursuing these two leads. My general question will be: How did a culture that inaugurated, in the Western tradition, serious reflection about intellectual study and its relationship to the practical, conceive of that relationship? Or, to use the language of this tradition, what did the ancient Greek philosophers and poets say about the contribution of intellectual study to the good life for a human being? And how might an understanding of their debates help us to make progress on our contemporary issues?

Two distinctions will be crucial for our articulation of the question. The first is the distinction between the good of the individual and the good of a larger social unit of which individuals are members. For the Greeks it was always very important, as I shall later argue that it is for us, to ask whether the end of a form of inquiry was public or private; I shall suggest that their way of pursuing this question is a good guide for our contemporary discussions as well.

The second distinction is less obvious. I shall be speaking of the relationship between intellectual and philosophical study and the good life for a human being, between research and the fullness of human activity. There are, plainly, two different ways in which a form of study could make a contribution to the good life for an agent or a group. One way would be *instrumental*: the study is useful as a means in helping the agent to pursue other goals, as Thales' scientific study proved useful in his business ventures. It contributes to his good life in the way that a tool contributes to the production of an artifact. If a study has only instrumental value, the attainment of the goal removes all reason for pursuing the study; and it would be appropriate to substitute for the study any other instrumental means that promised to deliver the goal in an equally effective or more effective way. The ends of the agent's life, the things that have value in themselves, can be completely described and specified without mention of this study. Another way a study could contribute to a good life, however, would be by being, itself, a component part of that good life, an intrinsically valuable part that gets promoted and arranged along with the other parts. In this case, the attainment of other ends would not remove all reason for pursuing the study, and a complete description of the ends of the life would include mention of the study. Thus, when someone maintains that a form of study should not be altogether useless but should make some contribution to the agent's life as a human being and citizen, it is not clear that this involves relegating the study to a purely instrumental role. It might make its useful contribution just by being pursued for its own sake, either by itself or along with other components. Or, of course, it might be both valuable for its own sake and useful toward the realization of other ends. What the person who so insisted *would* be ruling out would be any view in which the study was pursued just for study's sake and *not* as one component in a total good life. He or she would be ruling out any view according to which the study was chosen without reference to this general ethical and practical question. Notice, however, that once a study is valued in the second way, as a separate component in the good life, there arise possibilities of tension and competition with other ends that did not exist in the purely instrumental picture. These possibilities will concern us shortly.

My general thesis will be that the ancient Greeks, almost without exception in this period, defended some form of the view that intellectual study was appropriate and valuable only insofar as it made some contribution to the practical, that is, to the good lives of human beings. No poet, composer, historian, or philosopher could hope to win an audience without displaying the value of his works for and in the practical lives of citizens; no student of these subjects could expect to justify his activity without pointing to expected practical benefits. In short, the idea of art for art's sake, of art and study as simply forms of amusement, and of the "purity" of the humanities from practical concerns were completely unknown; or, rather, as soon as they were uttered they were most vigorously and generally denounced. There was, however—and this is the second major part of my thesis—a debate about the nature of the contribution to be made by poetry, music, and philosophy to the good life. I shall argue that in the period before Plato it was assumed that the function of study was (1) instrumental and (2) social or political: study educates young citizens to play a civic role in which study itself has no part; the ends of study are set from the outside and determine what form the study will take. Socrates and, even more clearly, Plato, by contrast, insisted that the benefits of philosophical inquiry were not just instrumental: for inquiring and contemplating are themselves activities of enormous intrinsic value, which play a role as central components in the best human life one could imagine. Questions about practical and political value were still not irrelevant to the theoretical disciplines: but now their practical value was inseparable from the fact that they were theoretical disciplines pursued for their own sake alone. I shall examine Aristotle's complex position on these questions, particularly as they concern the practical role of ethical inquiry. Finally, I shall end with the reaction of Epicurus against these philosophers' defense of the separate intrinsic value of their pursuits, examining his claim that no form of study is of any worth unless it has direct instrumental relevance to the attainment of the happy life for the individual. For this reaction, though it might in one way seem to signal a return to the old education, breaks with the entirety of the preceding tradition in its emphasis upon individual rather than communal ends; it leads, for the first time, to the establishment of a school that isolates itself from the city and whose inquiries do not aim at any political or social goal. In short, I shall be arguing that the separation between study and the practical that gives our term *applied* its force for us was not a datum of the intellectual life of our tradition. It was gradual, it had a complex origin, and it was always a matter for the most serious controversy. In a concluding section I shall try to say what light I think all this sheds on our current questions and plans.

Before we begin, one historical point. In bringing Greek debates to bear on contemporary issues I shall use the word *humanities*. In the period that I shall discuss, however, there was in fact no distinction that corresponded to our distinction between science and the humanities. The Hellenistic period, with which I shall be concerned at the very end of my historical remarks, knew a three-part division of philosophical studies into logic, physics (or natural philosophy), and ethics. Aristotle, earlier, distinguished inquiries into two broad groups: those that were in his own sense scientific, that is, capable of being systematized in a hierarchical deductive structure starting from first principles, and those that could not or should not be so systematized. In the former group were included all the natural sciences, metaphysics, general philosophy of nature, perhaps also the general study of life or soul; in the latter category, ethical and political theory. He also made a somewhat different distinction between studies whose primary aim was theoretical and studies whose end was practical; we shall later be exploring that distinction. But prior to Aristotle even these divisions were unknown. Instead there was only the more general division between *paideia*, i.e. those studies that were traditionally taken to form a necessary part of a young gentleman's education, and more specialized studies that were not a part of this traditional curriculum. *Paideia* included forms of physical training and also a certain sort of study of music, poetry, and history; thus it included a part of what we take to constitute the humanities. It did not include a more technical study of language; it did not include the more exacting varieties of historical inquiry; it did not include the systematic and theoretical study of ethical and political questions; and, above all, it did not include the metaphysical, epistemological, and natural-scientific inquiries that lay at the heart of the tradition of Greek philosophy, both before and after this period. Thus it will be difficult to draw parallels in an illuminating way. I shall try to do so by asking about the social role of the forms of study that we now associate with the term *humanities*: above all, the study of poetry and music and the philosophical study of ethics and politics. But since scientific and mathematical study ranked, for the greatest philosophers, as paradigms of intellectual and philosophical inquiry generally, I shall, in following their arguments, speak at times of forms of study that do not fall under the humanities as we construe them.

THE OLD EDUCATION

In the fifth century B.C., the "Great Age of Athens," young citizens did pursue what we might describe anachronistically as a form of humanistic education: an education, that is, that included, in addition to rigorous physical training, a training in poetry, music, dance, and most probably some form of political and social history. From the surviving descriptions of this education, *paideia*, it is quite clear that its aim was, in everything, the production of good citizens, sound in both body and character. An Aristophanic character succinctly describes it as "the education that reared the men who fought at Marathon"[3]. The function of poetry and music in this education was to subserve the purposes of civic

---

[3]*Clouds* 986.

acculturation, both providing examples of traditional conceptions of good behavior and at the same time inspiring, through stirring rhythm and melody, attachment to those conceptions. In the *Clouds*, a play in which the primary point is to ridicule and denounce a faddish intellectualism that seems to be destroying the old *paideia*, a character gives a nostalgic paean to the old ways that is, through historical accident, also one of our very few descriptions of how these ways worked[4]. Boys, he says, walked to the lyre-teacher through the streets in neat rows, braving the snow in light clothing. When they got there they sang songs learned by heart, in the mode traditional for that sort of song, handed down through generations. Examples of such songs are "Athena fearful sacker of cities," and "From afar came the cry." The function of such songs, plainly, was to instill patriotism, civic values, and a warlike spirit. Their role was at one and the same time both educational and motivational: they provided examples of virtuous civic behavior and through their stirring rhythm and melody inspired attachment to the conception of good action illustrated in the examples.

There comes next a passage of considerable interest for us. The speaker says that any boy who played around with the melody or added in any ornamentation that was not in the traditional version would get a thorough beating, on the grounds that he was dishonoring the Muses. It is known that traditional Greek music subserved closely the content of the text: one note to one syllable was the rule, so that the message would be plain to all. The innovative schoolboy is dishonoring the Muses and perverting the traditional function of music by pursuing ornament for its own sake, in a way that detracted from the patriotic and social function of the text. Revealingly, the speaker adds that this bad schoolboy resembles "those people nowadays"; and we know in fact that in the time of Aristophanes there was a heated debate about whether music might to this extent be pursued and studied separately from the text. Poets such as Timotheus and Euripides had sought technical elaboration in a way that seemed to some remote from the traditional practical and instrumental functions. Here the conservative character reminds us that the education that made his city great was one in which any such innovator would have gotten a beating. (The rest of the play makes fun of the civically useless pursuit of linguistic study, biology, meteorology, and theoretical ethics.) The only legitimate function of art and study is social, and not only social, but thoroughly instrumental to civic purposes that can be defined and specified without mention of art. The ends of artistic activity are given to art from the outside, by the political needs of the day.

---

[4]*Clouds* 961 ff.

This Aristophanic character may or may not be describing historical reality with precision. He is, clearly, expressing a social conception of the function of education that had widespread support. It is worth noting here that, so far as we can tell, even the innovators whom he castigates felt it important to defend their enterprise in social and instrumental terms. Although we lack direct evidence on this point, the debate between Aeschylus and Euripides depicted in another play of Aristophanes, the *Frogs*, shows *both* poets defending their quite different styles with reference to the good of the city. The play concerns a visit to the underworld. The city is (as it really was) in a time of upheaval; it is in desperate need of teaching and good advice. Its three greatest tragic poets are all dead. Dionysus, the god of tragic and comic poetry, undertakes a journey to the underworld in order to bring back a major poet to fill this advisory role. From the beginning it is assumed, first, that the tragic poets are the major ethical and political teachers of the culture, and, second, that their central function as poets is to provide such teaching. The ensuing contest of poetic value between the dead poets Aeschylus and Euripides centers around their ethical contributions. Neither one of them so much as suggests that this is the wrong way to assess poetry. Aeschylus states emphatically that the dramatic poets are, as it were, an adult citizen's teachers. Little boys have a schoolmaster to teach them about morals, adults have the poets.[5] The poets, then, have a heavy responsibility to provide good ethical teaching. He clearly believes, with the *Clouds* character, that the function of such teaching is both to provide examples of virtue and to inspire the love of virtue; he uses his grandiose language and stirring, incantatory rhythms to this latter end.

More surprisingly for us, Euripides, the alleged innovator, agrees thoroughly with this general idea about education. To the question "For what should we admire the poets?" he answers, "For sagacity and good advice, because we make human beings in cities better".[6] He defends his stylistic innovations on the grounds that they help poetry engage and interest the ordinary person by appealing to that person's taste for the new, clear, and clever. He denounces the grandiose verse of Aeschylus as boring bombast that could not perform an ethical function well because nobody could understand it and nobody would want to make the effort. In short, the debate, even about rather technical matters of style, is conducted along ethical and practical lines: poetry is an instrument of separate social ends. If Euripides' own true attitude on this issue must remain unclear, we can at least say that even a hostile critic does

[5]*Frogs* 1053–54.
[6]*Frogs* 1008–10.

not charge him with an art-for-art's sake attitude (even though the charge of *apragmosunē*, civic indifference and uselessness, is one that Aristophanes is quite capable of making and frequently does make). I think we can conclude at least that an art-for-art's sake attitude did not have sufficiently widespread or serious support that an appeal to it would be judged helpful to one's case.

I have concentrated on the social function of the study of poetry and music. I have more briefly mentioned the study of language and of scientific matters. It is of interest for our purposes to mention here that among theoretical and scientific studies at this period there was one that was continually ridiculed and denounced because of its obvious lack of practical value, and there were two whose value as studies was never challenged because of their self-evident practical value. Linguistics, or the technical study of language, looked plainly silly. Linguistic competence was a paradigm of something that is naturally and successfully acquired without teaching of a formal kind. Nothing more than a native speaker's competence was of any use to the citizen; so the theoretical study of linguistic forms seemed a waste of time. The plainly useful studies, on the other hand, were medicine and political-military history. In these two cases, once again, we see that the idea of pursuing knowledge just for its own sake was altogether absent. The doctors continually defend their art by pointing to its direct practical usefulness. The idea of a theoretical study of medicine or biology without direct application to the curing of disease and the saving of lives is never entertained; and the moment a medical conception becomes so abstract that its application to particular cases is unclear, it becomes the target of ridicule. The great historian Thucydides, father of the serious and exact study of the past and therefore of our discipline of history itself, takes it for granted that there ought to be an ethical and social function for such a pursuit. His problem is, how to defend his newly tough and arduous procedures with reference to this function, in a context in which the telling of traditional stories had usually been taken to be history enough for social needs. Thucydides defends his choice of period and of method by the famous claim that exact knowledge of past events will be "useful," will contribute to our ability to handle our future, in that human matters happen repeatedly in more or less the same way. For this reason, his history is "a possession for always," rather than merely "a showpiece for the present." It is clear that Thucydides does not think he can defend his new interest in precision as a scholarly value in itself. He feels himself vulnerable to the charge of producing something that is merely ornamental, and he is determined to refute that charge. His study must be commended with reference to the social and political ends that are the proper ends of any study; these ends do not include the pursuit of historical knowledge as a component part.

Let us review our argument up to this point. I have claimed that the group of studies that were the ancestors of our humanities—and, indeed, of other more scientific studies as well—were agreed, in fifth-century Greece, to have a purely instrumental function. They were *useful*, ethically and socially—either because they motivated and educated young people toward mature social values or because they reinforced and supported these values in adults, or because they provided information that was in some other way useful to the political and ethical ends of the city. Thus Thales could defend his astronomical interests only by pointing to his achievements in predicting the olive crop, or to similar socially productive applications of scientific skill. (There is another story in defense of Thales: he helped King Croesus cross the Halys river by diverting its channel.) Any intellectual or artist who could not put his studies in some fruitful instrumental relationship to civic goals that were themselves separate from science and study would have a hard time defending his claim to teach and would be regarded as an altogether parasitic and dangerous character. Thus what would be foreign to this culture would not be the idea of a practical function for the humanities. It would be the idea that there was any legitimate purpose for these studies *besides* their practical function. In the first century A.D., the Greek geographer Strabo, writing in criticism of a more recent view that the only legitimate purpose for poetry and art was delight, invokes the ancients on his side, in a way that confirms these claims:

> Every poet, according to Eratosthenes, aims at entertainment, not instruction. The ancients held a different view. They regarded poetry as a sort of primary philosophy, which was supposed to introduce us to life from our childhood, and teach us about character, emotion, and action in a pleasurable way. . . . This is why Greek communities give children their first education through poetry, not for simple "entertainment" of course, but for moral improvement. Even the musicians lay claim to this, when they teach plucking the strings with the fingers, or playing the lyre or *aulos*; they are, as they say, educators and correctors of character.[7]

We can focus the difference between the Greek fifth century and our own day by asking what possibility most worried the Greeks when they thought about the social role of study. We are, perhaps, above all worried—and with justification—by the thought that the humanities will be coopted for political ends and turned aside from their own even-handed and disinterested pursuit of knowledge. These Greeks were

[7]Strabo 1.2.3, translated by D. A. Russell and M. Winterbottom, *Ancient Literary Criticism* (Oxford: Oxford University Press, 1972), p. 300.

worried by an altogether different picture: the picture of a clever young man with a flabby ill-trained body and an equally flabby character, who has learned all sorts of facts and many clever tricks of argumentation— the young man, that is, who has acquired knowledge through study not incorporated in, not subservient to, the ends of *paideia*. This young man, who appears frequently in the comedies of Aristophanes, has, as the *Clouds* speaker warns us, a pale face, thin shoulders, a narrow chest, large genitals, and a large tongue.[8] He knows how to argue about lots of things, but not how to be loyal to anything. He is a danger because he has acquired learning without its "application." Or rather, having pursued learning for itself, he is now all too ready to "apply" it to the pursuit of his own selfish ends. He knows too much to be docile, but he does not know what to care about or how to be a good person. It is the idea of this culture that this separation of learning from acculturation and social motivation would mean the downfall of the city.

SOCRATES AND PLATO

With Socrates and Plato we see a shift in this picture. But we must be careful to say what this shift is *not*. It is not, by any means, a shift over to the view that study should be pursued for its own sake without reference to ethical ends. Socrates and Plato insist just as firmly as did the tradition that preceded them on the idea that any form of study is only as worthy as is its contribution to the good human life. To ask about the ethical function of study is just as important for them as for their predecessors. Furthermore, both Socrates and Plato insist, like their predecessors, on the great instrumental value of certain sorts of study in getting people to become good citizens. But they add something further. They add the point that engaging in inquiry is itself one *way* of leading a good life as a human being and a citizen. The internal ends of inquiry are themselves of intrinsic value.

Socrates famously insisted on the ethical value of self-knowledge and self-inquiry. The unexamined life, he declared, is not worth living for a human being. Through his use of the *elenchos*, or dialectical cross-examination, he persistently tried to generate this sort of self-inquiry in people of all kinds, dislodging them from their ethical complacency and showing them that they knew far less, even about their own ethical beliefs, than they thought they knew. Clearly, in Socrates' view, this examining and self-examining have instrumental value: by becoming clearer about the nature of his or her ethical beliefs and commitments,

[8]*Clouds* 1011–23.

the examined person will achieve a greater internal consistency and will probably choose and act better as a result. Thus Socrates can claim that his techniques have contributed to the improvement of public life. He compares himself to a gadfly on a noble but sluggish horse, the Athenian democracy; this image shows us the instrumental benefits he claims for inquiry which rouses democracy to a more effective pursuit of its own values.

But, equally clearly, this image captures only a part of Socrates' aim. His unrestricted claim for the value of inquiry, with regard both to himself and to others, suggests that he believes it to have an ethical value that transcends instrumentality. He does not commend examination only to bad people, or only to confused people; he commends it to each and every person; and he himself tirelessly pursues it in himself, even though he is a far more than usually virtuous person and citizen. This looks like a departure from the ordinary view that study is a kind of tool to be used at a certain stage in one's life and then disregarded. The life without it is one that Socrates would not consider worth living at any time. How, then, does Socratic inquiry go beyond tool-like usefulness? Most of all, in its capacity for revealing, delineating, refining goals and ends themselves. A good tool is applied to a job that has been thoroughly set up and described beforehand; a tool is good because it performs the set-up function well. The old education was, in effect, a tool of the standing conception of values and ends. Socratic inquiry, however, gets people to work on the content of their values themselves. Although the material of inquiry is always the beliefs of the interlocutor, it frequently emerges that the most important beliefs about value and worth lie buried beneath layers of convention or fashion. People do not always say what they most deeply mean when questioned about the good. Inquiry cannot function as a tool because the end or goal becomes evident only as a result of inquiry; inquiry does not turn up means to a preset end, but rather works out the best specification of the end. And, beyond this, it may also be that, for Socrates, inquiry has an intrinsic value all its own, even once the ethical ends of life are well clarified. Certainly he does not cease its pursuit upon arriving at a well-articulated ethical conception; and he declares that no life would be worth living without it.

Now clearly the function of Socratic inquiry is thoroughly ethical and political: never does he suggest that self-study or any other sort of study is to be pursued in a way that severs it from the general aspiration to lead a good human life in a city. He is suspicious of natural-science inquiries that do not link their findings to ethical aims. And he tirelessly opposes sophistical and immoralist types who allege that the proper function of learning is the advancement of our self-interested ends, apart from those of the city. But in our aspiration to live a good human life, inquiry becomes an activity that we seek out for reasons that go beyond its immediate civic usefulness. It is no wonder that this view was greeted with suspicion in Athenian culture. For the idea that inquiry has its own separate value gives rise, as Socrates' critics sensed, to a troublesome possibility: that inquiry might make claims that would take people away from other areas of value. And the idea that inquiry, not the conventional wisdom, will provide people with the truest and best account of their values was greeted, as one might expect, with suspicion and hostility. Plato's dialogues give evidence that Socrates was both mocked as uselessly impractical and feared as an influence that would either distract people from political functions or, still worse, turn them against time-honored civic values. Aristophanes' *Frogs* concludes its poetic competition with a praise of the civic activity of Aeschylus in particular, tragic poetry in general, contrasting it with the ethically useless and/or dangerous pursuit of wisdom that is ascribed to Socrates:

> This man here [Aeschylus], because of his practical wisdom, is going back home again, to the good of all citizens, to the good of his own relatives and friends, because of his intelligence. Then it is well not to sit chattering with Socrates, casting poetry aside and leaving the important themes of tragic art. To spend one's time idly in imposing discourse and foolish verbal scratchings is the sign of a deranged man.[9]

Notice how Socratic discourse is here taken to be "idle," a kind of babbling or chattering indulged in for its own sake. This is presumably because its *use*, the *good* of it in conventional civic terms, cannot directly be seen. Its separateness—both its claim to reformulate ends and its claim to *be* an end—makes it dangerously unreliable. Socrates is at pains to emphasize that he does not urge people to neglect conventional civic duty. But it seems right to suggest that a Socratic attitude to inquiry opens up the possibility of conflicts that might lead to this situation. We shall return to this at length in our concluding section.

Plato pressed Socrates' defense of the intrinsic value of intellectual activity much further. Unlike Socrates, he had a serious and deep interest in the sciences, and especially in mathematics. Frequently it is these disciplines that he has most in view when he speaks of the value of theoretical intellectual pursuits. About Plato's position on intellectual study I want to argue three points: First, that he retains a strong interest in answering this culture's demand for an instrumental defense of pursuits such as philosophy and mathematics; he insists that, far from being useless as many people suppose, they have a direct instrumental contribution to make to political and social life. Second, he is equally con-

---

[9]*Frogs* 1485–99.

cerned to argue that their value goes well beyond their usefulness; indeed, that their great importance is precisely that, unlike many other human pursuits, they have a value that is not simply a function of their usefulness. Third, that this value is, nonetheless, still conceived itself in ethical terms: it is value *as* a component in a good life. Thus his talk of intrinsic value remains within his culture's traditional organizing question about study, namely, what contribution does it have to make to human lives?

First, the point about use. Plato is well aware that the philosopher and the mathematician are widely regarded as useless people, people whose social contribution is at best nil, at worst negative, because they encourage neglect of practical affairs. In a number of dialogues, in particular in the *Gorgias*, he vividly depicts the attack on Socrates from this point of view. And yet in the *Republic* he defends the view that cities will be adequately governed only when philosophers, thoroughly trained in mathematics and dialectic, have been made their rulers. The force of his audience's expectations can be seen in the defensive way in which he articulates these proposals. The suggestion that mathematics should be an essential part of a future ruler's education is introduced as something that "the many" will surely oppose on the grounds that mathematical studies are useless; it is defended on grounds that the many could themselves accept, by insisting on their high instrumental usefulness. Glaucon, the interlocutor, anxiously tries to point to the immediate usefulness of mathematics in agriculture, navigation, and military strategy. Socrates tells him that there is a more general and basic argument from use, since mathematics is good for developing the soul's powers of discernment in any area whatever:

> I am amused, I said, that you seem to be afraid of the many, in case they should think that you are prescribing useless studies. It is no trivial matter at all, but a difficult one, to realize that there is in the soul of each of us an organ or instrument that is purified and rekindled by mathematical studies, when it has been destroyed and blinded by our ordinary pursuits, an organ whose preservation is worth more than ten thousand eyes, for by it alone is the truth seen. Those who share this belief will think your proposal surpassingly good; those who have never had any perception of these things will probably think that you are talking nonsense—for they don't see any other advantage worth speaking of in these pursuits.[10]

The proposal that philosophers should be rulers of the city is, of course, even more controversial. When Socrates brings it forward, he calls it "the greatest wave of paradox" and says that he expects to be washed away on "billows of laughter and scorn." For how can it be

---

[10]*Republic* 527DE.

correct to say that philosophers can and must rule, when it is the popular belief that

> of those who turn to philosophy, not merely touching upon it to complete their education and dropping it while still young, but lingering too long in the study of it, the majority become cranks, not to say rascals, and those accounted the finest spirits among them are still rendered useless to society by the pursuit which you commend?[11]

Socrates devotes much long and careful argument to answering these instrumental worries, describing the cognitive competence of his philosophers and showing how this could in fact be of the highest practical value. It is significant, too, that he has already made a rather non-Socratic concession to traditional ways by insisting on the necessity of the old-style *paideia* as the first stage in the education of future philosophers. In short, then, Plato does not ignore or dismiss his audience's demand to know the *advantage*, for the city, of any study that will be undertaken. He accepts and attempts to satisfy that demand. He breaks with tradition, so far, only in that he believes the highest instrumental value to reside in studies that have frequently been derided as useless.

But of course mathematics and philosophy are not valuable only for their consequences. First of all, it is only these studies that permit the correct apprehension and specification of ethical ends themselves. The reason why the philosopher must rule is that only he or she will have the understanding of what justice and goodness are that is necessary to govern a city well. Thus, although philosophy in a sense responds to concerns that come from outside it, fulfilling the ordinary person's demand for justice and good government, it does not confine itself to the ordinary person's understanding of justice; it will provide a superior account of what it is. Then, too, these studies have enormous intrinsic value, apart from any contribution they make to other ends. The *Republic* as a whole is structured around the contrast between instrumental and intrinsic value. Glaucon's initial challenge to Socrates was that he show justice and just activity to be good not only for their consequences but in and of themselves. And the activity of the philosopher, who is, paradigmatically, the just person, is clearly defended as having high value in itself. Philosophical study is not something you do just in order to achieve something further; it is the chief component of the best life that there is. It is not necessarily bound up with need and the fulfillment of need; it is chosen in and by itself. Even if studies had no consequences beyond themselves, it would still be rational to pursue them because of what they themselves are. In fact, it is argued that what makes philosophical and scientific study different from just about everything else

---

[11]*Republic* 487CD, trans. C. Shorey.

that we pursue is that its value *is* independent in this way from needs and interests. These activities would look good and valuable even to a being who needed nothing at all, because they are so intrinsically wonderful. By arguing in this way, Plato insists that his tradition has been looking at the life of the intellect in too narrow a manner, searching only for instrumental value in studies when, in fact, this instrumental value, although high, is not at all the greatest part of their contribution to the good life. Their most special contribution is to be the sort of thing that goes beyond instrumentality. And this leads to an antitraditional ranking of the arts and sciences in which the most practically useful branches of science, which traditionally fared well in ethical debate, appear lower than the more abstract: pure math is preferred to applied math, geometry to architecture.

It is crucial to stress that all of this scrutiny of studies and all of this ranking goes on thoroughly *within* the general ethical question, what is the good life for a human being. Mathematics is defended for its role in a good life, not as something that has no relevance at all to ethical aims. Plato's interest in the intrinsic value of intellectual studies is not an interest in art for art's sake or science for science's sake. It is an ethical interest, broadly construed. He wants, however, to insist that not all ethical interest is reducible to interest in usefulness; some (the highest) ethical interests are interests in an activity for its own sake alone. In one way he is breaking with his tradition; in another, he is accepting the tradition's general attitude toward study and only pointing out to it that it has had too narrow an understanding of its own ethical project.

This break, however, gives rise to a notorious problem. If study is supremely valuable in and of itself, if, as Plato argues, it is the best and finest thing a human being can do, then it is suddenly unclear why the philosopher will choose to use his or her time in ruling the city. The ethical value of the study remains firm; its communal and social role is in jeopardy. The philosophers of the *Republic* have useful knowledge, knowledge without which the city cannot be governed well. But they prefer to remain apart from the city, performing their contemplative activity without the distractions and dilutions imposed upon that activity by social life. The separateness of the value of contemplation gives rise to a tension between the pursuit of that value and the fulfillment of social ends. The philosophers must be forced to return to the city, and when they do they regard their task not as something fine or beautiful but as a necessity. Plato's argument concedes that the fears of his culture are not groundless. Give study its proper honor as something intrinsically fine, remove it from subservience to externally generated ends and allow it to form, and be, its own, and you have the ingredients of a deep conflict of values. This is the only case, it seems, in which Plato acknowledges the possibility of tragedy.

ARISTOTLE

In many ways Aristotle's discussion of the value of philosophical study continues and develops Plato's. He insists on the usefulness of various forms of intellectual endeavor and he insists that their value in our lives is not exhausted by instrumental usefulness. But in an extremely important and influential break with the previous tradition, Aristotle casts the question of intrinsic value in a new light by separating the forms of inquiry into two broad groups: those whose end is the improvement of some aspect of practice and those which have as their end theoretical understanding alone. In the *Eudemian Ethics* he writes that some sciences, for example astronomy and geometry, have only knowing and understanding as their proper ends.[12] There are, on the other hand, other forms of inquiry whose proper end is something practical over and above the knowledge gained through inquiry: such studies are medicine and ethics: "For we aim not to know what courage is but to be courageous, not to know what justice is but to be just—just as we aim to be healthy rather than to know what health is, and to be in a good condition rather than to know what good condition is."[13] Aristotle is not saying that the practical arts do not acquire knowledge or that the natural sciences cannot have practical application; he explicitly asserts the latter point,[14] and the former he clearly believes. What his talk of the *telos* of a discipline seems to mean is that this is the primary thing we are striving for in pursuing the discipline, the thing that gives that discipline its point and importance in our lives. We would and do, as he insists in *Metaphysics* I, pursue the study of astronomy and mathematics with alacrity for the sake of understanding alone. We do not demand of mathematicians that they improve our lives. Although they might incidentally do so, our assessment of them as mathematicians is based solely upon their contribution to the advancement of understanding. The same is not true of medicine: we assess doctors as good doctors not on the grounds that they are knowledgeable or get theoretically elegant results, but on the grounds that they are good at curing; we give their science as a whole its place of respect in the community because of its relation to health, a practical good. So much, he is claiming, is true of the philosophical study of ethics: if it makes human lives no better, it will be deservedly ignored; and intellectual sophistication alone does not make a practitioner a good one.

Now it is most important to stress that when Aristotle says that the end of ethical study is *practical* and that his ethical lectures are *useful* he

---

[12]*Eudemian Ethics* 1215b15–17.
[13]Ibid. 1216b22–25.
[14]Ibid. 1216b15–18.

is not returning to the traditional instrumentalist conception. The end
is practice, but the study is not simply a tool. It does not just provide
means to an end that could be fully identified apart from it. The help
offered centrally involves specification of ends themselves: both individual clarification concerning ends and communal agreement or at-
tunement. (These goals go together for Aristotle, in that what the individual comes to see more clearly is a conception of the good that he
received from society and according to which he intends to live in society;
the communal agreement is arrived at as a result of the reciprocal scrutiny
and clarification of different individual proposals.) In the *Nicomachean
Ethics* he uses an image from archery to illustrate the practical contribution of his arguments: "Won't the knowledge of it [*sc.* the good] make
a great shift in the balance where life is concerned, and won't we, like
archers with a target before us, be more likely to hit on what is appropriate?"[15] Ethical injury is presumably not *supplying* a target where one
was previously altogether absent. (Later Aristotle explicitly tells us that
the audience for his books should be reasonably mature people with
well-formed characters.) But such archers can be helped to get a clearer
view of their target—of their aims and the way in which they stand to
one another—by a theoretical discussion of the sort that Aristotle will
present. Ethical study shows us more clearly *what* the target *is*; this will
improve practice by making us more discriminating, more confident,
more reliably accurate in choice. In a most important passage of the
Eudemian Ethics Aristotle tells us more about how specifically philosophical argument might be thought to advance these aims:

> Concerning all these things we must try to seek conviction through argu-
> ments, using the appearances as our witnesses and standards. For it would
> be best of all if all human beings could come into an evident communal
> agreement with what we shall say, but if not that all should agree in some
> way. And this they will do if they are led carefully until they shift their
> position. For everyone has something of his own to contribute to the truth,
> and it is from these that we go on to give a sort of demonstration about these
> things. For from what is said truly but not clearly, as we advance, we will
> also get clarity, always moving from what is usually said in a jumbled fashion
> to a more perspicuous view. There is a difference in every inquiry between
> arguments that are said in a philosophical way and those that are not. Hence
> we must not think that it is superfluous for the political person to engage in
> the sort of reflection that makes perspicuous not only the *that* but also the
> *why*: for this is the contribution of the philosopher in each area.[16]

To be clear about our ends we must progress beyond the hasty and
confused modes of ordinary discourse, toward greater clarity and per-
spicuity. But this progress requires the sort of argument that sorts things

---

[15]*Nicomachean Ethics* 1094a22–24.
[16]*Eudemian Ethics* 1216a26–39.

out and clarifies, that leads people to shift their alleged ground by pointing to inconsistencies in their system of beliefs, that makes evident not only the fact of our commitments, but also their *why*, that is, how they contribute to one another and to the good life in general. He tells us unabashedly that to give this sort of discourse is the business of the professional philosopher and that this is why the philosopher is a useful person to have around. After this passage he goes on to warn the reader that clarity and elegance are not *sufficient* for practical value. You have to be on your guard, he says, against the sort of philosopher who argues clearly but is lacking in the proper connectedness to human experience. Some pupils are led astray by such people, thinking that "to use arguments and to say nothing at random is the mark of the philosopher"[17]: they thus allow themselves to be influenced by jejune and irrelevant glibness. But we should not let the emptiness of some ethical discourse give practical philosophy a bad name; properly done, it makes an important and irreplaceable contribution.

I have described Aristotle's position on practical philosophy at length because I believe it to be one of the best accounts of this topic ever produced; I shall return to it in my concluding section. But if we now turn to Aristotle's other group of inquiries, we discover that Aristotle breaks with instrumentalism in a deeper and more radical way. He does not exactly sever the pursuit of understanding in these cases from the overarching ethical question about the best life, for he defends theoretical inquiry and contemplation as prominent constituents of the best life for a human being. In fact, he holds the desire for understanding to be one of the basic and deepest natural desires of the human being. The *Metaphysics* begins with these famous words:

> All human beings naturally reach out for knowledge. There is evidence of this in the love of the senses. For even apart from their use they are loved for themselves, and the sense of sight above all others. For not only for the sake of action, but even when we are not going to act, we choose seeing above just about anything else. The reason for this is that it, above all, makes us apprehend things and shows us many distinctions.[18]

The instrumentalist tradition is implicitly criticized here for having neglected one of our most powerful original motives, the motive that above all others led us to study in the first place. Repeatedly in his scientific works Aristotle pursues this theme, defending the value and beauty of astronomy, of biology, of the study of any order or structure in the world of nature, no matter how humble. His protreptic to biology in the first book of the *Parts of Animals* insists that even this apparently some-

---

[17]Ibid. 1217a1–2.
[18]*Metaphysics* 980a23–28.

what disgusting study has great intrinsic value and beauty because we are learning something true about the order of the natural world. He does not seem to feel constrained, as an earlier Greek doctor or scientist might have, to indicate the practical benefits of his own research. Research, evidently, is an end in itself.

Aristotle attempts, in the ethical works, to show how the architectonic management of practical wisdom can both maintain the dignity of reflection and keep it within its managerial domain (it "arranges" for theoretical activity to exist without "giving orders to it"). Nevertheless, it is clear that the thoroughgoing unity of politics and science that existed even in Plato's ideal city is no longer present. Even if we should believe that the difficult remarks in the *Nicomachean Ethics* X about the choice between a life centered around contemplation and a life of social excellence are in several ways inconsistent with material elsewhere that defends as best a life in which these two elements are harmoniously related (an interpretative problem by now notorious), we must acknowledge that Aristotle's conception of *theoria's* independence and intrinsic value contains implicitly the possibility of a serious tension between the two elements. And it is clear, too, that Aristotle himself found it quite possible to pursue inquiry throughout his life in a context rather far removed from civic and political concerns. His researches were accomplished in exile in Asia Minor; and at Athens, as a resident alien, he lacked Socrates' and Plato's intimate connection to the daily life of the city. He had this position of necessity, it is true; but he fostered a spirit of scholarly autonomy in his school as well. Here we find the first beginnings of some of the hallmarks of the scholarship we know: the first library, the first organized collaborative research programs aimed at the complete mapping of a field, apparently for the sake of knowledge only. To Aristotle, then, we can trace our modern idea of pure inquiry—and the problems about interrelation and application which arise with the birth of that idea and which have played such a large role in the tradition of Western thought about the humanities.

EPICURUS

We move now to the last major figure whom I want to study here, one whose views were of considerable influence for centuries and who has captured the imaginations of influential thinkers of later date— especially Karl Marx, who wrote his doctoral dissertation on his thought. I want to end with Epicurus, since he returns us in a sense to the place where we began, that is, to a thoroughgoing subordination of theory to practice. Epicurus was a missionary philosopher, one who was deeply moved by human suffering wherever he encountered it, in male and female, slave and free, high-born or low. To him the only problem worth worrying about was how to rid human beings of their suffering, both physiological and, more importantly, psychological. The only legitimate function of the intellectual and philosophical life, of any of the studies which we now associate with the humanities or with the sciences, was the removal of suffering, the promotion of a happy life free from disturbance. He argued three things: (1) that the study of Epicurean philosophy was necessary for a happy human life; (2) that it was sufficient for a happy life, if sufficiently pursued and practiced; (3) that there was no other reason to pursue any of these studies. These arguments constituted a scathing attack upon Platonism and the Platonist's attachment to the pure pursuit of science and mathematics. Epicurus is reported to have said of Plato's pursuit of the *kalon* (the beautiful or noble) in and of itself, "I spit on the *kalon*." And his utter contempt for mathematics and mathematicians is legendary. Why, then, did some intellectual studies fare better?

According to Epicurus, most of the disturbances and anxieties that plague human life are caused by false beliefs. These beliefs are of many kinds; but chief among them are false beliefs about the gods, about the badness of death, about the terrors of the afterlife. Because of these beliefs, human beings are continually in the grip of painful anxiety. Certain sorts of studies do nothing to relieve anxiety. Logic and mathematics are of no use at all. Certain sorts of poetry and music are actually harmful, as the Epicurean poet Lucretius shows when he imagines people whose fear of death is increased by poignant literature about loss and grief. But certain sorts of studies can, on the other hand, have such a powerful positive effect upon the soul that they are like a drug for its anxieties. These studies would include the knowledge of the material composition of the human soul, of the impossibility of survival after death; they would include a new theology that would depict the gods as benign and noninterventionistic. These studies, carefully and thoroughly pursued, simply wipe out anxiety and troublesome longings by wiping out the false beliefs on which those feelings are based. Epicurus speaks of his philosophy as a form of medical treatment. His first four "Principal Sayings" were called the Tetrapharmakos, or "Four-fold Drug." And the general features of the therapeutic process are set forth in his *Letter to Menoiceus* with reference to the treatment of the fear of death:

> Correct apprehension of the fact that death is nothing to us makes mortal life enjoyable, not by adding on some limitless time, but by taking away the deep longing for immortality. For nothing is fearful in life to the person who is genuinely convinced that there is nothing fearful in not living.[19]

---

[19]*Letter to Menoiceus*, 124.

Correction of belief through study works on the emotions, removing not only the justification for the feeling, but the feeling itself. The great importance of this process as a cause of happiness is set out later in the same letter:

> It is not drinking and continual feasting, nor is it enjoyment of boys and women nor of fish and the other things offered by an expensive table that make the pleasant life: it is sober reasoning that searches out the causes of all pursuit and avoidance and drives out the beliefs from which a great disturbance seizes the soul.[20]

Once again, we see that study works by driving out beliefs; but the removal of these beliefs guarantees, in turn, the removal of certain disturbances and bad desires.

Epicurus clearly thought that this happy condition could not be attained without Epicurean philosophical study. One of the Principal Sayings is, "It is necessary to reason concerning the end that is there in nature and concerning every clear evidence to which we refer our beliefs. Otherwise everything will be full of confusion and disturbance." He also assures us repeatedly that this pursuit of philosophy is sufficient for happy life. But it is important to insist that Epicurean philosophy does not produce happy life by being, itself, a valuable thing. What is valued is the condition of null disturbance or pain; philosophy is only an instrumental means to that condition. Another of the Principal Sayings concludes, "If we were not in any way burdened by anxiety about the heavens and about death, that it might be something for us, and also by our lack of precise knowledge concerning the boundaries of the pains and desires, then we would have no need of the study of nature."

In short, Epicurus rates the instrumental value of philosophy very high. And he finds instrumental value in places where the earlier tradition had been slow to see it: namely, in the detailed study of nature and of human and animal physiology. The Epicurean curriculum was vastly more complicated and technical than the one described in Aristophanes. In the second century A.D., a firmly Epicurean gentleman in Asia Minor, called Diogenes of Oenoanda, wanted to put up on the edge of his property a billboard inscription that would proclaim to passersby the saving truths of Epicureanism, much in the manner of a religious billboard in our culture. But unlike our religious billboards, Diogenes' inscription had to contain a lot of highly technical material, since all of this was necessary, in the Epicurean view, for the production of happy life. The bronze inscription he erected is among the largest ever unearthed. But at the end of all this we must insist that Epicurus was no more interested than was Aristophanes' nostalgic old speaker

---

[20]Ibid, 132.

in the elaboration of learning and research for its own sake. He was not interested in it even as a constituent part of a good life. Like the Greek gentleman of the fifth century, he insisted that education was at best worthless, at worst pernicious and harmful, unless it contributed directly to a good that was separate from it.

We might now appear to have returned to the old education—but with an enormous difference. The old education asked that the ends of study be the ends of the city. When it spoke of use and advantage in connection with a form of study, it was advantage for a group, or for the human individual *qua* member of that group. Epicurus subordinates all communal and relational values to the ends of the single individual; the city, as far as he is concerned, has failed to provide a safe and happy context for human life. He urges that education sever itself from the anxieties and upheavals of the city in order to serve individual happiness more efficiently. Thus, if in one way he returns to an older conception of education, there is another way in which he breaks decisively with one of the deepest Greek views concerning education, inaugurating a characteristic modern picture of educational activity: namely, that it goes on in a place that is a sanctuary from public life, protected from its stresses and its claims.

I have said that it was Plato and, even more clearly, Aristotle, who began the move toward pure inquiry, severing research from ethical and political aims. But Aristotle still organized intellectual activity within a complex human social life. His view that the human being is by nature a social creature prevented him from urging human beings to pursue inquiry in disregard of the ends of the group. The final cutting of the bond that had held inquiry together with the practical required, ultimately, the denial of this Aristotelian view. Epicurus did not separate theory from practice. But he severed both theory and practice from the city; and it was this move that was necessary and pivotal in preparing the way for the modern ideal of the "ivory tower."

THE PRACTICAL HUMANITIES

This has been a complicated story. It may not yet be fully clear where it is heading and how it illuminates our own questions. Frequently, however, the stories we tell ourselves when we pose these questions are too simple. One of the most important reasons for turning from the questions to their history is to return ourselves to a sense of the complexity both of the questions and of the alternatives available for answering them. When we ask how and whether the study of philosophy and literature can make a contribution to practice, these ancient Greek debates have, I shall now claim, a good deal to offer us.

When we examine the story that has been all too simply set out here, one thing we grasp immediately is that the idea that the study of the humanities can be practical is no new or faddish idea. It is the idea with which the tradition that began the serious study of humanistic subjects operated from its beginnings. From the point of view of the classical tradition, the idea that is strange is the idea that education might be severed from the aspiration to live well as a human being and citizen. We have seen how long and tortuous a process was required before the elements of this idea began to be articulated. And we can see that Aristotle's views about the separateness and purity of inquiry, which strike us as normal and natural, were in his culture anomalous.

But if we are encouraged by this thought to look to the Greeks for guidance in applying the humanities to various aspects of human practical life, the tradition confronts us at this point with a variety of complicated questions. First, implicit in my story is a question about the ends of the educational project: Are they to be individual or communal? As we teach people moral reasoning and other related subjects, do we think of ourselves as aiming above all at the enrichment of the lives of individuals or instead at the improvement of the quality of public life? These alternatives are, of course, not exclusive; but in some contexts they can generate conflicting demands. The kind of education in the humanities that would most enrich the life of the individual doctor, businessman, or lawyer might not be exactly the same kind that would most enhance the quality of that person's public contribution. A doctor who learns to care about Plato, or Henry James, or Schubert may through these attachments develop a richer set of responses to human life; she may see and feel more, and more appropriately, and have a better individual human life as a result. It does not follow that these studies will be conducive to her making the kind of tough and quick decision that is required of doctors if the overall practice of medicine is to be as helpful as possible. So we need to think carefully about whom we are serving, and whose ends we are promoting when we teach what we teach.

As we grapple with this difficult question, the Greek tradition offers us some encouragement. For no matter how much they differ, Socrates and Aristotle in particular share, and defend with argument, the view that the public and the private, properly understood, do not come apart in this way. The best citizen and lawmaker will be one who has done a kind of philosophical and intellectual work that goes well beyond instrumentality: who has learned to ask hard questions concerning the ends of human life and their relationship to one another and to pursue these questions with tough and rigorous argument. But this is also, they argue, what any individual ought to do in order to live well. Living well cannot be separated from political attachments and ends, nor can the political do without the sort of clarification and self-scrutiny that is at the heart of an individual's education for goodness. The story I have told shows us in how many ways this harmony could be upset, or its existence questioned. Socrates was charged with being a foe of the city; Plato acknowledged that the best individuals would have to be compelled to give themselves to public life; Aristotle described a theoretical life that was in deep and ongoing tension with the political life. But as we ponder the public function of humanistic study we have in their works a powerful defense of the idea that the enrichment of each private understanding is the best, if not the only, way to improve the level of judgment concerning difficult matters of public choice. A teacher of ethics who turns to Aristotle as a model could justly feel that her work with individuals on difficult ethical issues was at the same time an enrichment of individual lives and a valuable contribution to the public sphere.

The Greek tradition raises another important issue about the relationship of education to its ends. The Old Education assumed that the right way to approach the educator was with a preset account of the values and ends to be taught. The educator provided a useful *technē* or set of skills in the service of a goal defined by someone else. This made it easy to measure the effectiveness of the educator's function, but it drastically limited his contribution. Socrates, Plato, and Aristotle saw in education the potential for a much more creative task. Instead of simply providing a set of means toward ends that he or she does not shape, the educator becomes involved in asking about the very nature of the ends of human life. His or her contribution illuminates and clarifies the nature of human values. This task requires, clearly, both more time and more freedom than the former one. Its direction is less clear, its practical contribution harder to assess. It can easily be made to appear vulnerable to charges of emptiness and uselessness, as both fifth-century and Epicurean attacks on philosophy show us. One of the most important choices before us today, as we design any kind of applied humanities program, is the choice between these two conceptions of the educator's function. When the philosopher or professor of literature goes over to the medical school to teach ethics or poetry, is he or she simply fulfilling a set of demands articulated by professors and students of medicine— for example, providing young doctors with some efficient decision strategies that will work well in a moment of crisis? Or will it be open to that professor to question the student's current understanding of his or her ends? To use literature or philosophy to generate uncertainty and surprise, to open up for the student a new understanding of value? If, as humanists, we insist that only the latter conception does justice to our sense of the power and richness of our subject, we should be prepared to encounter resistance. For as the story of Socrates shows, there are many busy professionals who open their arms to education until it begins to ask too many questions.

But Socrates and Aristotle both would vigorously insist that it is only by undertaking this more ambitious and elusive task that the humanities can make a really worthy and distinctive practical contribution. If we conceive of the philosopher as a character with a useful *technē* that can be applied to practice without altering ends, we will miss the best thing humanistic study can do for the culture, namely, to make it examine itself concerning its most basic values. It will be asked—as it was asked of both of these thinkers—what is the source of the philosopher's or humanist's authority to do any such thing. To this question Aristotle's reply seems to me a good one. The philosopher is the character whose professional experience in and attachment to clarity, consistency, and careful, sensitive description puts him or her in a good position to help us advance from the "jumble" of our ordinary self-understanding to "a more perspicuous view." He works with the material of the pupil's beliefs and contributes nothing fundamentally new; but his scrupulousness about method helps us all toward shared goals through an articulated vision of the "target" that we have already before us. This may seem like a modest role for a professional to play. But it seems to me both a deeper and a more exciting role than the instrumental and technical role given to humanistic professionals in some discussions of the applied humanities. I see no reason why we should not be able to play this role; and I think we should insist on playing this role, rather than accepting a narrower and more instrumental conception of our task. Ancient Greek conceptions, especially those of Socrates and Aristotle, appear to be good exemplars.

Finally there is the intrinsic value of humanistic study. Those of us who worry about what we are doing when we teach in the practical sphere and who would like to insist, as we do so, that humanistic study is more than a useful thing, is something of beauty and value in its own right, can identify our questioning with the criticism of the Old Education that began with Socrates and was further developed in both Plato and Aristotle. We can claim, then, that we have not really brought the full contribution of our disciplines into the practical sphere if we have not brought their internal value and beauty. If we have not conveyed to our students the sense that literature and philosophy are wonderful and wonderfully worth doing, we have taught only a diminished and impoverished version of what we do. The Greek thinkers remind us that to insist upon this intrinsic value need not be to abstract from ethical and practical questions: for we can insist that these studies have practical value as constituent parts in the best life for a human being. We can insist, as Plato and Aristotle did, that the instrumental and the intrinsic value of these pursuits usually go together: you make better citizens with richer public as well as private lives when you teach them to respect these pursuits for their own sake. But we will have to acknowledge that there are times when these two sorts of value may come to be in tension with one another, when the committed pursuit of humanistic value and truth may lead into areas that are useless, or even dangerous, for the public culture.

If we believe, then, that the practical humanities should be more than tools, if we want to insist both on their power to deliberate about ends and on their intrinsic value, one of our urgent tasks ought to be to insist, as we work, on the maintenance of stringent safeguards against the exploitation, deformation, and persecution of the humanities by external political and social demands. And here our tradition of ivory-tower autonomy has left us better prepared, perhaps, than the more socially immersed thinkers of ancient Greek culture. When these thinkers wanted to protect their studies from encroachment, their culture, with its consistently instrumentalist tradition, offered them few resources. Socrates drank the hemlock. Plato's attempt to found a philosophical city ended in failure and confusion. Aristotle died of stomach trouble after leaving Athens suddenly under threat of political persecution. He said that he left because he did not want the Athenians "to commit a second crime against philosophy." Only Epicurus, who refused political commitments and attachments, escaped having his activity as a thinker disrupted by political pressures. He found, in his garden far from the city, the tranquility he sought. These examples should make us suitably wary as we work toward a form of humanistic teaching that will be practical in the richest and most valuable way.[21]

---

[21]I find this sketch unfortunately simple and coarse. I have treated the same issues more fully in other writings, which also contain many references to excellent discussions by other authors. For the Old Education, see my "Aristophanes and Socrates on Learning Practical Wisdom," *Yale Classical Studies* 26 (1981); for Plato's views of instrumental and intrinsic value, see chapters 4 and 5 of *The Fragility of Goodness: Luck and Ethics in Greek Tragedy and Philosophy*, forthcoming, 1985, Cambridge University Press; for Aristotle's views, see my "Aristotle," in *Ancient Writers*, edited by T. J. Luce (New York: Charles Scribner's Sons, 1982), pp. 377–416, a general introduction to Aristotle's thought with full bibliography; on the debate between Aristotle and Epicurus about the value of philosophical argument for practice, see my "Therapeutic Arguments: Epicurus and Aristotle," forthcoming in the *The Norms of Nature*, edited by M. Schofield and G. Striker (Cambridge: Cambridge University Press, 1985).

Except where noted, all translations are my own.

CHAPTER 2

Storm over the Humanities
The Sources of Conflict

DAVID LITTLE

Whatever one may think, finally, of William Bennett's recent tenure at the National Endowment for the Humanities,[1] he has succeeded in generating a welcome discussion of the purposes of humanistic study. His proposal for shifting emphasis away from sponsoring programs that relate the humanities to public policy and toward programs that treat humanistic study as edifying for its own sake deserves the serious attention it has received from scholars and professionals in the field of public support for the humanities.

There is, nevertheless, something rather odd about one prominent feature of the discussion. It is the categorical tone of the various claims and counterclaims about what really constitutes humanistic study, or what its real purpose is. Such disputes are reminiscent of arguments over what the real purpose of religious devotion or artistic endeavor is. It is not that disputes of this sort are meaningless. It is only that the claims of the different proponents rest on conflicting normative beliefs that are usually unexpressed and undefended. Like the two neighbors contending heatedly across the back fence, the proponents are arguing from different premises.

Bennett's idea that "the purpose of learning is to save the soul and enlarge the mind," as he puts it, or that "intellectual refinement and

---

[1]William J. Bennett, "The Shattered Humanities," *American Association of Higher Education Bulletin* (February, 1983), p. 3.

DAVID LITTLE • Department of Religious Studies, University of Virginia, Charlottesville, Virginia 22903.

spiritual elevation are the traditional goals of the humanities, and should remain so" evokes in his hands one sort of ideal image with its own decided assumptions about what counts as spiritual and intellectual fulfillment. The assumptions imply a spirit of social and political detachment, a sense, primarily, of inward or deeply personal liberation.

It is surely because Bennett himself is committed to the underlying assumptions and their implications that he takes the dim view he does of humanists spending a great deal of time worrying over how to relate their subjects to public policy. Otherwise, he might draw a different conclusion from the fact that they are not uniformly good at illuminating policy questions. He might lament that state of affairs and admonish humanists to pull up their socks and undertake to improve their competence in policy matters.

However, if, in fact, the true goal of humanistic study is inward cultivation, if it is, in Bennett's words "developing a sensibility" or certain broad "qualities of mind and heart," then there is of course no good reason for humanists to occupy their time and energy with the ins and outs of public policy. Well and good. But a nagging question remains: How can we be sure Bennett's assertion about the real point of humanistic study is correct?

At the same time, we experience similar uncertainty when we listen to Bennett's critics. We would like more evidence than we receive when, for example, we are told by Bruce Sievers that "attention to policy questions in civil life . . . lies at the heart of traditional humanistic concerns."[2] Is that claim so clearly beyond dispute?

It is true that figures like Aristotle, Erasmus, and Thomas Hobbes, whose interests and ways of doing things are normally regarded as the fit subject of humanistic study, devoted attention to the organization and conduct of civil life. Aristotle, after all, wrote the *Ethics* and the *Politics*; Erasmus wrote *The Education of the Christian Prince*; and Hobbes wrote the *Leviathan*, the *Citizen*, and other books on political life. There is every reason to believe that all three would be fully disposed to draw practical conclusions from their general principles concerning issues of policy in the fields of education, taxation, punishment, and the like.

However, it is still an open question just how close to the heart of traditional humanistic endeavor such concerns really are. With all his interest in civil life, Aristotle, toward the end of both the *Ethics* and the *Politics*, gives unmistakable priority to the contemplative life, the inner

[2]Bruce Sievers, "In Praise of Public Policy," *Federation Reports*, IV, 1 (March/April 1983), p. 10.

life of mind and spirit, over social relations of any sort.[3] Erasmus may have written a treatise on the Christian prince, but by no stretch of the imagination were such affairs at the center of his interest.[4]

In Hobbes's case, our uncertainty is of a different order. At least Robert Bellah, in his essay, "The Humanities and Social Vision,"[5] questions Hobbes's right to be considered a part of the humanistic tradition at all. That is because humanistic study for Bellah is really about reverence for tradition, and Hobbes's theories are antitraditional. In short, if Bellah is correct, then Hobbes is an "anti-humanist," as presumably, are all subsequent philosophers and others who have not exorcised Hobbes's ghost from their thinking. Therefore, however, preoccupied with civil life Hobbes may have been, his brand of political reflection would not, in Bellah's view, represent the humanist spirit anyway; it would certainly not lie "at the heart of traditional humanistic concerns."

In other words, we can, apparently, only begin to identify with confidence those whose work and interests represent the heart of humanistic study, once we have made up our minds who counts as a real humanist. I need only add that, as with Bennett and Sievers, we are left to wonder a bit at the assurance with which Bellah lays down the law in respect to what is and what is not the true spirit of humanistic study.

My belief is that, historically considered, there is a deep ambivalence in the tradition of humanistic inquiry over what the real point of studying history, philosophy, literature, art, and religious thought is. Though by now attitudes have no doubt fragmented even further, the initial ambivalence or "great divide" can be traced to the sixteenth century and to a deep conflict, putting it heavy-handedly, between Renaissance and Reformation.

On this subject, the conclusions of Ernst Troeltsch and Max Weber are illuminating. In particular, they emphasize the large difference be-

---

[3]See Aristotle, *Nicomachean Ethics* (New York: Bobbs-Merrill Co., 1962), Ch. X. pp. 288–295; *Politics* (New York: Oxford University Press, 1962), Bk. VII, Ch. III, p. 289. Arthur Adkins, in his definitive study of Greek values, *Merit and Responsibility* (Chicago: University of Chicago Press, 1975), summarizes Aristotle's position well: "On Aristotle's principles, it seems impossible to persuade anyone who could now be solving a particular geometrical problem, thereby serving the highest kind of *eudaimonia*, that he should instead perform some moral act, since this would secure him only an inferior kind of *eudaimonia*, and *eudaimonia* is universally admitted to be the end of life" (pp. 345–6).

[4]See the introductory remarks of Lester K. Born, translator and editor, *The Education of the Christian Prince* (New York: Columbia University Press, 1963): "Steeped in the atmosphere and life of classical antiquity as he was, [Erasmus] came to feel that his life was one of mental, not physical, activity" (p. 20).

[5]Robert Bellah, Chapter 7 of this volume.

tween Renaissance thought and Reformation, especially Calvinist, thought over the concept of *vocation*. Troeltsch writes:

> The Renaissance's affirmation of the world is in no way bound up with the concept of calling which became for Protestantism the synthesis of the world and asceticism. Indeed, the Renaissance does not in principle at all recognize the concept of the calling . . . ; it means the emancipation of a free, aesthetically oriented education, of free inquiry, of personal self-revelation and self-cultivation from all the bonds of a scheme of callings deemed appropriate to civil and economic society. . . . The Renaissance goal is . . . the man of culture, mentally and spiritually free, the exact opposite of the man who has a calling or who is a specialist [in the world].[6]

The Renaissance ideal of the inwardly liberated, ultimately detached "virtuosi of the intellectual and artistic life" produces an "aristocracy of culture" that *devalues the significance of political and commercial vocations and thus systematically diverts the energies of humanistic study away from the moral supervision of "life in the world."*

There were essentially three different ways in which the moral and spiritual devaluation of civil and commercial life might be expressed. The first was in the form of Aristotelian enlightenment, according to which, as I pointed out earlier, the life of self-absorbed contemplation takes final priority over all kinds of social interaction. The second is in the form of Renaissance Platonism, which, as Oskar Kristeller has pointed out, was "individualistic rather than political," or, at most, stressed love and friendship among a small group of persons bound together "in the contemplative life."[7]

Finally, the moral and spiritual devaluation of civil and commercial life might take the form of deliberately setting aside moral and religious

---

[6]Ernst Troeltsch, "Renaissance and Reformation," unpublished translation by Henry A. Finch of "Renaissance und Reformation," in *Aufsätze zur Geistesgeschiche und Religionssoziologie* (Tübingen: J. C. B. Mohr, 1925), pp. 261–296.

[7]See Paul Oskar Kristeller, "Renaissance Platonism," in Wallace K. Ferguson et al., *Facets of the Renaissance* (New York: Harper & Row, 1959), pp. 117–119. Writes Kristeller: "Yet unlike Bacon and his modern followers, the Renaissance Platonists were no activists. Their ideal was that of the contemplative life, and their moral thought was dominated by the spiritual experience of an inner ascent which leads the soul through several degrees of knowledge and of love to the immediate vision and enjoyment of God. The entire meaning of human life is understood with reference to this ultimate experience, and insofar as the final vision of God seems to be attainable in this life, at least for a few persons and for a short while, the Renaissance Platonists reveal themselves as the successors not only of the ancient Neoplatonists, but also of the medieval mystics and spirituals" (p. 117).

Troeltsch suggests that even Thomas More, who, in *Utopia*, takes up a social subject, characteristically articulates his observations "outside of all real context" (p. 20). Cf. Max Weber, *Economy and Society* (New York: Bedminister Press, 1968), II, pp. 513–514, for similar comments concerning Renaissance humanism.

prescriptions when it comes to matters of this world, and especially to affairs of state. That attitude characterizes the "chain of thought," as Troeltsch correctly saw, running from Machiavelli to Hobbes. In his classic study, *Machiavelli and the Renaissance*, Federico Chabod captures the spirit of this third option:

> Nothing is further from Machiavelli's mind than to undermine common morality, replacing it with a new ethic; instead, he says that in public affairs the only thing that counts is the political criterion, by which he abides: let those who wish to remain faithful to the precepts of morality concern themselves with other things, not with politics.[8]

Hobbes did Machiavelli one better. Fully convinced as he was that religious and moral disputes were the cause of civil strife and disorder and thus that such beliefs were a positive detriment to civil life, Hobbes set out to place government and the direction of public policy on a footing entirely independent of religious and moral belief—namely, on the solid rock of self-interest. With Hobbes, the disjunction between civil order and the moral and spiritual life was complete.[9]

The point is that whichever of the three options is preferred, and there are no doubt important differences among them, they all ultimately

[8]Federico Chabod, *Machiavelli and the Renaissance* (New York: Harper & Row, 1958), p. 142. Against scholars like Isaiah Berlin ("The Question of Machiavelli," *New York Review of Books* (November 4, 1971) who have argued that Machiavelli intended to create a new "pagan ethic" with service to the state as the central value, Chabod is undoubtedly right to portray Machiavelli's position in "transmoral" terms. Machiavelli frequently recommends that morality, which is otherwise to be observed, must, on occasion, be disregarded and "transcended" in the interests of political success. Moreover, Chabod's formulation is superior, in general, to Michael Walzer's interpretation in "Political Action: The Problem of Dirty Hands," *Philosophy and Public Affairs* (Winter, 1973) 2, no. 2, pp. 175–177, which characterizes Machiavelli's attitude toward politics and morality in terms of the category of "excuse." According to Walzer, Machiavelli acknowledges "the existence of moral standards" (p. 175) but is ready to excuse a deceitful and cruel politician if he is politically effective. However, as Walzer himself admits, there is no sign of moral regret or reluctance that Machiavelli's politicians must "learn how not to be good." There is no sign of these things, I would suggest, because when it comes to politics, as Chabod indicates, moral concerns are decidedly of secondary significance for Machiavelli. Contrary to Walzer, Machiavelli's politician is not so much excused as *exempted* from normal concerns—a very different notion.

[9]See J. W. N. Watkins, *Hobbes's System of Ideas* (London: Hutchinson University Library, 1965) for an able discussion of Hobbes's "deconstruction" of morality. "[Hobbes's] civil philosophy will set out from an account of men as they would be if civil society were entirely dissolved. They are egocentric, restlessly ambitious, and lonely; though their bodies collide, their minds never meet. The scarcity of resources in a state of nature forces men to competitive strife; and competitive strife causes their resources to be very scarce indeed. They are imagined to be equipped with a moral vocabulary; but there are no objective moral properties to regulate its employment, no natural standards of good and bad; their moralizing talk rather tends to intensify their conflicts" (pp. 163–4).

carry the same message: The attempt to organize force, power, and wealth according to religious and moral prescriptions is not, at the end of the day, a fully appropriate subject for the humanistically educated individual. Such a concern is, finally, beneath the aristocrat of culture.

Weber and Troeltsch argued that a profoundly different attitude toward these matters emerged in the Reformation, and particularly on the Reformed or Calvinist-Puritan side. Out of that tradition emerged what Weber referred to as the "inner-worldly Protestant ascetics." These were, in effect, "worldly monks" whose vocation it was, now that the door to the monastery had been slammed by the Reformers, to pour their considerable moral and spiritual energies into worldly vocations, into economic and political activity.[10]

In that respect, these Protestant ascetics moved directly against the spirit of the Renaissance. Far from devaluing the effort to organize and direct force, power, and wealth in keeping with spiritual and moral insight, the Calvinists were consumed with doing just that. For them there was no higher priority than translating their faith into institutional terms, or than offering extensive and rather detailed practical guidance in the "cases of conscience" that confronted the devout in their daily lives.

Well over a third of the final version of Calvin's *Institutes of the Christian Religion* is devoted to questions of ecclesiastical order, with some very prominent and influential attention given to civil order in the last chapter. And Calvin leaves no doubt that his purpose in the *Institutes* is to direct attention away from speculative and contemplative theoretical reflection and toward "practical theology." His aim, as Weber understood, was to harness religious and moral reflection to "the disciplining and methodical organization of the whole pattern of [vocational] life."

The preoccupation of Calvin's followers with the issues of civil and ecclesiastical order—Knox in Scotland, the Huguenots in France, the Puritans in England and America, together with their passion for producing books on casuistry—attests to the power and persistence of this distinctive vision of the spiritual life.

But what is for us especially interesting about this Calvinist vision of true vocation is its attitude toward learning, toward humanistic study. Calvin was himself a product of Renaissance training. His use of original languages, his approach to textual interpretation, his deep acquaintance with classical authors, his style of writing are inconceivable apart from

---

[10]Troeltsch was greatly influenced by Max Weber's famous essay, *The Protestant Ethic and the Spirit of Capitalism*, in regard to the development of the spirit of "inner-worldly asceticism" and the importance of the Reformation (especially the Reformed side) in this development.

his humanistic education.[11] The same is of course true of English and American Puritanism. As Weber puts it:

> The great men of the Puritan movement were thoroughly steeped in the culture of the Renaissance. The sermons of the Presbyterian divines abound with classical allusions, and even the Radical [Puritans], although they objected to it, were not ashamed to display that kind of learning in theological polemics. Perhaps no country was ever so full of graduates as New England in the first generation of its existence.[12]

In connection with Weber's last comment, it is well to recall that the founding of Harvard College was one of the first items of business for the New England settlers and that the curriculum followed a rather conventional humanistic pattern. Moreover, to an important extent, the Puritan emphasis upon humanistic training or "liberal education" became the inspiration and the model for the proliferation of Protestant colleges across the land from the seventeenth to the nineteenth centuries.

On the other hand, if the affirmation of humanistic study is unmistakable, it is equally clear that for these Protestant ascetics the real purpose of humanistic education was systematically different from the purposes we earlier identified with the Renaissance. The original objective for establishing Harvard College was vocational through and through, as a contemporary observer reported. Along with the demand for training learned ministers, wrote Jonathan Mitchell, there is a "need for learning and education to accomplish persons for the magistracy and other civil offices."[13]

If the Puritans admired humanistic learning and praised the skills and techniques of logic, rhetoric, exegesis, and so on that went along with it, they were at the same time deeply apprehensive about the temptations to contemplative self-indulgence that lay in wait for the unsuspecting student. That radical Calvinist, Roger Williams, expressed these pervasive Puritan suspicions with characteristic bluntness:

> As to the name 'scholar,' [which] although as to humane learning [is] in many ways lawful, [when] it is appropriated to such as practice the ministry [, as] 'have been at the universities' (as they say), it is a sacrilegious and thieving title . . . . As to their monkish and idle course of life, partly so genteel and stately, partly so vain and supersititious, . . . it is a disgraceful

---

[11]The classic discussion of Calvin's humanistic background is Josef Bohatec's *Calvin und Budé* (Graz: Hermann Böhlaus, 1950), but cf. Quirinius Breen, *Christianity and Humanism* (Grand Rapids, Mich.: William B. Eerdmans Publishing Co., 1968), esp. Chapter 4, "John Calvin and the Rhetorical Tradition."

[12]Weber, *The Protestant Ethic and the Spirit of Capitalism* (New York: Charles Scribner's Sons, 1958), p. 168.

[13]Cited in Samuel Eliot Morison, *Founding of Harvard College* (Cambridge: Harvard University Press, 1935), I, p. 249.

and unworthy act [for them] to set a finger in any pains or labor. But the church is built upon the foundation of the Apostles and prophets, who were laborers, fishermen, tentmakers, Jesus Christ (although the Prince of life, yet) a poor carpenter, the chief cornerstone.[14]

Williams here calls attention to the ultimate Puritan fear: that the universities, in their search for "intellectual refinement and spiritual elevation," might become a sort of secular monastery, absorbed in the contemplative enlightenment of the individual or a small group and creating thereby an aristocracy of culture, idle and above it all, condescendingly indifferent to the cause of industrious, vigilant, down-to-earth, day-by-day life in the world.

Learning is legitimate so long as it is put to active and self-conscious use in guiding and controlling power and coercive force in civil life, in producing and distributing wealth in economic life, and in harnessing erotic power in family life. Calvinists did not reject humane learning, as they did not reject the ascetic calling. They transformed both in endeavoring to transform the world.

I am suggesting, then, that as we gather to debate the role of the humanities in relation to questions of public policy, we are the inheritors, particularly in this culture, of a profound and pervasive ambivalence toward what the real purpose or the heart of humanistic learning in fact is. It is, I submit, the great divide between Renaissance and Reformation that continues to fuel our own disputes.

Now if I am right, the first lesson is to acknowledge this deep cultural ambivalence and thus come to understand the sources and reasons for the conflicting visions and impulses that underlie the current storm over the humanities. That will mean, at least in the first instance, less inclination simply to choose up sides and batter away and a greater readiness to examine critically and reflectively (as humanists are supposed to do) what the respective advantages and disadvantages of these very different traditions are.

It will also mean having to reflect more systematically than I have observed in the discussion so far what reasons might be given for preferring one tradition over the other or possibly for working out some combination. Such reflection is unavoidable if, as I have suggested, it is no longer possible to speak dogmatically about the real purpose or the heart of humanistic study.

The second, and related, lesson is to begin to cultivate a spirit of tolerance and pluralism in approaching the question of the humanities and public policy. It will immediately occur to us that the Calvinist

---

[14]Cited in Perry Miller, *Roger Williams: His Contribution to the American Tradition* (New York: Atheneum, 1962), pp. 201–202.

attitude toward humane learning, uncontested and unchecked, can easily degenerate, as it did in many places, into thought control and indoctrination. Without restraint, it can also foster, as it has, a wooden and legalistic method of applying moral norms to civil, economic, and family life. The ways in which public policy was discussed and directed in Geneva, Edinburgh, and Massachusetts Bay at the hands of humanists of a Calvinist stripe must give us pause.

Indeed, a strong dose of learning for its own sake, of learning that is distinctly impractical and unuseful, of learning that is not vocationally oriented (as we would say), is a bracing antidote to the dogmatism and "utilitarian worldliness" (as Weber called it) of one side, anyway, of the Calvinist tradition.

At the same time, there are, it seems to me, equally distressing liabilities attached to the "aristocracy of culture," that were inspired in its various forms by the Renaissance. (Here I freely confess my own adherence to what I hope is a chastened brand of Calvinism.) Roger Williams had a point. Uncontested and unchecked, humanistic learning can become disabling and diverting in respect to the crying moral issues of our time—the issues of public policy, that is. If it is not careful, the academy does indeed tempt its inhabitants to a kind of cultivated condescension and self-satisfied indifference toward the menial problems of the vocational world—the regulation of armed force and weapons, the administration and direction of political power, the distribution of wealth, the allocation and disposition of medical resources.

By conspiring in various ways to cut the nerve of sustained and sophisticated moral and spiritual reflection on such questions, some of the representatives of the Renaissance among us have made it more difficult to begin to integrate vocational, including professional, education with serious and elaborate humanistic training. In fact, such an attitude simply serves to isolate humanistic study even further by laying down the law that humane learning must be concerned only with developing sensibilities and creating general frameworks of thought and broad qualities of mind.

Just as the Renaissance tradition has helped to keep the Calvinists honest, there is need, to my mind, for the influence to work the other way, as well. Given our heritage in this country, there is no obvious justification for dictating one and only one real purpose of humanistic study. Why not several real purposes at once, by means of a division of labor?

As Troeltsch saw, that sort of pluralistic approach, which encourages accomodation and mutual correction on both sides, had already begun to emerge in the seventeenth century, especially in England, and gained momentum by the time of the Enlightenment. Figures like John

Milton and John Locke had a foot in either camp. For both of them, Renaissance learning helped to relax the rigors of Calvinism. At the same time, each sought unremittingly to apply his adjusted version of Puritan faith and morals to the order of civil, economic, family, and church life. There is no other way to read Milton's defense of divorce in his pamphlet, *The Doctrine and Discipline of Divorce Restored to the Good of Both Sexes*, or his call for church reform in *The Reason of Church-government*, or his assault on traditionalism in *The Tenure of Kings and Magistrates*, to mention only a few of his remarkable essays on public policy issues.

Nor, having read the *Second Treatise on Government* in the light of the *Letters on Toleration* and the *Reasonableness of Christianity*, may we possibly doubt the Puritan sources of Locke's thought. Here is a man who is consumed by the Puritan impulse to address and reconstitute political, economic, and family vocations in a covenantal image. Although both Milton and Locke are deeply influenced by humane learning, they are as far from the typical attitudes of the Renaissance toward civil and commercial life as was Calvin himself.

Troeltsch's interesting generalizations about the Enlightenment extend this theme of interaction between the two traditions:

> The Enlightenment is closely allied to the Renaissance by a secular optimistic spirit, by the ideal of humanity realizable in this world (the ideal having its source in reason), and further, by filiation to Renaissance philosophy; and above all by adherence to the new science of nature created by the Renaissance. But in addition to the foregoing sources, the Enlightenment receives a part of its energies and goals from individualistic Protestantism successful in England, from the struggle of Calvinism for freedom of religious faith and for the people's liberty, and from the sober Protestant earnestness and utilitarianism of the ethics of the calling . . . . [In that tradition] the Enlightenment is democratic and engaged in building or gaining power, not like the Renaissance, which was aristocratic and [socially] parasitic. Consequently, [in contrast to the Renaissance] the Enlightenment . . . [is] a constructive and programmatic force sociologically.[15]

I am advocating, I suppose, that we, from our vantage point, keep the interaction going. I recommend that NEH and the state councils continue to encourage programs that represent both traditions. We should, I would have thought, resist any pressure toward forcing a choice. We may make room, for example, for a program funded last year by the Virginia Foundation entitled "The Ancient World," which was billed as considering "issues in art history and archeology in order to promote an exchange of ideas among all students of ancient culture." Nothing could be closer to the spirit of the Renaissance. At the same time, we

---

[15]Troeltsch, "Renaissance and Reformation," pp. 23–24.

may make room for conferences on "The Ethics of Land-Use," or "Ethics and City Politics," or "Ethics and Journalism," such as have also been funded by the Virginia Foundation. These all were in the vocational direction and quite appropriately, in my judgment.

Having uttered a plea for diversity, may I close with a word of bias. The fact that humanists sometimes fall flat on their faces when called upon to address policy matters ought to prompt us not to discontinue such programs, but both to improve them and to develop supplementary projects that begin to train humanities people who have the will and the aptitude to think with sophistication about the problems of policy.

I am currently involved in writing a book on human rights, a subject that is surely of the deepest significance from the point of view of the humanities. After considerable research, I have come to the conclusion that until I have spent sufficient time and effort finding out about the human rights policy process (as we might call it), any carefully formed philosophical arguments I may put forward will be "as a noisy gong or a clanging cymbal." I emphatically do not believe that well-crafted philosophical discussions of these questions are beside the point. Indeed, policy experts and decision makers can—sometimes by their own admission—use a dose of moral reasoning. Still, it is highly unlikely that unless one takes the shape and constraints of vocational life seriously, moral reflection will be of much use. Programs that increase the exposure of the humanist to the shape and constraints of the policy-making vocations would be all to the good. I hasten to add that I make this recommendation in regard simply to *one* of the appropriate tasks of the humanist, but *not* the only one.

May the storm over the humanities subside, and the conflicts give way to creative diversity.

CHAPTER 3

The Professionalization
of the Humanities

BRUCE KUKLICK

This chapter examines a major tradition of learned discourse in America from the seventeenth to the twentieth centuries and shows how our current understanding of the humanities emerged from it. This three-century tradition is defined by its central concern, the continuous tension between the eternal and the practical, the otherwordly and the wordly, in the discussions of the erudite.

Some of the learned in my tradition either claim (or live their lives in such a way as to suggest) that the higher learning is a good in itself, to be pursued without regard for anything but its own supposed intrinsic merits. Learned endeavor, on this view, has a transcendent value that needs no further justification. On the other hand, there have been repeated demands made for what we today call the application of the humanities to other more "relevant" fields of endeavor. Finally, some members of the tradition have persistently affirmed the role of learned discourse as the study that should suffuse life. In this last formulation that reconciles the first two positions, learned understanding is not irrelevant to practical affairs but only indirectly relevant. Its insights are not applied to everyday affairs because they are the background of educated involvement in life; they are not so much goods in themselves, irrespective of their function in the world, as necessary to all worldly goods.

If these strains in my tradition persist in America over three centuries, the form in which the strains are expressed changes. Different

BRUCE KUKLICK ● Department of History, University of Pennsylvania, Philadelphia, Pennsylvania 19104.

elite groups carry these impulses at different times and express them differently. And the social context in which the elites operate alters so that the ways in which the tensions are resolved differ in different periods.

I have used some simple conceptual slight of hand to make my thesis perhaps tautological, but I hope the tautology, if it is such, will be complex and interesting. For I have defined my tradition as that one that has tied our understanding of the here and now to what we perceive as more enduring and perennial issues. That is, the concerns of my tradition are just those that attempt to link the way we make our way in the world to the point of making our way. We must recognize that our present conception of the humanities is temporally bound; it will simply not do to assume that our contemporary academic conception— the humanities—is anything but a recent invention. At the same time I believe that at least in American cultural history of the last 350 years there is a set of abiding issues—the lasting interest in seeing how the infinite is lodged in the finite. If our present-day humanities derive from this interest, it follows that a tension is likely to exist between their theoretical and their this-worldly components. As a historian I want to show how these components connect to one another over a long period of time in which a changing cultural order has to embody certain tenacious human needs; and I want to evaluate how today's humanities emerged from this matrix.

Three periods of my tradition of learned understanding are worth examining. The first occurred in the colonies in the seventeenth and eighteenth centuries; the second occupied most of the nineteenth century; the third began in the last quarter of the nineteenth century and extends to the present, although it had transformed learned ideals by the interwar period. The first two periods form the historical backdrop to the third period, of the professionalization of the humanities, the formal topic of this paper.

THE SEVENTEENTH AND EIGHTEENTH CENTURIES

In the first period learned ideals were incarnated by the Puritans religious groups of New England. But speaking of the work of the Calvanist divines requires not just a grasp of divinity, of Calvinist theological ideas however much they have been stressed, but of the ministry as a social group. The clergy mediated conflicts between philosophic doctrine and the practicalities of the active pastorate. Calvinists in America negotiated issues between the preacher and his flock as well as between the authority of an individual congregation and the religious establishment. The church stood between the demands of the faith and the realities of the world.[1]

The American Puritans established themselves intellectually by criticizing what they saw as the Aristotelian logic-chopping of the scholastics. Philosophy had to be made the guide to life and the scholastics, so the Puritans held, in concentrating on certain aspects of Aristotle's logic, had removed philosophy from human affairs. On the contrary, Puritan leaders urged, rhetoric had to be elevated to an equal place with logic; people would then have the ability not only to grasp the truth but also to convince others of it. This so-called dialectic was a mode of analysis that enabled the learned to grasp the structure of certain propositions and if the propositions were true the structure of the world; *and* the compelling way of expressing these truths.[2]

This dialectic was the philosophic backbone to Protestant religion in the New World. Classical learning was put to use in a religious framework; the ancient languages were an adjunct to Biblical study. In a strict sense, then, the clergy were the preservers and transmitters of the classical heritage in America. In a wider sense the ministry was the principal upholder of the learned tradition we are examining: its perusal of the Bible was designed to explicate the appropriately ideal life man was to lead and to convey the point of leading such a life. But the ministers did not just expound higher truths. They were pastors concerned with the members of their congregations, absorbed in the needs of the church as a temporal institution as well as their parishioner's lives in the world. The Bible, as well as Calvinist theology, had to be made to fit the world, and vice versa. The clergy found its vocation in uneasily interpreting the sacred to the profane.

The controversies that have defined the early period of New England history are simultaneously social and intellectual, of the world and of the spirit. In the Antinomian controversy of the 1630s the ministerial elite fought to protect its position as the guardian of sacred truths against those who claimed that salvation was a private transaction between God and the individual, that the saved were beyond the laws of the church and the pastorate. As the custodian of the means of salvation, the established clergy responded, it had a responsibility for overseeing the

[1]See David Hall's discussion in *The Faithful Shepherd: A History of the New England Ministry in the Seventeenth Century* (Chapel Hill: University of North Carolina Press, 1972.)
[2]See Elizabeth Flower and Murray G. Murphey, *A History of Philosophy in America*, 2 vols. (New York: G. P. Putnam's, 1977), vol. 1, pp. 14–45.

process of salvation and, concomitantly, for checking natural man's evil impulses.[3]

The debate over the so-called Half-Way Convenant of the 1660s reflected somewhat different issues. Clergymen and parishioners arrayed themselves on different sides of the question of who should be admitted to the churches. Should the church be composed of all God-fearing and respectable people, or should membership require an actual experience of grace? In the seventeenth-century church membership was a potent affiliation, and New Englanders struggled for control of congregations. Narrower and wider conceptions of membership—over who could or could not belong—were theological as well as political issues.[4]

The Great Awakening of the 1730s and 1740s raised the same sorts of problems as did the Antinomian controversy and the Half-Way Covenant. Commentators have focused on the revivalist threat to the established clergy and the threat of the revivals themselves to stable and respectable churches, but for our purposes it is more striking simply to examine the career of Jonathan Edwards, the leading intellectual leader of the Awakening. Edwards became famous as a revival preacher, an activist proponent of vital religion in the 1730s. In the 1740s he wrote a number of treatises defending the revivals against both conservative criticisms *and* the orgiastic excesses of immoderate social revolutionaries. In the 1750s, after his own congregation had dismissed him, he spent his time in the then wilderness of Stockbridge, Massachusetts, composing dense treatises of Calvinist divinity in an attempt to make his theological formulations logically impregnable.

Edwards's career illustrates a central point I want to make about my tradition of learned discussion. He was first a practical evangelicalist whose job was, as he conceived it, to save souls. Later, during the Awakening, he wrote to defend his ideas of saving souls. By the end of his life Edwards was writing philosophic tomes about the Calvinist world view. Clergymen in New England did not all have careers that transversed these three positions—the practical, the theoretical, and the combination of the two. But Edwards's life does convey how the clergy in early America variously and not always comfortably developed the learned concerns I have specified.

From a narrow point of view the clergy's job was to deal with God,

---

[3]See William K. B. Stoever, *"A Faire and Easy Way to Heaven"* (Middletown, Connecticut: Wesleyan University Press, 1978).

[4]E. Brooks Holifield, *The Covenant Sealed: The Development of Puritan Sacramental Theology in Old and New England, 1570–1720* (New Haven: Yale University Press, 1974); Paul Lucas, *Valley of Discord: Church and Society Along the Connecticut River, 1636–1725* (Hanover, New Hampshire: University Press of New England, 1976); Robert Pope, *The Half-Way Covenant* (Princeton: Princeton University Press, 1969).

as did Edwards at the end of his life. Or clergy could be intensely worldly—as was Edwards as an active pastor at the start of his ministry. But the pastorate more often than not mediated between humanity and its creator—as did Edwards in the middle of his career. That is to say, the various New England cultural disputes in the seventeenth and eighteenth centuries reveal that, within the context of Calvinist religion, individuals could embrace the "extremes" to which I have pointed. Yet the mediating position was culturally central: the ministry in its various disputes tried to adjudicate the demands of this life and those of the life of the spirit.

Some commentators have urged that the political transformation of the late eighteenth century had its roots in the revivalism of Edwards: the impetus to the revolutionary and constitutional periods was the democratic and leveling experiences of the religious awakenings. That is, American culture can be construed as more or less monolithic, its concerns being transformed from a religious into a political direction.[5] What is more useful to say for our present purposes is that religion in the earlier period and the culturally dominant politics of 1763–1800 *both* had worldly and otherworldly dimensions.

We may concede that theology declined in importance at the end of the eighteenth century and even that the political elite became the principal carriers of ancient learning. *The Federalist Papers* clearly suggests the use of classical sources as ways of learning how a polis ought to be governed. The founders were also part of my learned tradition in America: they were concerned both with political reality and with the ideals that political life set out to achieve. Franklin, Madison, and Adams—to name only three—had all imbibed a Calvinist view of man; they were not optimists about human nature. They viewed government as a limitedly effective but crucial means of social control. But they also hoped that an appropriate government might promote a way of life that would protect individuals from the worst abuses of an evil state. John Adams's remark is here critical:

> I must study politics and war, that my sons have liberty to study . . . mathematics and philosophy, geography, natural history, . . . navigation, commerce, and agriculture, in order to give their children a right to study painting, music, architecture, statuary, tapestry, and porcelain.[6]

---

[5]See Alan Heimert, *Religion and the American Mind from the Great Awakening to the Revolution* (Cambridge: Harvard University Press, 1965).
[6]John to Abigail Adams, n.d., 1780, in Adrienne Koch, ed., *The American Enlightenment* (New York: George Braziller, 1965), p. 188.

The founders, that is, also tried to bring together, in the political realm, the ends of life and the details of living.

I believe learned impulses in colonial America were crucially embodied by the clergy. But even if one accepts the conventional view that the late eighteenth century saw a transformation in American culture with Calvinist religion being replaced by more liberal creeds oriented to the concerns of politics, it is nonetheless clear that both joined practical and otherwordly notions. The divines were blessed or cursed by the mundane. The Founding Fathers could not escape the lure of the etherial.

THE NINETEENTH CENTURY

In my second period the learned tradition was still defended by the clergy, but the social form of this exemplification altered. In the eighteenth century the clergy's role was diffuse; in the nineteenth century it was fragmented and specialized. The later active pastorate diluted doctrinal discourse to preacherly eloquence. The nineteenth century was the era of American oratory; a new sort of divine emerged who swayed large audiences with watered-down homilies.[7] The teachers of this pastorate were those in control of the burgeoning system of divinity schools that grew up in the United States in the first quarter of the nineteenth century, the first professional schools of higher learning in the country. By the middle of the century these men had no knowledge of the clergy's daily rounds but were able to devote themselves entirely to the enterprise of systematic theology.

When theology thus withdrew from the center of the colleges to the margin of the academic community in a special school, the constitution of the tiny but growing American university was weakened insofar as it wanted to preserve its continuity with the past and to safeguard the tradition we have been discussing. In the ancient universities theology was responsible for animating schools of higher learning with a sense of their comprehensive calling. The professionalization of theology in America in the nineteenth century, on the one hand, and the disengagement of the active pastorate from speculation, on the other, were early and potent symbols of the fragmentation of knowledge and culture. Divinity-school theologians acquired the social role of speculation, the ministry that of applying this speculation. In between was

[7]Donald M. Scott, *From Office to Profession: The New England Ministry, 1750–1850* (Philadelphia: University of Pennsylvania Press, 1978); Ann Douglas, *The Feminization of American Culture* (New York: Knopf, 1977); Daniel Calhoun, *The Intelligence of a People* (Princeton: Princeton University Press, 1973).

the religious leadership comprising the college professoriate. Almost all of these men were ordained clergymen, but they did not have their own congregations, nor was their major concern the elaboration of systems of theology.

For the college professoriate the learned impulses were neither merely speculative nor merely applied; rather, they infused the careers of the college teachers. The teachers compromised the otherworldly and the this-wordly traditional extremes now instutitionally located in divinity schools and in the popular pulpit. The vagaries of the earlier learned enterprise yielded to specialization in the nineteenth century, but also to a specialist group that trod between the material and the spiritual. Socially located as an entity, the professoriate functioned to inculcate the dominant values of various local cultures; teachers fortified the norms of the educated classes, the established moral and religious conventions. Custodians of the truths essential to civilization, the functionaries of higher education conveyed them to the young men who would assume leadership in the United States. The culmination of collegiate training was the senior course in moral philosophy, taught by the college president, always a clergymen, but one whose expertise was in academic administration and philosophy (and not theology). This class rationalized man's duties and exhorted the young to carry them out. The philosopher-president explicated the hierarchical obligations growing from the family that led to the rules governing social life and political economy; and he demonstrated the religious ground of all obligation.[8] These principles were ingrained in every human heart but also had to be educated and cultivated. In the properly trained, understanding ruled the passions,and deferential patterns clarified life's duties. For the philosopher-president the education of character disclosed the seamless web of personal forms constituting virtue and making self-control possible.[9]

Lest I have given the impression that we have discovered the Golden Age of my American learned tradition, let us also remind ourselves that this mediating group of clerics has usually been excoriated by scholarly commentators. As one more astute critic has noted, their theorizing was filled with "the flat metallic taste of facile moralism and unacknowledged self-aggrandizement."[10] The collegians actively attended to public affairs

---

[8]See Bruce Kuklick, *Churchmen and Philosophers: From Jonathan Edwards to John Dewey, 1746–1934,* (New Haven: Yale University Press, 1985).

[9]Donald Meyer, *The Instructed Conscience* (Philadelphia: University of Pennsylvania Press, 1972); H. Wilson Smith, *Professors and Public Ethics* (Ithaca, New York: Cornell University Press, 1956).

[10]Robert Charles Post, "Studies in the Origins and Practice of the American Novel: Social Structure, Moral Reality, and Aesthetic Form," Ph. D. Dissertation, Harvard University, 1980, p. 19.

and schooled their students to attend. Believing informed discussion essential to the republic's health, and sanctioned as spokesmen for the upper middle class, they debated the great issues of the day. But their perspective on political and moral life was jejune. Although not removed from the world, the professoriate was not perspicacious about it. It distinguished between politics and public affairs, offering learned comment on the world without being of it. The collegians' own textbook analyses dissociated political morality from actual political life, or rather, perhaps, mirrored knowledge of only a narrow, restricted, and genteel life.[11]

THE PROFESSIONALIZATION OF THE HUMANITIES

My third era, its formative years being those from the 1880s to the 1920s, extends until the present. It is associated with the rise of the modern university and the professionalization of all of academic life. As I have suggested, this view overlooks the professionalizing drive in theology that occurred in the early nineteenth century. But the conventional wisdom does expose aspects of intellectual life that are common to everyone connected with the higher learning today.

During the late nineteenth century the university as we understand it—the social organization defining the modern professoriate—came into existence. Amateur intellectuals, those without an institutional basis, all but disappeared, as the university came to be the sole focus in the production and distribution of knowledge. Various areas of study hived off from older and vaguer "departments" of inquiry, and scholarly disciplines were established as limited fields of knowledge in the university, distinguished by special techniques and an accepted set of doctrines. Academic departments grew up, and disciplinary integrity was defined by the number of positions in a given field the university would finance. Teachers were trained and placed in this field by an intensified apprenticeship leading to the doctorate and appointment as a college professor. The proliferation of universities and the enlargement of a new educational bureaucracy also contributed to the evolution of a novel twentieth-century way of life within which careers could be made. The professional grades centering on the concept of tenure were codified. An arcane disciplinary language, professional associations, and scholarly journals became common. Academics learned to consult, to raise funds, to receive grants, and to inhabit research centers of various sorts that live on the social edge of the university and participate in the culture of expertise.

[11]Meyer, *Instructed Conscience*, pp. 103–107, 114; Smith, *Professors*, pp. 25–27.

There were gains and losses in this process. Wealth, family, and gentility became inadequate to guarantee a successful life in the literary and cultural world. Appraisals of merit were more frequently made by the impersonal consensus of experts and came to depend on evaluations of published writing. Ministerial training ceased to be the *sine qua non* for having something to say about moral and social problems. Newly independent and qualified researchers explored the unknown territories of their terrains of inquiry in detail. On the other hand professionalization—that is, what I have been describing—painfully restricted the field of vision—and the visions—of its practitioners. To make a long story short here, the revolution in higher education and scholarship provoked the credible lament that we now know more and more about less and less.

I want to consider these developments in the somewhat wider perspective of what I call the ideal of applied science that dominated the emergence of the research university. In this period not only did religious training become inessential for higher learning but the ministry also lost its long control of collegiate education—dating back to the early seventeenth century—to a new breed of academic administrators. Like their predecessors, these administrators believed that higher education served the nation, but their idea of the nation's future was different. Post–Civil War America would be a business culture requiring many kinds of skilled men. As a repository for the knowledge an advancing and complex society would need, the university would train them. The new captions of erudition—symbolized by Charles William Eliot, the M.I.T. chemist who led Harvard for forty years—conceived the modern university as a group of associated schools wherein scholars of diverse interests would prepare students for leadership in American life. Believing that social usefulness and truth-seeking were compatible, they asked their publics not to look for immediate returns from universities; but they were convinced that an institution engaged in liberal studies would produce public-spirited, service-oriented men. Modern education would foster open minds and broad sympathies, not detatched scholarship. Although the universities would not be practical in a shallow sense, they would be scientific in the sense of wedding theory and practice. The American administrators specifically rejected the German conception of "pure" research; instead, when they imported conceptions of German scholarship they joined them to ideas of cultural serviceability.

The faith in all areas of academic life in this vaguely defined notion of science to solve ethical, social, and political problems was unbounded. This faith extended to what we today think of as the hard sciences that were justified not as yielding pure and applied research in the contemporary sense, but as all being somehow socially serviceable. Moreover, the academics who created the social sciences astutely conceived their own scholarly spheres on this model: they were systematic and objective yet also useful for practical problem solving. For my purposes what is important to remember is that professionalization took place within the context of this emphasis on applied science, the key to understanding the legitimate role of the university in society.[12]

CONTEMPORARY HUMANITIES AND SOCIAL SCIENCE

I have argued that in the earlier nineteenth century learned ideals were centrally embodied in academic moral philosophy. Today we would best comprehend this old discipline as an omnibus study of the social sciences conceived as explicitly normative. In the late nineteenth century various of the social sicence disciplines—economics, political, anthropology, and sociology—emerged out of the old moral philosophy. The other branch of nineteenth-century philosophy was called intellectual philosophy—composed of logic, epistemology, and metaphysics. And out of it developed what we think of today as philosophy *and* psychology: the latter was the empirical and practical study of the mind. What I am consequently asserting, then, is that the heart of the nineteenth-century learned impulse is the ultimate locus of contemporary social science. But the meaning of this fact requires greater elaboration.

The invention of the contemporary social sciences from the core of the learned areas of collegiate inquiry must also be seen in conjunction with the professional growth of what we *now* call the humanities. History had a minor belletristic role in the nineteenth-century college curriculum. As the old moral philosophy fragmented, history grew rapidly as an independent discipline absorbing, most significantly, those aspects of the study of politics and economics that had a past dimension. Indeed, history's ambiguous status—now categorized as a humanity, now as a social science—flows from its old association both with moral philosophy and with the minor field of nineteenth-century literary inquiry. The latter is contemporary humanistic history; the former is the social science component of history today. The modern languages and English as humanistic disciplines were almost completely the creation of the profession-

---

[12]These issues are discussed in relation to philosophy in Bruce Kuklick, *The Rise of American Philosophy* (New Haven: Yale University Press, 1977). But there is an entire literature on professionalization, a good bibliography for which (through 1975) is given in Carol S. Gruber, *Mars and Minerva: World War I and the Uses of the Higher Learning in America* (Baton Rouge: Louisiana State University Press, 1975), pp. 10–45, 261–81. For some doubts about the idea and further references see the essay by Laurence Veysey cited below.

alizing drive. Belles lettres were admitted late into the college curriculum as electives, but politically astute academics gave them credibility because of the late-nineteenth and early-twentieth century focus on the modern world as worthy of study.

The rise of English and modern languages accordingly came at the expense of the classical languages, and the place of classics in the humanities spectrum is perhaps the most striking illustration of the point I want to make. In the eighteenth century the ancient languages in America were a necessary prerequisite to all learned endeavor: they were the medium in which the West's concern for the connection of the here and now to the abiding was preserved, transmitted, and carried on. In the nineteenth century as the new learning eroded the absolute hegemony of the classical languages, philology emerged in the United States as the scholarly study of ancient languages. But it was also the professional analogue to moral philosophy. Theologians pursued philology as a means of understanding the most accurate and warranted interpretation of the Bible; mastery of Greek, Latin, and Hebrew was the key to comprehending sacred texts that unlocked the meaning of life. In this well-defined sense classical studies were a precondition to the work of the erudite. But as the study of language progressed in the nineteenth century, and the learned came to believe that language was more than a calculating device, philology's independent status developed and rose. Language was central to grasping man's nature and his knowledge of the physical and moral world; and philology was the principal and most high-powered study of language. Moral philosophy was the student's entree into learned ideals, philology the scholar's. By the beginning of the twentieth century, however, when philology or classics began to be recognized as a humanity in our current sense, it had ceased to have this wide-ranging, speculative import. In the twentieth century, classics became philological in the contemporary sense: the exact, antiquarian, and careful analysis of "dead" languages.[13]

In an important essay Laurence Veysey has argued that our current conception of the humanities came into existence after World War I when an ill-assorted and ragtag collection of academic disciplines banded together to protect their fields from the encroachment of the much better organized sciences and social sciences. Our current conception of the humanities, says Veysey, must be analyzed socially and politically: it is

---

[13]Jerry Wayne Brown, *The Rise of Biblical Criticism in America, 1800–1870* (Middletown Connecticut: Wesleyan University Press, 1969); for the later period see the discussions and citations in *The Divided Mind of Protestant America, 1880–1930* (University, Alabama: University of Alabama Press, 1982), pp. 14–41.

the product of disciplinary imperatives and social forces at work in the university as well as an unchanging, genteel, elitist, cultural context, exclusivist and socially pretentious.[14]

This examination is attractive and compelling, but its refreshing cynicism must be tempered by understanding a larger piece of institutional history and by realizing that it is possible to be too cynical. Let me recall some salient features of those disciplines organized as the humanities. By and large they were composed of the least worldly leavings in the university, after the hiving off of the social sciences. As I have written, the social sciences evolved from the older moral and intellectual philosophy, which spawned all those disciplinary studies of the human world that most easily fit the stress of the new universities on applied science. What was left could not be easily applied: for example, what we now call the humanistic discipline of philosophy proper—logic, epistemology, metaphysics. History made overtures to social science to the extent that it had roots in the old moral philosophy; its humanistic aspect came from its peripheral and effete literary role in the nineteenth-century college. Indeed, history and the modern languages were deemed inessential to the antebellum American college because they were vulgar—not vulgar in the sense that they were too practical for the professoriate to study, but vulgar in the sense that it was considered unnecessary for them to be studied by a professoriate at all. They were added to curricula as a concession to belletristic interests. Once the passage of time helped to give modern languages even a bit of veneer that attached to the classics, they became more pertinent to the concerns of the university. But they, along with the classics, had little claim to being an applied science and thus with philosophy and history (in its humanistice aspect) were relegated to the humanities.

The emergence of the humanities in the United States has little to do with the antiorthodox religious impulse associated with Renaissance Humanism. Rather, in America the humanities arose from the stronghold of orthodoxy. The nineteenth-century clergy gave birth to our current social sciences and, almost as an afterthought, our current humanities.

I originally defined learned impulses in the religious tradition I am surveying as those associated with linking abiding queries to the problems of daily life, and I contended that tension was always bound to exist between the worldly and the otherworldly. In the United States in

---

[14]Laurence Veysey, "The Plural Organized Worlds of the Humanities," in *The Organization of Knowledge in Modern America, 1860–1920*, ed. Alexandra Oleson and John Voss (Baltimore: Johns Hopkins University Press, 1979), pp. 51–106. Veysey pays lip service to a more complex intellectual analysis, but its substance is missing in this essay.

the nineteenth century the otherworldly pull existed in divinity schools, the worldly in the pulpit; learned impulses infused life in the work of the clerical professoriate. By the first third of the twentieth century divinity was not an important study, nor was the pulpit a significant public platform. The professoriate in the modern university was still the locus of the learned enterprise, but professionalization and homage to applied science had exacerbated the conflict between the relevant and the otherworldly claims of the learned ideals. The social scientists took over the relevant aspects of these ideals; what was called the humanities took over the otherworldly. That is, from my perspective the learned endeavor today embraces in two separate areas what in the nineteenth century was one. The social sciences codify the practical, the humanities the eternal dimensions of the old moral philosophy. The impulse to proclaim the purity of scholarship for its own sake became a barricade for humanists to protect themselves; and the claim that social science could resolve practical problems was a barricade for social scientists to protect themselves. The first group justified its claim on the university budget by its intrinsic worth, the second group by its instrumental worth. The view that the aim of the learned tradition we have been discussing should be to infuse life became more difficult to maintain. In the twentieth-century West it was harder to yoke the enduringly spiritual to the day-to-day material. The blunted sensibility of the social scientist was matched by the pompous arrogance of the humanist. Each needed a better half but could see in the available partner only a mortal enemy rather than a mate.

This is not to deny that within the contemporary social sciences and humanities the missing impulse did not develop. The connection of social science to the social order in terms of both research agenda and cognitive content appears to me undeniable. But many social scientists stalwartly affirmed a belief in a "value-free" social science. That is, they believed in a discipline that might theorize about culture but, in crucial ways, be independent of culture. Social scientists had a yen for the otherworldly in the sense of an objective realm free of the mark of social contamination. Social workers, public policy professionals, and so on might apply the results of social science, but these results, many argued, were transtemporal and transcultural. In the contemporary humanities, the emphasis on methodology and theory reflects an interest in establishing a scientific basis for, say, literary studies. Although distinctive, the humanities might then take their place among the applied sciences, making progress and advancing to new insights. The (unfortunate) chronic reinterpretation of texts might then yield to genuine knowledge. The desperate attempts by the humanities to appear relevant is another aspect of this institutionalized dilemma.

In this bureaucratic context it is not surprising that scholars concerned with less schizophrenic renderings of the learned heritage I have traced have today engaged in humanistic social science or called for the applied humanities. But this outcome of the heritage may mirror more a symptom of the disease than its cure.

PART II

The Humanities in Theory and Practice

CHAPTER 4

Theory and Application in Science and the Humanities

EDWIN T. LAYTON, JR.

One of the ways to conceptualize the relations between theory and practice in the humanities is the "engineering model." That is, one can assume that the relations between science and engineering are in some important ways similar to those between the humanities and their applications. As Arthur Caplan has pointed out, an engineering model involves at least three basic assumptions:

1. There is a body of knowledge in which it is possible to become expert. It should be added, of course, that the knowledge or "theory" is true and that it gives a correct description of the area of application under consideration.
2. It is further assumed that this theory can be applied in a more or less mechanical way by making deductions from it.
3. It is assumed that the decision or application can be carried out in a value-free manner. This involves not merely impartiality, but a certain neutrality in relation to the problem and the goals to which it is associated.[1]

Those who employ the engineering model usually make implicit use of a widespread theory of science–technology relations. According to this theory technology is applied science. Advances in engineering depend upon prior advances in basic science, and the task of the engineer

[1]Arthur L. Caplan, "Mechanics on Duty: The Limitations of a Technical Definition of Moral Expertise for Work in Applied Ethics," *Canadian Journal of Philosophy*, Supplementary Volume (1982), p. 8.

EDWIN T. LAYTON, JR. ● Department of Mechanical Engineering, University of Minnesota, Minneapolis, Minnesota 55455.

is to understand this science and apply it properly to practical problems. Thus the humanist who applies ethical theory is assumed to be functioning in a manner similar to that of the engineer in relationship to scientific theory.

There is, however, a serious objection to the engineering model. Recent research has raised doubt about the adequacy of the "applied science" theory of the relations of science and technology. If the engineering model does not work for engineering, why should it be assumed to work for the humanities? Studies of the relations of science and technology have revealed a hitherto unexpected complexity and many paradoxes. It is not always helpful to think of technology as applied science. Nevertheless, there are useful analogies between theory and practice in science and the humanities. But first it will be necessary to examine the traditional applied science model and the objections that have arisen to it. It is hoped that the newer perspectives of the relations between science and technology will prove to be suggestive for the problem of the humanities and their applications.

Vannevar Bush provided one of the clearest statements of the applied science theory of technology. Bush held that "basic research leads to new knowledge. It provides scientific capital. It creates the fund from which the practical applications of knowledge must be drawn." And Bush concluded that new products and processes depend on new principles and conceptions "which . . . are painstakingly developed by research in the purest realms of science."[2] Bush was one of the principal architects of America's postwar science policy; similar ideas have been used to defend undirected basic research elsewhere as well. A British government document upheld basic research on the grounds that "this constitutes the fount of all new knowledge, without which the opportunities for further technical progress must eventually become exhausted."[3] Through the efforts of Bush and other spokesmen of the scientific community, the applied science theory of technology has become very widespread. It contains two critical propositions. First, advances in basic science are necessary to advances in technology and engineering. Second, the theory holds that basic research in science is the source of the new knowledge needed by technology. Without these infusions of knowledge technology would come grinding to a halt like a giant locomotive that has run out of fuel.

The applied science theory of technology became popular despite the fact that it was not supported by critical research. When the theory

[2]Vannevar Bush, *Science, the Endless Frontier: A Report to the President* (Washington, D.C.: U. S. Government Printing Office, 1945), pp. 13–14.
[3]Central Advisory Council for Science and Technology, *Technological Innovation in Britain* (London: HMSO, 1968), p. 4.

was tested it failed dismally. One of the first of these tests was a report of the Materials Advisory Board of the National Academy of Sciences. The Academy kept editorial control but delegated the case studies to technical personnel with first-hand information. The editors constructed an elaborate seven-stage model which assumed an orderly sequence from basic science to engineering application. None of the case studies selected for study fit this model, however.[4] This report may have influenced a much larger study, Project Hindsight, conducted by the Department of Defense. The investigators spent forty man-years in study. They isolated 700 key "events" critical to the development of twenty important weapons systems. These events were then classified as either technological or scientific: if scientific they were further subdivided into mission-oriented and undirected research. Of all events 91 percent were classified as technological; only 9 percent fell into the science category. Within the latter group, 8.7 percent of the events were applied science; only 0.3 percent, or two events, were credited to undirected research.[5]

The results of Project Hindsight produced something of a furor in the scientific community. The National Science Foundation commissioned its own study with the acronym TRACES. It studied five recent innovations (increased to ten by a follow-up study). By extending the time horizon backwards, TRACES demonstrated the relevance of prior scientific research for a selected number of important technological innovations.[6] Both studies were open to methodological questions. The TRACES study did not fully support an innovations "chain" moving from pure or basic science to applied science to engineering application. In some cases technological events came before basic scientific ones.

If nothing else, Hindsight and TRACES stimulated a great deal of work in innovations studies. In general, the results have not supported the applied science theory of technological change. A British study directed by J. Langrish and others was one of the most impressive of the studies which cast serious doubt upon the existence of a "linear-sequential" chain leading from basic science to industrial innovation.[7] The

[4]Materials Advisory Board, *Report of the Ad Hoc Committee on Principles of Research–Engineering Interaction* (National Academy of Sciences–National Research Council, publication MAB-222-M, 1966).

[5]Chalmers W. Sherwin and Raymond S. Isenson, "Project Hindsight," *Science*, 156 (June 23, 1967), pp. 1571–77.

[6]Illinois Institute of Technology Research Institute, *Technology in Retrospect and Critical Events in Science*, 2 vols. (Chicago: IIT Research Institute, 1968). The original traces study of five innovations was extended to ten in a follow-up, Battelle Memorial Institute, Columbus Laboratories, *Interactions of Science and Technology in the Innovative Process: Some Case Studies* (Columbus, Ohio: Battelle Memorial Institute, 1973).

[7]J. Langrish, M. Gibbons, W. G. Evans, and F. R. Jevons, *Wealth from Knowledge* (London: 1972).

largest sample of innovations studied was in another NSF-funded investigation by Sumner Myers and D. G. Marquis. They found that most of their innovations did not originate in systematic research of any kind, but that most began with a technological idea of some sort or other. They found that the great majority did not involve systematic research at any stage of their development. Where research was involved, in most cases the technological idea stimulated the research, and not vice versa.[8]

Innovations studies have produced a rather confusing situation. At one level it appears to be quite obvious that advances in mathematics, physics, and chemistry have played a vital role in the development of technology. One does not have to look far to discover evidence of the influence of these and other sciences upon the engineering literature. Yet, at another level, innovation, basic scientific theory does not appear to have played the direct role implied by the applied science model. Clearly, there is a flaw in the common theory of the interaction of science and technology.

The idea that technology is applied science is quite recent in historical terms. It is absent in classical antiquity and the Middle Ages. Thus we find Aristotle drawing a sharp line between science and technology, since the former dealt with things that existed of necessity and the latter did not. Aristotle classified technology with the arts. He held that:

> Now since architecture is an art and is essentially a reasoned state of capacity to make, and there is neither any art that is not such a state nor any such state that is not an art, *art* is identical with a state of capacity to make, involving a true course of reasoning.[9]

Clearly, natural philosophy is not a capacity to make.

Aristotle's definition of art, if it does apply to modern technology, raises doubts concerning the validity of the applied science theory of technology. Indeed, it appears that the first assumption of the engineering model does not hold for engineering. For although there can be no doubt that classical physics constitutes a true theory, engineers have often questioned just how adequate the theory is for technology. One

---

[8]Sumner Myers and D. G. Marquis, *Successful Industrial Innovations*, National Science Foundation Report, NSF 69-17 (Washington, D.C., 1969). Marquis and Myers found that of the large sample of innovations studied, only about 5 percent had had their origin in an idea produced by systematic research, but that 15 percent of the innovations were in some way facilitated by systematic research (Table 19, p. 46).

[9]Richard McKeon, ed., *Introduction to Aristotle* (New York: Modern Library, 1947), p. 427. For the larger context of Aristotle's practical and ethical concerns, see Martha C. Nussbaum, "Historical Conceptions of the Humanities and Their Relationship to Society," Chapter 1 in this volume.

of the fundamental points raised by engineers concerned the idealizations of natural phenomena which underlie many of the laws of classical physics. Scientists were forced to simplify or "idealize" their picture of reality out of sheer necessity. Things like "fluid resistance" were not understood until the present century, with the development of boundary layer theory in fluid mechanics by Ludwig Prandtl and his followers. One of Prandtl's students, Theodore Von Kármán, showed that although the formula for fluid resistance developed by Newton was of no use to millers and shipwrights, it could be applied in some circumstances to supersonic flight, where the mutual attractions of the particles of fluid can be neglected.[10]

Even in those cases in which all relevant parameters can be taken into account, the classical physicist still resorted to idealization, because extra complexities often have the effect of converting soluable linear equations into insoluable nonlinear ones. Thus a second driving force behind idealization has been the need to linearize equations in order to make them soluable. As two contemporary mathematicians have observed:

> The classical methods of mathematical physics have often used linearization, and we have become accustomed to idealizations of natural phenomena which are frequently made for the sake of arriving at explicit solutions. One assumes ideal homogeneous and uniform fluids, no friction, perfect insulation, isotropic media, weightless and perfectly rigid objects, molecules that are infinitely small solid spheres, and collisions of zero time duration.[11]

We may summarize by saying that classical physics provided engineering with a true but idealized and incomplete body of theory. In many cases the idealized theory provided useful approximations, but in many others even this was not the case. The things left out of classical physics, such as friction, imperfect elasticity, and fluid resistance are often not epiphenomena to the engineer, as they are to the physicist, but the very essence of the technological problem. No one doubts that in an important sense Galileo's discovery of the parabolic shape of projectile trajectories was important. But this "law" is true only under ideal conditions of zero fluid or air resistance (i.e., in a vacuum). For gunners, however, the actual trajectories of projectiles in air was and is essential. The effects of air resistance are so great that this is in fact the crux of the problem.

The idealization of physical science had important consequences for engineering. It meant that the basic scientific theory provided by physics

[10]Theordore Von Kármán, "Isaac Newton and Aerodynamics," *Journal of the Aeronautical Sciences*, 9 (December, 1942), pp. 521–22, 548.
[11]Thomas L. Saaty and Joseph Bram, *Nonlinear Mathematics* (New York: McGraw-Hill, 1946), p. ix.

was incomplete and failed in many critical cases to provide a sufficiently accurate picture of technological reality. (This of course means that the first assumption of the engineering model does not apply to engineering itself.) Engineers found that if they wanted a science adequate to their needs they would have to build it themselves by adapting for their own purposes the theoretical and experimental methods of science. In doing this, engineers converted engineering into a scientific profession.

The role of science in technology might be approached by examining one of the best-known examples of the applied science myth. And this is the myth of James Watt's alleged dependence upon the prior scientific work of Joseph Black. Clearly, Watt's improvement of the steam engine by his invention of the separate condenser was pivotal in the history of technology. By the applied science theory an improvement in the steam engine would be expected to be an application of some prior advance in basic scientific theory. And scientists and historians of science have shown amazing persistence in attempting to interpret Watt's invention in these terms. The myth is that Watt got his idea from Joseph Black's discovery of the principle of latent heat. The myth was first started in Watt's own lifetime and he was at some pains to refute it. Watt's own words are significant:

> Although Dr. Black's theory of latent heat did not *suggest* my improvements on the steam-engine, yet the knowledge upon various subjects which he was pleased to communicate to me, and the correct modes of reasoning, and of making experiments of which he set me the example, certainly conduced very much to facilitate the progress of my inventions.[12]

It is interesting that although this myth has been repeatedly refuted since the time of Watt, it keeps blossoming forth again in the literature. The recent work of Donald Cardwell has, I hope, led to a decisive refutation. One of the most interesting parts of Cardwell's refutation was his demonstration that Watt was an important scientist in his own right and one of the founders of the science of thermodynamics.[13] Black's theory had no influence on his invention. But as Watt pointed out, he did derive modes of reasoning and of making experiments from Black.

The myth of Watt suggests one of the things that is wrong with the applied science theory of technological change. It is a hierarchical model which assumes that scientists and engineers constitute a single team or community, with a sharp division of labor. The scientists do the thinking and provide the knowledge, which the technologists then apply. This

---

[12]Quoted in Donald Fleming, "Latent Heat and the Invention of the Watt Engine," in Otto Mayr, ed., *Philosophers and Machines* (New York: Science History Publications, 1976), p. 123.

[13]D. S. L. Cardwell, *From Watt to Clausius, the Rise of Thermodynamics in the Early Industrial Age* (Ithaca: Cornell University Press, 1971), pp. 480–485.

implies a hierarchical subordination of technology to science. The hierarchical model portrays technology as a machine shop attached to an information retrieval system. But it is a fundamental fact of common observation that scientists and engineers are not part of a single community. Each has its own professional associations, its knowledge-producing institutions, and its degrees and patterns of recruitment. The communities of science and technology are enormously complex. But there is one great thread of simplicity that runs through the institutional maze. And that is that scientific professional associations greatly value knowing, whereas engineering and other technological associations place greater value upon doing or practice. These differences are built into the reward systems and other social controls adopted by these professions. The differences in value serve to direct particular communities toward their own specific needs. Thus we have medical scientists, engineering scientists, and agricultural scientists whose professional loyalties serve to direct their work to serve the needs of practice. Scientific communities have different needs, and they have social mechanisms which define good scientific work in terms of these community needs.

The existence of different needs accounts for the fact that science and technology evolved into two interacting communities rather than a single monolithic one. As technologists, such as Watt, came to need science, they were compelled to generate their own. Scientists, such as Galileo, often provided critical stimulus and guidance. But in the end technologists had to adopt the theoretical and experimental methods of science and adapt them to their own needs in order to generate the scientific knowledge needed by technology. To do this technologists had to borrow not only methods but institutions and values from science. In effect technology became a mirror-image twin of the scientific community. For each function, institution, or value of the scientific community an analog appeared in technology. But a subtle yet irreconcilable difference persisted, analogous to the change in parity between mirror images. That is, even when they may share the same values (such as knowing and doing) the communities of science and technology reverse their rank order. Thus any model of science and technology must take into account the interactions between two broad communities separated by different values, goals, and needs.

An interactive model of science and technology makes it possible to eliminate some of the paradoxes in the theories of their relations. It eliminates the apparent paradox that as technology becomes more scientific its scientific nature is seemingly harder to demonstrate. This is, in part, a result of trying to reduce the enormously complex set of all interactions between two autonomous communities to one particular form of interaction. In particular, technological change was to be explained where an advance in one of the basic sciences found direct application in a technological innovation. Although this type of interaction does take place, the innovation studies suggest that it is not typical. But there are many other types of interaction. Engineers, for example, nurture a growing cluster of sciences or "theories" such as the strength of materials and the theory of structures which are directly relevant to their professional needs. In the first instance, one would expect that engineers would have recourse to these sciences as their primary source of scientific knowledge.

The engineering sciences, in the end, came to differ in subtle, but significant ways from the basic sciences. One of the most important differences in the engineering sciences is that these sciences place much less reliance upon deduction. They are much stronger upon empirical induction. In many cases, these empirical results bear virtually no relation to the hypothetico-deductive structure so prominent in classical physics. Historically, engineers often first tried to use deductive theories, but found that they were not sufficiently accurate to guide practice. As a result engineers resorted to empirical formulas. A leading American hydraulic engineer, James B. Francis, after reviewing existing theories for the flow of water over weirs, concluded:

> The results, however, of these numerous labors, is far from satisfactory to the practical engineer. On a careful review of all that has been done, he finds that the rules given for his use, are founded on the single natural law governing the velocity of fluids, known as the theorem of Torricelli; omitting, in consequence of the extreme complexity of the subject, all consideration of many other circumstances, which, it is well known, materially affect the flow of water through orifices.[14]

Francis responded to this situation by developing his own empirical formula. Other engineers followed suit. With the advance of engineering sciences in depth and sophistication, the role of empirical formulas has been somewhat reduced. But they are still widely used and important.

There has been a great advance in the utility of theory in engineering in the last generation. The problem for theory in engineering lies with the complexity of engineering problems; the engineer cannot arbitrarily simplify the problem as can the physicist. For a sufficiently complete description of a real physical system the equations are usually nonlinear. In practice this means that there are no general solutions. Particular solutions can be calculated by tedious numerical methods. The computer has greatly facilitated the use of theory in engineering. With an appro-

---

[14]James B. Francis, *Lowell Hydraulic Experiments*, 2nd ed. (New York: D. Van Nostrand, 1868), p. 71.

priate program, numerical solutions can be derived, and they are being used more widely.[15]

But despite the remarkable advances in engineering theory since the Second World War, empirical methods are still primary. The enormous complexity of engineering problems makes it difficult to sort out all the physical effects that may be involved. Engineering innovations still require a tedious and time-consuming process of development, involving model testing and other empirical procedures. The experimental methods employed by engineers are not always closely linked to theories. Indeed, as Walter Vincenti has pointed out, engineers have developed empirical methods that are entirely independent of theory.[16]

To conclude, the engineering sciences enable technologists to close the gap between idealized physical theories and the actual phenomena under study. But because of the inherent complexity of the problems with which engineers must deal, the engineering approach is still largely empirical. Engineers still tend to view deduction from theory with a certain skepticism. The strong empirical bias within the practice of the engineering sciences makes a deductive model quite inappropriate for understanding how engineering operates. Thus actual engineering practice is not in accord with the first two assumptions of the engineering model. The theory provided by classical physics is neither adequate nor sufficiently accurate, and engineers have had to develop their own body of theory. The second assumption of the engineering model also fails. The engineering sciences that evolved to bridge the gap between theory and practice cannot, in general, be employed by a more or less mechanical deduction from theory. Instead the approach tends to be empirical and inductive rather than deductive and theoretical.

If the first two assumptions of the engineering model turn out not to apply to the realities of engineering and its relation to science, then what of the third? This states that technology can be applied in an impartial, value-neutral way, a way that is indifferent to the ends involved. If engineers did no more than apply science this might be reasonably correct. And the formula "technology is applied science" does contain a great deal of truth, if one does not place artificial restrictions on the source and nature of the science that engineers employ. But although such a formulation contains a great deal of truth, it is still

[15]This is based on interviews with many engineers, for example with Suhas V. Patankar, March 17, 1983. Patankar is well known for the numerical methods he has developed for solving problems in heat and mass transfer.

[16]Walter G. Vincenti, "The Air-Propeller Tests of W. F. Durand and E. P. Lesley: A Case Study in Technological Methodology," *Technology and Culture*, 20 (October, 1979), pp. 712–751.

essentially false. Despite the rising importance of analysis, the "bottom line" in engineering is still the act of synthesis which produces a working system of some sort. And the process that produces these artifacts or systems is called design; it is the crucial act of engineering synthesis. Or, to put the matter differently, there is a central element in engineering that is not reducible to natural philosophy. And this is precisely engineering design, the vital act of synthesis that produces the end products of engineering activity.

The primacy of design in engineering is of long standing. The earliest engineering notebooks going back to the sketchbook of Villard de Honnecourt were essentially portfolios of design. The scientific elements of technology were much slower to develop. But despite the growing importance of science, engineering design has continued to play a critical role in engineering. Indeed, design has long been considered the most characteristic part of engineering. When American engineering societies attempted to set down the specific membership criteria for defining the full-fledged professional engineer they did so in terms of design. The true professional engineer is one qualified to design. The engineers' criterion of "ability to design" is virtually identical both in form and substance to Aristotle's "state of capacity to make, involving a true course of reasoning."[17]

Whatever design may involve, it cannot be value-neutral or indifferent to ends. That is, engineering design does not fit the third assumption of the engineering model. Design is the adaptation of means to achieve some preconceived end. It is by its very nature goal-directed. Nor can it be value-neutral. For design involves making choices, choices that have both social and technical implications. And each choice leads to further choices. There must be some sort of criteria for making these choices. Thus design is goal-directed and permeated with value judgments at all levels. Design is also active, not passive. It involves doing or making something, worldly activities incompatible with passive impartiality assumed in the engineering model.[18]

One of the crucial differences between the old and the new methods of design consists of the explicit recognition of the value judgments that must be built into technological systems. In the older design methodology the designer employed a conceptual or mathematical model of the system which would allow the appropriate scientific laws to be applied. Thus the engineering sciences include idealized models of beams, tur-

[17]Edwin T. Layton, Jr., *The Revolt of the Engineers: Social Responsibility and the American Engineering Profession* (Cleveland: Case Western Reserve University Press, 1971), pp. 26–27, 30, 39, 49, 51, 80, 88–89. See also the reference in note 8.
[18]Thomas T. Woodson, *Introduction to Engineering Design* (New York: McGraw-Hill, 1966), pp. 3–4, 204, *passim*.

bines, heat engines and the like. These models had the effect of placing an emphasis upon the physical constraints; values and economics were treated as externalities. In the modern approach a very different type of systems model is constructed, called the "criterion function" (or "objective function"). In this case the technological system is expressed as a summation of separate terms. Each term consists of a criterion variable (x_i) which stands for a function the system is expected to perform, multiplied by a weighing coefficient (a_i) which expresses the relative importance or value assigned to the criterion. Thus one ends with a function in the form of $\Sigma a_i x_i$. By appropriate methodology this function can then be optimized.

This systems approach to design has several features worth noting. It explicitly subordinates science to values. As the author of perhaps the foremost text on engineering design, Thomas Woodson, notes:

> If this expression $\Sigma a_i x_i$ is a reasonable symbolic model of the system at what point do all the other mathematical models of system behavior fit? How about circuit analysis, thermodynamics, feedback control and stability, structural integrity, materials and process analysis? Are all these rigorous mathematical tools to be subjugated to subjective decisions from the top? The answer is, of course, that they are subjugated; but that as tools they do fit in at lower levels of the design process, aiding in producing adequate decision-making information.[19]

Woodson is very clear: engineering designs are not objective "scientific" givens which stand outside culture. Engineering artifacts are cultural products in which all manner of values may have an influence. Thus, as Woodson notes:

> As we look behind the scenes, we find major influences on decision-making coming from the individual's own value system, from that of his organization, and from the culture, as well as from technology.[20]

With the criterion function we have clearly come a long way from the rather naive theory that science makes discoveries which engineering applies, and to which humanity must willy nilly conform. It is clear from this perspective why humanists have done so poorly with technology. They have been led astray by a common misconception that confuses science and technology. Thus, the three characteristics of the engineering model of the relations of theory to practice delineated by Arthur Caplan all turn out to be false for engineering and its relation to science. Why then should such models be considered to apply to the relations of theory to practice in the humanities?

---

[19]Ibid., p. 205. It is interesting to note that the "rigorous mathematical tools" cited are all engineering sciences.
[20]Ibid., p. 204.

Though the engineering model fails, there are some useful analogies with engineering which may be suggestive in developing an understanding of the relations of theory to practice in the humanities. Engineering design, in particular, has much in common with the purposive social action with which the applied humanities are so critically concerned. Herbert Simon is one of the important modern students of engineering design. Simon has argued that engineering design is only a special case of a general type of thought characteristic of the professions. He has maintained:

> Engineers are not the only professional designers. Everyone designs who devises courses of action aimed at changing existing situations into preferred ones. The intellectual activity that produces material artifacts is no different fundamentally from the one that prescribes remedies for sick patients . . . . Design so construed is the core of all professional training; it is the principal mark that distinguishes the professions from the sciences.[21]

In this view there are many parallels between applied humanities in engineering and other professions. But it should be noted at the outset that the biomedical and legal fields are far more advanced in terms of ethical theory and applied humanities generally. That is, those concerned with applied ethics in engineering, a relatively underdeveloped field, have more to learn from these humanistically more developed fields than vice versa.

But some of the unique characteristics of the relations of engineering and science are highly suggestive. The theory that technology is applied science is a hierarchical theory; the engineering model would bring this into the relations of the humanities and the professions. Nothing could be more pernicious. First, hierarchical theories, whether for science or the humanities, are arrogant and elitist. They imply that one field is somehow superior to another. And this attitude, whether expressed by scientists or by humanists is likely to antagonize professional men and make cooperation with them more difficult.

Instead of thinking of medicine, law, and engineering as being in some way dependent upon a comprehensive theory in the humanities, one might think of the role of the humanist as comparable in some ways to that of the engineering consultant. The "client" in this case is usually a corporation, often a large and powerful one with its own staff of experts. In general, therefore, the consultant in engineering is not just an expert in a particular technical field. To function successfully, the consultant must be intimately familiar with the social, economic, and technical context of the problem. Most engineering consultants were

---

[21]Herbert Simon, *The Sciences of the Artificial* (Cambridge, Mass.: M.I.T. Press, 1969), pp. 55–56.

employed by the industry they serve at an earlier stage in their careers. Thus they have two levels of expertise. The same duality is highly desirable in the humanist who would seek to advise the professions. Obviously humanists cannot easily become physicians, nor can they practice medicine. But they can immerse themselves in the profession and its practice. One way to do this is to work, at least for part of one's career, in a professional organization such as an engineering department or a medical school.

The engineering consultant provides other possible analogies for the applied humanities. As Caplan has noted, moral philosophers admit that their role is more that of moral diagnosis than moral judgment. That is, they point out moral issues that have been missed, or anticipate issues before they occur, and they provide a proper classification for moral problems which do occur in day-to-day practice.[22] In fact, this is the role often followed by engineering consultants. To cite a case known to the author, one consultant was brought in because of noise coming from a factory smokestack. The consultant first identified the problem as one of periodic vibration in fluid flow. This then suggested a solution. But his work also suggested that other apparatus was susceptible to the same problem and that plans the company had underway might well produce the same noise problem all over again. The engineering consultant typically serves as diagnostician and advisor; he or she seldom sits in judgment.

The case of engineering and science serves to reinforce those writers in applied ethics who have already come to stress the vital importance of a thorough understanding of the context of ethical decisions. There are no doubt many important differences between theories in the humanities and in the sciences. But the example of scientific theory in relation to technology provides many parallels. Clearly gunners would not have been well advised to follow Galileo's projectile theory. Newton's theory was an improvement over that of Galileo, since he did attempt to include resisting media in his theory; unfortunately, he was not completely successful. The humanist would not want to be in the position of a follower of Galileo or of Newton trying to get gunners to use a theory that is not appropriate as a guide to practice. Only intimate knowledge, usually gained at first hand, will allow the practitioner to know how properly to apply this theory to practical conditions.

Engineering suggests several of the criteria needed for the successful application of theory to practice. All of these have been previously recognized by applied humanists; none is totally new. But the engineering–science division does suggest something that is, I believe, not an-

---

[22]Caplan, pp. 13–15, 17.

ticipated in the literature of applied ethics. That is that the conditions for the successful application of humanities to professions are also the conditions which have often led to the creation of autonomous sub-professions. Since we are dealing with an analogy, this is not a prediction. Will applied humanists sever at least some of their ties with parent humanistic disciplines? Will they form their own professional associations and perhaps seek separate graduate departments in universities to train future practitioners? The analogy with science and engineering does suggest that application requires some separation, but it does not predict the precise form of this separation. But those who would apply ethics must immerse themselves in medicine, engineering, or another of the professions. More than this, they must become morally engaged and committed to the profession and its problems. An ivory tower neutrality will not do. The need to master a novel context as well as the implicit value commitments provides the basis for some sort of separation between applied humanities and their parent disciplines. I should like to suggest that they already do in fact constitute subdisciplines. The existence of institutions such as the Hastings Center suggests that subdisciplines are already taking shape. Precisely what this shape will be we do not know, but the emergent institutional structure suggests that quasi-autonomous subdisciplines of the humanities will play an increased role in the future of applied humanities.

CHAPTER 5

Applied Ethics and the Sociology of the Humanities

J. B. SCHNEEWIND

A rather specific sociological situation gives rise to the topic of this paper and the others in this current Hastings Center volume. The situation may be described as follows. A large number of people in positions of authority either by virtue of acknowledged expertise or as a result of political processes must now make decisions which have several striking features. First, the decisions are to be publicly known, that is, known not only to those immediately affected by them but also to others whose concern may be a matter of principle rather than of individual involvement. Second, the decisions are problematic, and not just for technical reasons. Often the decision maker is not sure just what is the morally right thing to do; and if he or she is not uncertain, there are others who will find the decision problematic. Third, there is no code, or set of rules or norms, which is at once strong enough to guide and justify the decisions and widely enough accepted to guarantee that if decisions are made in accordance with it critical scrutiny will be satisfied. Nor are there traditional figures of authority who could do by personal advice and defense what a formal code might do impersonally. As a result, decision-making authorities and experts, pressed by those affected by their decisions and by others concerned about them, are coming to be willing, if not exactly eager, to find some sort of third party whose mediation and advice would be acceptable to themselves as well as to those directly affected by their decisions. They express interest in this for those preparing to enter into decision-making positions as well as for themselves; and students, either as potential holders of such posi-

J. B. SCHNEEWIND ● Department of Philosophy, The Johns Hopkins University, Baltimore, Maryland 21218.

tions or as sharing concerns about the decisions, look for education which will help them with these problems.

Historically speaking, I think this is rather a new situation. I shall not however discuss its causes. I propose rather to discuss the facts that people identifying themselves as coming from the humanities have stepped forward to fill the role of third parties, have been reasonably successful in gaining acceptance in this role, and think of their success as at least in part due to their training in and affiliation with the humanities.[1] There are a fair number of people involved in teaching such subjects and even in doing such work now, and they have created many of the paraphernalia of institutionalization: conferences, journals, courses, internships, degrees. It seems possible that we are seeing the formation of a new field of endeavor, which may in time come into maturity as an independent field of endeavor, making claim to its own standards and its own methods. Such claims are not lacking for applied ethics. This kind of growth of a new field has happened before, of course, most frequently when some branch of philosophy has burst its original bounds and become an autonomous science. Applied humanities began as applied ethics, and that in turn was initially simply an outgrowth of traditional moral philosophy. Should we view the spread of this movement as the first steps of yet another child of philosophy, tottering on its way to self-reliance, to the usual accompaniment of increasing scorn for its elderly parent? Without trying to answer this question, I do want to ask: what is it about the humanities that makes it possible for people with humanistic backgrounds to take on the role of third parties in the sorts of disagreements I have very briefly described?

I

It would help us to answer this question if we could find an account of the humanities which reflected both the humanists' view of their work and what the general public thinks it is. But this is not easy to do, despite the fact that, as John Higham has pointed out, "the belief that knowledge and the students thereof are divisible into two bodies, one scientific, the other 'humanistic', is . . . one of the constitutive ideas that frame con-

---

[1]"Loevinsohn particularly stresses the linguistic facility that has carried over from his philosophical work. In a last-minute fight over the wording of an amendment . . . he was . . . asked on short notice to come up with 'a verbal formula that got most of what we wanted while avoiding an objection raised by the administration.' Within moments the new language was in place, and Loevinsohn says: 'I couldn't have done it so quickly without training in linguistic philosophy'." In *QQ, Report from the Center for Philosophy and Public Policy*, College Park, Md., vol. 3, no. 1, pp. 9–10.

temporary intellectual life."[2] The well-known list of subjects given in the law which set up the National Endowment for the Humanities does not readily suggest such an account. President Reagan tells us that "it is the humanities . . . that provide the intellectual underpinnings for our values as a civilization. And deepen our understanding and appreciation of truth, beauty, adventure, art, and, yes, peace."[3] But this view—aside from the qualms it causes about the role of argumentative apologist in which it casts the humanist—fails to accommodate the longstanding and still powerful tradition which sees humanists as opposed to, and even subversive of, accepted cultural values. Nor do older conventional treatments of the humanities[4] do much to give us a rationale for the NEH list. Probably nothing can do so. For the list springs not from some deep insight into the nature of learning, but from the history of academic organization and also—for example, in its exclusion of the creative and performing arts—from the political exigencies connected with starting a new federal agency. If we are to get some help with our questions, we must look further.

Academic disciplines, like other occupational groups centering on knowledge, define themselves in several ways. Their own view of their history plays a role in their self-definition, but not a dominant one: thus we do not today confine the humanities to the founding discipline of the original humanists, the study of the Greek and Roman classics. What is more important is the discipline's sense of the kind of knowledge on which it centers, the way such knowledge is developed and used, and methods and possible extent of its dissemination. But no one discipline can define itself in isolation from others, for all make claims to possess certain areas of knowledge, and these claims overlap. Every time a new field wins general recognition it forces a reassessment and redefinition of older fields. We thus understand any one discipline, or set of disciplines, only by seeing the differences generally accepted as existing between it and the others. An important part of the difference is constituted by the position occupied by a discipline in the society's hierarchy of prestige and power. New areas sometimes displace old ones, as the sciences did the humanities; at other times they are kept comfortably below them, as medicine has kept nursing subordinate. We need to look at the humanities in this light, and particularly in the light of American views of the sciences.

[2]John Higham, *Writing American History* (Bloomington: Indiana University Press, 1970), p. 6.
[3]Quoted in *Proceedings and Address of the American Philosophical Association*, vol. 56, no. 3, p. 377.
[4]Such as that in the thoughtful book by Howard Mumford Jones, *One Great Society* (New York: Harcourt, Brace & Company, 1959).

For this reason I will begin with a reminder that the notion of science current in the United States is narrower than that long used and still largely current in other societies. "The restrictive meanings of 'science'," says Fritz Machlup,

> limiting the term to empirical, positive (nonnormative), operational, falsifi- able propositions, or even to systematic study of natural (nonsocietal, non- cultural) phenomena are confined to Anglo-American parlance. In French, German, Italian, Russian, Japanese, and most other languages, the words for 'science' stand for *systems of knowledge acquired by sustained study*. . . . There is no difference in these languages between scientists and scholars. . . . This is reflected in the organization of the academies of sciences in many countries.[5]

The narrower sense of *science* was enshrined in John Stuart Mill's *System of Logic* (1842), one of the most widely read and influential writings of the nineteenth century. Mill not only gave a roughly positivistic inter- pretation of the physical sciences. He argued that the social sciences, or, as he called them, the moral sciences, could use the same methods the natural sciences use; and he ended his book with a chapter on the logic of practice, in which he gave classical expression to the view that values cannot be derived from, but must be brought to, the sciences. He thus provided an important impetus for separating the humanities, with their longstanding association with values, from the sciences—an impetus more successful in England and the United States than on the continent, where antipositivist movements had a power they never ac- quired here.

Intellectual groundings alone do not explain socially accepted groupings of disciplines, but I cannot try to trace the whole history of the separation of the humanities from the other disciplines here. Higham tells us that the crucial step in this country occurred in 1923, when the social science organizations broke away from the broadly conceived American Council of Learned Societies, which had been founded in 1919 to represent all the disciplines other than the natural sciences.[6] The aim of the social scientists was not to distance themselves from the natural sciences. It was rather to stress their distinctness from the older disci- plines, which were not value-free, did not have research programs, and were not cumulative and progressive in the way the social sciences thought they themselves were. As scientists both natural and social began to find positions, funding, and influence in government and in- dustry—aided in this by the needs generated by World War II—they came to feel themselves more and more different from the remaining

[5]Fritz Machlup, *Knowledge: Its Creation, Distribution, and Economic Significance*, vol. 1 (Prince- ton: Princeton University Press, 1980) pp. 67–68.
[6]Higham, pp. 16–17.

areas of study, which had not yet overcome the longstanding American separation of academics from the centers of power.[7] They also came to dominate the curriculum. Their disciplines were ratified by society as being useful; they led to jobs; they provided the training necessary for entry into professional school; and they had to be taught in sequential order. The natural sciences still maintain precedence on these points over the social. But as the tripartite grouping came to be institutionalized in academic administrative structures, in philanthropic foundations, and in the federal government, and as it spread to Europe, the humanities emerged as a collection of disciplines linked together largely because they lack the features present in the areas which had captured for themselves the eulogistic name of "science." And as the social sciences move away from their alliance with positivism, even this defining distinction becomes, in Geertz's term, "blurred."[8]

II

We might hope to find a more positive characterization of the humanities by looking at the beliefs and attitudes of those who most obviously make their careers in them—members of humanities departments. But research on the sociology of academe has not specifically investigated or factored out the humanists to any very helpful extent. We have ample data about the more obvious characteristics of the profession. Between 1938 and 1980 some 76,000 Ph.D.'s were awarded in the humanities, here taken to include history, art history, music, speech and theater, philosophy, classical and modern languages and literatures, and "other humanities" (e.g. library and archival science).[9] This compares with about 265,000 doctorates in science and engineering and 102,500 in the social sciences. History alone accounts for about 21,000 Ph.D.'s. So if history is counted, as some people count it, with the social sciences, then the sciences and engineering are close to five times as large as the humanities, the social sciences over twice as large. Although

[7]I am indebted here and generally to Edward Shils, *The Constitution of Society* (Chicago: The University of Chicago Press, 1983), especially Chapters 8 and 10.
[8]Clifford Geertz, "Blurred Genres: The Refiguration of Social Thought," in *American Scholar*, vol. 49, no. 2, pp. 165–79; and see, more generally, his *The Interpretation of Cultures*, (New York: Basic Books, 1973).
[9]Data in this paragraph are taken from *Science, Engineering, and Humanities Doctorates in the United States, 1981 Profile* (Washington D.C., National Academy Press, 1982) published for the National Research Council, Betty D. Maxwell, Project Director. I have also consulted the *1979 Profile* and Frank J. Atelsek and Irene L. Gomberg, *Selected Characteristics of Full-Time Humanities Faculty, Fall 1979*, Higher Education Panel Reports no. 51, August, 1981, American Council on Education.

the sciences are more heavily male than the humanities (sciences 87.6 percent, humanities 72.8 percent), the latter are more nearly all white (sciences 87.5 percent, humanities 92.1 percent). The scientists have a slightly higher employment rate than the humanists and are far more widely dispersed outside the teaching world. Educational institutions employ only 53 percent of scientists but 85 percent of those in the humanities. In the past few years there has been some increase in nonacademic employment of humanists, a slightly higher percentage of those who got their degrees after 1975 being employed in such jobs than of those with earlier doctorates. We cannot tell from the data how many of these nonacademic jobs are in applied humanities.

Various studies by Seymour Martin Lipset and Everett Carll Ladd, Jr., help us to fill in the picture a little despite their lack of interest in breaking down their data, in most areas, to show the peculiarities of humanists. In "The Changing Social Origins of American Academics"[10] they present evidence to show that despite the enlargement of faculties since the 1960s and the effort to open them to groups previously excluded from membership by racist, sexist, and other prejudices, there has been little increase in the extent to which faculty members are drawn from blue collar and low income families. In fact the proportion of faculty members describing themselves as coming from poor families declined somewhat between 1969 and 1975, the dates of the surveys. In the humanities, art historians, archaeologists, and classicists used to come largely from families with substantial wealth. Although this is less true today, the change is apparently not significant enough to show up in large-scale data of the kind Lipset and Ladd collect. Particularly among younger faculty members, they detect an increase in the numbers reporting their families as wealthy, and they conclude that "the expanding profession has been recruiting from the more privileged sectors." This, they note, is in striking contrast to the business world, where there has been a marked increase in the employment of people from lower economic levels.[11] Their surveys confirm the impression any experienced academic will have, that the numbers of women, Jews, and Catholics have increased significantly, and that the numbers of academic minority group members have not increased nearly so much. Lipset and Ladd give an interesting differentiation of Protestants on faculties, showing that Congregationalists, Presbyterians, and Episcopalians are represented in far higher numbers than their presence in the American population generally would indicate. They add that Baptists and Roman

[10]In Robert K. Merton, James S. Coleman, and Peter Rossi, eds., *Qualitative and Quantitative Social Research*, New York, 1979.
[11]Merton et al., pp. 322–323.

Catholics are under-represented by this criterion. I would hazard the guess that what this adds up to is that faculties have achieved little if any increase in the presence of people who are likely to bring values into the academic world that are not already dominant there.

About those values Lipset and Ladd do have some things to tell us, and here they are rather more specific about humanists as a special group. They have argued in several places that social scientists and humanists are far more liberal, on general political affairs, than the population at large, and more liberal than any of their other academic colleagues. The social scientists come in first on various measures of liberality, the humanists second, natural scientists rank in about the middle of the academic world, and those in business, engineering, agriculture, and other applied fields are most strongly conservative.[12] Correlated with political liberalism, their data indicate high academic achievement, as viewed by the academic world itself, in terms of publications, grants, and honors. Lipset has argued in a separate paper that the members of elite disciplinary academies are more liberal than even their successful counterparts who are at the very top of the slippery pole.[13] Finally, Lipset and Ladd have investigated the extent to which various faculty groups would describe themselves as intellectuals, scholars, scientists, professionals, or teachers. They take an intellectual to be not simply one engaged in learned or technical professions but one who has a general and probably doctrinaire stand on political and social issues. They found that humanists are more willing than any other academic group to think of themselves as intellectuals—and also more willing to think of themselves as teachers. Of humanists, 21 percent accept the label "intellectual," but only 14 percent of social scientists, 6 percent of natural scientists, and 5 percent in the professions.[14]

III

Little of this information is surprising, and still less of it offers any clues as to why humanists should be able to step into the role of third party consultants in difficult moral issues. Of course those humanists

[12]Everett Carll Ladd, Jr., and Seymour Martin Lipset, *The Divided Academy* (New York: McGraw Hill, 1975), p. 60, and the whole of Chapter 3. These two authors also published reports on the constitution of faculties in *The Chronicle of Higher Education*, September 15, 1975–May 24, 1976, and October 3, 1977–April 24, 1978. In most of these no special data concerning humanists are given.

[13]Seymour Martin Lipset, "The Academic Mind at the Top," *Public Opinion Quarterly*, vol. 46, pp. 143–68.

[14]Lipset and Ladd, *The Chronicle of Higher Education*, vol. XII, no. 8, p. 14.

who think of themselves as intellectuals may believe they have something of great value to offer. But the question is not whether they do or not, but why they, or other humanists, might be accepted as having some sort of right to speak out on such issues, or some kind of special authority.

The answer is not difficult when what we have in mind is the application of historical techniques to matters of immediate public concern. Here we have a fairly straightforward case of applied humanities, or social science if you prefer. Whatever the uses to which public history or corporate historians are put, whatever the controversies surrounding the training of personnel for such positions, the cognitive core is the same as that in academic history itself, and the notion of putting these skills to work in a practical setting is fairly unproblematic. The problematic cases are those in which decisions strongly affected by values and morality are at issue, and it is on these that I will concentrate. I will therefore in what follows not be considering history as a humanistic discipline—not because it matters whether we call it one or not, but simply because the distinctive humanistic subjects involved in the disputes I have in mind are philosophy and literature, and perhaps to a lesser extent art history.

The question is whether there is some sense of the humanities, shared by humanists and the public, which might help to explain why the latter would be prepared to think of the former as pertinent authorities from whom assistance might be expected in difficult decisions of the sort I have described. I think there is, although like almost everything about the identity of the humanities the matter is controversial (and perhaps a willingness to engage in just such controversies is a mark of a humanist).

First, then, in philosophy and literature and the study of the arts the work of humanists is very much bound to certain central texts or objects: books, pictures, statues, pieces of music, plays—for convenience I shall use the word *text* to refer to all of them. Being a classicist is most simply defined as being a student of the work of Homer and Aeschylus and Vergil and people like that. To be a philosopher is to be able to understand and talk about the things Plato and Descartes and Kant wrote, and problems like theirs. There are of course numerous specialists within the humanities who do not deal directly with the texts. Numismatists, epigraphers, symbolic logicians, and linguists serve others as well as those who work with our texts, but they are classed as humanists because of their connection with work on those texts. History itself does not (except in the branch of intellectual history) deal with the texts either; but, like the other disciplines I have just mentioned, it is valuable, indeed indispensable to those who do.

Second, the humanities deal with subjects which are supposed to be directly interesting and accessible to the general educated public, and ideally to every person. Poems, plays, novels, pictures, philosophical view of life, we suppose, do not require the introduction given in a classroom and can certainly go on being a part of a life after formal education is finished. No doubt the social and natural sciences expect that the general public will be interested in their recent developments. But there is an important difference, which I would put this way. In the humanities the *very same texts* (in the broad sense) which we study are what we suppose the general public is interested in and can benefit from. We think that they and we will, or anyway should, have a core of common knowledge or a common range of acquaintance with texts. Then the difference between them and us is just that we have spent more time and trouble thinking and talking about those texts than the nonprofessional reader of them. We know more, but we know more about something about which the public knows something. This fact and the equally significant fact that we train our successors largely by making them read our central texts help to bring out one difference between the sciences and some, at least, of the humanities. Natural and social scientists are not trained by studying the classical writings of their discipline's past. They do not expect those texts to be the bridge between themselves and the nonprofessional with an interest in science. And in fact when texts in the sciences come to be of interest to people outside the field, it is often a sign that they are coming to be treated as literature or as some other concern of the humanities. Thus Freud is of less interest to psychologists now than he is to philosophers and literary critics; and it is not the historians of Rome who write about Gibbon, but the students of narrative form or of historiography.

Third, the texts which are central to the public view of our identity and to our own view are inextricably and essentially involved with the deepest of human values and meanings and significances. They require not only understanding but assessment. And we must offer assessment in areas of considerable complexity and controversy, where there is no settled method or set of methods, and no question of abandoning these issues and these modes of discourse for others which might be value-neutral and with which we could be assured of growing consensus from generation to generation. There is certainly progress in the establishment of verbally exact texts or precisely dated artifacts, or in knowledge of the context of a writer's work or in the grasp of a painter's political aims. But insofar as humanists work with texts, it seems to be of the essence of our work that we are involved with contested interpretations and revisable evaluations. It is no accident, as the phrase goes, that there should be "revolutions" in the assessment of thinkers like Hegel and

Nietzsche, and comparable alterations in the way we view artists and composers. The endless possibility of such revolutions is one of the things that distinguishes humanistic scholarship from the work of dogmatists and apologists, who may very well discuss some of the same texts we discuss but who cannot take them, as we do, to be challengeable through and through.

These three features do not define the humanities. They do not characterize all, perhaps not even a majority, of faculty members in humanities departments. I have no statistics on which to base the claim that a great many such faculty members do nonetheless think of themselves in these terms. And I have no special data to show that these are the terms of the public understanding of the humanities. On this last matter, however, there is a fact of some significance which may help. For various reasons philosophy and some aspects of the study of literature have become very technical in the past few decades. Philosophers have developed research programs addressed almost entirely to problems of interest to other professional philosophers with similar programs, and for a while the old common problems of philosophy were dismissed as not intelligible or not worthwhile. The public response to this was interesting. When a science begins, it is rarely so technical that it cannot be understood by the lay public; indeed much of the scientific work of previous centuries was done by wealthy amateurs. But when a science takes off and becomes too difficult for the lay enthusiast to follow, the public sees the development as a sign that the scientists are doing what they ought to do and that progress is being made. Not so with the increased technicality of philosophy: rightly or wrongly—and I am not concerned with this question—the public felt that philosophers were ceasing to do what they ought and that so far from progress being made, there was reason for concern for the health and even the existence of the subject. There have been similar, if milder, complaints about some sorts of literary criticism. But complaints of this sort would not exist, would indeed be incomprehensible, unless the public had a view of the humanities which included something like the features I have sketched.

My suggestion, then, is that these three features explain why the humanities can be seen as providing appropriate education for people who propose to serve as third parties giving advice and enlightenment about the difficult value problems that seem to arise so frequently in our times. The humanities are not value-neutral, in the way the social sciences claim to be. But the texts with which we work, as we work with them, are not and cannot be identified with the beliefs of any special group or the ideology of any class. Our teaching is directed at showing, among other things, that texts which may seem inaccessible or unrelated to our lives are not so; and in the course of doing this we must suggest that the complexities and difficulties in the texts may be matched by those in our lives. Although as teachers we are more expert at reading our texts than the students are, there is no clear structure of authority in the humanities. We ask students to respond to the texts with their own intelligence and sensibility, not to take some reading as definitively established. The very fact that makes humanists the target of jokes and criticism when we are compared with scientists—that we do not seem to settle issues, that we make so little progress—makes our work an appropriate model for the real issues of morality. For morality itself does not make much progress either. The basic principles stay pretty much the same; the difficulties arise in interpreting them in new and changing situations. Critics from the left and the right will dispute this description of humanistic work, saying that we are really masking ideological positions, either forwarding class privilege or subverting established order. I think these criticisms wide of the mark; but although they deserve an examination, I cannot give it here. Instead I shall merely point out that if the public generally sees the humanities in the way I have suggested, then it is not implausible to suggest that at present the public believes that in them we have the main cultural repository of texts dealing with complex issues of value, and in the humanists the sole body of people educated to think about those issues from a nonpartisan point of view.

IV

I turn now to applied humanities, and more specifically to applied ethics. How are we to look at the production and use of knowledge in this enterprise? How are its relations with established disciplines to be understood? I will discuss, in order to reject, three answers to these questions and will end by proposing an answer I think is slightly— perhaps only slightly—better.

We might be tempted at first to think of those in applied ethics as being like intellectuals in politics. But although humanities professors may like to think of themselves as intellectuals, this would describe at most a small segment of those with interests in applied humanities. The intellectual in politics has an abstract program relating to the social structure and political operation of society as a whole and is making an effort to bring about large-scale changes. There are relatively large-scale or programmatic implications in many of the activities of applied humanists—in the ecology groups, for example—but what seems more evident is a willingness to work with existing authorities at piecemeal reform and at the mitigation of some of the worse examples of harmful action. The vast bulk of the discussions published as applied ethics deal with carefully circumscribed issues and display no general theoretical approach to society as a whole. Applied humanists do not look much like the intellectual in politics.

They also do not look very much like engineers, who are sometimes said to apply pure scientific theories to particular practical problems. The excellent paper Professor Layton presented to this group casts doubt on the general claim that technology advanced by application of theory to practice. But if the model is inaccurate even on its home territory, it is in even worse shape with respect to applied ethics. For in the first place there are no theories coming from the humanities which are in any way as clear, definite, and well established as those provided by the sciences. And in the second place, insofar as philosophy provides theories clear enough to lead to definite solutions to practical issues, the use actually made of them in applied ethics is very far from this. My first point perhaps need not be defended here. The second can be supported by a review of the now very numerous texts in applied ethics.[15] I hardly need say that these texts may not show us what would occur in an actual situation in which a humanist is a consultant on a live issue. But they hold up a pedagogical model which shapes the ideas students have of applying ethics, and they reflect what teachers want to present. In these texts, whatever their differences, it is clear that theory plays second fiddle to case studies. It does so in two respects. First, relatively little space, sometimes even none, is given to presentations of abstract philosophical theories of ethics. In Bandman and Bandman, *Bioethics and Human Rights*, about fifty pages out of 360 are given to general accounts of rights; the remainder are dedicated to discussion of very specific health care issues. Barry, in *Moral Aspects of Health Care*, writes thirty pages summarizing egoism, utilitarianism, nonconsequentialism (Kant, Ross, Rawls) and Roman Catholic natural law theory. The rest of his 450 pages is devoted to special issues. A similar pattern is found in Munson's

---

[15]My remarks in this and the following paragraph are based on examination of the following volumes: Elsie L. Bandman and Bertram Bandman, *Bioethics and Human Rights* (Boston: Little Brown and Company, 1978); Vincent Barry, *Moral Aspects of Health Care* (Belmont, CA: Wadsworth Publishing Co., 1982); Michael D. Bayles and Kenneth Henley, *Right Conduct: Theories and Applications* (New York: Random House, 1983); Tom L. Beauchamp and Terry P. Pinkard, *Ethics and Public Policy* (Englewood Cliffs, NJ: Prentice Hall, 1983); Baruch Brody, *Ethics and Its Applications* (New York: Harcourt Brace Jovanovich, 1983); Virginia Held, *Property, Profits, and Economic Justice* (Belmont, CA: Wadsworth Publishing Co., 1980); Thomas A. Mappes and Jane S. Zembaty, *Social Ethics* (New York: McGraw Hill, 1982); Ronald Munson, *Intervention and Reflection: Basic Issues in Medical Ethics* (Belmont, CA: Wadsworth Publishing Co., 1983); James Rachels, *Moral Problems* (New York: Harper & Row, 1979); Charles L. Reid, *Choice and Action* (New York: Macmillan, 1981); Earl E. Shelp, *Justice and Health Care* (Dordrecht: D. Reidel, 1981); Richard A. Wasserstrom, *Today's Moral Problems* (New York: Macmillan, 1979).

Intervention and Reflection. Some books present more theory: Reid, *Choice and Action*, and Bayles and Henley, *Right Conduct*, devote just under half their space to excerpts from well-known theoretical writings before moving on to selections on specific moral issues. But a number of books give no space at all to expositions of general theory. This is true, for example, of Beauchamp and Pinkard, *Ethics and Public Policy*; Mappes and Zembaty, *Social Ethics*; and Wasserstrom, *Today's Moral Problems*. No doubt books like those in the last category are often used in conjunction with readings of a purely theoretical nature; but there is nothing to prevent a teacher from making one of them the sole source of class readings.

The second way in which theory takes a back seat is in the use that is made of it. The most extreme example of this that I know of is Brody's recent *Ethics and Its Applications*. In this 200-page volume, Brody gives eight pages to explaining the nature of philosophy, of theoretical ethics, and of applied ethics. He gives ten pages each to consequentialism and rule-based morality, listing their strengths and weaknesses and adding exercises stressing the pros and cons as well as the way each view would work out on specific issues. In the following chapters he discusses criminal justice, the distribution of wealth, suicide, abortion and other life and death issues, and autonomy and paternalism. For each topic he presents a utilitarian view in one chapter and a deontological view in another, concluding each such chapter with a review. The review tells us in every case that the conclusions drawn from the theory are in many respects controversial and are meant to challenge us to think about accepted institutions or about the views drawn from the other theory. But although Brody is extreme in the clarity and balance with which he manages to refrain from endorsing any moral conclusions whatsoever, he is in principle doing no more than the other texts, which always supply a carefully balanced diet of pros and cons for every theory and for every issue. What is being taught, and what is held up as what ought to be taught, is not that we can expect philosophers to come up with theories from which answers can be derived. It is that the to and fro of argument is what matters. After my description of the ways in which certain humanists work, this should not seem anomalous. My point is simply that it hardly shows applied ethics as following the conventional idea of theory and practice in engineering.

If applied humanists were intellectuals in politics or moral engineers there would be a clear way of distinguishing their work from that of humanists in the "pure" fields from which they derived their theoretical orientation. On another view of applied humanities, this distinction could not really be drawn. It is sometimes supposed that the point of having professors of English or philosophy in medical and business schools is simply to enlighten the professional students, to remind them of the complexities of life, and to hone their moral sensibilities by having them probe ethical issues through case studies and novels and poems, preferably dealing with doctors and stockbrokers so as to keep them awake. Whatever the merits of this approach to improving professional morals, it does not yield a distinctive way of generating or using knowledge. It is simply doing later what we always thought was done earlier, in college or even in high school. Those who advocate this approach do so for reasons which reinforce the belief that this yields no distinctive enterprise of applied humanities. When William Bennett, for example, says that "the humanities provide us with an indispensable framework for the civilized development of public policy" and follows this by telling us that they do so not by discussing specific topical issues but "by developing a sensibility, a moral and imaginative framework for action" his aim is not to recommend the creation of more and more courses on special problems in applied ethics. Quite the contrary: it is to urge humanists to stick to their traditional topics if they wish to have the appropriate sort of impact on public policy.[16] Whatever the merits of his position, it is clear that we cannot find in it a model for understanding applied humanities as a new and separate undertaking.

V

If applied humanities is to become a separate and ultimately autonomous field, it must embody some ways of producing or using or disseminating humanistic knowledge that will distinguish it from the older disciplines from which it stems. As a conclusion to this paper I will suggest a way of looking at the enterprise that would show how it does so and will consider a few of the consequences if this view of applied humanities should prove to be correct.

My suggestion is that we think of applied ethics as being like certain aspects of what is done by nurses and social workers. In both these fields, problems arise because people in positions of authority make important decisions involving the lives and well-being of others who are not in positions of authority. Often the decisions—a doctor's prescription for a course of treatment, a new law about the conditions for receipt of welfare payments—do not take account of all the details of individual cases. Given the family situation of a patient, a certain treatment cannot be carried out; given the realities of the lives of the poor, those conditions make no sense as tests for eligibility. Social workers

[16]William Bennett, "The Public Life of the Humanities," copy of typescript for delivery on January 14, 1983, at American Conference of Academic Deans, Washington, D.C.

and nurses must then try to make adjustments to accommodate the needs and demands on both sides. They must try either to convince the authority to alter the decision or to make those affected understand why things have to be like that. They must look after the individuals touched by abstract or impersonal decisions and try to affect the decision makers so that they can make their decisions with fuller knowledge of their effects than they would otherwise have had. Thus in addition to their central task of offering direct care and service to patients and clients, nurses and social workers have a two-way mediatorial role. That role is heavily dependent on the knowledge they acquire and on how they use it.

Nurses and social workers receive very similar kinds of professional training. Both professions require practitioners to be knowledgeable about a wide variety of subjects which are specialities for others: for nurses, anatomy, physiology, biology, pharmacology, numerous aspects of medicine, health and professional legislation, and the structure of health services; for social workers, social policy and its history, human development, psychiatric theory, therapeutic models, economics, political science, administration and management theory, community development, a good deal of law, and the whole structure of public and private charitable organizations. Both require a substantial amount of practical experience as part of the training. Students of both sorts usually feel that they are being asked to learn too much abstract theoretical material and prefer the practicum to the classroom. In both professions practitioners must learn a very large amount on the job, since the details of institutions and systems vary considerably but must be mastered if optimal service is to be rendered. And much of what nurses and social workers know is the kind of practical expertise that comes from years of coping with the realities of their work.

In the use no less than in the acquisition of knowledge the two professions are also alike. Practitioners must use a certain amount of knowledge which overlaps with the knowledge of those who are the decision makers in the system in which they work. But they must not use so much that they are seen as threatening the knowledge-based authority of those in command. Practitioners must also acquire a good deal of perfectly ordinary knowlege about the details of the lives of their clients or their patients. To do this they must keep themselves from falling victim to their own technical knowledge and their socialization into the use of the jargon of their profession. But then they must be able to translate this knowledge into the system's own vocabulary in order to bring it to bear on the decisions that affect the patients or clients. In carrying out orders and in trying to affect orders, the professional must tread a fine line between being solely the tool of the system and being solely the advocate of the client or patient. The nurse and social worker must be able to see both sides of the issues that arise, must know how to explain them to those in various positions within the system, and must be able to help arrive at a resolution of difficulties which is acceptable to all concerned. It is recognized in the training of social workers and nurses that one of their major functions is teaching: teaching clients the intricacies of their entitlements and of the welfare system, teaching patients how to maintain their own health. The teaching function works up as well as down: those in superior positions are taught as well as those affected by their decisions, even if the teaching of the decision makers is less overt.

I hope it will not seem that I have merely caricatured the aspect of social work and nursing to which I want to compare the work of the applied moralist. I think the mediatorial relation to authorities and those affected by them is present and important in all three cases. And it appears to me that this way of looking at applied ethics helps us understand a good bit about it. The work experience of those actually employed as moralists in government or business and the educational patterns which are becoming more and more marked as these topics come to be more widely taught both indicate that applied ethics is serving a mediatorial function. This illuminates the facts I noted earlier about the textbooks now appearing. Like nurses and social workers, those interested in applied ethics do not want too much in the way of pure theory. They want to get into the details of the issues that interest them. And they are pleased rather than not that mastery of those details requires them to delve into a large number of subjects which humanists ordinarily never touch. The indecisiveness of the texts is also illuminated. The function of applied ethics is not so much to find the "right answer" to a hard and complex moral question as to make all those involved in the issue see all the bearings and implications of their views and feel that their concerns are appreciated and understood by everyone else who is involved (and no doubt the quality of the moral decisions is often improved in the process). Given the analogy I am drawing, it seems quite in order that in a new program in applied philosophy at Bowling Green State University an internship is a major component and that the director of the program should hold that "the key to bridging the gap between philosophy and nonacademic careers is an internship."[17] I should think that those engaged as moralists in nonacademic settings and in professional schools could supply a wealth of anecdotal evidence to confirm that they must, like the nurse or social worker, walk

---

[17]Louis I. Katzner, *Applied Philosophy and Graduate Programs*, a report prepared by the Department of Philosophy, Bowling Green State University, 1982, p. 10.

a thin line between becoming a mouthpiece for the system in which they work and being distrusted as a partisan advocate for those affected by it. Finally, it is striking that nurses and social workers spend a good deal of time worrying about their own professional identities. They do so largely because they cannot define, as precisely as can those in the so-called pure disciplines, their relations to the knowledge which provides them with the abilities and the authority to do the work they do. Discussions at the Hastings Institute suggest that perhaps those in applied ethics have the same worries, and for the same reasons.

This way of viewing applied ethics allows us, then, to give an account of how its practitioners differ from old-fashioned humanists in relation to the acquisition and use of knowledge. It does not tell us— how could it?—whether applied ethics is on the way to becoming an independent field. A difference between social workers and nurses and those in applied ethics is relevant here. The former, in addition to the mediating role I have ascribed to them, perform services which are indispensable to the systems in which they work; the latter do not. The moralists are therefore in a far more precarious position than the service professionals. They represent a new sort of threat to the authority of those whose orders and decisions are dominant within a system, and if they establish themselves as permanent fixtures there will have to be a corresponding redefinition of the roles of those authorities. Mediation and compromise are part of the way in which an open moral community like ours, lacking fixed doctrinal or personal sources of moral guidance, manages to continue as one community. As long as American society remains distrustful of authority, it may continue to support the movement toward applied ethics. Whether, in that case, the moralists will find their historic ties to the humanities stronger than the professional ties they will develop to the decision makers with whom they work or whether they will develop an autonomous identity are questions I cannot presume to answer.

PART III

The Humanities and Public Life

CHAPTER 6

The Humanities and Public Policy

DANIEL CALLAHAN

If Jimmy the Greek had been willing a decade ago to give odds on the
likelihood of an eventual union between the humanities and public policy, they would have been favorable to the hopeful gambler, at least
even money and perhaps even better. Had he talked only with those in
the humanities, he might have been unwilling to lay odds at all, so
bright was the picture. The humanities were staging a fast break of classic
proportions, moving aggressively out of the academy into the mainstream. The budget of the National Endowment for the Humanities was
on the rise, the NEH state programs would shortly be under a mandate
to focus their grants on policy issues, and a large number of humanists
were beginning to focus on topical social, moral, and political problems.

Jimmy the Greek's only hesitation might have come from conversations with those in the field of public policy. Although they would
doubtless have expressed pleasure at the prospect of being courted by
the humanities, they might also have been scratching their heads trying
to surmise just what the humanities have to do with cost–benefit analysis, linear programming, decision trees, and the mathematical models
of macroanalysis. It is only because Jimmy the Greek might have sensed
some bemusement from the policy side that he would have reduced the
odds to something less than a sure thing. Furthermore, as a hesitant
and careful man, trained to discount the enthusiasm of trainers and
managers, he would have paid heed to some lockerroom muttering in
the humanities themselves. Was not all of this new zealotry, some were
whispering, just one more sign of the lingering illness of the 1960s, that
cancerous pandering to the mob summed up in the detestable word
relevance? Still, despite reasons for hesitation here and there, the pros-

DANIEL CALLAHAN ● The Hastings Center, Hastings-on-Hudson, New York 10706.

pects for what we were in those days told was the most important kind of relationship, a "meaningful" one, were good.

As it turned out, for reasons now known only to him, Jimmy the Greek never did publish odds on the future of the relationship, whether of the meaningful or other varieties. It is just as well that he did not. Only too soon did those in the humanities fall to squabbling openly about the public policy forays, the NEH rescinded its order giving priority to public policy in state programs, and the Heritage Foundation prepared the way for the 1980s by deploring the capitulation of the humanities to debased taste and popular fashion. Moreover, even a glance at the typical curriculum in a school of public policy still shows a presence of the humanities about equal to that of the place of regression analysis in the works of Michel Foucault and Jacques Derrida. One way or another, then, what began on a hopeful note has now been slowed to a somewhat faltering, hesitant pace.

What went wrong, and what might be done about it? I start with the assumption that the desire to find a way of relating the humanities and public policy was and is perfectly legitimate. So far as I know, no one has flatly denied the pertinence of the humanities to public policy concerns. It is the nature of that pertinence that is in question. If a fundamental purpose of the humanities is to reflect upon and to attempt to understand the human condition, to explore questions of ends, meanings, interpretations, justifications, past memories and present purposes, then how can they fail to have something of value for the formation of public policy? If a basic purpose of public policy is that of finding ways to devise a more just, humane, and sensitive economic and political order, how can that not, in turn, be pertinent to the work of the humanities?

Quite apart from some failed or second-rate efforts, there have been at least two serious challenges to those assumptions. The first, from the side of the humanities, is that they are not, of their nature, suitable for the solution of the daily dilemmas of political and economic life. They seek not instantly usable practical knowledge of the kind needed to build bridges, balance budgets, or create jobs, but that deeper and different knowledge necessary for human self-understanding, an understanding reflected primarily in the great written texts of the past, whether historical, literary, or philosophical. As the principal vehicle by which tradition is kept alive, by which the ultimate ends of life are kept in the forefront, by which the heights and depths of human experience over time are kept before our eyes, the humanities speak to that which is most central and abiding in our life together. Such a position does not entail an indifference on the part of those in the humanities to matters of public policy. It only entails a distinction between the two spheres.

The humanities cannot be true to themselves if they take on public policy issues, by their nature transitory, technical, and political. It is, moreover, pretentious and dilettantish for those in the humanities to believe they can effectively work with policy matters. They have neither the professional qualifications nor the practical experience to do so.[1]

The assumption of a fruitful relationship has been no less challenged by many within the policy sphere, though their stance is often more implicit than explicit. In a democratic system, it is the political process that determines the goods and values to be sought in society. Although the question of what those goods and values ought to be is serious and basic, the role of the policy analyst is to serve that system by helping it to function effectively. That is essentially a technical, not a philosophical or theoretical, task. Once a commitment has been made to devise, say, a welfare program for the poor, alternative strategies must be weighed to determine which policy option would best achieve that end, how the chosen option could be financed and implemented, and what criteria ought to be used in evaluating its effectiveness once it is in place. Those technical tasks do not imply indifference to the larger questions of the human good. They imply only that some should have the training and experience necessary to implement the concrete details of those goals that society chooses; practical, not theoretical, reason is needed. Inevitably, the analyst must live in a world of trade-offs (a term that is not despised), seeking not the larger truths—a task best left to the sciences and the humanities—but those smaller truths that result from the give-and-take, the clash of values and interests, that are the stuff of daily life in a well-functioning, pluralistic democracy.[2]

Those are the principal objections to a close bond between the humanities and public policy. Although different, they suggest a basic agreement between core perspectives on the humanities and public policy. Both perspectives share the belief that they are engaged in different enterprises and that each, in its own right, is valuable and worthy. They also share the belief that their mutual tasks are best kept separate. Neither field will gain by merging the two enterprises, and society as a whole will not benefit by a confusing of two distinct realms of thought and activity. The result will be neither good humanities nor good public policy.

That is a persuasive argument. It bespeaks a desire to preserve the

---

[1]See, for example, "Serving Two Masters," by Robert Hollander, *VFHPP* (Newsletter of the Virginia Foundation for the Humanities and Public Policy), (Winter 1980–82), pp. 1–4; and William J. Bennett, "The Public Life of the Humanities," an address delivered at the annual meeting of the American Conference of Academic Deans, January 14, 1983.

[2]Cf. Edith Stokey and Richard Zeckhauser, *A Primer for Policy Analysis* (W. W. Norton: New York, 1978).

integrity of different spheres of human activity yet also recognizes that they serve equally valid purposes. It takes seriously the view that the humanities and public policy will of necessity have different standards of excellence and craft, different methodological criteria, and different though complementary roles to play in the culture.

Nonetheless, for all of its power, I believe it is a viewpoint that ought to be rejected. But how, if it is to be rejected, can that be done in a way that takes serious account of a fundamental truth embedded in the objections to a rapprochement: that the humanities and public policy are distinct realms? For the moment, I will leave that question dangling in the air, working my way toward it by constructing a different image of a possible relationship between the humanities and public policy. I will do so by beginning with a few things I have learned in recent years about the practice of public policy analysis, trying to see to what extent some internal struggles in that field can provide an opening for the humanities. For I have come to think that the critical issue is not only how we ought to understand the humanities (the most common entry point), but how we ought also to understand public policy analysis and policymaking. Under some construals of policy work, the humanities and public policy do properly belong in separate realms; but under others, they can share many affinities and a close relationship is possible.

A first step in making some sense of the possibilities is to observe that the expression *public policy* is, in fact, much too loose to be of great help. More helpful would be to distinguish among *public policy, public policy analysis*, and *public policymaking*.

Public policy can be understood as the aggregate collection of those actions undertaken by government, either by omission or commission, to advance the welfare of its citizens and the protection and advancement of its national interests. Those actions encompass legislation, administrative regulations, court decisions, and so on. Although of course not everything that the government fails to do—its acts of omission—can also be called a matter of public policy, there are a number of such issues that work themselves into the public policy realm by virture of the fact that a national debate or a legislative or judicial ruling determines that the government ought to remain free of involvement with them. Debate over abortion or other issues thought to be pertinent either to private morality or to the operation of the economic marketplace might be examples there. In general, public policy will reflect the competition of values and interests, of tradition and modernity, of ideals and reality.

Public policy analysis can be understood as an analytical and disciplined effort to articulate the practical alternatives open to government in implementing public policy commitments. Its purpose has commonly been understood as that of understanding the process by which policy is made, of studying the various possibilities for public policy initiatives, of exploring the potential consequences of different policy options, and of determining the most feasible means of achieving political, economic, or social goals. An essential purpose of policy analysis is to set the stage for policymaking. Policy analysis is typically carried out by advisors or consultants to those who actually make policy.

Public policymaking is the actual act of making a policy choice or implementing a policy option. The understanding of public policy or an analysis of policy choices is not in itself to make policy. Policymaking, by contrast, can be seen as the final outcome of understanding or analysis. Here, decision, judgment, action, and choice are the dominant features. They will be part and parcel of the political process, encompassing struggles over different conceptions of the national interest and human welfare.

Those distinctions are worth keeping in mind. Instead of asking in an abstract and general way how the humanities and public policy ought to or could be joined, we can ask somewhat more specific questions; and we may also discover not one role for the humanities but a plurality of possible roles.

At first glance, it might seem that the only, or most appropriate, relationship should take place in the arena of public policy in general. Indeed, it is at that level that the going is easiest and most congenial for those in the humanities. What ought to be the proper end of man and how ought public policy and government to serve that end? What is a just society? How much freedom ought people to have? What ought to be the role of tradition in shaping political and social institutions? In short, at this level one can appropriately ask and grapple with the oldest, most enduring, and deepest questions of human concern, both to the humanities and public policy. Once can also ask and answer those questions in a radical or utopian way, putting aside (if only temporarily) issues of feasibility; Plato's *Republic* and More's *Utopia* are classic illustrations.

With public policy analysis, we move into a somewhat different realm. Here one must begin talking about and analyzing particular and concrete policies. The question is not what is justice, but rather what would be a just economic, or immigration, or housing policy—in this society at this time in history? Should there be laws regulating abortion, or drugs, or interstate commerce? How should a tax code be written to stimulate investment yet not unfairly discriminate against small business?

A notable feature of public policy analysis is that if it is to be done well it must recognize the existence of constraints. At that point, the going can become more complicated and problematic for those from the humanities, whose imaginations can roam widely withouut regard for immediate application. But the public policy analyst has to exist in actual societies and in devising particular policies must be aware of and pragmatically responsive to political realities. One must ask not only what might be ideal, but what is feasible; not only about tradition in general, but about the pertinence of particular traditions to particular problems. One must move down a notch from the highest theory to a lower level, and one must move out of the past or utopian future and into the present. Inevitably, public policy analysis must also move a step closer to action and away from contemplation and reflection. The *is* and the *ought* begin to jostle each other more closely. The humanist must not only understand the great ideas and deepest memories but also grapple with contemporary facts.

Yet even as those shifts are made policy analysis is still analysis and not final choice or decision making. It is still thinking and not acting. Accordingly, policymaking is the arena of action. Here elected and appointed officials pass legislation, issue rules, and pronounce juridical decisions. This is not the humanistic arena as such. But it is here, finally, that one would most hope to see the impact of the humanities, to see whether the actions reflect high values, display well-tutored moral and historical sensibilities and vision, and advance human welfare and self-understanding.

At this level, expertise disappears. Knowledge is important, but no less important are character and vision. Also, if it is true as is sometimes said that the people get the kind of leaders they deserve, then their moral and social formation will show in the kinds of people they elect to represent them. If in one sense the humanities have the least to contribute at the actual policymaking level, in another sense they have everything to do with the formation of the viewpoints, perspectives, and character of those who actually make the decisions. If those who make decisions have not been nourished with history, tradition, civic values, and moral perspectives, it will show.

Much of the discussion of the relationship between the humanities and public policy in recent years has focused on the relationship between the humanities and public policy analysis; and that new emphasis complements a long-standing interest in public policy writ large. It is at the analysis level that the possibilities are in some way the freshest for a more direct role for the humanities in the formation of public policy. It is there that the humanities can have the most direct contact with the policy process and specific policy issues. The encounter between those in the humanities and those in public policy analysis can take place in a variety of ways. It can encompass the encounter of one discipline with another, of philosophy with, say, economics; or, more broadly, of one way of looking at the world versus another—the qualitative versus the quantitative; and emphasis on ends (appropriate to the humanities) versus an emphasis on means (characteristic of the policy sciences); a focus on ideals and possibilities over against insistent social or political obstructions. Those are all fruitful tensions.

At the risk of considerable oversimplification, I will sketch briefly what I believe to be a central argument now taking place within the field of public policy analysis. It has considerable bearing on future relations with the humanities. The early history of policy analysis—which can be traced back to the even earlier emergence of the social sciences as a distinct set of disciplines trying self-consciously to distinguish themselves from the humanities—showed a strong dedication to bringing the findings of the social sciences to bear on matters of public policy. The social sciences came to understand their purpose to be that of the scientific study of human behavior, both individual and social. The guiding conviction was that such study could develop empirical theories and laws comparable to those found in the more established natural and biological sciences. It was only a small step from that belief to the further conviction that the social sciences could make significant contributions to issues of public policy. If a public policy is to be designed in a rational way, then it should draw upon that most rational of all fields, the sciences, to gain a better understanding of human behavior in social and political settings. Implicit in that aspiration was the premise that it is not the business of science to devise normative goals and ends. At its best and most rigorous, science is value-free.[3]

Working with that set of convictions, the social sciences were brought increasingly to bear on policy issues, reaching a high point during the 1960s when social science knowledge was applied to a variety of domestic welfare and defense programs. The question of the relationship of ends and means was central to that agenda, but it was decided decisively in the direction of an emphasis on means. Once ends have been determined externally by the political process, then it only makes sense to be rational, efficient, and sensitive to the probabilities of human behavior—that is, to be carefully attentive to means and to bring to bear on them the full range of scientific knowledge and rational methodologies.

There is no need to relate in any detail, and once again, the various criticisms of that approach that began to emerge during the 1970s. Not only was there an outpouring of attacks on the conceit of a value-free science, there was no less strong an emphasis on denying the sharp bifurcation of ends and means. In response to those criticisms, the mainstream tradition introduced some modifications. It still rests upon science

[3]For a general discussion and analysis of this viewpoint, see Harold D. Lasswell, *A Pre-View of Policy Sciences* (New York: American Elsevier, 1971); and Robert A. Scott and Arnold R. Shore, *Why Sociology Does Not Apply* (New York: American Elsevier, 1979).

and instrumental rationality. But it has been modified in the sense that even those who remain in that tradition are now prepared to agree that science can become interwoven with the values, that ends will inevitably play some part in the shaping of means (and vice versa), and that the borderline between facts and values is not sharply demarcated.

This modified approach is well expressed in the opening pages of Edith Stokey's and Richard Zeckhauser's book, *A Primer for Policy Analysis*:

> Most of the materials in this book are equally applicable to a socialist, cap-
> italist, or mixed-enterprise society, to a democracy or a dictatorship, indeed,
> wherever hard policy choices must be made. In deciding whether a vaccine
> should be used to halt the spread of a threatened epidemic we need not
> worry about the political or economic ideology of those innoculated. Nor will
> the optimal scheduling for refuse trucks depend on whether it is capitalist
> or socialist trash that is being collected. Questions of values are, nevertheless,
> a critical and inevitable part of policy analysis. . . . The very nature of the
> tools and concepts we expound reflects a philosophical bias in the particular
> set of ethical concerns. For one thing, the subject itself, policy analysis, is a
> discipline for working within a political and economic system, not for chang-
> ing it. For another, we follow in the predominant western intellectual tra-
> dition of recent centuries, which regards the well being of individuals as the
> ultimate objective of public policy.[4]

The initial foray of some early explorers from the humanities into policy analysis found passages of that kind—and the tradition of policy analysis which they embody, modified or not—fair game. Laurence Tribe and a number of others pointed out that the technocratic approach to policy embodied in the mainline tradition of policy analysis was simply naive in attempting to work with a positivistic model, insensitive to the implications of trying to separate ends and means, and ultimately a hazard of the first order to democratic societies, whose life should be left in the hands of citizens rather than turned over to experts. In short, the basic premises of the entire enterprise were rejected.

Out of debates within the policy field, and perhaps reacting to the various criticisms, two important alternative approaches to policy ques-
tions emerged. The first, represented by the work of such figures as Jurgen Habermas, Richard Bernstein, and those who have come to be called "interpretive" social scientists, argued not only that a different, less positivistic, notion of the social sciences was required but that the kind of social inquiry necessary for the making of public policy had to combine the perspectives of both the sciences and the humanities, and more the latter than the former.[5] The second model, quite distinct, saw a move away from an understanding of policy analysis as scientific in

---

[4]Stokey and Zeckhauser, p. 4.
[5]See especially Richard J. Bernstein, *The Restructuring of Social and Political Theory* (New York: Harcourt Brace Jovanovich, 1976).

nature, to an understanding of it as essentially an art or craft. As Aaron Wildavsky has put it:

> Policy analysis is an art. Its subjects are public problems that must be solved at least tentatively to be understood. . . . The technical base of policy analysis is weak. In part, its limitations are those of social science: innumerable discreet propositions, of varying validity and uncertain applicability, occasionally touching but not necessarily related, like beads on a string. Its strengths lie in the ability to make a little knowledge go a long way by combining an understanding of the constraints of the situation with the ability to explore the environment constructively. Unlike social science, however, policy analysis must be prescriptive; arguments about correct policy, which deal with the future, cannot help but be willful and therefore political.[6]

Or, in another formulation, Charles E. Lindblom and David K. Cohen argue, in *Usable Knowledge:*

> PSI [Professional Social Inquiry] is one method among several of providing information and analysis to the extent that they are required. Information and analysis provide only one route because . . . a great deal of the world's problem solving is and ought to be accomplished through various forms of social interaction that substitutes action for thought, understanding, or analysis. Information and analysis are not a universal or categorical prescription for social problem solving. In addition, PSI is only one among several analytical methods, because other forms of information and analysis—ordinary knowledge and casual analysis foremost among them—are often sufficient or better than PSI for social problem solving.[7]

Policy is best formulated by the interaction of special and general knowledge, of reason and passion, of citizens and experts.

It is important to distinguish between the different routes taken by the interpretive social scientists on the one hand and those whom (for lack of a better term) I will call the "interactionists" on the other. The former group has by now actively engaged the interest of those in the humanities, and it is a congenial route for many to take. Interpretive social science works at a high theoretical level, tries to grapple with some old and central human questions, is suitably hostile to bureaucratic liberalism, and remains well clear of the day-to-day grime of "trade-off" thinking and politics. It is a thriving endeavor, although one that has remained almost exclusively within the university, at least in the United States.

Far less well explored by those in the humanities have been the implications of the interactionist perspective, in part, I suspect, because this point of view does not have the transcendental spirit and aspirations

---

[6]Aaron Wildavsky, *Speaking Truth to Power: The Art and Craft of Policy Analysis* (Boston: Little, Brown, 1979), pp. 15–16.
[7]Charles E. Lindblom and David K. Cohen, *Usable Knowledge: Social Science and Social Problem Solving* (New Haven: Yale University Press, 1979), p. 10.

of interpretive social science and gives no field—neither the sciences nor the humanities—a favored position. It takes seriously the notion that politics is a combination of fervently sought but usually unrealized ideals, of unremitting trench warfare, and of that classic form of comedy which becomes indistinguishable from tragedy. It is a form of policy analysis that is willing to get its hands dirty, that is inclined to incrementalism rather than revolution or radical reform, and that is as skeptical of the Zeckhausers and Stokeys of the policy science academy as it is of the Bernstein and Habermas critical theory academy.

In trying to think about these two models of public policy analysis and how some mix of them might best relate to the humanities, I am tempted by the old cliché of the high road and the low road. On the face of it, interpretive social sciences takes the high road. It can thus readily make common cause with the humanities, the history of which is that of the highest of all high roads. But the trouble with high roads, whatever their beauty, is that they do not pass through the cities and the towns, are not hampered by stop lights, and view the places where people live from afar. The trouble with low roads, by contrast, is that one can readily become habituated and deadened to their clutter and impediments. It is that perception, I suspect, that, even were it better known, would probably stimulate some distaste on the part of the humanities for the low road of the interactionist approach. It is one thing to think deeply and reflectively about the human condition; that is appropriate to the humanities. It is quite another actually to mix it up personally and directly with that mob of policy analysts, government bureaucrats, and politicians who overflow the sidewalks of the towns; that is not appropriate for the humanities.

I want to contend, however, that the humanities have a place on both the high and the low road and furthermore that a great contribution the humanities can make is to help cut a path between the two roads. Some should hack out the path from the top down, if that is where they find it congenial to begin, and others from the bottom up. But whatever the starting point, I believe those in the humanities will be failing in their civic duties and in their duties toward the humanities if they do not make the work of path-cutting part of their mission. And since I am generously assigning duties to the humanities, I will evenhandedly assign a few to the policy analysts. They also must cut a path, between the high road of interpretive sociology and the low road of interactionist analysis; and each must also, as is now happening to some extent, continue to nip at the heels of the mainstream scientific tradition. If that should happen, then the humanities and the policy arts could find a new and fresher common cause. They will inevitably find themselves hacking through the same undergrowth.

But enough of my cartographic and bushwacker metaphors. Just how might any of this be accomplished? Here I will, once again, take my lead from the debate within the field of policy studies. Central to that debate have been discussions of, first, the proper relationship between the social sciences and policymaking and, second, very closely related, the relationship of the social scientist to the policy analyst or policymaker. As I describe that discussion, I will allude to analogous issues within the humanities; the parallels are striking, as are the problems raised.

Robert Mayer has very nicely summarized four different models of the social science–policymaking relationship. One of the models is that of the *social engineer:*

> This model involves the social scientist working with the decisionmaker in the direct application of existing theoretical knowledge to produce answers to policy questions. The engineer works on whatever problems are assigned or defined by the policymaker, leaving the selection of goals and objectives outside the utilization process. . . . In its most extreme form, the social engineer becomes a 'hand maiden' or mandarin of the decisionmaker.[8]

The closest analogue to this model within the humanities might be that notion of applied ethics which sees its task as the straight-out application of prominent moral theories drawn, say, from Kant, Mill, or John Rawls to the moral dilemmas of personal or professional life—a generally ill-fated venture, I might add.[9] In its more debased form, it would not even try to make judgments about the validity of the theories; it would simply say, "if one is a utilitarian, then X would be the proper conclusion"; or, "if one is a deontologist, then Y would be the proper conclusion." Value-free ethics! The analogy is all the more pertinent when the humanist passively allows professionals in other fields solely to define the key issues of moral or social concern.

Another route is that of the *clinical model,* first propounded by Alvin Gouldner:

> In this model the social scientist interacts with the decisionmaker in all phases of the decisionmaking process. He assists in the clarification of goals and objectives, we as well as in proposing appropriate programs and in evaluating them.[10]

---

[8]Robert J. Mayer, "Social Science and Institutional Change," (Rockville, MD.: National Institute of Mental Health, n.d.), p. 95.

[9]Arthur Caplan has tellingly criticized the engineering model in ethics in "Mechanics on Duty: The Limitations of a Technical Definition of Moral Expertise for Work in Applied Ethics," *Canadian Journal of Philosophy* Supplementary Volume VIII (1982), pp. 1–17.

[10]Mayer, p. 95.

The analog that comes to mind in the humanities would be that of the historian- or philosopher-in-residence programs in hospitals, legislatures, or government agencies.

Still another model has come to be called the *enlightenment model:* it

> is one in which the social scientist develops a series of broad scale studies of complex social systems. . . . These studies result in bodies of data and new modes by which society can evaluate its present goals and objectives and develop new ones. The impact of the social sciences is indirect rather than direct. While working on the same issues being dealt with by the policymaker, but independently of the latter, social scientists have a good deal of freedom to define problems and pursue inquiries on their own initiative.[11]

The humanities parallel suggested here is that of the academic who chooses for his or her work some current policy issues but who would only, on occasion, care to spend time with policymakers or observe the policy process at first hand. It is the theoretical part of the problem that is comparatively more interesting than the clinical or actual setting and resolution of the problem.

Still another possibility is what Mayer calls the *nonparticipation model:* Here it would be

> argued that social scientists should not attempt to influence policymaking through participation in any government-sponsored activity. . . . Social scientists should continue to write and do research as independent academicians. To the extent that their results are useful, they will be picked up in the policymaking process.[12]

I would want to amend this category by suggesting that the nonparticipation model would really encompass the work of those who have no special interest in policy issues at all. They would have no objection to a policymaker's picking up their work but would not seek it and would strenuously object if even a comma was changed. Their work would have to be taken pure or not taken at all. The humanities analog, I suppose, would be the view that the humanities are essentially academic disciplines the only task of which is to preserve and advance the tradition of scholarship and learning—only that and nothing more.

Finally, I would add still another model to Robert Mayer's list, one suggested by Edwin Layton, that of the *sub-interdisciplinary model.*[13] By this I mean the development of a special field of study, one that draws upon mainstream theoretical and disciplinary work in more than one field but becomes its own discipline, set apart from the parent disciplines. The humanities example would be that of professionalized public

[11]Ibid., p. 96.
[12]Ibid., p. 96.
[13]Edwin T. Layton, Jr., "Theory and Application in Science and the Humanities," Chapter 4 in this volume.

social history or disciplinary bioethics, marked by its own journals, associations, and standards of excellence.

Each of these models, in addition to its concept of how the social sciences and policymaking ought to interact, has often something implicit, but now and then explicit, to say about how the individual social scientist ought to interact personally with policy analysts and politicians. They run the gamut from paid handmaiden through cautious, somewhat wary relationships, to a resolute refusal to have any dealings at all with workaday policy people. At stake are different notions of what might compromise the integrity of their own field, commitments, and training. The social engineer senses no threat to integrity at all. He is glad to have the opportunity to put his field to the service of policy. At the other extreme would be those who do not think any noncompromising relationship is possible at all; one should just stay away. In between are those who believe one can virtuously work in the policy arena if care is taken to avoid occasions of sin. I do not think I need spell out the humanities analogs here.

The point I want to draw from a recounting of the various possible models is twofold. First, with the exception of the engineering model, none of the others needs be out of bounds for the relationship between the humanities and public policy. Each has its problems, but none is inherently dangerous to a preservation and enrichment of the best that the humanities can offer. The nonparticipation model carries with it the hazard of wholly sundering the humanities and civic life; at best, it would simply shower learning and wisdom on the populace, indifferent to its consequences. But that hazard is slight compared to that engendered by the engineering model. The latter fundamentally subverts the necessary independence and integrity of the humanities. My second point is that there is a place both for a humanities equivalent of the high road of interpretive sociology and for the low road of the interactionists. But on one condition only—that each realizes its need to take account of, and attempt to work toward, those on the other road.

So far, I have suggested that distinctions must be made among the various levels at which policy can be understood—public policy, public policy analysis, and public policymaking—and among the various types of relationships that might exist between the humanities and public policy analysis. I do not believe there is any reason why there cannot be a plurality of possible ways for the humanities to interact with policy questions, as long as they can avoid some pitfalls. The first is that they not play the handmaiden role—there must always be some critical distance. The second is that the humanities not succumb to pretentiousness, either that of believing they have the final wisdom (or the exclusive means of seeking it) and theirs is the purer life and vocation or that of thinking that their disciplinary work has an elegance, thoughtfulness, and rigor that are infinitely superior to the muddling through of the policy process. That is a particular danger to be noted in the creation of sub–interdisciplinary fields. It is tempting to think that special fields could be carved out in the humanities that would bring to policy matters a kind of intellectual elegance now lacking and requiring only that certain aspects of the humanities be made considerably tighter than would otherwise be the case in their general parent disciplines.

I believe that those from the humanities with an interest in policy questions must on occasion mix it up in the trenches of political life. The purpose of this is not only to gain a bit of credibility for themselves in the eyes of those who work out in the world of politics and policy, but in order better to understand themselves and the limitations and possibilities of their own disciplines. The humanities are about the only academic fields that do not traffic much beyond the academy. They should on occasion, if only because those in the humanities need to have their own imaginations and disciplinary potentialities stretched. A steady diet of confronting only students, rather than trying themselves to grapple directly with the problems, is likely to leave them intellectually anemic, far more prone to note and comment on the work of their colleagues than to focus on those larger human questions that provide the fundamental motivation behind the humanities in the first place.

If it is true that policy analysis and policymaking, but particularly the latter, are in essence oriented toward action and not toward thought or theory, then it is possible to agree that there is a basic difference between the sphere of the humanities and that of policy. In that sense, the critics of attempts to join the fields are correct. But that is not the end of the matter. There are two important, indispensable contributions the humanities have to make to policy issues. The first contribution is that of the formation of character. The humanities have an important and traditional role to play in helping to form the traits and virtues necessary for citizens to make sound and sensitive judgments. If policymaking is an art, oriented toward action, then inevitably character, fundamental sensitivities, basic human decencies will count very heavily. The second, no less important, contribution is that of providing alternative perspectives, frameworks, and vision. It is an inherent hazard of policy analysis and policymaking to neglect the larger schemes and problems of human life in order to solve immediate problems and meet clamorous demands. The humanities, by reminding people of tradition, of ends and purposes, can provide an important and necessary corrective.

Finally, however, I doubt that anything of value can effectively be done by the humanities unless those whose calling it is to work within them form their own character and take seriously just what it is the humanities are all about. The greatest deformation of the humanities has been to turn them into one more set of specialized disciplines, particularly in their aping of the sciences or by retreating into the pleasure of the humanities as into exotic crossword puzzles. The first people those in the humanities have to deal with are themselves. They cannot provide insight for others unless they are able to generate it for themselves. Too much of the work of the humanities, and those in the humanities, is divorced from life. If a fundamental purpose of the humanities is to foster human understanding, then this sense of purpose must also stimulate an effort at self-understanding on the part of those in the humanities.

There is for those in the humanities a great deal of worry about the integrity of the various disciplines, and particularly their integrity when moving in the public policy arena. The worry is that somehow they will sell their souls for the instant relevance of policy issues, or will sell out their methodological souls for the less elegant, less careful ways of policy formation. I suppose that is a hazard. But the greater hazard is that those in the humanities will forget that they are meant to generate wisdom and insight, vision and perspective. And that is what policy most urgently requires.

CHAPTER 7

The Humanities and Social Vision

ROBERT N. BELLAH

The very wording of the topic I have been invited to discuss, "The Humanities and Social Vision," suggests that there are two quite different things that must somehow be brought into relationship. If one understands the humanities to be that one of the tripartite divisions of the university that concerns itself with the study of historical texts and social vision to be the society's understanding of itself and what it ought to be, then indeed there is a very problematic relationship between the two. If one sees the humanities, however, as the tradition of self-understanding of the society itself, then where else would one go for a vision of what the society is and ought to be? The same issue arises with the term *applied humanities*. If one sees the humanities as a form of pure knowledge of a body of objective fact, then indeed it would take a special effort to apply it. But if with Hans-Georg Gadamer we see that "application is neither a subsequent nor a merely occasional part of the phenomenon of understanding, but co-determines it as a whole from the beginning,"[1] then *applied humanities* is a redundant expression: it is in the nature of the humanities to be applied. Yet it is clear that today the notion of the humanities as a form of practical reason, *phronesis*, in Aristotle's sense, is not readily intelligible. Rather, our discourse is governed by the great dichotomies between theory and practice, fact and

---

[1] Hans-Georg Gadamer, *Truth and Method* (New York: Seabury Press, 1975), p. 289. Gadamer is perhaps the most powerful exponent of a view of the "human sciences" (a term that includes the humanities and a bit more besides) as inherently applied. He equates the human sciences with Aristotelian practical reason. Perhaps the key section is "The hermeneutic relevance of Aristotle," pp. 278–289.

ROBERT N. BELLAH ● Department of Sociology, University of California, California 94720.

value. It is the pure cognition of natural science that is only subsequently applied to practical matters that is our model of intellectual inquiry. From this point of view what is more natural than that the humanities as a form of pure knowledge, and the vision of what society is and ought to be, would be only very problematically related. It was not always thus.

Although the term the *humanities* makes us think first of all of the university as the locus of concern, and it is of the university that I will mainly be speaking, I would like to point out that in the history of the West until quite recently the humanities were involved much more directly in social thought and action. *Civic humanism* is a somewhat vague term but it does point to the fact that political and social thought from the Middle Ages to the nineteenth century was profoundly affected by classical models and texts. The American and French Revolutions were undertaken with classical and especially Roman models in mind. Social vision was for centuries closely linked to and largely an expression of what we now call the humanities. And, although theology was always considered something different from the humanities, the links between the two were quite important for social vision. The political writings of Thomas Aquinas as well as those of John Calvin can correctly be called expressions of Christian humanism because of their blending of biblical and classical inspiration. Not only the republic of Geneva but the New England colonies gave expression to a Christian humanist social vision. And when Samuel Adams called the new American republic a "Christian Sparta" he was describing both what he saw and what he thought ought to be. Today our political action and social thought are not exactly animated by humanist visions (although unconsciously more may survive than we are aware of) and the humanities are indeed seen largely in the context of university life, but there too great changes have occurred.

We imagine that the university stretches back with great continuity for almost a thousand years, and so in a sense it does. But the contemporary university is very different from the university of a hundred years ago, and if we go back 150 years we are indeed in a different world, a world in which the humanities meant quite simply Greek and Latin, or, at Edinburgh, simply Latin, for that is what the Professor of Humanity taught. The humanities then did not include modern languages, the fine arts, religious studies (*divinity* was clearly a contrast term to *humanity* and applied to the biblical as opposed to the classical side of our cultural heritage), or even philosophy or history except as they are contained in the classical authors.

But although the humanities then contained a great deal less than now, they also in another sense contained a great deal more. For the humanities were a form of *paideia*, a normative preparation for a form of life, embedded in a set of social practices. A proper study of the humanities was the necessary preparation for a cultivated gentleman so that he might take his place in society. Further, and in keeping with the place of the university in the education of an elite stratum of society, the humanities were a preparation for political leadership. The ancient connection between rhetoric and political leadership was still alive in the nineteenth century. We all know this, are a bit nostalgic for it, yet are perfectly aware that the humanities today are preparing neither cultivated gentlemen nor political leaders. I suppose if we ask what we are doing we must say that we are preparing people in the technical study of various kinds of texts or, in the case of nonprofessionals, teaching them to appreciate certain texts the importance of which we cannot always terribly well defend.

It may be instructive to see how Arthur Sutherland Pigott Woodhouse, Professor of English at the University of Toronto from 1938 to 1964, grappled with these issues in the article "Humanities" in the *Encyclopedia Britannica* (1967 edition). He insisted that the humanities, even today after their enormous expansion, still have a normative component, though he was defensive about that assertion:

> Well into the 19th century the humanities, still mainly represented by Greek and Latin, constituted with mathematics the staple of liberal education. The 19th century, which witnessed a great expansion of and within the humanistic disciplines, also witnessed the inevitable loss of their monopoly before the advance of the sciences and social sciences. These disciplines have indeed brought within the scheme of formal education knowledge essential to an understanding of the world we live in and useful for various practical ends; but (as Matthew Arnold observed in "Literature and Science") science is apt to content itself with the steady accumulation of knowledge, while the humanities have failed unless, in addition, they bring some accession of wisdom, some recognizable cultivation of intellect, imagination and sensibility, and some preparation for what the Greeks called the good life. This conception of the humanities and their role is true to the tradition from Cicero onward; but it sometimes invites misapprehension.[2]

Woodhouse's worry about misapprehension is instructive for it shows how difficult it was by the mid-twentieth century to justify anything normative in the university curriculum. His defense goes as far as he can carry it to bring the humanities into the orbit of the scientific and liberal, in the modern sense of the word, ethos of the contemporary university without abandoning his own commitment:

> The gravest danger in the demands made upon the humanities, and the opportunities opening before them, lies in the possible misapprehension regarding their role, hinted above, and what that role entails. This misap-

---

[2]Arthur Sutherland Pigott Woodhouse, "Humanities," *Encyclopaedia Britannica* (Chicago: Encyclopaedia Britannica, Inc., 1967), p. 827b.

prehension, in a word, is to suppose that the humanities can reach their end by indoctrination concealed as intellectual discipline. If the humanities are indeed normative, if they mold the mind and sensibility of the student and bring an accession of wisdom, it is by virtue of their subject matter, of the ideas which they present or evoke and the experiences to which they give him entry; and these ideas and experiences achieve their full effect only as they are examined critically, evaluated, and by the student made his own.[3]

The very nervous intrusion of the word normative in this passage suggests what is new in the modern context that Woodhouse had to face in order to hold onto the older conception. In that older conception it would be assumed that one studied Cicero or Plutarch in order to become a more virtuous person and act more wisely in the spheres of state and society. "Critical evaluation" and the "normative" were not separated. Woodhouse wanted to retain that older view even though he recognized that in the modern university the humanities have become a collection of technical and professional academic disciplines. It is here that the relation to social vision comes to a head. If the humanities do indeed bring "an accession of wisdom," then application and social vision are intrinsic products of their study. If, however, the humanities are technical disciplines, it requires a special effort to see how they might be applied or have any relation to social vision.

If for Woodhouse something seemed vaguely amiss, for Walter Jackson Bate, Kingsley Porter University Professor at Harvard, something has gone very much awry. In an article in the September–October 1982 issue of *Harvard Magazine*, ominously entitled "The Crisis in English Studies," Bate begins: "The humanities are not merely entering, they are plunging into their worst state of crisis since the modern university was formed a century ago, in the 1880s."[4] Bate's fundamental understanding of the humanities, which he traces to "the great Renaissance concept of *litterae humaniores*, 'humane letters'," is very close to that of Woodhouse. He sees them as taking the experience of the classical world in a way that intermeshes literature, history, and philosophy and doing so "with the hope of forming that mysterious, all-important thing called character as well as the generally educated mind."[5] He sees that great mission as first endangered and then nearly shattered by developments occurring in the universities since the 1880s.

Bate singles out two tendencies that were destructive of the larger humanistic mission. One was the emphasis, ultimately stemming from Romanticism, toward the personal and the idiosyncratic. In this ten-

[3]Ibid., p. 827c.
[4]W. Jackson Bate, "The Crisis in English Studies," *Harvard Magazine* 85 (September–October, 1982), p. 46.
[5]Ibid., p. 47.

dency, aestheticism replaced the larger concern with ethical and public meanings and eventually led to a concentration on form for its own sake. The other tendency he calls "organized (in fact, militantly organized) academic specialism." Here the prototype was the natural sciences, although Bate argues that the intellectual rationale for specialization in the sciences was often lacking in the humanities, where becoming an "authority" on an ever more delimited field of knowledge became an end in itself. Formalism and specialization, taking somewhat new forms, have only increased since World War II, says Bate. The vast overproduction of Ph.D.'s to meet the needs of expanding universities encouraged shallowness, but the present lean period, instead of reversing older negative trends, is only adding further destructive ones, especially the temptations toward puffing the curriculum with whatever trendy subjects might attract students and toward asserting a new esoteric "theory" in the humanities that makes extravagant claims and shows few results.

Yet for all the devastation he portrays, Bate is remarkably optimistic at the end of his essay, asserting once again the old humanistic ideal:

> The subject matter—the world's great literature—is unrivaled. All we need is the chance and the imagination to help it work upon the minds and characters of the millions of students to whom we are responsible. Ask that the people you are now breeding up in departments, and to whom you now give tenure appointments, be capable of this.

He calls finally for "a combination of some creative specialism (inevitable in the modern world) with the range and general power of both character and mind that we have been trying to form and develop."[6]

Woodhouse spoke of wisdom; Bate speaks of character. But is it so clear that "the world's great literature" today (no longer the Greek and Latin classics), even well taught, produces anything we would really recognize as wisdom or character? Lionel Trilling in an extraordinary essay entitled "On the Teaching of Modern Literature" describes the hesitation of his own department at Columbia in teaching the modern masterpieces to undergraduates and his own feelings of discomfort, when teaching the course, in exposing young men and women of good family to the great rebels against bourgeois morality, finally, according to Trilling, against culture itself. To reduce the great iconoclasts to the proprieties of the lecture hall and the examination room is finally absurd: "Compare Yeats, Gide, Lawrence, and Eliot in the use which they make of the theme of sexuality to criticize the deficiencies of modern culture. Support your statement by specific references to the work of each author. [Time: one hour.]"[7] And although Trilling is finally dismayed more by

---

[6]Ibid., p. 53.
[7]Lionel Trilling, *Beyond Culture* (New York: Harcourt Brace Jovanovich, 1965), pp. 10–11.

the many students who absorb the rebels with the same equanimity with which they absorb everything else than by the few who find them alien and incomprehensible, we can ask what kind of wisdom and character can result from an education in which Dante and Baudelaire, Nietzsche and Aristotle all have equal standing? The traditional humanities were based on a canon of classics, certainly not without inner tensions, but with something of an integrated moral world view. Modern literature has produced anticlassics and an anticanon. Today there are many who are at sea with respect to both canon and anticanon, who see no basis for giving any texts a preferential status. And yet today I think there is great anxiety as to what might count as a basis for the wisdom and character of which the humanists have so long talked. Recently, while sitting in on a meeting of the advisory committee of the California Council of the Humanities, I was told that what secondary school humanities teachers most wanted from us was a list of books that they could feel sure deserved to be taught. When I lectured at Harvard in November of 1982, I learned of the dismay of the students at the cacophony of the new core curriculum and the wish for something more definite.

This long pedagogical prolegomenon may seem like a diversion but I believe it is directly related to my topic. If the humanities are to help us with social vision it will not be, I believe, through the application of technical humanistic disciplines to specific problems of social policy. It will be through a reappropriation of the right relation between the humanities and the practice of life. That indeed is the problem.

Perhaps it is easiest for us to see a critical role for the humanities in providing us with something like a social vision, for criticism is so much a part of the ethos of the contemporary university. The humanities can provide us with a critical perspective on our own culture by holding up to us the image of another culture. That image allows us both to see the limitation of our own culture and to imagine other possibilities for ourselves. Trilling suggests that a classical education, in its last days, when it no longer had much connection with the practice of life, yet still lingered on in schools and universities, played such a role. Of Freud, who kept his schoolboy diary in Greek, Trilling writes,

> who can say what part in his self-respect, in his ability to move to a point beyond the reach of the surrounding dominant culture, was played by the old classical education, with its image of *the other culture*, the ideal culture, that wonderful imagined culture of the ancient world which no one but schoolboys, schoolmasters, scholars, and poets believed in?"[8]

Today there is no one "other" culture that stands in splendid difference and implicit criticism of our own, with which all educated per-

[8]Ibid., p. 97.

sons are familiar, and not just with its dry contours but with its myths, its heroes, its climactic historical moments. Today the student is inundated with possible other cultures that classicists, anthropologists, Sinologists, Indologists, and so on are prepared to purvey to him, although usually through an elaborate critical apparatus that, for all but the most imaginative students, is more apt to keep them at a distance than bring them alive. The enormous increase in our ability to reconstruct sensitively an extraordinary range of human cultures both contemporary and historical is certainly a cultural resource of the greatest importance. Still it is not so clear how to bring that resource to bear on our current social reality, even though I believe that many individuals have found important resources of meaning for their own lives in such studies.

Louis Dumont is one of the few who have thought seriously about the systematic use of comparative studies to illuminate the presuppositions of our own culture. He points out that unless we can get outside our ideology "we remain caught within it as the very medium of our thought."[9]

Dumont has worked primarily from his own deep knowledge of India, gained from anthropological field study and historical documents. In looking at the modern West from the point of view of India, Dumont argues that it is the modern West that is radically aberrant, not only in comparison with India, but with all the traditional cultures of the world. What he singles out particularly are our individualism and our utilitarianism, which he sees emerging from the triumph of what he calls "economic ideology" in the West in the seventeenth and eighteenth centuries.

Dumont's argument only reinforces what students of modernity have been saying with increasing clarity for some time: that the social thought that emerged in the West in the seventeenth and eighteenth centuries is markedly discontinuous with older Western traditions and that the conceptions of human action contained in this ideology have become part of the common sense of the more developed Western societies in the nineteenth and twentieth centuries. The new philosophy saw individuals not primarily as members of a community, as the older religious and political traditions had done, but as separate bits of matter in motion, each driven by will and passion, especially the fear of harm and the desire for comfort.[10] This new way of thinking was radically subversive of older conceptions of social order. In the new conception, society lacked any organic value. It was merely an association created

[9]Louis Dumont, *From Mandeville to Marx: The Genesis and Triumph of Economic Ideology* (Chicago: University of Chicago Press, 1977), p. 27.
[10]See William M. Sullivan, *Reconstructing Public Philosophy* (Berkeley: University of California Press, 1982), p. 19 and *passim*.

by contracting individuals to further their own quite heterogeneous ends. This new philosophy is the classical form of liberalism, the ideology of economic man, what can be called utilitarian individualism.

Utilitarian individualism was profoundly subversive of tradition and of the humanities as the locus of tradition, even though it took a long time for this to be fully evident. The individual and his interests are the new source of value, and no tradition or canon can have any validity if it conflicts with that. Hobbes began already in the seventeenth century the work of ideology critique, telling us to look at any book or speech to see how it serves the author's or speaker's interest. He even went so far as to say that someone would argue the untruth of two plus two equals four if it served his interest to do so. The received canon that was the core of Western culture had been changed many times before the seventeenth century. The changes were mainly through loss on the one hand and accretion on the other. The triumph of Christianity led to the addition of many new works to the canon and the revaluation of others. But now something new had occurred. The entire canon was devalued by Hobbes in the name of individual interest and scientific reason. He specifically claimed that his own work replaced all previous works on the study of man. His appeal to the logic of science casts a shadow over tradition, canon, and the humanities that has not lifted to this day.

A reaction against the harshness and narrowness of utilitarian individualism set in quite early, already by the eighteenth century. This movement accepted the individualistic assumptions of its predecessor but insisted on seeing something more in the individual heart than exclusive self-regard and the pursuit of self-interest. It recognized powerful emotions, feelings, and sentiments that created sympathy for nature and other persons. This movement, called in its early phases Romanticism, we may speak of as expressive individualism. It has accompanied utilitarian individualism, in a variety of forms, ever since, partly as critic, partly as complement.

On the face of it, it would appear that expressive individualism, particularly in its early form of Romanticism, was much more sympathetic to tradition and to the humanities as the carriers and expression of tradition. Indeed, the Romantic movement stimulated a new sophistication in the study of tradition and a fascination with history. Yet expressive individualism, like utilitarian individualism, had no commitment to traditional forms in themselves. The individual self and its rich array of feeling remained the criterion for the choice of what in the past might be of interest. The powerful movement of historicism, associated with such great figures as Schleiermacher and Dilthey, found history finally to be an expression of "life" which could be reanimated in the present by the sufficiently sympathetic student of culture. Romanticism, because of its lack of commitment to anything beyond individual expression, was finally just as subversive to the ideas of tradition and canon as utilitarian individualism. But unlike utilitarian individualism with its fascination with science, expressive individualism, in turning the attention of the individual to one or another aspect of tradition or period of the past, left open at least the possibility of a new commitment that would genuinely embody a cultural form.

Particularly among the educated classes, utilitarian and expressive individualism have shunted aside biblical religion and civic humanism, although these genuine traditions have never ceased to carry some cultural influence. It is worth mentioning that the ideologies of utilitarian and expressive individualism were not a product of the universities and were for a long time distinctly uncongenial not only to faculties of divinity but also to faculties of, in the older sense, the humanities. It was not really until the rise of the great research universities at the end of the last century that they gained a major foothold in higher education at all and not until the massification of higher education after World War II (at least in America) that they replaced older conceptions of college education; and not until the last twenty years have they become the ethos of primary and secondary education (again, in America) as well. This triumph of the individualist ideologies in education has led, I believe, to questions about the very meaning of the humanities, to the notion of "applying" the humanities, and to the question of whether the humanities have anything to offer by way of social vision.

The primary problem that the triumph of the individualist ideologies raises for the humanities is our relation to the past, to time and memory. All cultures outside the modern West have viewed the past, our memory of the past, in a word, tradition, as a primary cultural resource, probably *the* primary cultural resource. The modern individualist ideologies are almost by definition antitraditional, or, I would say, inimical to memory. It is not that modern culture, certainly modern academic culture, wishes to remain ignorant of the past. We now know more or can know more about the past than anyone has ever been able to know before. But our relation to the past is different from that of traditional cultures. Traditional cultures remember the past in order to incorporate it. We remember the past in order to abolish it.[11]

Utilitarian individualism's negative attitude toward the past is ev-

---

[11]On tradition and modern hostility to tradition see Edward Shils, *Tradition*, (Chicago: University of Chicago Press, 1981).

ident in its ideal picture of the self, defined so aptly recently by Michael Sandel (in *Liberalism and the Limits of Justice*) as "the unencumbered self."[12] According to Hobbes, we are creatures of need and desire engaged in a restless pursuit of "power after power, that endeth only in death." Nature, society, and other individuals are all only instruments to our self-interest. All previous notions of morality, of the Good, of political philosophy, are fallacious and distracting. We must build a society on the basis of self-interest and its regulation alone. Like other social scientists, generation after generation after him, Hobbes informs us that we have no need of the books of his predecessors, now that society is set on a scientific foundation. It is striking that Locke, so concerned with legitimating the revolution of 1688, never mentions the traditional "rights of Englishmen." His *Two Treatises of Government* are concerned to attack a defense of monarchy based on patriarchal tradition and replace it with one based on the needs and desires of contracting, unencumbered individuals. Modern social science has taken an inflexibly negative view of traditional moral, social and political thought, which it considers either wrong or totally superceded. Of course, the contrast of traditional and modern is central to the social science vocabulary, with the negative implication concerning traditional thought that it is by definition unscientific. When the social scientist wants to be charitable toward premodern social thought it may be called, interestingly enough, *humanistic*, usually as dismissive a term as *traditional*.

The ethos of utilitarian individualism has, of course, for a long time been seeping into the humanistic disciplines themselves, however much initially humanists may have resisted the new tendencies. The most obvious influence is the questioning of all received opinion. Thus, even in the case where tradition itself is the object of study, tradition as a living reality is viewed with the utmost suspicion and scepticism. Every text, every event, is to be considered on its own terms, so far as the investigator can get at it with the most sophisticated possible critical methods. If a scholar can overturn received opinion and offer a revised view, then he has scored his greatest coup. A relentless historicizing, even beginning as early as the Renaissance, although increasing our knowledge, has pushed the past ever farther away from us. In remembering too much, it has come close to destroying any practical memory at all.

Expressive individualism in its post-Romantic forms has exploded the past in a somewhat different way. It too works with the ideal of an unencumbered self, but here the encumbrances to be eliminated are not

[12]Michael Sandel, *Liberalism and the Limits of Justice* (Cambridge: Cambridge University Press, 1982), p. 90 and elsewhere.

restraints on the pursuit of self-interest but limits on the expression of authentic feeling. The great modernist writers were trying to free themselves from every constraint of convention and routine, to discover the depths of true individuality. Walter Benjamin suggests that this quest ends in a situation in which only the intensity of the atomized individual's sensations are real to him. In a discussion of Baudelaire and Proust, Benjamin distinguishes this sensation, which is close to a form of psychic "shock," from genuine experience, which is always rooted in a living relation to the past. Benjamin writes:

> Where there is experience in the strict sense of the word, certain contents of the individual past combine with material of the collective past. The rituals with their ceremonies, their festivals (quite probably nowhere recalled in Proust's work) kept producing the amalgamation of these two elements of memory over and over again. They triggered recollection at certain times and remained handles of memory for a lifetime.[13]

Proust, having lost those handles, engages in an effort to remember the purely personal, which becomes endless and compulsive, replacing the living of life with the work of recollection. As Benjamin puts it, "For the important thing for the remembering author is not what he experienced, but the weaving of his memory, the Penelope work of recollection. Or should one call it, rather, a Penelope work of forgetting?"[14] The great masters of suspicion, Marx and Nietzsche and Freud, tell us to suspect every received category of interpretation for our lives as expressions of oppression, repression, or false consciousness. The great remembering task of psychoanalysis itself is to liberate us from our past, not initiate us into it; to destroy repressive memory so that we can live in the present, not provide us with a creative memory that we can use to understand the present.

Expressive individualism has spawned a whole generation of culture critics as diverse as Herbert Marcuse, Norman O. Brown, Michel Foucault, and Lionel Trilling and has profoundly influenced our attitudes toward literature and tradition. Trilling is a particularly instructive example. In *Beyond Culture* he shows how the tradition of the revolt against culture has itself become a culture, a tradition of being antitraditional, that is established, particularly in academia, and so inhibits genuine individual autonomy. He resolutely calls for the resumption of the quest for autonomy, insisting on the priority of the individual over culture, yet unaccountably summons up reason as an ally, as though reason were not itself a cultural form.

If our foray into cultural criticism is correct and there are indeed

---

[13]Walter Benjamin, *Illuminations* (London: Jonathan Cape, 1970), p. 161.
[14]Ibid., p. 204.

major forms of modern ideology, forms ascendant in the university, that destroy effective memory, then we may begin to see why the humanities are in crisis and have difficulty producing either wisdom or character. For it is precisely through the transmission of a living memory that those functions have always been performed, to the degree that they have been performed at all. But when the humanities become "disciplines" armed with "methodologies" and "critical perspectives" that call into question the validity of any tradition, they cannot transmit a living memory; they dynamite it.

There are two aspects of the transmission of a living memory which the humanities as presently constituted have difficulty understanding, much less communicating, that I would like to discuss before turning to the reality of our present situation and considering how the humanities might contribute to social vision. These two aspects involve narrative and practice.

Scientific description communicates truth by maximizing the difference between observer and observed, attempting to arrive at a picture of the object as little contaminated by subjectivity as possible. Narrative attempts to communicate truth by pulling the reader or hearer, so far as possible, into the narrative itself. Through the process of identification narrative attempts to shape the subjective feelings of the hearer so that they are appropriate to the form of the narrative. This is true whether the narrative is historical, mythical, or fictional. Scientific description attempts to control the interference of the environment by decontaminating the object. Narrative attempts to control the interference of the environment by drawing the subject into another world, the world of the narrative, the world of memory.

The great culture-shaping narratives have seldom been reassuring. Whether they recount the lives of heroes, saints, and sages or whether they recount the history of cities and peoples, they are often disturbing. The memories they communicate are often, from the point of view of contemporary reality, dangerous. (Johann Baptist Metz has spoken eloquently of the "dangerous memories" transmitted in the Christian tradition.[15]) The lives (and deaths) of Socrates and Jesus are disturbing, unsettling. The stories of the great paradigmatic cities, Jerusalem, Athens and Rome, are far from reassuring.

If narrative is a form of mimesis of historical or paradigmatic events, it also leads to mimesis in the hearer, not in the form of copying, but of *productive imagination*, as Paul Ricoeur has recently pointed out.[16] This

---

[15]Johann Baptist Metz, *Faith in History and Society* (New York: Seabury Press, 1980), Chapter 5 and elsewhere.

[16]Paul Ricoeur, *Hermeneutics and the Human Sciences* (Cambridge: Cambridge University Press, 1981), p. 293.

leads to my next point: the relation of memory and narrative to practice. But first let me point out how difficult it is for the humanities, seen as disciplines in a university, itself seen as a place for the production of objective knowledge, to communicate genuine narrative. Where critical examination has come loose from the normative and the teacher has lost all conviction as to whether anything of normative value is being taught, then it becomes difficult for the student imaginatively to live the story. The formative power of narrative is left, unexamined, to television, rock music, and the movies. The student has difficulty feeling any connection to what is analyzed in the classroom. Narratives become objects, along with all other objects, to be decontaminated, mounted, and hung as specimens in a museum. If, in spite of everything, students insist on identifying with them and living them we are more apt to be baffled than pleased.

As I have already implied, the transmission of living memory in traditional cultures is never an end in itself. Memory is valuable only insofar as it shapes practice. This it does first of all through ritual, as the quotation from Walter Benjamin, cited above, suggests. Ritual is a category singularly difficult for a utilitarian culture, a culture that despises memory, to understand. To say that something is a ritual or only a ritual is to indicate finally that it is of no importance. To this point of view the existence of religious ritual, civic ritual, and academic ritual is explained as the vestigial survival of what is no longer necessary. Yet ritual is, as Benjamin pointed out, critical in the process of transmission of living memory and the meshing of individual and social memory. Ritual involves the dramatic reenactment of the paradigmatic narrative. Holidays often involve a calling to mind and an acting out of what is memorialized or commemorated. "Do this in remembrance of me."

But, as a utilitarian view of ritual fails to understand, and the actual performance of ritual in any culture often fails to realize, the ritual action, the mimesis, ought not to be confined to the ritual situation itself. It is intended to conform the participating individuals and the community of participation itself to a ritual pattern that must then be creatively applied to the whole of life. That is what it means to say that living tradition is productive of character and wisdom. Practical activity in the world—economic, political, social—cannot simply be read off from the ritual. But the ritual and the narrative it reenacts carry a perspective (often disturbing) relative to which action in the midst of present reality, with all its complexity, can be evaluated and imaginative possibilities envisaged. It is through this process of memory, narrative, and practice that tradition has led to social vision. But again what have the humanities today to do with all this, especially with ritual and practice? Even to talk about it raises Woodhouse's specter of indoctrination.

From the point of view of where we actually are what is there to say? The first thing I would say is that wherever there is any living memory it should be nurtured. For those who still view the humanities as having something to do with the "accession of wisdom" or the formation of character, I think it is time to make common cause with divinity. Divinity has finally become part of the humanities in most campuses in the form of "religious studies." This was long resisted in many places precisely because of the fear of indoctrination. Unfortunately, from my point of view, there is presently little such danger from religious studies, where the process of museumification has gone as far as in the other humanities. Yet we should not forget that most American universities and colleges were founded by religious bodies and that in some smaller denominational colleges something like a living memory of that fact survives. Indeed it survives, rather surprisingly, in the heart of one of our greatest research universities, Harvard. Memorial Church, where in 1982 I gave the William Belden Noble lectures, sits in the middle of Harvard Yard and is to this day a house of Christian worship, though apparently during the Conant years it almost ceased to be one. An anachronism and an embarrassment, I am sure, to most of the Harvard faculty, Memorial Church and the few hundred who gather there each week manage to keep some living link between the Harvard of today and the original Harvard of John Winthrop. Even the great state universities that lack chapels of their own are usually ringed with churches, Newman Centers and Hillel Houses. It is my feeling that those institutions are more integral to the health and even the survival of the universities than most today might imagine.

There is another aspect of living memory that does not find the university a very comfortable home today, although it is rooted in important ways precisely in the humanities rather than in divinity, and that is the memory of the republic in which we live. That the republic in its origins was deeply entwined with the tradition of civic humanism is something most of us know. That this creates a living link between us as humanists and the republic we live in is something we less often think about. That our very form of governance is itself linked to the larger political order in which we live is also something we do not often consider. Eva Brann, in her remarkable book *Paradoxes of Education in a Republic*, puts it well and in a way consonant with my own argument about memory, narrative, and practice:

> Precisely because these little republics [the universities] are not self-sufficient, they need a ground from which to draw life, and that ground is the larger republic. There is something inexpressibly foolish in the sight of an institution bent on ignoring or despising its own source. That educational communities should foster reverence for the Republic seems to me obvious. *In extremis,*

radical reflection and civic reverence might indeed appear to be irreconcilable, yet the founder of all inquiry reconciled them precisely in his death: He was condemned to die because he refused to cease asking questions, and he was executed because he declined to flout his city's laws by running away. (Plato, *Apology* 37c; *Crito* 52c.)[17]

If religious and political piety may have more to do with the health and survival of the university than most of us presently presume and should be nurtured rather than repressed, then how much the more the central piety of intellectual life itself, the search for that which is intrinsically good and true. This is the life of theory, in the classical sense of contemplation, where the concern is with ends, not means. We have almost successfully banished concerns about ends from our public life. If we manage to banish them from our intellectual life the result will be somber indeed and we might as well forget talk about social vision. Wilfred Smith puts the issue very succinctly:

> If truth is not transcendentally good; if "values" are merely what (-ever) is valued rather than what is in fact valuable; if the a-moral impersonalism of objective sciences is our only knowledge; if the rational is the instrumental; if being human has no intrinsic or absolute or higher or even shared purpose, only individual purposes; then there is no reason why the university should continue to have loyalty and consensus within, respect without, freedom from tight state control. Efficiency management for externally imposed objectives would be its rational role.[18]

I have tried to argue that the modern individualist ideologies that so dominate our consciousness and our universities are destructive of living memory and so of social vision, for social vision cannot be manufactured on the basis of present need or feeling alone but always involves an effort to discern what is good in itself and how that might be embodied. Tradition as living memory is not, as its modernist critics believe, the mindless repetition of the past, but the creative reappropriation of the past in the context of present reality. Thus a sense of the past and a sense of the future are intrinsically related: if we destroy one we destroy the other.

Clearly I am calling for the revival of tradition and wondering where in the university that revival might take root. I have been particularly concerned with Western traditions, older than the modern individualist ideologies, that still survive as living practices even if pushed more and more to the peripheries, because realistically I think they still have the best chance of speaking to us. I do not mean, however, to overlook the

---

[17]Eva T. H. Brann, *Paradoxes of Education in a Republic* (Chicago: University of Chicago Press, 1979), p. 147.
[18]Wilfred Cantwell Smith, Review of *The Anatomy of Academe* by Murray G. Ross, *Dalhousie Review* 57 (1977), p. 548.

plethora of traditions of which we now have knowledge. In principle, today, all traditions are our traditions.[19] There is an enormous problem of knowledge overload and the creative management of pluralism, but I am convinced that we cannot hermetically return to some "pure" (it was never pure) Western tradition. The traditions of the world, in narrative and even in practice, are available to us and we ignore that fact to our great loss. Nor do I wish simply to deny *in toto* the achievements of the modern ideologies. We are all, like it or not, modern men and women. We do not really wish to abandon the many liberations that have come with modernity. As Hegel saw, the problem is not to abolish modernity but to incorporate it into a living practice; not to renounce freedom but to situate it.[20] As Hegel also saw, that will not be possible without a living sense of the entire human journey. In the very teeth of modernity we must say, I believe, that tradition is an indispensable source of human existence and that if we kill it we commit suicide.

Yet the question remains, how? Daniel Callahan has recently asked that question in a searching review article entitled "Tradition and the Moral Life."[21] I cannot here reproduce the complexity of his argument but only allude to the questions he asks of those who take a position similar to my own. May it not be already too late to revive the traditions we treasure? Is there not a *via media* between tradition and modernity, a "moderate individualisim"? My answer to the second question is that there is a moderate individualism to the extent that radical individualism is an untenable position and so necessarily involves some symbiosis with at least remnants of tradition. As Peter Berger said, "A totally modern society would be a science-fiction nightmare."[22] But I believe that unless modern individualism is subjected to a radical critique and altered in important respects the symbiosis will be unstable. The pressure of modern individualism is toward the relentless destruction of tradition, suicidal though that may be.

To the first question, as to whether it is not already too late, I am sure I do not know the answer. But I do believe that it is at least possible that the answer is no. It is possible to reappropriate tradition and canon in a way true both to our past and our present reality. It will require an unprecedented degree of openness, for the tradition is the human tradition and the canon contains all works that can still speak to us. There

---

[19]No one has seen this more clearly or expressed it better than Wilfred Cantwell Smith in *Towards a World Theology* (Philadelphia: Westminster Press, 1981).

[20]See Charles Taylor, *Hegel and Modern Society* (Cambridge: Cambridge University Press, 1979), Chapter 3.

[21]Daniel Callahan, "Tradition and the Moral Life," *The Hastings Center Report*, December, 1982.

[22]Peter Berger, *The Homeless Mind* (New York: Vintage Books, 1974), p. 229.

must of course be selections, subtraditions, canons within the canon, but the boundaries should be left open and subject to change. To make such an operation viable we would have to reject the antitraditional bias of modern thought even as we seek to appropriate the antitraditional traditions as themselves traditions from which we have to learn. We can teach both Aristotle and Nietzsche, not as specimens to be dissected, but as texts that speak to us and force us to clarify who we are.

If all this is possible it will only be because we have become convinced that modern individualism is false. We are not "unencumbered selves" who then choose what to believe and what to be loyal to. We are social and cultural beings constituted by our past and only able to understand ourselves and our future in constant conversation with our past. Memory and hope belong together. An unencumbered self has neither.

CHAPTER 8

The Humanities and the Social Sciences
Reconstructing a Public Philosophy

BRUCE JENNINGS AND KENNETH PREWITT

I

It is now a commonplace to point out that scholarly knowledge and research have inevitable social consequences and effects. Even the most theoretical and abstract research takes place in a public world of ideas, traditions, and problems—a public world that in turn shapes and is shaped by that research. Intellectually and sociologically, if not physically, the scholar's study and the scientist's laboratory are exceedingly crowded places indeed. Recognizing this, no branch of learning can now avoid perplexing questions about the social meaning and effects of scholarly knowledge. The debates concerning the nature of "applied knowledge" now surfacing in the humanities are not unlike those that have been going on for a very long time in the natural sciences and the social sciences. For the question in each case is not whether knowledge can be (will be) applied, but how its application will be carried through and to what ends. To take the question of application seriously is to suppose that the inevitable social effects of disciplinary knowledge can, at least to some extent, be intelligently foreseen and directed toward constructive human goals.

Generally speaking, in the natural sciences the "how" of application is well understood and easily demonstrable. Few would dispute the validity and importance of applied science; in physics, chemistry, and biology the interconnections between theory and applications, discovery

BRUCE JENNINGS ● The Hastings Center, Hastings-on-Hudson, New York, 10706.
KENNETH PREWITT ● Social Science Research Council, New York, New York, 10016.

and products, are clear. It is when the ends of application are feared—monstrous weapons, environmental damage, the growing potential for genetic engineering—that the most difficult questions are raised.

In the social sciences, by contrast, both the ends and the means of application are still open to dispute. Social scientists are still working out what application means and identifying the "for instances" which will convince skeptics that the social sciences offer practical benefits to society. Various attempts to apply social scientific theories, models, and research findings to the formation of public policies have become deeply ingrained in the postwar governance of the liberal welfare state and in the political management of advanced capitalist economies. Nonetheless, applied social science continues to be faulted simultaneously for triviality *and* for having a substantial if, to some, distorting influence in social affairs and public matters. This is a telling commentary on the still indeterminate status of the social sciences as theoretical and applied disciplines.

But if social scientists are becoming increasingly perplexed about the relationship between disciplinary scholarship and applied studies in their fields, humanists are faced with an even deeper set of doubts and suspicions which have their roots in the cultural history of the humanities since the Enlightenment. For one thing, many humanists are wary of the "engineering model" of application, traditionally presented as the linkage between theoretical knowledge and practical applications in the natural sciences and which, at least until recently, the social sciences have sought to implement for their own fields. For another, humanists have been put off by the baldly utilitarian and instrumentalist conception of knowledge that they—not always mistakenly—see lurking behind programs for the development of applied studies. Humanistic scholarship has always had to struggle for recognition, support, and validation in the highly pragmatic, action-oriented cultural ethos of modern industrial society. The legacy of these longstanding and continuing battles—especially in America, the quintessentially "modern" society—still complicates the current discussion of applied work in the humanities. Some commentators, such as Robert Bellah, have attempted to recast the entire framework of this debate by arguing that, properly understood, the humanities are inherently applied or practical modes of knowledge, by nature more akin to *phronesis* than to *theoria* in Aristotle's sense.[1] But most humanists generally agree that, however we construe the notion of an applied humanities and however strongly we may want to support and encourage applied studies in philosophy, history, and other fields, it is important to insist that the value of these disciplines

[1] Robert N. Bellah, Chapter 7 of this volume.

does not and should not rest solely on their application to the immediate, practical concerns of society.

The purpose of this chapter is to suggest a viable conception of the means and ends of application in the humanities (and the social sciences) by examining the past and present relationships between the humanities and the social sciences. We believe that, even by themselves, both social scientific knowledge and humanistic knowledge have potentially important practical applications.

Our main concern, however, is to suggest that the recently emerging interconnections between the humanities and the social sciences—the blending of their approaches in the interpretation of human conduct and sociocultural phenomena—hold the key to a critically important application for these disciplines. We have in mind the contribution that the interpretive disciplines of the social sciences and the humanities can make, and should be making, to the reconstruction of a public philosophy to inform the governance of modern liberal society. These disciplines can contribute to the reconstruction of a public philosophy by articulating—through their studies of cultural traditions, symbolic meaning, political, economic, and social structures, and patterns of purposive human conduct—a richer understanding of human nature and a teleological, normative conception of the human good. By articulating, that is to say, a richer "philosophical anthropology" as the theoretical groundwork for a shared public philosophy.

As we, echoing Walter Lippmann, will be using the term, a public philosophy does not directly provide specific answers to particular questions of public policy. It does not mandate any particular political program in detail, establish social priorities, or determine cultural agendas. Rather, a public philosophy provides a normative framework, a climate of civility or civic concern, and an animating vision of human possibility and social order within which legitimate political procedures can operate and substantive policy choices can be framed, debated, and peacefully resolved. Without a guiding public philosophy, governance in an open, democratic society will inevitably be stymied and confused; without a coherent, widely shared commitment to a public philosophy, a liberal democratic polity lacks a sense of common purpose and shared endeavor, the legitimacy of the political process erodes, and the essential discourse among citizens and their representatives can find no common idiom.

To suggest that it is the task, indeed the calling, of the social sciences and the humanities to provide a philosophical anthropology as the basis for a public philosophy is to reject the notion which views applied knowledge as a form of social scientific or humanistic "social engineering." The linkage between a philosophical anthropology and a public philosophy is neither as direct and mechanistic as engineering nor as indirect and diffuse as a banal notion of enlightenment—that is, simply adding willy-nilly to the general stock of ideas—that is often counterposed to the engineering model. This linkage, which we cannot fully flesh out but only invoke here, is a middle ground between the attempt to propose solutions to specific, technical policy problems and general reflection on "timeless" themes and universal principles. If social scientists too often quest in vain for the former, humanists too often sell themselves short— and their disciplines and their republic—by settling for the latter. If social scientists think of application only in the engineering sense, they will but partially and inadequately fulfill their intellectual mission. Similarly, if humanists take recourse only in assertions about general enlightenment, fretful about references to more direct application, they will cut themselves off from an opportunity to help our society sort out its intrinsic possibilities and likely limits. Tending to the public philosophy, and the philosophical anthropology on which it necessarily rests, is a mission which can be shared by the social sciences and the humanities. Such a shared mission will on the one hand protect social science from a narrow and technocratic view of application and on the other urge humanists to rethink their civic responsibilities. Both scholarly endeavors would be healthier as a result.

The initial question is whether the social sciences and the humanities can get together.

II

The humanities and the social sciences share a common subject matter and many overlapping concerns in their study of human activity. Both aspire to deepen and to broaden our insight into the multifaceted reality of the human condition. Both expand the limits of our cultural horizons and enrich our self-understanding as socially and historically situated beings. Both take the realm of human artifice and performance as the primary locus of inquiry, exploring the meanings that adhere in the interactions among persons, the forms and conditions of those meanings, and the embodiment of ideas in texts and institutions which mediate the social relationships among individuals and the material relationships between persons and their natural environment.

In the pursuit of these common objectives, the humanities and the social sciences do of course differ in the categories they employ and in the themes they characteristically emphasize. The humanities tend to throw the particularity of individuals—their originality, their style, their creativity and causal efficacy as agents—into bold relief against a distant background of collective, historical, or material forces. For their part, the social sciences tend to highlight precisely those general background conditions and structures that both make individual particularity possible and serve to limit it. Nonetheless, these differences do not obviate the common interests of the humanities and the social sciences. Were these common interests better understood and more thoughtfully acted upon, the humanities' characteristic emphasis on human agency and the social sciences' characteristic emphasis on the context of agency would be reciprocally illuminating, allowing the two families of discourse in concert to comment more intelligently on the human condition than either has been able to do separately.

And at present there is a renewed appreciation of the common bonds. Most, if not all, social scientific and humanistic disciplines have lately been caught up in a process of theoretical realignment and methodological turmoil, reflecting in part an uncertainty about next steps in disciplinary development. We have entered a period of what Clifford Geertz has aptly called "blurred genres"; disciplinary boundaries that once appeared firmly entrenched are breaking down, and new patterns of research are forming, based upon problems and metaphors that shuttle between and confound old dividing lines.[2]

Before they could be blurred, genre distinctions between the approaches, idioms, and methods belonging to the humanities and those belonging to the social sciences had to be well established and influential. And so they were, and still are. These distinctions grew up because they were instrumental to the refinement of scholarship and the advancement of knowledge, much as the division of labor and specialization of function are linked to efficiency and productivity. As historians of the natural sciences have pointed out, when the researchers in a particular field of study settle on their own "paradigm" or "disciplinary matrix" and organize themselves into a sociologically isolated group with its own internal communication network and distinctive terminology, they achieve a remarkable focusing of energy. Freed from the continual need to reexamine epistemological or ontological questions and absolved from the obligation to communicate directly with a general audience, scientists have broken their research down into subfields and examined each with a depth never before achieved. Much the same impulse—and some of the same effects—has been present in the social sciences for some time and, to a lesser extent, in some areas of the humanities. The result (in both the natural and the human sciences) has been an information explosion. We now know far more about human behavior and social phe-

---

[2]"Blurred Genres: The Refiguration of Social Thought," *The American Scholar*, vol. 49, no. 2 (Spring, 1980), pp. 165–179.

nomena than ever before—"know," in the sense that we now have far more information about, and multiple interpretations of, human activities in nearly every time and place.

The often cited irony, of course, is that an abundance of information about and interpretations of human activity does not necessarily generate a coherent intellectual framework within which specialized knowledge could be melded into an orderly and meaningful whole. A century of increasing specialization and compartmentalization in human studies has done more than break the links between the social sciences and the humanities. It seems to have obstructed the kind of comprehensive vision of human nature and society that those intellectuals in earlier periods, who were the precursors of modern day humanists and social scientists, offered the public culture of their age. The roots of this condition are to be found in the path toward a certain organization of science that the social sciences have taken.

When the natural sciences beginning in the seventeenth century embarked upon the path of disciplinary specialization, they largely jettisoned their older concern with cosmology and natural philosophy. The corresponding move by the modern social sciences has been to abandon their concern with what we have called philosophical anthropology. But if modern culture can adjust without undue trauma to the demise of cosmology, it is not so clear that culture can so easily accommodate the demise of philosophical anthropology. To view the physical universe as a mechanistic arrangement devoid of telos or immanent meaning is one thing; to view the social universe in that way is quite another. For the better part of the last century, social science has flirted with that picture of the social universe just as many in the humanities and the arts have been haunted by it. Now many social scientists are rapidly breaking off that flirtation. They are returning apace to something resembling the older discourse of philosophical anthropology.

It is too early to tell what will come of this. It may constitute nothing more than a passing fad or a temporary burst of unusual daring and ecclecticism. Moreover, the danger raised by blurred genres is blurred vision. As disciplinary forms give way to more fluid patterns and protocols of inquiry, the intellectual virtues of disciplined analysis, observation, and critical judgment will be put to the test and will need new standards and criteria of assessment to sustain them.[3] But if it is too early to say that a viable new restructuring of human studies has been achieved and its perils avoided, it is also too early, in our judgment, to call for retrenchment. The air is already too full of manifestos on both

---

[3]Richard J. Bernstein, *Beyond Objectivism and Relativism* (Philadelphia: University of Pennsylvania Press, 1983).

sides. It is not our intention here either to embrace uncritically all the initiatives now taking place between the humanities and the social sciences nor to join in the disciplinary backlash against such initiatives. What is needed—and what we do propose—is to step back and examine the promise offered by the newly emerging connections between the humanities and the social sciences.

III

Every culture distinguishes among its various bodies of intellectual and practical knowlege, and some cultures—those more advanced in this sense—also create a second-order interpretation of these distinctions, classifying bodies of knowledge within some abstract schema and hierarchically ordering them according to normative principles of epistemological, moral, or utilitarian value. For the members of any given culture at a particular time, these classificatory schemata and ordering principles are enormously significant—albeit largely unperceived and unquestioned—because they condition the intent and production of knowledge and the way it is used. They affect the social relationship of one group of knowers to another. They provide, so to speak, a "grammar" for the languages of science, art, and craft. Similarly, for the student of a culture, its classificatory schemata and ordering principles are deeply revealing; they offer clues concerning the fundamental assumptions human beings make about their own capacities and limitations and about the ways in which reality can be broken up into different orders, each submitting itself to human knowledge in different ways.

We broach this very large topic here to make a more modest, but still important, point. Neither the historical development of the social sciences nor that of the humanities can be understood in isolation from one another or strictly on their own terms. The rise of the modern social sciences from the mid-nineteenth to the mid-twentieth century grew out of a more general reorganization of knowledge that simultaneously transformed the character of the humanities. From this point on the humanities and the social sciences have often defined themselves in terms of their differences from to one another, as well as in terms of their relationship to the natural sciences.

The present trend toward a less adversarial relationship between the humanities and the social sciences indicates two important developments in our cultural system of knowledge. The first is that natural science—or, more precisely, the positivist interpretation of natural science—no longer rules supreme in our culture's hierarchy of knowledge and no longer serves as the universally acknowledged standard against which all other claims to valid "cognitively significant" knowledge must be measured. And the second development, already alluded to above, is that neither the humanities nor the social sciences can find in their opposition to one other a serviceable basis for their own cultural legitimacy and intellectual rationale.

For more than a century, the social sciences have justified their independence and existence by claiming to offer an "objective," applicable kind of knowledge about human things that the humanities could not provide. During the same period the humanities, when pressed, have claimed the superiority of their distinctive and more explicitly value-laden approach to the study of the human condition. Each of these claims is untenable. Each overestimates the promise and misconstrues the character of the disciplines they purport to defend.

How did these claims arise? And why have they misfired?

The quest for a systematic understanding of the nature and functioning of human society is a very old intellectual adventure. From one point of view, the history of the social sciences corresponds to the history of western social and political philosophy. Plato in the *Republic* and Aristotle in the *Politics* established a tradition of discourse to which the modern social sciences still belong; they formulated interconnected and fundamental questions that social scientists still pose and attempt to answer. Nonetheless, to focus exclusively on the continuity of this Great Tradition is to overlook three things of equal, or greater, importance about the social sciences, namely, (1) their overriding self-consciousness of their own modernity; (2) their founding sense of the inadequacy of traditional social theory; and (3) their attempt, in breaking with that tradition, to inaugurate a kind of social inquiry at once more solidly established epistemologically and more powerful as an instrument of social control.

These three elements of the modern orientation in the social sciences grew out of a more comprehensive reordering of knowledge that took place in the nineteenth century, for it was then that the social sciences began to coalesce into the disciplinary pattern still operative today.[4] During this period a new cultural ideal of knowledge emerged. This ideal, called Science, was based on the empiricist doctrine that sense perception is the basis of all human knowledge and that through controlled observation general laws of cause and effect could be discovered which would mirror in human language and thought the true structure

---

[4]For a general account of this reordering of knowledge, see Maurice Mandelbaum, *History, Man and Reason: A Study in Nineteenth Century Thought* (Baltimore: The Johns Hopkins University Press, 1971). For an account of the influence of positivism in social science, see Anthony Giddens, "Positivism and Its Critics," in *Studies in Social and Political Theory* (New York: Basic Books, 1977), pp. 29–88.

of external reality itself. So conceived, science was placed at the top of the intellectual hierarchy, supplanting religious revelation, aesthetic imagination, and practical common wisdom, and relegating them, as it were, to the epistemological dust bin of superstition, metaphysics, and subjective illusion. Moreover, since it was widely held that the natural sciences—preeminently Newtonian physics—came closest to realizing this ideal of science, many thinkers concluded that other disciplines must henceforth adopt the methods and stance of the natural sciences if they were to achieve a sound footing and discover the truth about their objects of study.

Debates surrounding this ideal of science and its relation to other modes of knowledge dominated nineteenth-century intellectual life. These debates pitted *positivism*—a philosophical elaboration of the ideal of science—against its conservative and radical critics: traditionalists, literary romantics, philosophical idealists, and so on. The subsequent development and consciously articulated rationales of both the social sciences and the humanities were deeply influenced by their respective reactions to the positivist conception of science and by their attempts to carve out a place for themselves in the new order of knowledge over which science reigned. It is here, then, in their differing reactions to the intellectual challenge posed by science and by the complex industrial, technological civilization being produced by the applications of science, that one finds the source of the divergence of the social sciences and the humanities. In order to understand the course of this divergence, we need only take quick note of three general features of positivism having to do with the epistemological and the ethical stance of the knowing subject vis-à-vis the object of knowledge.

First, nineteenth-century positivism was a deeply skeptical and anti-traditional doctrine. Its first impulse was to sweep aside all received doctrines and all claims to truth based solely on the authority of canonical belief or established practice. In this, its image of the knowing subject was highly individualistic and even heroic. If the human intellect could free itself from the fetters of accumulated belief and dogma; if, like Descartes in the *Meditations*, it could dig down to some bedrock of certainty and then logically and methodically rebuild a body of knowledge, it could know the truth.

Second, following from this demanding image of scientific discovery, positivism was equally severe in its demands on the mental discipline of the knowing subject. Not only must scientists avoid sources of error coming from outside, they must also control or suppress sources of bias within themselves. This does not mean that science, even according to the positivist account, must be a cold, passionless endeavor. But it does mean that the scientist qua scientist must establish an emotional distance from the phenomena he or she studies. For positivism, the first virtue is objectivity or value neutrality; the cardinal sin is to allow judgments of value or preference to influence one's analysis of facts.

Third, positivism externalized the relationship between the knowing subject and the object of knowledge. That is, the activity of science was ontologically separated from the reality it studied; it observed that reality but did not in any important or essential way participate in it. This doctrine (which was derived from the seventeenth century shift from a teleological and Christian cosmology to a mechanistic cosmology)[5] meant that the objects of scientific knowledge were things to be described, manipulated, and controlled. Scientists can have no human (or spiritual) relationship with their objects of study, for that would involve anthropomorphic project and myth. Moreover, the practice of science did not, in and of itself, either depend upon or enhance the broadly human or spiritual qualities of the scientist. To hold that science was related to the spiritual qualities of scientists both threatened the objectivity of science and, even worse, led back in the direction of alchemy, which was for positivism the very archetype of pseudoscience.

The nineteenth-century positivist ideal of science posed an especially acute challenge to the humanities because, even though modeled on the physical sciences, it claimed to establish the valid criteria for *all* knowledge. During the two preceding centuries when the natural sciences broke away from their moorings in ancient natural philosophy, the humanities had concomitantly established themselves in the study of human or cultural phenomena. If, as the custodians and transmitters of ancient learning, the humanities had no important contribution to make in the study of nature because ancient knowledge contained no serviceable truth for such a study, then at least they remained germane to the study of culture, where ancient knowledge was still thought to contain unsurpassed wisdom and insight. At least in the domain of human studies, if modern knowledge were to progress, it would have to remain firmly rooted in an ongoing tradition of discourse established by classical sources. So long as that conception held, the humanities' intellectual rationale remained secure in their vast, if bounded, area of study. Nineteenth-century positivism shattered that nature–culture dualism and with it the heretofore stable détente between the humanities and the sciences.

By challenging ancient learning across the board, positivism pro-

---

[5]Cf. E. A. Burtt, *The Metaphysical Foundations of Modern Science*, rev. ed. (1932), (Garden City, NY: Doubleday Anchor Books, 1954); and Charles Taylor, *Hegel* (Cambridge: Cambridge University Press, 1975), pp. 3–50.

posed to extend its conception of the distinctively modern mode of knowledge, Science, into the study of society, culture, history, and human behavior. The nineteenth-century social sciences arose in an effort to carry out precisely that program. This established the terms and the stakes of the contest between the humanities and the social sciences that we have inherited and are only now beginning to reassess. It also marked out two divergent paths along which the humanities and the social sciences would subsequently attempt to locate their distinctive identities and intellectual missions in modern society.

Broadly speaking, the humanities responded to the challenge of positivism in two ways. First, they defended the validity of classical learning and came to underscore several attendant conceptions upon which the value of a continuing study of classical knowledge seemed to depend. The most important of these conceptions were: a frankly normative (and, some would say, elitist) concept of high culture or civilization; the notion of a canon of texts representing, in Matthew Arnold's memorable phrase, "the best which has been thought and said" on topics of perennial human concern; and finally the importance of preserving cultural traditions when industrial capitalism was relentlessly sweeping those traditions aside in favor of an uninhibited pursuit of material self-interest.

Each of these conceptions—high culture, the canon, and tradition— rested on an assertion which the humanities began to call upon with renewed emphasis in order to defend their rightful place in the republic of letters. That assertion was the moral authority inherent in those portions of the western cultural tradition that the humanities were most concerned to preserve and transmit. At stake was the continued authority of the humanistic canon and the normative significance of those texts; not only the significance of their substantive content, but also and more importantly the significance of the standards of judgment, the sensibility, and the imaginative reach they exemplify.

The second aspect of the humanities' two-pronged response to the challenge of positivism centered not so much on the continuing validity and importance of the subject matter they studied as on the moral and psychological effects of that study itself. And it is here that the modern self-understanding of the humanities took shape most clearly as a reaction against the positivist conception of the relationship between the knowing subject and the object of knowledge sketched above.

Against the skeptical and heroic stance prescribed by positivism, defenders of the humanities insisted that human wisdom and creativity were not the *sui generis* products of a lonely human intellect unencumbered by past culture, but were achievements that could arise only out of a deep and critical engagement with received traditions of discourse.

Against the purported objectivity and value neutrality of modern science, the humanities stressed the value-laden character of human knowledge and the crucial need for an education geared toward the cultivated refinement of normative sensibility and judgment rather than the repression or methodological avoidance of them.

Finally, the defenders of the humanities argued that the "objectifying" attitude inherent in the positivistic account of the relationship between the knowing subject and the object of knowledge was misleading and pernicious when applied to the domain of human studies. When studying other human beings and the products of their activities, the humanists argued, one should adopt an essentially moral stance toward the persons and events in question, seeing the "other" as a human *subject* to be understood and evaluated as a cultural agent rather than as a human *object* to be explained and controlled as a natural thing.[6] This humanistic stance would keep the distinctively human qualities of the past—or present—persons and events being studied at the center of attention. In this way, our appreciation of the richness and diversity of the human condition would not be lost in an ill-conceived attempt to reduce human doings to a master set of uniform conditions and universal laws. It would thereby enhance our own highest human qualities, enriching our capacity to reach outside our own parochial experience and concerns and refining those capacities of imagination and sensibility wherein both reason and feeling are united and expressed.

With arguments roughly along these lines, the humanities in the nineteenth century began to redefine and extend their intellectual rationale and their claim to an essential place in the new order of knowledge. Over time this defense has proved relatively successful; although the first aspect of this defense—based on the authority of a canonical tradition—has always left the humanities open to attacks motivated by populism and cultural pluralism alike, while its second aspect—the humanizing function of the study of the humanities—has tended to promise more than it can deliver.

More important for our purposes here, though, is the fact that this defense of the humanities has tended to cut them off from the broadly political activities and concerns of modern society. In reacting to the challenge of positivism, the modern defenders of the humanities have inadvertently or, with Matthew Arnold, deliberately conceded that modern science alone can provide instrumental or "applicable" knowledge for the solution of social problems. In rendering unto science that

---

[6]Edward Shils captures the tensions between the social sciences and the humanities in this regard. Cf. *The Calling of Sociology and Other Essays on the Pursuit of Learning* (Chicago: University of Chicago Press, 1980), pp. 3–92.

which is science's, the humanities have left themselves in a predicament that scholars are only now beginning to untangle.

For their part, the social sciences were also shaped by their response to the challenge of positivism; shaped, that is, as much by their affirmation of that challenge as the humanities were by their negation of it. But in recalling the fact that the social sciences arose out of an attempt to extend the positivist ideal of science into the domain of human studies, we tend to neglect an equally important part of the story: namely, the fact that many of the founding figures of modern social science (Comte, Spenser, Marx, Durkheim, Weber, Boas) were also motivated by their dissatisfaction with the self-understanding of the humanities that was developing in that period and by their belief that the humanities, so understood, could not offer the knowledge necessary to cope with the unprecedented conditions and demands of the modern age.[7]

Nineteenth-century social science (especially sociology) thus emerged with its own two-pronged defense and promise. First, qua science, it aspired to begin the long process of social description and explanation that would eventually produce the psychological and sociological laws that would better enable us to predict and control (or at least manage) human behavior. Second, against what was perceived as the excessive subjectivism of romanticism and artistic culture generally, social science aimed to provide a more adequate comprehension of the modern human condition, a comprehension based on an understanding of the collective, institutional forces shaping the activity and even the self-identity of the modern individual.

IV

This, then, is a very general sketch of some of the principal arguments and considerations that have been the source of the tension between the humanities and the social sciences. However, especially during the last ten years, the various rationales for the humanities and the social sciences discussed in the preceding pages have come to seem deeply problematical and even incoherent. Arguments that stood as largely unquestioned dogma as recently as the 1950s and early 1960s have come unraveled as each field has failed to live up to the expectations these arguments engendered.

The rationale and purpose of the humanities have been unsettled in two ways. First, there has been an almost complete loss of faith in

[7]Anthony Giddens, *Capitalism and Modern Social Theory* (Cambridge: Cambridge University Press, 1971); and Sheldon S. Wolin, *Politics and Vision* (Boston: Little, Brown, 1960), pp. 286–434.

the existence, or even the possibility, of a stable, authoritative canon. This is due only in part to the widespread skepticism and ethical relativism of our time. Most of the leading humanists have abandoned any attempt to construct and prescribe such a canon. Instead, they have turned to the much more open-textured process of examining the various systems of literary meaning and artistic taste and the temporal rise and fall of particular works within those systems.[8] Moreover, most humanists have also abandoned their claim to provide a single, authoritative interpretation of any text, whether canonical or not, and have produced instead a vast array of critical theories in which interpretation is seen as an activity that cannot, in principle, ever be complete.

Second, at least some humanists, such as the British critic, George Steiner, have begun to draw back from the straightforward claim that the study of the humanities is in and of itself a humanizing experience. "Unlike Matthew Arnold and unlike Dr. Leavis," Steiner has written,

> I find myself unable to assert confidently that the humanities humanize. Indeed, I would go further: it is at least conceivable that the focusing of consciousness on a written text, which is the substance of our training and pursuit, diminishes the sharpness and readiness of our actual moral response. . . . Thus there may be a covert, betraying link between the cultivation of aesthetic response and the potential of personal inhumanity. What then are we doing when we study and teach literature?[9]

Intellectual presumptions and methodological strategies in the social sciences have also been subjected to skeptical questioning, as the positivist tradition has failed to produce anything like the dominant paradigm or set of general predictive laws which were once expected. Questioning has emerged in part from within the social sciences themselves. For instance, the search for a scientific language that would describe the invariant features of social behavior, as perhaps best illustrated in Parsonian pattern variables, was never accepted by the area studies tradition in its search for an ever deeper understanding of particular culture forms and culturally prescribed behavior.[10] Local traditions and historically rooted habits took scholars away from the abstractions of general theory. Thus, under prodding from area scholars, social science has looked less for invariant behavior and more at temporal and spatial boundary conditions, turning away from covering laws and back toward history.

---

[8]Jonathan Culler, *The Pursuit of Signs* (Ithaca, NY: Cornell University Press, 1981), pp. 18–43.

[9]*Language and Silence: Essays on Language, Literature, and the Inhuman* (New York: Atheneum, 1972), p. 61.

[10]For a recent summary statement, see Philip A. Kuhn, "Area Studies and the Disciplines," *The Bulletin of The American Academy of Arts and Sciences*, vol. 37, no. 4 (January 1984), pp. 5–8.

Area scholarship is not the only internal source of disenchantment with positivism. The human consequences of the self-fulfilling prophesy hypothesis, as described in Merton's classic essay, remind us that the way in which social science describes the world has an independent and at times substantial influence on the world.[11] This suggests that social science is not outside of but very much part of the phenomena under investigation. With this realization has come skepticism toward the positivist assumption that the activity of science is ontologically separate from that which it studies. Moreover, social scientists have come to understand that they initially encountered the natural science model through philosophers—such as Hempel, Popper, Cohen, and Nagel—rather than through direct acquaintance with the scientific process itself. The enormously influential writings of the post-positivist generation of philosophers, historians, and sociologists of natural science have now taught social scientists that the hypothetical-deductive model was never an accurate empirical statement of what went on in the labs of physicists, biologists, and chemists and thus could hardly be the only approach for psychologists or economists.[12]

Social science has also been transformed from without, especially by the realization that external events are much less amenable to prediction and control than an earlier and more optimistic view of social science theory promised. The intellectual collapse of modernization theory is a case in point. History refused to obey the laws of the theory. For instance, Rostow's stages of economic growth notwithstanding, there is no inevitable progression in the growth of GNP among the preindustrial societies, and if there are cases of growth, there have been as many or more cases of economic stagnation and even decay. The political science version of modernization held that democratic political stability and economic development would be mutually reinforcing, but events have now demonstrated that rapid growth has covaried as frequently with authoritarian regimes (Taiwan, South Korea, South Africa, Argentina, pre-Khomeni Iran) as with regimes based on competitive elections and widespread civil liberties.

Yet another disquieting encounter with history is captured in the "end of ideology" discussion, which held sway in intellectual circles a few decades ago. The assertion that advanced industrial societies had

[11]Robert K. Merton, "The Self-Fulfilling Prophecy," *The Antioch Review* (Summer 1948), pp. 193–210.

[12]On recent developments in the philosophy of science, see Frederick Suppe, "The Search for Philosophic Understanding of Scientific Theories" and "Afterward—1977" in *The Structure of Scientific Theories*, ed. by F. Suppe, 2nd ed. (Urbana, Ill.: University of Illinois Press, 1977), pp. 3–241, 617–730. Cf. also Harold I. Brown, *Perception, Theory, and Commitment: The New Philosophy of Science* (Chicago: University of Chicago Press, 1977).

come to an end of ideology in politics was companion to the larger quest for social engineering, which found political and social scientific expression in policy studies and social experiments. And although policy studies have instructed society about the dimensions of social problems and have helped leaders evaluate policy interventions, we have a much more modest view of "problem solving through social engineering" than held sway only two decades ago. In part, this modest view results from an important social science idea, the notion that aspiration levels have no fixed zero point. People build on past accomplishments and therefore continually change the terms of what is acceptable policy. That tuberculosis is no longer a killing disease does not make us patient with the slow progress of cancer research. The research in human engineering models that allows mere mortals to fly jumbo jets helps increase the complexity of man–machine systems which must be managed. These medical and technical illustrations have their analogs in social systems, producing transformations which, far from bringing an end to ideology, keep the political conflict process alive and in a constant state of change. Politics is not a process, we now see, that can be neutralized or brought to heel through the technocratic application of social science theory.

V

The serious rapprochement now occurring between the social sciences and the humanities is not an ordinary instance of interdisciplinary cooperation on a few limited themes. The prospects are much broader and much deeper. If genres are blurring, it is because many disciplines are undergoing internal transformations leading to overlap, intersection, and reconstitution. Neither the social sciences nor the humanities are likely to emerge from the present period of intellectual ferment dominated by their present disciplinary lines.

Indeed, it is probably misleading to refer to the relationship between "the social sciences" and "the humanities." Less misleading would be the observation that in important areas of research there is now a blending of perspectives which previously were kept separate. Certain characteristically social scientific questions are being explored with traditional humanistic categories, and vice versa. These developments present the opportunity for the humanities and the social sciences *together* to rejoin the civic conversation of our political culture. We believe that these developments are intellectually significant because they contain the promise of a fruitful and exciting new generation of scholarship and research; research leading, as we have said, to an enhanced understanding of the forms and conditions of being human (philosophical anthropology) and a clearer vision of those goods intrinsic to the human estate.

Moreover, and even more important, these developments are socially significant because they are arising at a time when the need for a newly articulated public philosophy is becoming increasingly evident.

Philosophical liberalism broadly defined has historically provided an integrative, secular public philosophy in the United States.[13] Underlying the most dominant traditions of constitutional jurisprudence, political ideology, and economic theory, philosophical liberalism—and its core notions of individual liberty, civil rights, toleration, freedom of expression, equality of opportunity, and progressive self-realization— has provided a vision of the good society and the fundamental social contract. Founded on a philosophical anthropology stemming from the rationalism, empiricism, and individualism of the Enlightenment (and earlier seventeenth-century sources), philosophical liberalism has been the normative framework within which political leaders and citizens have fashioned the priorities and purposes to be served by government and the other major institutions of society.

Like any other viable public philosophy or integrative intellectual tradition, liberalism has not been static; nor has it been free from political and moral blind spots. As America has developed from an agrarian, precapitalist society into a world power and a technologically and economically complex welfare state, liberalism has been remarkably successful in adjusting to social change and holding out an evolving framework of social consensus within which national governing coalitions could form and reform in response to changing distributions of social and economic power. Throughout, liberalism has exemplified the dynamic pattern that is, we believe, the hallmark of any viable, living public philosophy. That pattern involves a tacking back and forth between a conceptual analysis of normative principles and ideals and a descriptive analysis of the sociological conditions under which those ideals could be realized in existing institutions.[14]

In making these adjustments in a dialectical process of conceptual

---

[13]For overviews of philosophical liberalism, see John Plamenatz, "Liberalism," *Dictionary of the History of Ideas*, 4 vols. (New York: Scribner's, 1973), III, pp. 36–61; R. D. Cumming, *Human Nature and History: A Study of the Development of Liberal Political Thought*, 2 vols. (Chicago: University of Chicago Press, 1969); C. B. Macpherson, *The Life and Times of Liberal Democracy* (Oxford: Oxford University Press, 1977); and Amy Gutmann, *Liberal Equality* (Cambridge: Cambridge University Press, 1980), pp. 1–47.

For a history of American liberalism, see Theodore J. Lowi, *The End of Liberalism*, 2nd ed. (New York: Norton, 1979), pp. 3–66.

[14]The changing liberal understanding of the concept of private property in a corporate economy and the changing understanding of the relationship between private property, individual liberty, and political power are examples of the process we have in mind here. Cf. Michael B. Levy, "Illiberal Liberalism: The New Property as Strategy," *The Review of Politics*, vol. 45, no. 4 (October, 1983), pp. 576–594; and more generally, Charles E. Lindblom, *Politics and Markets* (New York: Basic Books, 1977).

reformulation and institutional reform, the liberal public philosophy has been informed by a stock of scholarly knowledge drawn from the social sciences and the humanities. But, for reasons we have tried to clarify in this essay, neither social scientific nor humanistic research did much to challenge the basic philosophical anthropology upon which the liberal public philosophy has rested.

The crisis currently facing philosophical liberalism as a public philosophy has been a long time coming. Writing in the 1950s, at a time when liberal public philosophy was arguably at its apex in the United States, two extraordinarily perceptive social commentators—applied humanists *avant la lettre*—, Walter Lippmann and Lionel Trilling, were already sounding notes of alarm. Lippmann was concerned with the challenges to liberalism posed by the great transformations of the first half of the twentieth century—the two world wars, the depression, the breakup of the colonial empires, the triumphs of Marxism. Cautiously optimistic, he still held out hope that the traditions of liberal civility, swept away abroad and eroding at home, could be revitalized.[15] For his part, Trilling was troubled by what he perceived as the atrophy of moral sensibility and imagination in modern liberal culture, but he too was still persuaded of the possibility for cultural and artistic renewal.[16]

Thirty years later the warnings remain, but the optimism has faded. In the wake of social militancy, ecological concerns, the persistence of racism and xenophobia, economic stagnation, and a host of other traumas in recent decades, American society has experienced a frustration of social expectations, a political fragmentation, and a kind of "zero-sum" economic conflict that the traditional liberal public philosophy seems unable to contain.[17]

This, then, is the measure of the challenge facing the application of social scientific and humanistic knowledge today. The task facing a united humanistic and social scientific inquiry is nothing less than the reconstitution of a philosophical anthropology for a new public philosophy. Such a new public philosophy—we continue to hope—will retain the essential values of philosophical liberalism and liberal democracy. But it must be based on a substantial modification of the possessive indi-

[15]Walter Lippmann, *Essays in The Public Philosophy* (New York: New American Library, 1955).

[16]Lionel Trilling, *The Liberal Imagination* (New York: Harcourt Brace Jovanovich, 1979).

[17]Various diagnoses of the problems facing liberal public philosophy can be found in: Theodore J. Lowi, *The End of Liberalism*, esp. pp. 271–314; Lester C. Thurow, *The Zero Sum Society* (New York: Basic Books, 1980); Samuel P. Huntington, *American Politics and the Promise of Disharmony* (Cambridge, MA: Harvard University Press, 1981); William M. Sullivan, *Reconstructing Public Philosophy* (Berkeley: University of California Press, 1982); Douglas Maclean and Claudia Mills, eds., *Liberalism Reconsidered* (Totowa, NJ: Roman and Allanheld, 1983).

vidualism and hedonistic rationalism which are simply no longer tenable components of the liberal theory of human nature.

The range of questions the humanities and the social sciences must ask in their quest for a new philosophical anthropology and in their support for a new public philosophy is very broad. Included among the most perplexing and pressing of these questions are the following: What are the limits of tolerance? What is the proper role of this nation in the family of nations? In what ways is one generation prepared to forego immediate benefits in order to protect the economy or the environment for future generations? How might leaders assess the unintended consequences of social reform? Can the true costs of externalities be captured in a market economy? How does a multiracial, multilingual, and multiethnic population interpret what is thought to be a shared text? Can the great forces of modern times—science, technology, and bureaucracy—be governed under constitutions mostly concerned with the relation of the citizen to the state?

Answering the kinds of questions posed above is part and parcel of the dynamic process of building a revitalized public philosophy, the process of alternating between a conceptual analysis of normative principles and a descriptive analysis of the sociological conditions under which these principles could be realized in existing or reformed institutions. The kind of united humanistic and social scientific analysis that the blurred genres of new research are beginning to make possible can play an essential role in this process. This, and not the simplistic conceits of social engineering or scholarly detachment, is a notion of application fit for the social sciences and the humanities of today and tomorrow.

CHAPTER 9

The Humanities and the Media

MARK CRISPIN MILLER

As we begin, in a cursory way, to analyze the relationship between the humanities and "the media," we are struck at once by the fact that there does not seem to be one. Surely no two modern cultural entities could have less to do with one another, or diverge more widely in their respective programs. As a curricular sequence or idea, the humanities supposedly conduce to a refinement of the human essence, or *humanitas*; and this exalted project, this pursuit of individual cultivation, depends upon a deep, respectful knowledge of the greatest texts and a deliberate avoidance of the commercial world with its distractions and debasements. On the other hand, "the media" would seem, in every sense, entirely inimical to this ideal and idealistic plan of education. Whereas the end of the humanities must be humanity itself, what we call *the media* has, in at least two important senses, no end. First of all, it is a *means*, as the derivation suggests. Secondly, however, and paradoxically, the media, although merely instrumental, is apparently a means to no end whatever, the flood of sounds and images apparently *endless*—both boundless and interminable. Moreover, whereas the humanities, engaged in their enhancement of the individual spirit, supposedly transcend the defilements of *negotium*, the media is pervasively commercial, its tone and messages determined by those corporate interests, vague yet inescapable, that monopolize it.

From what we might call the humanistic point-of-view, then, the relationship between the humanities and the media is entirely negative, not really a relationship at all, in fact, since the humanities remain unsullied and detached while the media encroaches upon everything else, "and universal Darkness buries all"—all, that is, except the humanities

MARK CRISPIN MILLER • Department of Writing Seminars, The Johns Hopkins University, Baltimore, Maryland 21218.

and their adherents. It is this attitude of revulsion and disdain—an attitude far too complex for us to trace its history in this essay—that has underlain much of our humanistic thinking, both public and private, about the media. Indeed, it might even be argued that the humanities' identity, such as it is, has been forged (by humanists) in meticulous opposition to precisely those forces which the term *media* now contains and expresses: the public appetite for meretricious entertainments; sensationalistic spectacle; the crude practical demands of Big Business.

Although it is true that most humanists regard themselves as somehow separate from the influence of the media, however, and their work as somehow elevated high above it, this does not mean that the relationship between the humanities and the media is either as simple or as flattering to humanists as the foregoing account implies. For there has been an actual relationship between the two, a relationship both complex and entangling, not merely negative, as between pursuer and pursued, but close, subtle, and complicitous, as between, say, a tyrant and the priests who, although surrounded by the growing evidence of his criminal influence, persist in their purely abstract preachments about some other, better world.

What, then, is the nature of this relationship? We might suggest that if the humanities have indeed been defined in opposition to those forces that have been unified and consummated in the media, then the humanities cannot possibly exist apart from those forces, without which the humanities would, as a category, cease to be. Such an argument is clearly too abstract to be entirely illuminating. However, although it will not suffice to tell us just how the humanities have become entangled with the media, this argument does point us toward a problem that is more concrete and is directly relevant to an analysis of the strange relationship between these two seemingly disjunct categories.

WHAT ARE THE HUMANITIES?

Whether or not the humanities exist by virtue of their opposition to the media, the fact remains that the humanities do not comprise, express, or promulgate any coherent values or world view but constitute an entity only in the vaguest curricular sense. That pure humanistic point-of-view described above, in other words, with its stern commitment to the ideal of *paideia*, no longer predominates throughout today's so-called humanities, which can be considered a modern entity only insofar as they are no longer based on the defunct principles of Renaissance humanism. Indeed, at its most influential or controversial, the current spirit of the humanities is purposely antihumanistic. Enlightened by a variety of recent Continental doctrines (or anti-doctrines), most noteworthy literary theorists, along with representatives of other humanistic disciplines, continue to question and reject the whole range of assumptions that once comprised what we now recognize as a mere vulnerable ideology, the ideology of humanism. Professional humanists now subvert the notion of a "human essence" and deny the status of "the greatest texts," often as wholeheartedly as their more credulous predecessors once reconfirmed those categories.

Such revisionism, or demythologizing, obtains primarily in the most sophisticated humanities departments, while elsewhere the original ideology remains widespread, still a powerful force, even if expressed with a new defensiveness. Between these two camps, as diversely constituted as each may be, there is now a tremendous struggle, not always explicit, but always bitter and wholly unavoidable. Indeed, the current climate of the humanities has been determined by the intensity of this pervasive schism, which is evidenced in various ways and settings. Most frequently, perhaps, the schism will manifest itself within particular departments, as a generational conflict between the elder faculty, who cling to the anachronistic faith, and the younger members, who bring to bear on their research and teaching many of the new assumptions. More generally, the schism, at least insofar as it involves literary study and philosophy, has been expressed in terms of a sort of quasi-national rift, between those who subscribe to one or another (or all) of the methods or approaches imported from France and those who align themselves (even if unwittingly) with various British traditions.

Of course, this ideological battle is much more complex than the word *schism* may imply, for it is not a simple face-off between two opposed and equal sides, nor is it, in all of its manifestations, necessarily a clean conflict between the Old Guard and the avant-garde. First of all, neither side is homogeneous. Although often considered by its adversaries (and even, all too often, but its own least reflective adherents) as a united front, the ostensible avant-garde is actually comprised of positions, concerns, and assumptions not only diverse but often mutually contradictory: Derridean deconstruction, neo-Freudianism, Marxisms of various conflicting kinds, feminism, semiotics, and so on, are all simply not to be reconciled, however easy it may be to create the illusion of a unified position through a journalistic stroke of punctuation, as when we read in, say, *The Village Voice* of some "Marxist/structuralist/feminist" claim or attitude. Whether evoked admiringly, by the wary faddist eager to align himself with some many-pronged intellectual assault, or whether, contrarily, it expresses a conservative's disgust at an apparent alliance of disreputable factions, the illusory conglomeration that is meant to represent the academic avant-garde merely annihilates the threat which it would seem to amplify, by submerging pointed and specific arguments within an amorphous vision of spreading opposition. Similarly, those who resist or attack the disparate claims advanced by the innovators do not cohere into a perfect ideological monad but express through their resistance a range of beliefs, some political, some philosophical, and some, of course, mere unconsidered preconception.

Although neither side is neatly coherent, however, it would be an overstatement to assert that each of the two assortments of combatants is so richly, confusedly diverse that there is actually no ultimate and basic split, but a sprawling intellectual melee, many arguments and counterarguments all going on at once, yet contained within the profession which they vivify. For there is a single profound division between two very different sets of attitudes, however meticulously we must qualify our descriptions of each general stance. To put it over-simply, there is a fundamental and irreconcileable disagreement between those who, on the one hand, believe in absolute values, historical progress, and art as a means of direct moral betterment and those who, on the other hand, deny and seek to invalidate such metaphysical conceptions. Although this distinction is important, however, it is also so hard to apply to reality as to be almost useless. First of all, such terms as *absolute values* and *progress* are ambiguous enough to have precious meanings of entirely different kinds for, say, a Maoist, a liberal Democrat, and a radical feminist, respectively. Furthermore, even the most ardent deconstructionist, if studied carefully, will himself betray a bias toward the metaphysical, and so, although it is theoretically necessary, the above distinction, when applied to the current situation, does not enable us to locate every argument on one side or the other of some clear boundary line but merely serves to illuminate a number of pressing questions and concerns.

In trying to sort out the deep convolvement between the humanities and the media, then, we must first understand the real incoherence, at this historical moment, of what we still call *the humanities*. This effort at comprehension will not only enable us to grasp our own uncertain situation(s) as humanists but will also help us, indirectly, to grasp that process, or interference, or reflection, or display, to which we give that misleading name, *the media*. For in taking pains to convey the full complexity of any social, cultural, historical, or intellectual reality, we necessarily acknowledge some definitive tendencies of the media through our implicit efforts to thwart them. Despite its various pretenses at pure objectivity the media is not transpicuous, presents us with nothing in its immediate condition, but at once translates whatever it seizes upon into some simple, vivid, and apparently familiar pattern, some tidbit (so to speak) that has a powerful taste but goes down easily, so that we may then gulp down another such morsel, then another. It is this continual reduction, effected conjointly—indeed, monolithically—by television, the newspapers, and the newsmagazines, against which we struggle whenever we try to express the subtleties of any complicated entity. For instance, each of the simplistic schemata which I rejected above in my (necessarily crude) account of the humanities today represents some well-worn rhetorical or narrative device used by the media in its project of total simplification: the image of a humanistic professoriate entirely homogeneous in its highbrow unworldliness; the facile division of an ideological crisis into two sides or viewpoints labeled "liberal" and "conservative" or "rising generation" and "Old Guard"; the emphasis on the grand diversity of a given group or moment, which is thereby automatically protected from critical scrutiny, as somehow too thrillingly vast and vital to be comprehended (except by the reporter who thus applauds it).

WHAT IS THE MEDIA?

If a tendency to oversimplify is one definitive feature of the media, then we will find it increasingly difficult, as our world becomes more and more thoroughly saturated and determined by the media, to explain—or even to conceive—*any* complex notion. Our struggle to account for the humanities is in fact a single manifestation of a general cerebral and linguistic struggle that can only become more intense as we persist in trying to think and speak in a world regulated by television and its products. And under such conditions it becomes especially difficult to comprehend the media at all, for the media does not just oversimplify itself in its self-representation but automatically *conceals* its own influence in the very process of extending it. If we are to understand just how we humanists ought to regard and approach the media, we must first attempt something like a definition of this elusive, all-pervasive force.

What, then, *is* the media? Raymond Williams tells us that the word, derived from the Latin *medium*, "middle," first came into regular English usage in the late sixteenth century, carrying "the sense of an intervening or intermediate agency or substance." In the eighteenth century, there emerged the conventional use of *medium* to refer to newspapers, and this particular use evolved until "the description of a newspaper as a medium of advertising became common [in the early 20th century]." Then: "Media became widely used when broadcasting as well as the press had become important in communications; it was then the necessary general word. Mass media, media people, media agencies, media studies followed."[1]

This succinct conclusion to Williams' brief and learned history contains a crucial fact about the media, as both a term and a reality: the media finally entered common parlance just at that moment when the media became the overarching, inescapable system that contains us now—the epithet was generated by its own vague, omnipresent referent. (Specifically, it was the immense celebrity of Marshall McLuhan in the mid-1960s that occasioned the wide dissemination of the term.) This odd feature of the epithet's history suggests the crucial characteristic of the media itself: its incessant, automatic self-reference. The media both reflects back on itself and defines itself. It shows us nothing but its own images of everything and simultaneously establishes the very terms in which we think and talk about it.

Now, in order to appreciate the enormous influence of this self-referentiality, we must establish both the scope and the perfect homogeneity of the media. When people talk about the media, they are usually referring to the so-called communications industry, that nexus of corporate agencies the function of which is the generation of narratives and images for mass consumption: television, newspapers, newsmagazines. Of course, we generally use "the media" to refer to those agencies or agents who purport to record the news; the movies, for example, are not normally considered as part of what we call the media. However, it is not just the news which the media broadcasts or publicizes—that is, not just reflections on or of events that are supposed to have some political and/or economic significance—but other, less momentous images and facts as well, the various faces, names, occurrences whose only reason for celebrity (as has been said so often) is their celebrity. Or, to put it more accurately (and disquietingly), the media creates an inchoate display in which "newsworthiness" is entirely arbitrary, in which the latest rock group, candy bar or movie appears no less important than a recession, war or natural disaster; so that the putative seriousness of major stories finally disappears into that vivid, spurious fuss the maintenance of which is actually the only purpose of the media. In other words, despite the largely journalistic connotations of this epithet, the media, the ultimate function of its referent is not to inform us, but to induce us to consume. Each of the seemingly disparate components of the media are actually united by this imperative. Thus the hardware and the employees of *People* magazine, ABC News, *The New York Times*, and

[1]Raymond Williams, *Keywords: A Vocabulary of Culture and Society* (New York: Oxford University Press, 1976), p. 169.

Cable News Network, for example, are all, in effect, indistinguishable, as indistinct from one another as, increasingly, all those employees from all that hardware.

The media, then, is actually a monolith, even if the word denoting it is in the plural form. Moreover, this monolith is at once so vast and so convincing that it has determined the ways in which we perceive and contemplate it; or rather, it reflects the kind of consciousness that has formed it and that it now reinforces. In other words, the fact that the media has named itself is highly significant, for it provides one subtle instance of this baffling pattern: the media itself generates those criteria of so-called objectivity that actually *prevent* us from discerning it. It is itself the basis of our perceptions of it and of the world which it has altered, which it keeps altering. In short, the central and definitive quality of the media is also the very quality that prevents our clear perception of the media—its *illegibility*.

THE IMPLICIT POSITIVISM OF THE MEDIA

If the media is both all-pervasive and illegible, the humanist confronted with (and superannuated by) its influence is obliged to muster all of his or her interpretive powers in an effort to combat that influence. For the illegibility of the media is not absolute but superficial, and the consequence of our trying to understand the media in the very terms which have empowered the media in the first place. If we try to stand *outside* the media, however, we will be able to perceive and demonstrate the strategies whereby it both extends and hides its power. In other words, we must exert precisely those analytical capacities that distinguish us from our colleagues in the sciences, in order to read through the media, that is, to discern both the nexus of imperatives whereby the media affects us, and the ways in which the media simultaneously obscures those imperatives.

Let us begin by returning to that delusory epithet, *the media*. What might it tell us about its enormous referent? First, there is that vestigial plural ending, which suggests multiplicity where there is actually mere rigid uniformity. Thus the colloquial tendency to refer to the media as if it were a single entity suggests a wholly accurate inference, even if such usage is not grammatically correct. (It should be obvious by now that my own use of the term has been dictated by the same perception.) The media would have us see itself as many-sided, perspectively diverse, when in fact it is only many-headed.

And, as it does with itself, so does the media with everything which it reduces to its own few formulas; and it reduces everything. The world as seen on television and in the pages of *Newsweek* and the like is a world that initially appears to the wide-eyed consumer as a stunning cornucopia, the abundant contents of which, once soberly interpreted, immediately dwindle into sameness, contained as they are by the determining forms and repetitive narratives of the media that purports to be revealing them. This is not a recent phenomenon. The daily newspapers of the nineteenth century and later, with their every page arranged as a collage of fragmentary items, atomized the world into an unintelligible array of seemingly disparate names and happenings; and yet such apparent multiplicity was, in each case, actually a perfect unity, both formal and ideological, imposed by the newspaper on the vital data which it packaged for the reader. And now this same explosive yet reductive tendency recurs far more convincingly on television, which complements and threatens to replace the spatial fragmentation of the newspaper page with its own endless temporal sequencing, creating an ostensible diversity comprised of elements that are, in fact, identical, made fundamentally the same, visually, affectively, ideologically, by the system that presents them.

Moreover, television's process of reduction affects not just the mass of images that twinkle from our mass of video screens but also includes the world around those screens, and the coagulating audience that watches them. In approaching this development, we must move beyond mere quantitative inquiry—the amassment of statistics, formulaic "content analysis"—and transcend as well all blinkered perusal of historical and/or literary texts. Rather than continue to concentrate on such conventional inquiry and perusal, we must now use them as the basis for an interpretive effort far more adventurous and difficult, as we take the world around us for our text, in order to perceive how, in the age of television, life imitates artifice, as artifice pretends to life. More than any other medium, television feeds on those who use it; and, more than any other, this medium entices its users into feeding on itself. This mutual addiction has finally brought us to the point of supersaturation, for it has now become impossible to tell where television ends and the surrounding world begins. We and the medium are all but indistinct, having engaged over the last thirty years in a bewildering mutual pursuit, which has ended in our resembling images which are loosely based on television's image of ourselves: our public deportment, colloquial idiom and styles of humor, our values, ideals, capabilities, and pastimes have been variously altered by the inexhaustible box. Television has thus homogenized its viewers while celebrating their diversity in countless sentimental newscasts and commercials; and, as with the populace, so is it necessarily with our institutions, which the media has similarly narrowed and depleted. Television has all but displaced the remnant of our public life, consuming our politics, exhausting our literary culture, ruining cinema, ruining sports, and otherwise cancelling out variety precisely in the process of depicting and applauding it.

Although the media has thus reduced the world, it seems impossible to point this out without resorting to the devices of polemic (as I have just demonstrated). It sounds unreasonable, extreme, alarmist, when we deplore the influence of the media, or even mention it; but this apparent intemperance does not inhere in the critique of the media but is in fact imposed, both directly and obliquely, by the media on any such critique, because despite its devastations, the media always evinces an automatic credibility. This apparent trustworthiness arises from some further contradictory tendencies. As the media evokes multiplicity in the process of destroying it, that multiplicity remains believable, like all that the media represents, because, first of all, the media both depends on and perpetuates the myth of its own *transparency*.

This myth too is implicit in the epithet, which sustains the fiction that the media is comprised, to repeat Williams' formulation, of "intervening or intermediate agencies or substances," each a literal *medium*, purely instrumental and therefore innocent. And the myth also resonates in other of the verbal formulae whereby television implies the complete trustworthiness of the media, such as that familiar epithet for television, "our window on the world," or program titles like "You Are There," or "20/20," which suggests an eye with impeccable vision. That metaphoric eye, however, is meant to be conceived as disembodied, unattached to any contaminating consciousness, and therefore fit for use by us weak seers as a superior prosthesis. And the other organs of the media, advertising on and perhaps deriving their rhetorical devices from television, pretend to the same objectivity: "*Time* flies, and you are there," as one current television commercial for *Time* magazine puts it.

Whether it defines itself as a window or a perfect eye, the media implies that it does not generate its own peculiar images, that it generates, in fact, no images at all, but that it actually transmits material reality, that it "takes us on a visit" to whatever place it might be representing, that it "brought the war into our living rooms," and so on. Furthermore, this myth of transparency finds expression, not only in the various locutions of the media, but in daily journalistic practice. When it offers its version of the day's events, television persistently conceals its presence as a stimulus, as if it had not caused or even influenced what is "reports." This is a complicated fiction, related closely to still another myth inherent in the media, which is supposed to be not only transparent but also entirely *separable* from the reality which it determines. Of course, at this late date in the history of the media this myth necessarily demands the perpetuation of an absurdity; and yet the members of the media sustain this absurdity, not hypocritically, but quite sincerely, unshakeable in their deep faith in the mythology of their profession.

Although ostensibly objective, every newscast entails the full concealment of the minicams' inevitable impact on whomever it approaches out in public. Of course, it is unlikely that a group of men carrying video equipment could, in times like these, go about their business unobserved. Nevertheless, the media newsmen always imply that their equipment is invisible, that their intrusions make no difference, that what we see was going on before the crews arrived, by happenstance, to tape it. The reporters even depict themselves as absent when reporting on their presence, at which moments the absurdity becomes exquisite. This has become a commonplace of television "coverage": we are shown some footage of a lot of cameras shooting footage, while the correspondent blandly comments on all those media people on the scene, as if he were not one of them.

Aside from thus demonstrating both its own ostensible transparency and seeming separability from the world, television also implicitly reconfirms its own objectivity through the essential tone, or visual quality, of its own images, which, however dazzlingly diverse they may at first appear to the novice channel-changer, are all equally televisual in their unvarying coolness. This point demands elaboration. Television seems the perfect medium for seeing through the fictions of the world. Even at its noisiest and brightest, its vision is essentially a no-frills proposition, purporting to reveal the bare, immediate reality of things and selves. It is only the extraordinary visual event—the most opulent state occasion, the most gruesome sudden death, the most explicit personal sorrow— that can impress itself upon us through television's surface; and such rare impressions are, at that, mere momentary thrills, soon forgotten. For the most part, television seems always to be automatically interrogating what it shows us, implicitly discrediting its objects through its merciless scrutiny. Its subversive visual tone may well be the medium's primary determinant, since what we see on television is either calculated to derive an air to truthfulness from television's relentless gaze or else is carefully contrived to work *against* the medium's undercutting tendency. On the one hand, we have spectacles as seemingly unalike as "60 Minutes," "The People's Court," and Barbara Walters' "specials," as well as any regular newscast, all of which derive their apparent incisiveness from television's inquisitorial vision. On the other hand, we have the commercials and most other kinds of programs, all of which attempt to counteract or resist television's subversiveness through excessive stylization and unremitting sensationalism: high gloss, intense color, extreme close-ups, breathtaking zooms, and so on.

In effect, however, these two stylistic modes are identical, equalized by the incessant montage in which television presents and contains them. Ultimately, then, television's peculiar visual tone invites us to watch without intensity of any kind. We are numbed both by those images that seem to have been discredited by the medium's penetrating vision and by those vivid, hectoring images devised to withstand that penetration. All these images comprise an interminable process of hypnosis that implants no values, the purpose of which, rather, is to *discredit* every value that is foreign to itself—and value itself is foreign to television, whose vision is purely ironic and therefore finally nihilistic. It is too cool to encourage any form of life. Because its eye is inquisitorial or clinical, it is too jaded to appreciate those indefensible delusions that make us want to live—belief, desire, or any other ardor; intellectual commitment; self-esteem. Television apparently cuts through these insubstantialities, seeming to purify its objects; and yet these objects, televised, fail even to retain the special pleasures of their substance. Although television allures us with a universe of shining goods, it deprives material objects of their peculiar heft and tone; and although it ranges far and wide across the faces of mankind, it actually denudes us of significance by straining out the subtle features of every individuality. Pretending to show us the entire real world, television can only neutralize the vital motions that sustain identity, and represents this emptiness as Truth.

Thus the media realizes those positivistic assumptions that once motivated the engineers and scientists whose labors helped to make the media possible. Each of the aforementioned televisual tendencies repeats, and thereby reconfirms, some old tenet of positivism, the original program of which has been lucidly outlined by Bruce Jennings and Kenneth Prewitt in their essay for this volume. Television's clinical eye, for instance, at once recalls and manifests the positivistic urge to "sweep aside all received doctrines," to "dig down to some bedrock of certainty," and so on. Similarly, television's putative transparency recalls the "objectivity or value neutrality" of positivism, the first proponents of which believed that they were able and obliged to "control or suppress sources of bias within themselves." And television's presumed separability from its world recalls "the activity of science" as conceived by positivism, that is, as an enterprise "ontologically separated from the reality it studied; it observed that reality but did not—in any important or essential way—participate in it."[2]

These belated, automatic expressions of positivism define the tone of television's documentary mode, the custodians of which, as we have seen, corroborate this purely formal quality with their own professional

---

[2]"The Humanities and the Social Sciences: Reconstructing a Public Philosophy," Chapter 8 of this volume.

ideology. As bland and blow-dried as they are, the television newsmen mechanically evince all the hard-boiled savvy of those unkempt, cynical reporters in *The Front Page* and other such *hommages* to the newspaper world, so that it seems as if the coldly realistic vision of the media were not wholly formal, not a merely technological aura, but the deliberate, hard-won *weltanschauung* of a canny brotherhood. Thus television's newsmen purport to be resonsible for the very force that deprives them of all responsibility, reducing each of them to a mere onlooker, whose function is to stand there in the frame and look at things with the faint contempt and utter uninvolvement of the medium itself. They must, in other words, be as much like television as possible, which obligation instills and disseminates still another tenet of positivism, one made to seem more natural, less questionable, by virtue of its expression by, dispersal through a grimly visual medium. Just as the media poses as transparent, separable from the world which it presents, and relentlessly incisive, so too does it exalt the very basis of the positivist credo, the notion that *there is nothing that we cannot see and measure.*

By narrowing the range of all reality down to those few things which it can process, the media makes itself seem omnipresent and omniscient, able to miss or misinterpret nothing. Certainly the media is blind to anything that smacks of metaphysics, making the claims of mysticism, say, or conscience, or idealism, seem pointless and insane, however much it may attempt to hide its unbelief with maudlin commentaries on the plight of the Church behind the Iron Curtain. More crucial than such annihilation of the supramundane, however, are those dismissals whereby the media indirectly conceals its own predominance all around us, and within us. First, the media prevents our discerning its hegemony by attending only to specific instances, spurious particulars that each whizz past as if unrelated to any other things, as if unincluded in any historical continuum. Because the media rules out whatever cannot be bought or graphed, in other words, it discourages precisely the sort of dialectical thinking that might compass the large, elusive patterns of the media within society and culture. And, secondly, the positivist thrust of the media ensures our ignorance of the psychological, admitting as "causes" of behavior only those stark "factors" that can be easily tabulated, while denying the prevalence of the all-important unconscious, in whose obscure terrain the media erects, ever more efficiently, its own billboards and tollbooths.

THE EXPLICIT MODERNISM OF THE MEDIA

Thus far, it would seem that the media represents precisely the sort of old-fashioned scientism which today's more innovative humanists deride in their traditionalist opponents. Among the American students of Derrida *et les autres*, the term *positivist* functions as a derogatory catch-all, used often to dismiss a variety of methods and assumptions that continue to obtain among the (so to speak) humanistic derrière-garde. The notion, for instance, that texts contain specific meanings and that diligent criticism can make those meanings clear and unambiguous; the concomitant assumption that there is such a thing as truth, which reason can discover; the belief that each of us is a coherent self, unique and ontologically fixed, and somehow separate from the pervasive influences of class and culture: these and other such old notions are frequently condemned, with varying degrees of accuracy, as "positivistic." If we agree that there is indeed a positivistic animus behind a good many of those humanistic projects and beliefs that might be called conservative, it would therefore seem that, in attacking the media for its inherent positivism, we must ally ourselves with those humanists who purport to attack the same old animus as it is manifest among their colleagues.

However, such an alliance would be misconceived, not because there is no relation between the positivism that pervades the media and the ideology that impels the majority of the humanistic professoriate, but because the media, even while realizing the project of positivism, also realizes the opposite project. If the media constitutes a ceaseless caricature of the postures struck by old-fashioned scholars and scientists, in other words, it also caricatures the post-modernist impulses of those humanists who derogate those anachronistic figures. The media is simultaneously avant- and derrière-garde. It cannot be called either positivistic or modernistic because it is both at once, demonstrating the actual convolvement of two modes of thought that at first seem radically disjunct.

The media pursues what we might call the post-modernist critique of metaphysics, thereby realizing, albeit with a crude automaticity, the subtle deconstructionist intentions of Nietzsche, Heidegger, Derrida, and others. Within the world pervaded by the media, no humanistic essence is conceivable, nor can any entity retain its outlines as something privileged and impermeable, as if God-given. Despite its various pretenses at objective representation, its implicit claims to reveal everything, the media succeeds only in making everything equally obscure, partial, fragmentary. It explodes the daily world and the larger patterns of history into countless mysterious bits and pieces, which it then projects into every bedroom, onto every kitchen table, every newsstand, sustaining a tumultuous spectacle the only constant in which is *discontinuity*. Thus the media, although comprised of such prosaic elements as truncated newspaper stories, billboards half-glimpsed through windshields, and televised things and faces that abruptly metamorphose into other things, is as bold and baffling a modern artifact as anything created by Duchamp, John Cage, or Robbe-Grillet.

Within such a barrage, there are neither texts nor authors. Whereas the play or film is temporally discrete and must be mounted or projected in its own theater(s), the media, channelled largely through television, is a process that is itself more compelling than any of its constituent particles. In simply reading the paper, or watching television, it is this process that absorbs us, and not any one or another of such particles that engages us. And, whereas plays and films come to us as the works of specific authors, there are no such markedly unique and answerable authorities behind the media, which is a corporate construct, deriving much of its character, as we have seen, not from any supervisory human minds but from the forms through which such minds pretend to be autonomous.

This absence of manifest authority, moreover, not only makes discrete texts inconceivable as well as undesirable but also relates to an erasure more profound, more troubling: the erasure of the closed, fixed and self-sufficient personality. As processed by the media, and on television especially, such anachronistic inner-directed types immediately come across as ludicrous figures: pompous fools, cold prigs, tense neurotics, and so on. Thus the media not only proceeds without the evident influence of any overt authority but is also automatically subversive of any individual authority whatever, that is, any self sufficiently self-conscious and pronounced to resist the reductive current of the media. While it is dangerous for anyone represented by the media (and, by implication, anyone who watches what the media shows) to seem too inward, private, self-possessed, or otherwise eccentric, it seems safest, on the other hand, to become as affable, neutral, and forgettable as the majority of television's interchangeable performers. Responding to this imperative, which is all too often hidden by mechanical celebrations of diversity and cranky individualism, both those who perform for the media and those who gape for hours at the spectacle attempt alike to purify themselves of any psychic or sartorial abnormality, every odor, guilt, or passion, in order to become acceptably empty in the camera's ubiquitous, incisive eye.

Although it clearly works to the advantage of those industries that constitute and subsidize the media, this consumerist development—the slow extirpation of all resistant subjectivity—might be mistaken for a liberating movement, since it suggests the fulfillment of that antimetaphysical project toward which (it is often argued) all our great modern thinkers have contributed. Men, we have learned from these visionaries, are not each unique, self-enclosed, and self-determining, but the mere embodiments of historical and instinctual forces larger than themselves.

If the belief in personality is founded on a complex of outmoded lies, then the exposure and abandonment of all those lies must be a liberating action, a stepping, unencumbered, into the very present. And yet the media, although it has helped disburden us of our old-fashioned personalities, has hardly freed us but has merely replaced the old mythology with its own suasive messages and inescapable examples. Thus the media has demonstrated the dangers of that apparent intellectual progress in which the proponents of postmodernism have such great faith. On the one hand, writes Adorno, we must admit that "that which posits itself as 'I' is indeed mere prejudice, an ideological hypostatization of the abstract centres of domination, criticism of which demands the removal of the ideology of 'personality'. But its removal also makes the residue all the easier to dominate."[3] And so the media proves, by urging us to divest ourselves of all prior scruples, inhibitions, commitments and anxieties, so that we may become all that much more amenable to total domination by the media.

And this domination is effected, furthermore, through a kind of appeal that derives from yet another avant-gardist feature of the media. As we have seen, the documentary aspects of the media evince and reinforce a rigid positivism and therefore seem implicitly to validate a strict rationalism as the only proper attitude from which to observe the world. However, the media contains, in fact, comparatively few such documentary elements. Whereas the documentary images projected by the media seem rough, bleak, "natural," nearly all of what the media shows us seems, on the contrary, glossy, radiant, vivid, gorgeous, just as fantastic as those journalistic images seem mundane. And although those mundane images seem to appeal to our reason, addressing it straightforwardly with ostensible depictions of *what is*, the fantastic images that charge the television screen in most programs and in all commercials and that overwhelm the pages of our newspapers and newsmagazines assault the mind with threats and promises that are anything but rational, in an expert campaign of psychological warfare against ourselves.

The object of this campaign, of course, is to induce us to consume continually; and here, again, a corporate strategy reflects on, and in this case arose from, a progressive modern movement—the drive to understand the irrational bases of human action. One criterion of the most illuminating modern thought is its concern with those motivations which literary artists have recognized for centuries: fears and desires too deep for clear verbal formulation and therefore inaccessible to the purely ra-

---

[3]T. W. Adorno, *Minima Moralia*, tr. E. F. N. Jephcott (London: Verso Edition, 1978), p. 64.

tionalist philosophies of the Enlightenment. Nietzsche, then Freud and his disciples, and, more recently, such figures as Erving Goffman and Jacques Lacan, among others, have all worked variously to correct the Enlightenment bias toward pure reason, by pursuing the true, and therefore inexpressible, desires underlying our behavior. We humanists, of course, have studied the results of this modern scientific enterprise, but it is the corporations that have put them into practice, retaining veritable armies of industrial psychologists, motivational researchers, and advertising specialists, well-paid students of the irrational, whose function it has been to turn this great discovery of the psyche to the advantage of the powerful.

And it is the media that enables the powerful to wield this huge advantage, since it is through the media that our desires are both intensified and frustrated in ways that make us pay. However, to overemphasize the powerful would distract us from the objective autonomy of the media, the illegibility of which, we can now see, arises not from any corporate conspiracy but from the automatic interplay of those two modes—the documentary and the fantastic, or the positivistic and postmodernistic—that constitute the media. Through its barrage of suasive warnings and titillations, that is, the ads and all the material that interrupts and conduces to the ads, the media appeals precisely to that realm of mind which, according to the documentary world view, does not exist; and the larger, dialectical relationships between the ads and the material that surrounds them, between the media and us its viewers/victims, between us victims and the ads from which we hope for rescue even as they captivate us—all such entanglements remain invisible to us insofar as we accede to the assumptions of the media, for which nothing exists that its reporters or its clients cannot package.

THE HUMANITIES AGAINST THE MEDIA

Although it would evidence a naive faith in the power of the academic will to blame the media on our failures as humanists or to suggest that any efforts of our own could actually bring the media to a halt, it is still true that the media would not now be so mightily pervasive if humanists had long ago begun to read and therefore to resist it, teaching their students to do the same. For there can be no other means of escape from our entrapment by the media, which must either be actively criticized by its observers or else grow even larger and more influential. The so-called enlightenment model, according to which we might counteract the abuses of the media by placing humanistic experts in positions of power and influence throughout the pertinent industries, merely repeats the very problem which it purports to solve. It makes no difference whether the media now and then includes an injunction to social tolerance, or consistently depicts all ethnic types as wholly admirable, or represents the plight of the rape victim with all requisite sensitivity, since, even if the media is thus enlightened, it is still an overwhelming suasive force, demanding our perfect acquiescence. Because the media is by now autonomous, moreover, its tendencies determined by its technological forms and consumerist ideology, no individual attempts at intervention, however earnest, can alter it noticeably.

And, if a reformist effort from within cannot make up for the continued passivity of those who watch the media, then neither is mere cynical unbelief on the part of those watchers enough to make any difference. Indeed, it is precisely such inert skepticism that now sustains the media, the ads and shows of which tend to flatter this very attitude, thereby exploiting it. It is not that the habituated television viewer gazes at those images in a credulous rapture, as, say, a participant in the Nuremberg Rally might have gazed up at his Fuehrer. Rather, the viewer believes nothing that he sees and yet keeps watching, his weak skepticism threatening those sovereign images not at all, but only keeping the viewer himself from embracing any values that might strengthen him against the media. Sluggishly hungry, he is essentially overwhelmed by the very spectacle that he sees through and that keeps reassuring him that he sees through it.

There is no alternative, then, to our active, conscious interpretation of the media and its influence on our world; and it is just such interpretation that we humanists, and we alone in the academy, are (or ought to be) equipped to teach. Of course, in a culture dominated by the imperatives of business and distrustful of any intellectual endeavor that seems unscientific, interpretation, as opposed to physical research and solid scholarship, is necessarily a marginal activity: but this very marginality is proof of the real importance of interpretation, which will continue to be widely spurned as long as it threatens to make sense of things. That we humanists have failed to subject "the media" to our interpretive vision amounts to a form of criminal negligence. While the media is annually fortified by thousands of recruits who have studied under us as undergraduates, taking our courses in literary theory, art history, philosophy, semiotics, and so on, and thereby learning lessons which they later will apply as employees, we, their teachers, persist in ignoring the vast consequences of such application, although the media has all but superannuated us. We must therefore face the media, an orientation that will demand certain changes of approach and attitude within our profession.

First of all, it is no longer possible to regard the media as something too trivial and/or empty to merit serious consideration. This sort of attitude limits the thought primarily of those humanists who would be deemed, and who would deem themselves, as members of the so-called Old Guard. According to this attitude, the media is comprised of trash, mere cheap commodities, whereas what we call *art* is a haven furnished with far more expensive goods, worthy of protection and the tenderest ministrations. Of course, it is by thus separating art from its circumstances that we threaten it, for through this separation we not only silence the critique which art contains but also accede to the encroachment of those circumstances by refusing to read through them. More and more, it is the media that comprises those circumstances. By regarding the media as something like a vulgar neighborhood, as Pope and Wordsworth, say, regarded Smithfield, these supercilious humanists mistakenly regard its predominance as merely spatial, as if we might avoid the media just by steering clear of it; when in fact it is not some space that the media contaminates, but all consciousness, and so it is not possible to keep art works, or anything else, in some pure, isolated area.

While the more broadminded and adventurous among our humanists certainly do not thus loftily ignore the media, their discussion often has the same effect as their more snobbish counterparts' neglect. All too often, the critical discourse on the media or on "mass culture" is intended not so much to illuminate its subject, to restore those connections which the media systematically severs, but to use the subject for further obfuscation, as an occasion for priestly displays of impenetrable systematizing, and so on. This is hardly to derogate the attempts to articulate a theoretical comprehension of the media—efforts indispensable to anyone who would understand this elusive subject. Rather, my warning is intended to suggest that we draw distinctions between that theoretical analysis wherein the difficulty is the reflection of its subject's difficulty, and mere theorizing, wherein the difficulty is nothing more than a careerist gambit. That humanist who purports to criticize the media and the system that contains it but whose discourse serves no purpose but the dazzlement of a few colleagues ends up bolstering the reality which he claims to oppose. His performance draws its observers into a tiny circle of *cognoscenti* who thereby become mere professionals, and especially marginal at that. (This is often the case with the work of semioticians, whose ongoing effort at decipherment is basically quite valuable to anyone who would attempt to read the media. It is surely possible to preserve the illumination enabled by the semioticians without the pseudoscientific formulae that tend to hide it.)

Once humanists begin to face the media in a common effort to interpret it, they will begin to cohere just enough to attain to an identity.

And this identity will both enable and demand not only a new area for publications but—perhaps more importantly—a new pedagogical imperative. For productivity is not all: that community which we have lost through our compulsion to produce is surely the most important of the academy's attractions, although it has all but disappeared. We can best begin to regain something of that community, both within and ultimately outside the universities, by inaugurating programs in the interpretation of the media, which really means, as we have seen, the interpretation of our culture and its ideologies. All that undergraduates now study, in fact, would relate to their considerations of the media, which ought now to become not just an unacknowledged tyranny, but the subject of intensive study.

The establishment of such a pedagogical program, however, will depend on certain major alterations in our self-conceptions as humanists.

First, we must learn to read beyond the canon. Our aim should now be to teach an acute literacy that can decipher not only written masterpieces but the public world. That is, we must counteract the media by reading *consciously* its own *unconscious* messages and effects, as well as its many calculated solicitations. Although the media, through its positivist bias, implies that only the intended utterance is decipherable, we must recognize that intention can be unconscious as well as conscious and that every image, every gesture, even every event is saturated with significance that can be read. We must therefore attempt to read the world in reading any given text and learn therefrom to read the world, this world, as if it were a text, for the world has been all but transformed into one deft advertisement now that the media has insinuated its imperative into our landscape, our experience, our memories, our desires.

Secondly, if we are going to apply our hermeneutic methods to the world at large (a step that will alter those methods as it might alter this world), we must also begin to decompartmentalize our intellectual life. We must cease to regard our professional activities as determined by this or that specialist program and begin to meld the disciplines in our studies of the world. The divisions that currently obtain in the humanities are perhaps a practical necessity, defining various territories and enabling an amount of highly concentrated work, but we have internalized those professionalist distinctions so completely that our thinking is often as fragmented as the vision of the world presented by the media. Considering some aspect of the past or present, a humanist will often exert himself less to comprehend that aspect than to demonstrate his full compliance with the protocols of his particular discipline and his field within it, using his putative subject as an occasion for an exhibition of the signs of membership. It is now necessary to give up such self-reflexive professionalism and the often useless pluralism that preserves it. Because each of the disparate disciplines (of the social sciences and the humanities alike) can elucidate some specific features of the public world, all of them ought finally to inform each other, enabling us to read the media more boldly, if with somewhat less professional propriety.

CONCLUSION

However many cultural and/or sociopolitical purposes an applied humanities might fulfill, none can be adequately served before we come to grips with the enormous fact of the media. There can be no worthwhile political action that precedes a worthwhile political conception; but the media now makes politics itself inconceivable, as it proceeds to erase the memory of all prior worlds, subsumes every image of a bettered order into its own consumeristic exhibition, and translates the old paradigm of *homo sapiens* down into that ubiquitous new nullity, *homo sedens*. And the media pursues this program with precisely the same effectiveness and stealth with which it simultaneously depicts a world completely unaffected by its presence.

It is through its ingenious illegibility that the media succeeds, and so we will remain incapable of self-defense and then of self-definition as long as we continue not to read the media consciously. We humanists must apply our various disciplines—and others—by melding them into one wide-ranging and diverse interpretive attempt. But before we thus collaborate, directing our researches and establishing new curricula accordingly, we must recognize and transcend our prejudices. In order to comprehend the media, we must first admit that it is, although decentralized, nevertheless intended, highly legible, often artful, and that it therefore deserves—in fact, demands—the same kind of explicative zeal which we have hitherto reserved for our best texts. And once we thus agree that this commercial, suasive, public process requires our attentions, we will have to reconsider what we mean, what we have always meant by *the humanities*, which we must now regard as something other than a secular religion, a faith whose pieties demand that we ignore the very forces that are now completing its destruction.

PART IV

Applications of the Humanities in Medicine and Policy Analysis

CHAPTER 10

The Place of the Humanities in Medicine

ERIC J. CASSELL

INTRODUCTION

This chapter deals with the place of the humanities in medicine, past, present, and future. My general thesis is that not only have the humanities always had a place in medicine, but that they will play an increasingly important, necessary, and specific role, as medicine evolves beyond its present romance with technology toward a more balanced view of the origin and treatment of illness.

This discussion is based on certain assumptions about medicine. The first is that medicine is about the care of the sick; everything else is secondary to this goal. The second is that doctors treat patients, not diseases, and as a corollary that all medical care flows through the relationship between doctor and patient. My final assumption is that for doctors, the body has primacy.

The changes in medicine that are occurring today are part of a larger social upheaval that has been under way for more than twenty years. This social movement includes a turning away from science and technology—even, on occasion, from reason, itself.[1] But with time it will become apparent again that science and technology are not the enemies; and there will be a more widespread understanding that reason is not *inherently* atomistic or reductionist. Then the search for the solutions to the problems faced by medicine will inevitably involve the development

[1]Levi A. Olan, "A Preliminary Summing Up," in *A Rational Faith*, Jack Bemporad, ed. (New York: Ktav Publishing House, 1977), p. 194; Takeo Doi, *The Anatomy of Dependence* (Tokyo: Kodansha International, 1981), p. 148.

ERIC J. CASSELL • Department of Public Health, Cornell University, Medical College, New York, New York 10021.

of new and exciting intellectual tools. I believe that in the coming decades the humanities will find themselves increasingly engaged on this leading edge of medical progress.

EARLIER RELATIONSHIPS BETWEEN THE HUMANITIES AND MEDICINE

Medicine is one of the oldest learned professions. As idealized over the ages, a physician is someone who know more than merely recipes for the sick and has learned more than just the sciences of the body. In this view, a liberal education will increase physicians' understanding of and affection for the human condition. A somewhat less charitable explanation of why, historically, physicians have been broadly educated comes from the sociology of professions. In this interpretation, an aristocratic model limits access to membership, keeping medicine's product scarce and valuable.[2]

In the view of William Osler (who, probably more than any other physician, provided the model for the current form of medical education) to be a good physician *required* that one be broadly read and educated. Osler may have represented the ideal, but this ideal physician was rarely found in American medicine during the latter half of the nineteenth century or the beginning of the twentieth. At that time, physicians did not constitute an educated elite; instead, American medicine consisted primarily of poorly trained empirics with competing medical ideologies, such as homeopathy, allopathy, and osteopathy. Educated men, and a few women, were trained at the few good medical colleges, but many more doctors were graduated from proprietary schools, night schools, and short-lived medical institutions with few educational requirements. Many physicians were trained entirely by preceptorships.

German medicine had the greatest influence upon American medicine at the time, however, and in the German ideal education was extremely important. In contrast to more aristocratic British notions, however, this education was related to the concept of *bildung*—self-cultivation. In the ensuing reformation of American medicine, the primacy of the role of *education* in medical education was emphasized. Probably because of the influence of the German ideal, medical education was not seen merely as an initiation into a professional structure in conjuction with the acquisition of medical skills.

In the early twentieth century, American medicine was disorganized and backward in comparison with the medicine of Germany and Great

---

[2]Magali Sarfatti Larson, *The Rise of Professionalism: A Sociological Analysis* (Berkeley: University of California Press, 1977), p. 89.

Britain. As a result, Abraham Flexner's report to the Carnegie Foundation, recommending broad changes in the system of medical education, had a profound and widespread effect.[3] A basic tenet of the Flexner Report was that medical care should be thoroughly grounded in the sciences. It followed that medical education should heavily stress biomedical sciences. For this to be practical, students needed some knowledge of the sciences on entering medical school. As a result of the Flexner Report, proprietary medical schools disappeared, many medical schools became affiliated with universities, and some college training was required for entering medical students.

Early in the post-Flexner era the debate over the proper educational background for physicians began, and the tension between humanism and scientism has continued ever since. As Bruer has shown, commissions and reports, from the late 1920s to the present era, have championed liberal education over narrow vocationalism. Nonetheless, continuing surveys of medical school requirements testify to the lack of impact of such recommendations.[4]

George Engel has argued that Flexner meant to train medical students in the sciences in order to inculcate scientific thinking—forming hypotheses, gathering data, testing the hypotheses—rather than primarily to communicate scientific facts; Flexner's proposals, however, did not have this effect.[5] When the interpretations (or misinterpretations) of the Flexner Report were joined by a marked increase in the number of medical school applicants, the result was the all-too-familiar "premed syndrome": enormously competitive students fighting for admission to medical school, concerned with grades almost to the exclusion of any other educational goals, and concentrating almost entirely on the sciences in their premedical curriculum. Because of their belief that medical schools want only applicants who have majored in science, such students avoid humanities courses or take only required courses or those that can be expected to provide a good grade with little effort. Another factor that discourages premedical students from courses in the humanities is the necessity for taking sciences early in the college career in order to prepare for the Medical College Aptitude Tests (MCATs).

In addition to the effects of a large number of medical school applicants, difficulties for the humanities have been compounded by the

[3]Abraham Flexner, *Medical Education in the United States*, Report to the Carnegie Foundation for the Advancement of Teaching, 1910.

[4]John T. Bruer, "Premedical Education and the Humanities: A Survey," paper prepared for a conference on the humanities and Premedical Education, sponsored by the Rockefeller Foundation (February 25, 1980).

[5]George L. Engel, "Biomedicine's Failure to Achieve Flexnerian Standards of Education," in *Journal of Medical Education* 53 (1978), pp. 387–392.

national shift toward education in the sciences following the first Russian space flight and the current shortage of funds for education in general.

THE CURRENT SITUATION

At the present time the majority of American medical schools have some form of a program in the humanities. These vary from the full-fledged departments found in only four schools to the innumerable less formal, less helpful programs that have their home in other departments or in deans' offices. In addition, several schools have free-standing institutes that are closely attached to their schools of medicine. The Society for Health and Human Values periodically publishes reports on the state of human values teaching programs in the United States. Their most recent summary, *Human Values Teaching Programs for Health Professionals*, published in 1981, should be consulted for details.[6] The Institute on Human Values in Medicine and its staff maintain an active interest in this area, and constitute the single most valuable information resource.

With the exception of departments of the history of medicine, some of which have been in existence for many years, these programs began to come into being in the 1960s. The enthusiasm continued in the early 1970s, but progress has slowed recently. This may reflect a decrease in the amount of money available from grants and the institutions themselves; it might also represent what Daniel Callahan has termed the "ethics backlash." Although certain factors may have, in combination, diminished the continued rapid growth of programs, there is no sign of waning interest on the part of involved faculty or the students.

Let me illustrate with a description of a few programs:

- Pennsylvania State University—Hershey Medical Center. Program founded in 1967 (with the start of the medical center). This program has full departmental status and five full-time faculty members supported by the university budget and is completely integrated into the medical center functional and governance structure. Students are required to take at least two courses in the department during their medical school career. Courses are offered in death and dying, medicine and ethics, major medical novels, religion and medicine, philosophy of medicine, history and philosophy of genetics, and many more.

---

[6]Thomas K. McElhinny, *Human Values Teaching Programs for Health Professionals* (Ardmore, PA: Whitmore Publishing Co., 1981).

- State University of New York at Buffalo. Program founded in 1977. The Committee on Human Values and Medical Ethics is located in the dean's office from which it receives its funding. There are no full-time faculty. Teachers are drawn from those in the medical school who are committed to the program, as well as supporters in other schools and departments in the university. The committee offers an elective course for first-year medical students in addition to various lecture programs offered university-wide.
- Yale University. No formal program in the medical school and no medical school faculty. Courses in such topics as medical ethics and medicine and the law are given by the appropriate other schools of the university.
- Cornell University Medical College. Founded in 1979 as the Program for the Study of Ethics and Values in Medicine in the Department of Public Health. One faculty member supported primarily by grant funds. Elective course given in each of the four years.

As reported by the Institute of Human Values, four schools have departments of humanities, seven have departments of the history of medicine, three schools have divisions within other departments, twenty-three have programs located within other departments, eighteen medical schools have their humanities programs located in the dean's office, and fourteen others have various administrative structures.

WHAT THE HUMANITIES HAVE TO OFFER MEDICINE

Putting Living Persons Back into Medicine

Ideally, physicians should define their diagnostic and therapeutic goals in terms of the everyday life and function of individual patients. Unfortunately, this ideal is often failed. In part the problem arises because physicians are trained from the first days of medical school as though the knowledge they brought with them of everyday life and human function were irrelevant to medicine. Another obstacle is that doctors are not trained to include in their decision making the kind of "soft" and often subjective information that is relevant to the everyday life and function of such persons. Correction of these educational errors would do much to help change the physician's priorities in patient care.

I believe that an education that teaches how to apply knowledge of disease and the body to persons in their everyday life and function takes advantage of students' preexisting knowledge of the world as well as what they have learned of medical science. Teaching how to acquire knowledge of persons expands the students' knowledge and broadens the basis for the application of basic science and pathophysiology. Teaching physicians how to acquire, evaluate, measure, synthesize, and analyze information about both sick persons and their bodies provides them with the tools to gain the information about individual patients necessary to meet the ideal of care. Teaching doctors how to think about both the body and about the person—about objective and subjective date values, analytically and synthetically—allows them, in formulating the goals of patient care, to integrate their knowledge of medical science, the body, and the everyday life and function of the sick individual.

Although meeting this goal is desirable, it should be noted that the distance that physicians' training places between them and sick persons is a *necessary* component of medical education. Another word for this is depersonalization. In order to teach the sciences of medicine it is necessary to depersonalize the human body for medical students. Their cadavers, experimental physiology, pathology, indeed, all the preclinical studies provide a dehumanized arena in which to learn human biology. The body has yielded its secrets in a consistent manner only since experimental and statistical methods were developed that totally divorce scientific generalizations from the individuality of persons. Well-trained physicians are able to think in body terms—"think" heart, "think" kidney—completely apart from the fact that the kidney in question is John Smith's kidney and that what they are thinking is bad news for John Smith. On the other hand, effective physicians are able to bring the person, John Smith, back into the picture and make decisions that integrate facts about both the depersonalized kidney and the individual patient.

Literature

Superb training in the sciences of medicine is the hallmark of modern medical education. Unfortunately neither the need for *repersonalizing* the physician's knowledge nor methods for teaching the ability to apply the generalities of science to individual patients have made much headway in medical schools. There is reason to believe that training in the humanities might lead to these goals.

But what must be taught? That doctors take care of sick persons, not just their diseases? Why is not the saying of it the equivalent of teaching it? The problem to be overcome is not simply that the education of the medical students has dehumanized their knowledge but that in every encounter with a patient, the knowledge of the body that guides the examination—whether it be history-taking or physical examination—and the categories used by physicians to process the forthcoming information push the person of the patient into the background. Further, and equally important to remember, as physicians are working, they have no awareness that their actions and their modes of thought continually brush aside the person. Since, in common with everyone else, they have not been taught how to step out of themselves and watch their own actions, they cannot appreciate the impact of their words and manner.

Literature offers the opportunity to see the interplay of illness and individual, the role of physicians in the lives of others, the impact of their own medical knowledge on the doctors' personal lives, and the perception of physicians by lay people. Because literature is free of the constraints of the day-to-day world, it is able to offer a fuller picture of persons, their relations to objects, events, and other persons, of the world of the sick and the meaning of illness to individuals, of how compassion, empathy, mercy, and other moral qualities are expressed and how they affect others.

Humanists who teach in medical schools are often dismayed when they discover how single-minded medical students can be. Students are aware of the enormity of the responsibility that will be theirs all too soon. This generates an impatience with the humanities when they do not perceive them as adding to the store of knowledge required to be a good doctor—what their faculty believes to be of central importance, as judged by examination material, departmental curriculum time, relative status of faculty. The resistance of students can be overcome by imaginative courses that deal directly with medicine's concerns. The bibliography prepared by Joanne Trautman and Carol Pollard, *Literature and Medicine*, is a rich resource for those who wish to use literature in the teaching of medical students and need to isolate certain themes or find materials that are most apposite to specific areas.[7]

Kathryn Hunter has demonstrated, in her program at Morehouse, how the humanities (particularly literature) can reinforce the commitment of medical students to the goals of primary care.[8]

Sandra Bertman has used literature in a different sense, to affirm the legitimacy of students' own feelings in the painful interactions of medicine with human reality, such as death and loss, and to demonstrate

[7]Joanne Trautman and Carol Pollard, *Literature in Medicine* (Philadelphia: Society for Health and Human Values, 1975).
[8]Kathryn Hunter, "Morehouse Human Values in Medicine Program 1978–1980: Reinforcing a Commitment to Primary Care," in *Journal of Medical Education*, 57 (1982), pp. 121–123.

that what concerns the physician has been important to mankind through the ages. In respect to anatomy, she uses literature and the visual arts to explore the experience of dissections.[9]

An interesting collection of essays, *Medicine and Literature*, edited by Enid Rhodes Peschel, gives an idea of the widely different ways in which literature can be used to illuminate the medical experience and, conversely, the manner in which medical experience has been used by writers who were physicians and those who were not.[10] Anthony R. Moore, in *The Missing Medical Text*, demonstrates specifically how literature can be used to address aspects of physicianship not covered in the formal curriculum, to draw on the medical heritage that is recorded in literature, to heighten sensibilities for patient care and professional self-assessment, and to explore nonscientific ways of thinking and their importance in considering human issues. The book consists of short literary passages that illustrate specific topics—the patient's or the relatives' experience, portraits of doctors, ethical issues, and the like—and a transcription of students' discussion following a reading of the materials. Not only are the discussions interesting in themselves, but they give someone who is unfamiliar with teaching in a medical milieu an idea of medical students' interests and concerns.[11]

History

Medical students, and often their faculty, tend to believe that the history of medicine began the day they were born. Consequently their studies, their understanding of medical science, and their conception of the work of physicians have no historical context. One problem arises because depersonalization, a necessary part of medical education, is exaggerated by notions of medical science as timeless, objective, and value-free. In a world view that excludes the importance of persons, history is not welcome. Conversely, one cannot highly value personhood without also acknowledging the fact that persons *always* have histories. Whole human beings can never be discussed solely in the present tense.

---

[9]Sandra L. Bertman, "Communication With the Dead: An Ongoing Experience in Art, Literature, and Song," in *Between Life and Death*, Robert Kastenbaum, ed. (New York: Springer, 1979), p. 124 ff; Sandra L. Bergman, "The Language of Grief: Social Science Theories and Literary Practice," in *Mosaic* 14 (Winter 1982), pp. 153–163; Sandy Marks and Sandra Bertman, "Experiences of Learning About Death and Dying in the Undergraduate Anatomy Cirriculum," in *Journal of Medical Education*, 55 (1980), pp. 48–52.

[10]Enid Rhodes Peschel, ed., *Medicine and Literature* (New York: Neale Watson Academic Publications, 1980).

[11]Anthony R. Moore, *The Missing Medical Text* (Melbourne: Melbourne University Press, 1978).

Further, persons belong to families, and the family is an institution whose present is always indebted to the past and in thrall to the future.

It is only recently that medicine has begun to change toward a dominant concern with the sick person. Not only the person of the patient has been absent from medicine, but the person of the *physician* as well. Both patients and their physicians act as though technology made the diagnosis and cured the patient. In this belief, all physicians, to the extent that they know their medical science, are equivalent— individuals do not make a difference. This issue is complicated by a lack of synchronization in attitudes about the individuality of physicians as opposed to that of those in the mainstream of American society. From the 1930s through the 1940s there was much comment about the anomie imposed by the modern, increasingly technological, assembly-line industrial world. Later, the same kind of blurred individuality was denoted by the image of the "corporation man." During the same period, doctors were considered by many and believed themselves to be highly individualistic—whether they were clinicians or research scientists.

Since the 1950s, a new wave of individualism has emerged in American society, characterized by its uniquely inner-directed and personal nature. This change in self concept constitutes, I believe, a major social change that will have enduring effects. Now, however, the dominant society, having returned to its fundamental value of individualism, and distinguishing itself from the science and technology that saturates modern life, does not see *physicians* as distinct from *their* technology. This has led to the curious phenomenon of patients' demanding that they be treated as persons at the same time that they depersonalize their physicians! Medicine and physicians, however, are now also beginning to evolve to a point at which doctors will begin to understand that, *qua* doctors, they are distinct from their tools and their science.

Another difficulty that stems from teaching medicine without historical referents is a kind of cohort egocentricity—a belief that what we do today is the best that has ever been done, the most complete understanding of the human condition that has ever existed, and that (paradoxically) what we lack is just around the corner. In this view, history is merely the record of a never faltering climb to the (soon to be reached) summit of medical knowledge. When historical events are considered, they are judged by their contribution to the present. A problem caused by this approach is that physicians fail to understand that the profession and the work of individual physicians have always been subject to forces generated by the interaction between medicine and society.

Historians have agreed more about the importance of teaching history in medical school than about who should teach it and how. In the past, medical history was often the hobby of physicians with no special historical training. This created tensions between the amateur historians and those with professional training. The resolution of these conflicts seems at times to be more important to the contestants than medical history itself. However, when it comes to instructing medical students, as Hudson emphasized, quality of teaching is more important than who teaches. History is not seen as their most vital subject and their allegiance and attention must be *won*.[12]

This issue must be faced by all humanists who teach in medical schools: Are they there to teach medical students or to teach their individual subjects? The needs of the medical student are special and require that the teaching of the humanities be shaped to these special intellectual tasks. It is a necessary area of inquiry to find out exactly what is unique about their needs.

Understanding Time and Process

It never seems to occur to medical historians that anything but *medical* history should be part of the curriculum. History has a methodology and an understanding of *time* and *process* that are unique among the humanities. These two concepts play a vital role in clinical medicine. Central to taking care of the sick is understanding the history of their illnesses. Illnesses unfold over time and have contexts, a cast of characters (including, but rarely limited to, both the person and the body), occur at particular times and in particular places. Understanding the history of illness is a difficult task—even learning to present it well to other physicians takes years. Problems arise because patients' stories of their illnesses are not dispassionate expositions of a set of "facts." Rather, events in the body that are considered symptoms (in itself, a relative category) are perceived, organized, and described according to patients' perceptions of their meanings. Physicians taking the history from a patient must form hypotheses about the possible illness represented but must be careful not to allow their hypothesis to influence the data. Further, doctors must learn to test their diagnostic hypotheses as they obtain further historical information. Despite the difficulties inherent in the process of taking the history of illness from an individual patient, history taking is rarely taught in any systematic manner in medical schools. Yet, 80 percent or more of diagnoses are made on the basis of the patient's history. Unfortunately, most physicians are inexpert at

---

[12]Robert Hudson, "Goals in the Teaching of Medical History," in *Clio Medica* 10 (1975), pp. 153–160.

history taking. Thus, historians might have something special to contribute to teaching how to obtain, understand, and use the illness history. I am aware that historians may see this as neither their *métier* nor within their interests. Because illness is a process that takes place over time and presents itself in discrete, relatively short episodes, however, it lends itself to research on the dimension of time and the problems of thinking about process rather than about events. When disease concepts as we know them evolved in the nineteenth century, diseases were considered to be things that invaded patients. The progressive explication of their structural and biochemical basis did not change the sense that diseases were "things" that produced an "event." The great medical advances of this century, however, have focused on pathophysiology: how the body works in disease as contrasted to its normal function. Yet, pathophysiological thinking has failed to affect day-to-day clinical action as much as one would wish because of the difficulty of thinking about processes unfolding over time as opposed to static states. How does one teach physicians to think in process terms and deal with the dimension of real time? Because of the relevance of these issues to medicine, historians have something unique to learn from and to contribute to medicine.

Philosophy

Because of the growth of interest in ethics, philosophy is the humanist discipline that has made the greatest inroads in the medical curriculum during the present era. Courses on medical ethics are now given in most medical schools in the United States.

Edmund Pellegrino has stressed the important distinction between the liberal arts and the humanities:

> It is a common misconception that the humanities and the liberal arts are synonymous. The liberal arts are attitudes of mind, not disciplines or bodies of knowledge. They have since classical times been those intellectual skills needed to be a free man—not only in the political sense, but more critically in the sense of being free of the tyranny of other men's thinking and opinions, free to make up one's own position. The liberal arts comprise those skills most commonly associated with being human—the capability to think clearly and critically, to read and understand language, to write and speak clearly, to make moral judgements, to recognize the beautiful, and to possess a sense of the continuity between man's present and inherited past.[13]

---

[13]Edmund Pellegrino, "The Humanities in Medical Education," in *Mobius* 2 (1982), pp. 133–141.

Pellegrino has had more influence and written more, and more persuasively on the subject of the humanities in medicine than perhaps any other contemporary thinker.[14]

The liberal arts have something special to offer physicians if sick persons, rather than their diseases, are to be the new focus of medicine. Fresh concepts, skills and guidelines for behavior are necessary to supplement the strictly technical. In medicine, we do not simply describe the procedure for an appendectomy and then leave students to their own devices. We define appendicitis, base the definition on anatomy and pathology, demonstrate how it manifests itself, how the diagnosis is made, and how to treat it. Similarly, it is not sufficient to tell a student or physician to treat sick persons, not just their diseases. Without the necessary definitions, tools and skills, all that has been created is a moral injunction: "Go and do thou likewise." When a person fails to fulfill a moral injunction, he or she generally ends up taking the blame and feeling badly. This is frequently what occurs nowadays when physicians begin their internships. They are supposed to care about their patients as "persons," use their "feelings," and be "open" and communicative. Since they have had no specific training in this aspect of patient care, are overwhelmed by work, and are usually rewarded for technological rather than interpersonal skills, their sense of inadequacy may defeat their good intentions.

There have always been physicians who were extraordinarily adept at working with patients—taking histories, establishing rapport, achieving compliance with even the most unpleasant regimens, being sensitive to unspoken needs, providing empathetic support, communicating effectively, and even getting paid after the illness. This expertise, usually called "the art of medicine," is generally acquired after years of experience. Some doctors are more skilled with patients than others. Because of this, it is frequently said that the art of medicine is a matter of intuition and is unteachable. I am convinced that the art of medicine can be taught and studied in a systematic and disciplined manner.

The art of medicine is composed of abilities in four different interrelated areas: the ability to acquire and integrate subjective and objective information to make decisions in the best interests of the patient; the ability to strengthen and utilize the relationship between doctor and patient for therapeutic ends; the knowledge of how sick persons (and

---

[14]Edmund Pellegrino, "Educating the Humanist Physician," in *Journal of the American Medical Association* 227 (1974), p. 1288; Edmund Pellegrino, *Humanism and the Physician* (Knoxville, TN: University of Tennessee Press, 1979); Edmund Pellegrino, "The Clinical Arts and the Arts of the Word," in *Pharos* (Fall 1981), pp. 2–8.

doctors) behave; and finally, the central skill upon which all the others depend: effective communication.

The Workings of the Word

In the practice of medicine, communication skills are essential to the diagnostic and therapeutic process. Doctors should be able to establish their interest and concern for patients and should be attentive to their problems and anxieties. Indeed, the most common complaint that patients have about doctors is that they do not listen.

There is a deeper sense in which doctors must know how to speak and listen effectively. Speakers literally portray themselves when they speak. To tell someone about objects, events, or relationships is to tell the attentive listener about yourself. The choice of adjectives, adverbs, verbs, nouns, and pronouns "places" the speaker in relation to what is being described. If we believe that the nature of the person modifies the illness in its presentation, course, treatment, and outcome, then the kind of information that a patient's speech offers can be of importance to the physician. The spoken language is the most important tool in medicine; almost no diagnostic or therapeutic act occurs in its absence.

Given its importance in medicine, one would think that spoken language would have been subject to intense scrutiny. Yet the systematic study of natural conversation is relatively new. The basic difficulty derives from a fundamental and irreconcilable difference between language and other objects of scientific inquiry. Science has been successful because of scientists' ability to study simple, linear, cause-and-effect parts of more complex wholes, producing dyadic statements of the type "If A, then B." Language, however, is irreducibly triadic. Words do not merely stand for things. Words always stand for something *to someone*. The irreducible triangle consists of a word, what it stands for, and the person for whom it has that meaning.[15] Words can mean different things to different people. Since one cannot verify in objective terms what is going on inside another person's mind, the problem of personal meaning has proved impenetrable to "hard science."

Fortunately, all the features that make the spoken language opaque to science provide wonderful opportunities for clinicians. Human illness is, in fact, triadic in the same manner as language. Diseases, when isolated and confined to their afflicted cells, organs, or enzyme systems, are quite constant in the manner in which they express themselves. Each *illness* caused by a given disease is unique, however, differing from every

[15]Walker Percy, *The Message in the Bottle* (New York: Farrar, Straus and Giroux, 1975).

other illness episode because of the *person* in whom it occurs. Even when a disease recurs in the same person, the illness is changed by the fact that it *is* a recurrence; it now carries the associations and the history of the previous episode. The presentation, course, and outcome of a disease can be affected by whether the patient likes or fears physicians, believes in medication or abuses drugs, is brave or cowardly, is self-destructive or vain, has unconscious conflicts into which the illness does or does not fit. These features are part of the illness, for illness is not only a physical event but an event of meaning as well. The triadic nature of human illness makes the art of medicine vital; if every patient were the same, then merely to know the disease would be to know the illness.

Despite the obvious importance of spoken communication, few medical schools teach more than the rudiments of taking a history. None has attempted to teach not only the effective use of medical rhetoric, but its fundamentals in the same way that the fundamentals that underlie (say) methods of diagnosis are taught.

Even if students were able to employ the spoken language effectively, they would be hampered by lack of a descriptive language for recording or transmitting the information they would acquire. In contrast, when medical students are taught physical diagnosis they are also taught a descriptive language to record their findings and communicate them to other doctors. An acutely arthritic joint is "red, hot, swollen, and tender." If I add "exquisitely tender," a physician might suspect infection in the joint, or gout. I can go on to talk about wounds that are "red, swollen, and puckered around the sutures," or pus that has a "fecal odor," or even "tympanitic abdomen" (one that produces a drum-like sound when tapped with a finger) to make the point that physicians' language of description for physical phenomena is rich and communicative, allowing the reader or listener to visualize what the observer is characterizing without necessarily subscribing to the observer's conclusions. This richness is in sharp contrast to the poverty of words doctors use to portray persons. On their hospital charts, patients are often described as, for example, "depressed"—these same patients never seem to be sad, gloomy, melancholy, unhappy, down-at-the-mouth, or even blue. The word *depressed* is not very descriptive; it is also a diagnostic term with relatively precise meaning that often does not fit the patient so labeled.

Finding an appropriate language of description is not a minor matter. The genius of the disease theory is that it finally provided a basis for doctors to talk about sick persons using a commonly agreed upon language. Angina pectoris, coronary heart disease, rheumatic mitral valvular disease, oat cell carcinoma of the lung, and immune complex syndromes have common meanings wherever Western medicine is practiced because they are grounded in the anatomy and physiology of the body. Such linguistic precision became possible when doctors could agree not only on the words but also on the defining characteristics of the diseases indicated by their names. Finding a language of description for patients will certainly present difficulties if we require total agreement on definitions and nomenclatures. It simply cannot be done.

I think the solution to the problem of describing persons for medical practice is to use everyday language. Unfortunately, this does not end the problem. To say, for example, that a patient is "nasty, churlish and mean," certainly uses everyday language, but it does not solve the problem of definitions. What is the meaning of *churlish*? Because of the subjectivity of such words—because they are really words of opinion—they will not serve to describe persons for medical practice.

We need a model to point the way, and novelists would seem to be our best guides. Descriptive language is, of course, the writer's stock in trade. When Charles Dickens, for example, describes a character, he notes not only physical characteristics but also behavior. He describes bearing, demeanor, mannerisms, and habit of dress. From these small pieces of the total character we form an impression that supports speculation about some actions and manners as quite possible and others as improbable. Such details provide an enormous amount of information about a total person because people, in their dress, demeanor, gait, speech, facial expression, activities, work, in all of the characteristics that make up their persons, are *more*, rather than less, consistent. Even in an initial interview, the physician has the opportunity to observe a patient's physical appearance, dress, cosmetics and ornamentation, demeanor, speech, gait, and manner of sitting. This is certainly enough to characterize the mode by which a person presents himself or herself in a physician's office. With the exception for physical appearance, each facet is a *behavioral*, not an architectural, detail—even facial expression is an action.

Naturally, caution is necessary in interpreting and acting on the information provided by a patient's presentation and actions in the doctor's office. Some aspects of a person, such as sexual behavior, private fantasies, what is done in the intimacy of the home, or behavior during life-threatening illness, are not even open to educated speculation without very much more knowledge of the individual. Further, interpreting behavior can be open to many sources of error. Few would disagree, however, that accurate characterization of these aspects of human behavior would provide a good basis for representing an individual in words. Although an everyday language of description may not provide an infallible method of introducing the individual into the calculus of medical care, teaching medical students and physicians how to describe the persons for whom they provide care will surely improve that care. Medical students must be taught descriptive skills and learn a descriptive langauge. This task is natural to the humanities.

Learning to Reason

The practice of medicine requires not only communication skills but also the ability to reason carefully and make decisions. Here again, medical students receive little if any formal training. It is in this area of the liberal arts that philosophers have traditionally taught. Perhaps the best example of what and how to teach medical students is K. Danner Clouser, a philosopher who has been teaching in a medical school for more than a decade.[16]

Clouser teaches students to formulate a clinical problem based on the information from the patient's history, physical examination, laboratory tests, and X-ray examinations. Once a problem has been formulated, proceeding toward action requires the ability to analyze the problem over a period of time and synthesize new information. The analytic (reductive or scientific) thought that is employed in this process is familiar to most medical students. Active training is required, however, to improve their analytic skills and give them greater volitional control over their thinking. Teaching such skills is both important and difficult. A clinical case—the story of a sick person—is like a text in many respects. It is precisely the ability to deal with temporal aspects of a problem unfolding over time that marks good clinical thinking.

Medical students are generally more capable of thinking in a reductionist analytic manner then in a valuational mode. Valuational thought is a synthetic, integrative, constructionist method, whereby information is tested against previously held conceptions, meanings, and beliefs and, in the process, is assigned meanings. I believe physicians use these two interdependent but competing modes of thought, analytic and valuational, without awareness and thus are unable to take full advantage of both. For contemporary medical students, analytic thought is more robust and well developed. Valuational thought, dealing more with the moral and the personal, is less developed, and more private. The inability to think as well in valuational terms as analytic is unfortunate, because thinking of whole human beings in personal and moral terms requires valuational thinking. Human values cannot be arrived at by analytic thought. Thus, if students are to meet the needs of sick persons, in terms of the personal and the moral (not only their diseases), they

[16]K. Danner Clouser, "Philosophy and Medical Education," in *The Role of the Humanities in Medical Education*, Donnie J. Selfe, ed. (Norfolk, VA: Biomedical Ethics Program, Eastern Virginia Medical School, 1978).

must also be able to think in valuational terms. Because it is less well understood, teaching valuational thinking is much more difficult than teaching analytic thought. One method is to provide cases, replete with information about the person and the person's symptoms, and then ask the student to construct a story that tells in narrative form about the person *beyond* the information given. It is the effective use of narrative and metaphor that marks the ability to make wholes out of parts. Some stories will be more true to the information than others. Such a method of teaching thinking allows what Robert Belknap has called "the literary experiment" to be brought to bear: What would happen to the story— and consequently to the patient—if some of the facts were varied? It is valuational thought that most specifically allows the student's knowledge of everyday life and function to come into play in the care of patients. When both analytic (reductive) and valuational (synthetic) modes are brought together under conscious control, students are provided with powerful problem-solving tools.

One further goal in clinical thinking remains elusive. This is teaching physicians to weigh equally in their thought processes value-laden, or subjective, information and objective, or numerical, information. Until doctors can do this, until numerical data do not always win out over softer, more subjective information, the goal of treating sick persons rather than diseases will remain unrealized.

OBSTACLES TO A ROLE FOR THE HUMANITIES IN MEDICINE TODAY

Obstruction to the entrance of the humanities into the medical curriculum takes two forms.

First, the more general source of resistance: medical schools have relatively fixed curricula. Students *must* take certain core curriculum courses which have precedence over other educational endeavors: anatomy, physiology, biochemistry, microbiology, pathology, pharmacology. These basic sciences are the foundation of modern medicine. Anatomists, biochemists, and pathologists, like other educators, believe that no student can ever learn enough of their subject. Consequently most basic science departments believe they lack sufficient time in the core curriculum. Almost no department ever voluntarily surrenders curriculum time—spouses and all earthly possessions might be relinquished, but curriculum time never. If the humanities are to enter the core curriculum, something else has to go. Therefore, major curriculum reform is almost always necessary before humanities are successfully introduced into a medical school.

In most medical schools the clinical departments, especially medicine and surgery, have more power than do the basic science departments. The actual distribution of power can be quite different from the apparent distribution, however, and this will affect how change is carried out. The introduction of the humanities into the medical curriculum represents the kind of change that may alter the balance of power. Another factor holding back the introduction of the humanities is that the old established schools seem perpetually short of money and space, both of which are required when new subjects and faculty are introduced. Then there is just plain inertia, friend of the status quo and enemy of change.

Much of the resistance would disappear (given adequate funding and space) if humanists were content to teach an elective program and did not require core curriculum time. Funding agencies frequently do not believe that true change has taken place unless the core curriculum has changed. On the contrary, there are good reasons for *not* teaching core courses, reasons that can make electives more attractive and effective. A medical school class numbers about one hundred students. If they must all be taught—as in a core curriculum course—a lecture format must be chosen because of the few humanists on the faculty. Since lectures are not the best method of imparting the humanities, a seminar format is frequently used, requiring additional teachers. Such faculty often come from other departments, drawn by their commitment to the new program and their interest in the subject. If the course is standard humanist fare, those informal faculty members are often highly motivated and excellent.

If newer materials are to be taught, however, then using outside faculty not specifically trained in and committed to the new methods means that the course may drift back toward the conventional. This regression toward the mean will be hastened if the students are also not truly interested in the new approaches. Elective courses avoid both dangers. Enrollment can be kept small enough so that those who developed the course are the only teachers. Further, the students who elect the courses will be the ones who are interested—if the course is good, they will aid in its development and spread the word of its excellence. If the classes are a failure, total disaster is avoided and time is available for reconstruction. Gradually other faculty members will attend, and a cadre of teachers will develop who will help in the enlargement of the program. Over four or five years, a solid, well-tested and successful program can be developed which may be *invited* into the core curriculum. In medical schools, *change takes time*.

In addition, there are more important and specific obstacles that impede the introduction of the humanities into medical school teaching. Medicine and the humanities, particularly philosophy, have had a long-standing love–hate relationship. It is useful to understand the persistent belief that the antagonism between the humanities and medicine is a struggle between the real (medicine), and the nonreal (the humanities). Medicine deals with the realities of human biology, the body, and disease. It is (presently) founded on an atomistic rationalism, the reductionist methods of science, which have been enormously successful in comprehending the mechanisms of disease and providing tools for their relief. It views with suspicion and hostility attempts to understand these subjects based on pure hypothesis and on methods that are not grounded first and last on objectively verifiable observation. The humanities, all of them, are seen by many physicians to suffer from both defects. These objections cannot be dismissed; they must be acknowledged and dealt with.

If medicine dealt with the body alone, if what afflicted the sick person acted on the body and only the body, and if it were possible to intervene in the illness without the interventions taking place in the person who has the illness, then believing that medicine, or doctors, deal only with the real might be possible. But although medical science can abstract itself and deal solely with body parts, doctors who take care of patients do not have that luxury; they must work with people. Thus they are *always* faced with the *non*realities of their patients—the fears, desires, concerns, expectations, hopes, fantasies, and meanings which patients bring or attach to interactions with physicians—which always exist and which always influence their medical care. These realities, often called *psychosocial issues*, are better taught by literature and the other humanities.

The problem of dependence on speculation is not so easily dismissed. It must be emphasized, to medical students and faculty alike, that doctors cannot avoid such problems; they are inextricably bound up with the care of the sick. The choice is whether to employ the tools of the humanities that have been honed for centuries on just such questions or to allow doctors to pretend the issues do not exist or use underdeveloped and sloppy thinking to address them.

In the so-called new medical schools, founded within the past fifteen or twenty years, the humanities have received much greater acceptance, as a necessary part of the medical student's education. This is due, in part, to the fact that no entrenched curriculum priorities blocked their way. But more significant is the fact that these schools have stressed the importance of psychosocial issues, of treating the whole person, of emphasizing health rather than merely the treatment of disease. A commitment to these newer values in medicine is necessarily accompanied by a commitment to the importance of the humanities in medical education.

Humanists may not be thrilled at the idea of teaching the humanities in the manner we have discussed here. Teaching in the medical environment does not promise the usual academic rewards nor the company and comfort of like-minded (and similarly trained) colleagues. Since humanists' day-to-day tasks may diverge from their basic scholarly interests, publication becomes more difficult. Colleagues—peers and teachers alike—may look askance at their work.

Further, many humanists have followed the route of the sciences into analytic, reductionist methodologies; to such the kind of humanities teaching I am discussing will seem old-fashioned and uninteresting. In addition, to be successful in the medical environment, humanists must demonstrate the importance of their subjects *as medicine*. This is unattractive to faculty who believe that their subject matter is so intrinsically interesting that merely to make such knowledge available should guarantee student attention.

In the face of distaste on the part of humanists, it might seem unlikely that the humanities will ever enter contemporary medicine. To be crass, however, the money problems of many university departments of humanities suggest that if there are funds for humanists in medical schools, there will be humanists in medical schools.

New Challenges for the Humanities

I have presented the notion that the shift taking place in medicine is toward a focus on the sick person and away from an almost exclusive concern with disease. Fundamentally this change represents an increasing concern with wholeness and a turning away from atomistic thinking. It is one thing to be concerned with wholeness, however, but quite another to develop the intellectual tools to deal with it.

There are corollaries of the interest in wholes that demonstrate some of the problems that must be solved before physicians can deal effectively with whole persons. *Ambiguity* is the first of these. To make these points visually, I have used the device of showing color slides of a bouquet of flowers photographed daily from the time they were picked until utterly wilted, twelve days later. The bouquet of flowers presents a complex image that changes in many different ways over time. In contrast, I show a similar set of slides of three flowers photographed over the same time period. Here the changes are easier to keep track of. In their reduced complexity, the three flowers are to the bunch as understandings of body organs are to the whole person. Following the slides of the flowers are a set that show (only) the chest of a woman with cancer of the breast photographed daily from before her biopsy, to the bandaged torso following surgery, to the unveiling of the mutilated chest, to the evolution

of the wound. Then pictures of her face over the same period are projected. The effect is striking. Medicine's view of cancer of the breast
would appear to be captured by the pictures of the breasts. The deficiency of that perspective is driven home by the pictures of the woman's
face. But the face makes clear that science, as it is presently known in
medicine, cannot cope with the ambiguity that appears to be the inevitable companion of wholeness. What is her face telling us? What does
it mean? On the basis of what we see, what should we do? Is there only
one answer to each of these questions? If there are more answers than
one (and we know that to be true) are they the same for each observer,
or does the whole of which we are speaking in medicine necessarily
include the physician, or other caregiver as well as the sick person?
Currently, to tolerate such ambiguity in science would be an error in
reasoning. However, to eliminate the ambiguity in medicine eliminates
the richness and subtle complexity that expands the meaning of every
perception beyond the percept itself. Alas, this brings us no closer to
teaching physicians how to deal with such ambiguity *as a basis for action.*
Literary and artistic criticism deals with such ambiguity as its daily fare.
So it must be the case that in those disciplines, at least, the groundwork
has been laid from which a systematic understanding of ambiguity in
medicine might emerge. Perhaps more than a groundwork exists, but
what is lacking is the application to medicine and to the teaching of
medical students. This is one of medicine's challenges to the humanities.

Additional medical deficiencies exist that are dealt with better in
the humanities. For science, complexity is in part reduced by making
sharp distinctions: putting forth definitions of terms and situations that
allow of no overlap. Medical scientists characteristically disregard borderline states. They are put out of mind, or defined out of existence
because there are no good systems of thought to deal with them. Then
we act as if nondistinction did not exist. But there are situations wherein
such blinders become inadequate and we are brought sharply against
our inability to deal with nondistinction. Such a circumstance was brought
sharply into focus when ethicists tried to define the characteristics of
personhood that would provide a basis for deciding (say) when to turn
off a respirator. If certain criteria of personhood were met, for example
"awareness of self" or "cerebral function," then the patient should be
kept alive; if they were absent, then the patient might be allowed to
die.[17] No definitions of such terms can be made, however, that will
eliminate areas of nondistinction. Since doctors must act, and no action

---

[17]Joseph Fletcher, "Indicators of Humanhood: A Tentative Profile of Man," in *Hastings
Center Report* 2 (1972), pp. 1–4; Joseph Fletcher, "Four Indicators of Humanhood: The
Inquiry Matures," in *Hastings Center Report* 4 (1974), pp. 4–7.

seems possible based on nondistinction, the attempt to find precise "indicators of humanhood" fell by the wayside. The beauty of medicine as a force for intellectual change is that the deficiency of the original solution was quickly apparent when doctors tried to base their actions on it. Further, even though the proposal did not work, the problem did not go away; decisions are still required about individual patients on respirators.

Phrases like "awareness of self" and "cerebral function" turn out to be metaphors.[18] Metaphors may be a problem for medicine, but they are no strangers in literature. Thus again, the move toward dealing with wholeness raises problems not at all foreign to the humanities and in which progress in the humanities might be encouraged by the urgencies of medicine.

Medical science deals most often with static spatial concepts—with permanence and uniformity. To deal with whole persons necessitates coming to terms with the effect of the past, change, becoming, the unfolding novelty of future, uncertainty, of time itself. Understanding illness and health as processes means developing new ways of seeing and understanding what is happening to patients. Because science has been so successful in structural terms, one can understand the reluctance to stipulate the universe of medicine in anything so seemingly shaky and evanescent as the language of process. But the humanities, from poetry to history, have had to find a language for change and have dealt with it sufficiently to provide at least a beginning for medicine's excursion into these new areas.

CONCLUSION

This essay opened with the historical belief that the humanities is meant to provide broadly educated and humane physicians. It closes by presenting a future of medicine in which the humanities are necessary for progress to occur. Between the two is an entire spectrum of functions. Many humanists may believe that none of these are interesting—that nothing is offered that would warrant leaving the secure setting of university departments of humanities. On the other hand, universities in general and the humanities in particular are battered enough these days so that some humanists may want to try out the medical environment. Those who do will find challenge aplenty.

---

[18]Eric J. Cassell, "Moral Thought in Clinical Practice: Applying the Abstract to the Usual," in *Science, Ethics and Medicine*, Daniel Callahan and H. Tristram Engelhardt, eds. (The Hastings Center, 1976).

However, whether the humanities are ready or not, we in medicine need new tools and skills, insights and understandings, to pursue our goals. Thus, like it or not, interested or not, in the decades ahead medicine will pursue the humanists until they and the humanities produce what medicine needs. Because it can be found nowhere else.

CHAPTER 11

Policy Analysis and the Humanities
Contexts and Epiphanies

BRUCE L. PAYNE

Introduction

There is an offhand and unexpected revelation a little more than half way through *Lolita*. Nabokov's narrator, Humbert Humbert, has been telling the story of his sex-filled travels through the country he and Lolita had hardly even bothered to notice:

> The lovely, trustful, dreamy, enormous country that by then, in retrospect, was no more to us than a collection of dog-eared maps, ruined tour books, old tires, and her sobs in the night—every night, every night—the moment I feigned sleep.[1]

It is the first glimpse, and there are not many others, of a girl quite different from the lovely, shallow nymphet who likes Cokes and comic books and bad movies. In a moment, the reader's image of Lolita is transformed. An architecture of inference lies in ruins.

The crying implies a larger and more complicated emotional life than any reader is likely to have credited this girl with up to now. Crying asks for caring, a response that until this point one hardly thinks of making to Lolita. Humbert's pretense of sleep, hearing but doing nothing, is equally revealing. The utter self-absorption comes suddenly into focus, cruel and obsessive beyond any expectation. And this bit of candor paradoxically suggests how much he is not telling, giving us a glimpse of what the author is arranging in our minds.

With one selection of facts and our own biases we form quite plausible images of these characters. Another fact about Lolita, and a wholly

[1]Vladimir Nabokov, *The Annotated Lolita*, ed. Alfred Appel, Jr., (New York: 1970), p. 178.

BRUCE L. PAYNE ● Institute of Policy Sciences and Public Affairs, Duke University, Durham, North Carolina 27706.

different array of predispositions comes into play; another fact about Humbert, and we are led to question pretty deeply our previous assumptions about his moral condition and mental state.

All this is a typically Nabokovian sleight of hand and serves to validate Nabokov's claim that he could only use the word *reality* in quotation marks. The sense here is that the facts are elusive, that uncertainty and arbitrariness and subjectivity are present not only in our moral judgments, but also in our perceptions, our inferences, our frames of reference.

That Nabokov's characters are imagined does not at all weaken the analytic point: the stories we tell, the conclusions to which we come, are built of nothing more than selected particulars and the principles and pictures and stories we carry with us in our minds. With the addition of a few previously ignored or unknown facts, with an alternate angle of vision or another remembered image, we may find ourselves constructing a very different reality.

Teaching this story to policy students, teaching other stories to these very able students, I am struck by how often the crucial moments are missed. When later on the story becomes problematic, a few are driven back to see if there is something that they failed to notice. But readers even this attentive are relatively rare. Part of the problem is a kind of passivity, a lack of any habit of critical and reflective reading. It also appears that many students do not quite grasp the relevance, to their experience of reading, of what they already know and feel.

Tocqueville's assertion that there is nothing so difficult to comprehend as a fact[2] strikes my students as a very odd thing to say: theories and techniques may be quite difficult, but facts themselves seem easy. Tocqueville, however, was right. The facts are only to be comprehended in their contexts, in relation to many other facts, to what came before, and what surrounds, and what comes after. The fact of Lolita's sobbing changes everything, even Lolita—now suddenly Dolores, Dolores Haze, a person we had already met, but had not yet imagined.[3]

Good books in public policy seem to me as rare as first-rate novels, but in the few that are published comparable moments can be found, points at which the power of a single fact and the difficulty of comprehending it emerge with special clarity. Consider, for example, the fifth chapter of Charles Silberman's fine study, *Criminal Violence, Criminal Justice*. The preceding pages have been informative on the reality and the fear of crime in our cities and on the history of criminality, and have given us an essay on the relationship between poverty and crime. The

---

[2]Sheldon Wolin, "Political Theory as a Vocation," *American Political Science Review* 63 (December, 1969), p. 1073.
[3]And whose name, for all Nabokov's word play, we had not taken seriously.

fifth chapter is about race. It demonstrates, and then interprets, "the uncomfortable fact . . . that black offenders account for a disproportionate number of the crimes that evoke the most fear." Although there are no more crimes of property committed by blacks than by members of other groups in similar economic circumstances, homicide, forcible rape, robbery, and felonious assault are committed by blacks as much as four times as often as by Mexican-Americans or Puerto Ricans.[4]

Most of my students are surprised by the evidence. The uncareful readers among them want to attribute the overwhelming statistics to the effects of poverty, or to faulty reporting, or to the presumed hostility of a white legal system, objections all fully anticipated and cleanly answered in Silberman's text. For the succeeding sixty pages the reader is led to consider how a people not originally prone to violence came to have in the present time so many violent members. The explanations are chiefly historical. They deal with the uniquely violent treatment of the slaves and the special virulence of anti-black racism in much of America. Silberman reaches not only into history but into folklore and the work of black writers to see the shapes of rage and hear the growth of violent fantasies. He is careful to note that violence has increased elsewhere, that what he has to say tells only part of what has happened.

There is not much easy optimism left in this country about solving our crime and criminal justice problems, but Silberman's work is a nice corrective to such as remains, and a good beginning for students in the field who want to have some sense of what they are up against. More than anything else I know, it gives a sense of the size of the problem, and it offers a fine model for those who want to make effective use of history in thinking about policy, and a model as well of writing that is both tactful and scrupulous about matters of great public controversy.

There are other examples of varying size that might be brought on stage to introduce my subject, but these should serve. The humanities are important to policy analysis because they offer ways of thinking and moral insights, or because they suggest new ideas, or because they have necessary evidence about the particulars of some social problem. Pedagogically, the most precious things are probably those moments of epiphany when a student's emotional and intellectual world is suddenly, unexpectedly, enlarged.

THE MODESTY OF POLICY STUDIES

Policy studies began with a brash confidence in expertise, with the expectation that social science knowledge and sophisticated quantitative

---

[4]Charles E. Silberman, *Criminal Violence, Criminal Justice* (New York: Random House, 1978), pp. 160–167.

techniques would solve the most complicated problems facing the government—weapons acquisition, natural resources management, the redesign of welfare programs. Impatient with ideology, somewhat scornful of moral talk, and dubious about the relevance of the past, early policy analysts rarely looked to the humanities for anything at all. Over the past several years, however, the field has changed markedly. A measure of humility about what can be done is evident, and some policy analysts and teachers seem interested in considering what academic humanists might have to offer.

Public policy studies are relatively new to American higher education. Separate graduate schools of public policy have come into existence only in the last two decades; undergraduate majors and policy concentrations within majors (usually in economics or political science) are even newer. Yet the field is already a large one. Older schools of public administration have deepened their interests in public problem solving, adding training in economic analysis, statistics, computer modeling and the like. Many undergraduate programs have been fashioned by interdepartmental cooperation, without the necessity of many additional faculty members.

Training in policy analysis is popular partly because it seems to students to be effective preparation for a wide variety of interesting jobs in and out of government. Some students take policy courses because they are serious about public service, and others respond to the intrinsic fascination of government power. The public policy movement may also have been successful because of the large number of interesting and able teachers it has attracted, academics who like the opportunity for more direct connections with policymakers, who are eager to do as well as to teach.

A dozen years ago it seemed to many that public policy analysis as a field was going to be dominated by the economists, that the policy curriculum would come to have at its center the techniques of microeconomic analysis, and that its normative concerns would be limited principally to economic efficiency and one or another idea of equity. That expectation has not been fulfilled. Economics remains quite strong, but the field is, if anything, more diverse than it was.[5] At the same time,

---

[5]Many policy analysts remain deeply committed to the development and use of techniques drawn from economics, mathematics, operations research, and systems analysis. But even the most technically oriented of the recent introductory textbooks I have seen admits the broad eclecticism of the field, noting the "critical and inevitable role of values," although it limits normative concerns almost entirely to equity and efficiency. See Edith Stokey and Richard Zeckhauser, *A Primer for Policy Analysis* (New York: W. W. Norton, 1978), pp. 3–4, 257–290.

the idea of "the policy sciences" seems to have receded—policy studies and policy analysis are the characteristic phrases.[6]

As the field enlarges and the number of trained analysts increases, hopes for a full-fledged discipline of policy analysis, held largely by some of those more technically inclined, seem almost wholly to have ebbed. Recent writers speak more often of the "art" of analyzing policy.[7] They emphasize the guesswork involved in estimation and question the idea of "correct" or even "best" answers.[8] A sense of the limits of knowledge is evident too in recent discussions of "the pitfalls of analysis"[9] and in a greater degree of respect for the knowledge and capacities of public decision makers.[10] There is evident in recent policy research a deeper, more critical, more reflective interest in underlying theoretical problems, and a much greater modesty about what can be accomplished through research.[11]

What has been going on is no mere swing of intellectual fashion. A good many policy analysts have been pondering their experiences with bureaucrats and attending to some of the solidly researched and thoughtful portraits of policymakers that have been written in recent years.[12] They have also been listening to able critics within the field—Aaron Wildavsky, for one, who warned against the technocratic pre-

[6]Indeed the most thoughtful recent defense of the continuing vitality of the "policy sciences" makes clear the intellectual transition: "Human values are the crux of the policy sciences; problems for analysis are guided by the society at large, not by the theoretical inquiries of the scientific disciplines." Garry D. Brewer and Peter deLeon, *The Foundations of Policy Analysis* (Homewood, IL: Dorsey, 1983), p. 6. To be fair, this is not so far from what Harold Lasswell had in mind when he coined the phrase—but it is a long way from the scientistic and quantitative emphasis that characterized the early days of some of the major graduate public policy programs. But see also Ronald D. Brunner, "The Policy Sciences as Science," *Policy Sciences* 15 (1982), pp. 115–135.

[7]Peter W. House, *The Art of Policy Analysis* (Beverly Hills, CA: Sage Publications, 1982); Aaron Wildavsky, *Speaking Truth to Power: The Art and Craft of Policy Analysis* (Boston, MA: Little, Brown, 1979).

[8]See, e.g., Brewer and deLeon, p. 112.

[9]Giadomenico Majone and Edward S. Quade, eds., *Pitfalls of Analysis* (New York: John Wiley and Sons, 1980).

[10]See, e.g., Carol W. Weiss, *Social Science Research and Decisionmaking* (New York: Columbia University Press, 1980).

[11]It is instructive to compare the emphasis on theory in a recent evaluation studies yearbook with almost any earlier volume in the series: Ernest R. House *et al.*, eds., *Evaluation Studies Annual 7, 1982* (Beverly Hills, CA: Sage Publications, 1982). And see Philip M. Gregg, ed., *Problems of Theory in Policy Analysis* (Lexington, MA: Lexington Books, 1976); Martin Rein and Sheldon H. White, "Can Research Help Policy?" *Evaluation Studies Review Annual 3, 1978,* ed. Thomas Cook et al., pp. 24–41.

[12]Herbert Kaufman's handsomely written books may be among the most effective: see, e.g., *The Administrative Behavior of Federal Bureau Chiefs* (Washington, D.C.: The Brookings Institution, 1981).

tensions of some economists and systems analysts, and whose unheeded opposition to the Pentagon's overreliance on the techniques of systems analysts turned out to be prophetic.[13] The consistent failures of political and economic predictions have, meanwhile, convinced many analysts of the rightness of the view that most longterm predictions about politics are in principle illogical and therefore that no true science of policy-making is possible.[14]

The changed attitudes I am describing have by no means swept the field. Scorn for bureaucrats, and politics, and nonmarket solutions to policy problems, can still be heard from some policy economists. The time horizon in most teaching and analysis is limited, with little thought for problems beyond the "foreseeable future," sometimes extravagantly assumed to be as long as five years. Technical analytic modes continue to dominate curricula, and a certain "can-do" optimism is the most evident frame of mind. Still, the field seems both full of doubts and open to suggestion. New possibilities undoubtedly exist (the isle is full of noises).

Several scholars have published hopes that the art of policy analysis will be augmented by ideas and insights drawn from several areas within the disciplines we think of as humanities—history, philosophy and political theory, the criticism of literature and of art.[15] A sketch of some ways in which this is already happening will frame the varied modes and schemes and courses I envisage.

The most substantial group of academic humanists currently involved in policy schools and programs consists of the teachers of graduate and undergraduate courses in ethics and public policy. The numbers are not large. A 1978 survey showed that about 40 percent of the 134 responding schools and programs offered a course in ethics, with only a few offering more than one such course.[16] The reported courses cover a broad range of subjects: some concentrate on individual ethical

[13]Gregory Palmer, *The McNamara Strategy and the Vietnam War: Program Budgeting in the Pentagon, 1960–1968* (Westport, CT: Greenwood Press, 1978).

[14]Bertrand de Jouvenel, *The Art of Conjecture* (New York: Basic Books, 1967). See also Charles E. Lindblom and David K. Cohen, *Usable Knowledge: Social Science and Social Problem Solving* (New Haven: Yale University Press, 1979).

[15]David G. Smith, "Policy Analysis and Liberal Arts," in *Teaching Policy Studies*, ed. William D. Coplin (Lexington, MA: Lexington Books, 1978), pp. 37–43, (a cautious expression of hope, originally prepared for the Ford Foundation in 1975); Martin H. Krieger, "The Critique of Poor Reason: Using Literature to Teach Analysts," *Policy Analysis* 5, no. 4 (Fall 1979), pp. 505–520; William C. Havard, "Policy Sciences, the Humanities, and Political Coherence," in *The Ethical Dimension of Political Life*, ed. Francis Canavan (Durham, NC: Duke University Press, 1983).

[16]Joel L. Fleishman and Bruce L. Payne, *Ethical Dilemmas and the Education of Policymakers* (Hastings-on-Hudson, NY: The Hastings Center, 1980), p. 57.

problems, others on legal or political philosophy. A majority of those teaching these courses had studied political theory, but there were also teachers whose training was in philosophy or religion. Some unsystematic inquiry suggests that there has been a small increase since 1978 in the numbers.

No comparable figures are available for history courses and history teaching within the policy programs. There are a few, especially in the graduate policy schools (Harvard's JFK School of Government, the Rand Graduate Institute, Duke's Institute Policy Sciences and Public Affairs, and the Harriman School at SUNY, Stony Brook, all offer history courses).[17] At least one graduate program in history and public policy exists, and there appears to be a moderate level of interest in the possibility of history courses in several schools and programs that do not now have such courses. Those that have them now, however, are hardly likely to represent as many as a third of the total number. Courses are also taught at a very small number of institutions on aspects of the connection between policy and literature, or documentary photography.

Aside from the explicitly "humanistic" full-scale courses, there are some other interesting interconnections being made. Courses in criminal justice policy are often largely about the philosophical issues of punishment and responsibility; history plays a central role in many foreign policy courses; and the study of bureaucratic politics is freighted with ethical issues and questions of political theory to which some teachers pay close attention. History, ethics, and political theory are in fact pervasive concerns of most substantive work in policy studies. The important questions are whether these concerns are well enough understood by students, or by analysts, and whether more explicit work on them is better worth the necessary time than any of the knowledge and the skills we now impart.

I think policy students and analysts should be paying more attention to the insights and perspectives offered by the humanities. To that end we must consider the best ways of making use of what (and sometimes whom) these fields have to offer.

APPLYING THE HUMANITIES

In a recent speech, "The Public Life of the Humanities," William Bennett argued against the proposition that "humanists have a special

---

[17]These institutions have taken part, with several other graduate programs in business and in journalism, in the Uses of History Project, led by Professor Ernest May of Harvard and supported by the National Endowment for the Humanities.

insight into social and political problems," urging them instead to cultivate their older tasks, to teach the great books and nurture the "civilized framework on which public policy depends."[18] The defense of the tradition had a certain savor to it, and no one is likely to defend the practices he criticized most sharply—shallow applications of literature or philosophy, "humanistic perspectives" used to advance uninformed and oversimple solutions to complicated public questions. But Bennett's attack ignored at least one essential matter: there are fields in the humanities that are centrally and compellingly concerned with social and political problems—ethics, political theory, and history. Humanists from these fields will often have direct contributions to make in policy debates and studies, although the strength of their contributions will surely be greater if they are acquainted with relevant practical and social scientific knowledge.[19]

The notion of the applied humanities is nevertheless a slightly awkward one for many people, myself included. Humanistic knowledge is not used in the same way as the generalizations and discoveries of pure science, and *applied* prompts thoughts of ointments, or bandaids, or architectural ornamentation. But on balance no other terms seem to do as well in suggesting the kinds of activities I mean to urge—the effective use in relation to public policy of knowledge and insight from several fields in the humanities. Nor, on reflection, are the implicit imageries of therapy and rhetoric entirely inappropriate to the policy process.

A clear division of the field of the humanities into the socially useful and the personally valuable might seem better, but in fact no field, from history or philosophy to artistic criticism, fails to offer insights and knowledge of both these kinds.[20] What can more readily be distinguished are those areas within the humanities that are integral to the study and understanding, even necessary to the making, of policy, and those that are ordinarily suggestive, heuristically or critically valuable to people concerned with policy: recent history and political theory on the one hand, for example, metaphysics and art criticism on the other. For students, moreover, skills may be nearly as valuable as knowledge. Here the several humanistic disciplines share much that students of policy

---

[18]William J. Bennett, "The Public Life of the Humanities," delivered to the annual meeting of the American Conference of Academic Deans, Washington, D.C., January 1983.

[19]In spite of the recent speech, I find it hard to believe that Bennett has given up this position. See William J. Bennett, "The Humanities, the Universities, and Public Policy," in *The Humanist as Citizen*, ed. John Agresto and Peter Riesenberg, (Research Triangle Park, NC: National Humanities Center, 1981), pp. 188–201.

[20]Martin H. Krieger makes remarkable use of ideas drawn from art criticism here and there in his extraordinary and valuable book, *Advice and Planning* (Philadelphia: Temple University Press, 1981), e.g., p. 112.

are going to need: abilities to read insightfully, to write clearly and persuasively; competence in fashioning and testing arguments; some experience with the uses of passion and imagination.

This rough and ready categorizing may add definition to the concept of applied humanities, but its function here is chiefly to be an armature for a different, somewhat variegated argument, one aimed at changing what we teach in public policy studies.

Ethics

In the major political science departments during the Eisenhower years, political theory seemed irrelevant, almost antiquarian, and during the same period the prestige of ethics in American philosophy was hardly higher. The very possibility of moral philosophy was suspect. American triumphs of science and technology and organization, along with the self-confidence of the men who dominated these fields, help to explain some of this disesteem, and so too does the concurrent broadly based reaction against Fascist and Marxist ideologies and against ideology in general. Although American antitheoretical and antiintellectual prejudices also no doubt played a role, my sense is that the decisive factor in the weakening of these fields was the settled belief that knowledge implies certainty, that not knowing "for sure" is simply not knowing. Seen in this light, the decline of respect for moral inquiry and discourse had powerful internal causes—the ultimately unconvincing claims to moral certainty by both religious and secular moralists, and the generations of philosophic criticism that eventually and effectively undermined all such claims. It has taken some time for many thinkers to recover.

Policy studies was developed by people who saw the field of ethics at its weakest, people who distrusted ideology and were at best impatient with philosophy. Only a few followed with any care the gradual resurgence of serious work on ethics in several academic disciplines. To the others, professors who retained the positivism of their early training in social science theory, teaching ethics seemed mistaken. What could it be but fuzzy-minded or indoctrinating?

Those who have thought most seriously about the intellectual foundations of policy studies seem fairly decisively to have rejected this view. The head of the Rand Graduate Institute writes that a concern with normative issues, "with equity (in its widely varying interpretations and criteria), and with ethics and ethical dilemmas," is one of the field's identifying characteristics.[21] Several recent textbooks devote substantial

[21]Charles Wolf, Jr., "Policy Analysis and Public Management: Strengths and Limits," *Journal of Policy Analysis and Management* 1, no. 4 (1982), pp. 546–551.

space to ethics, and the policy journals show an increasing concern with ethical issues of various kinds.[22] There is, however, less clarity about how best to go about making ethics part of policy analysis. Some writers and teachers seem to believe that careful work on the values of efficiency and equity is most of what is needed. Others are principally concerned with the ethics of the analysts, still others with issues of democratic theory.

This new and growing interest in ethics is strengthened by the practical orientation of policy studies, for in the real world of governmental decision making ethical questions are pervasive and important. We must do better in preparing our students for these questions.

I think every policy student would benefit greatly from at least one course about policymaking in which ethical issues are the predominating explicit concerns. Such courses make it more likely, rather than less, that ethical questions will come up in other courses, and they usually give students some sense of the diverse resources of analysis and argumentation helpful in discovering the moral stakes of policy choice.[23]

Different kinds of ethics courses will no doubt prevail at different institutions, and that result seems beneficial. Those that deal with a broad range of values appear to me preferable to those limited mainly to problems of equity and economic efficiency,[24] and I also believe that the use of real cases, embedded whenever possible in some historical context, is superior to a more abstract and hypothetical approach.[25]

There is a recurrent temptation to work out systematic and elaborate frameworks for the application of normative criteria to policymaking or analysis.[26] My strong sense is that these are not likely to have much effect. Political theorists and others interested in bringing ethics to bear on policy would probably do better by trying to improve the existing ways in which values and moral rules are taken into account. This would

[22]Brewer and deLeon; Fred M. Frohock, *Public Policy: Scope and Logic* (Englewood Cliffs, NJ: Prentice-Hall, 1979); Duncan MacRae, Jr., and James A. Wilde, *Policy Analysis for Public Decision* (Belmont, CA: Wadsworth, 1979). Frank Fischer also notes the trend in the journals: *Politics, Values, and Public Policy: The Problem of Methodology* (Boulder, CO: Westview Press, 1980), pp. 2–3.

[23]For another, much more extensive, discussion of ethics teaching in policy analysis, see Joel L. Fleishman and Bruce L. Payne, pp. 15–56.

[24]MacRae and Wilde, pp. 45–70, work within these limits, but the care devoted to their thoughtfully chosen cases gives a special value to their textbook.

[25]A good example of a nicely complicated case is Dennis F. Thompson, "The Ethics of Social Experimentation: The Case of DIME," *Public Policy* 29, no. 3 (Summer 1981), pp. 369–398.

[26]This strikes me as the one failing of Frank Fischer's otherwise thoughtful and useful study, pp. 183–218.

mean, among other things, paying close attention to the ways in which ideology clarifies or obscures the moral stakes in this or that decision.[27]

In an earlier time, Plutarch and stories from the Bible were the main texts of ethical education for political leaders. Stories, and particularly interesting and memorable biographical stories, retain special advantages in teaching about ethics. William Greider's fine account of David Stockman in 1981 works wonderfully well in giving resonance and weight to essays about such subjects as deception, the ethics of analysis and advocacy, entitlements and fairness, private interests and the public good.[28]

Stories, philosophy, ideology, cases and moral theory will then be parts of any really fine courses. In what follows I have tried to make more specific the actual approaches and courses in ethics and policymaking that appear to me to be most promising.

Ethical Dilemmas of Individuals, Obligations and Interests

Policymakers live and work amid a variety of competing moral obligations. Accepting a public office means promising to fulfill its duties. One also owes allegiance to the constitution and the laws and has duties to superiors and subordinates. Officials are often bound by precedent and standard operating procedures, and by loyalties to political allies or to friends and family and community. Policymakers have a more general obligation to carry out the wishes of the people and to serve the common good.

This sketch understates the variety of responsibilities to which almost any policymaker is subject, but it may implicitly overemphasize the likelihood of conflict. Custom, law, and ideology share in marking out potential conflicts and guiding their resolution. Cabinet members, for example, have political obligations that would be improper for career servants; promises to political associates can hardly ever oblige a criminal act.

Competing obligations nevertheless engender recurrent and weighty problems. The temptation to leak a document, or falsify a record, or tell a lie may be particularly strong when such methods seem the only way to do a job as one has promised. Whether to act as the voters desire, or in their long-term best interests, is a repeated question for legislators.

---

[27]For an excellent and subtle defense of the uses of ideology, see Henry David Aiken, "Morality and Ideology," in *Ethics and Society*, ed. Richard T. De George (Garden City, NY: Doubleday, 1966).

[28]William Greider, *The Education of David Stockman and Other Americans* (New York: E. P. Dutton, 1981).

No one in the public office avoids facing such dilemmas. How can we prepare our students for them?

Here the main teaching objective is to bring as much as possible into consciousness. Students need to learn about the variety of obligations they will face, need to think in advance how some of the tougher conflicts might be met. Talking about competing obligations often ends up raising issues of democratic theory and constitutional law. It also reaches to fundamental issues of philosophy: Should I obey the law? When? Why?; What is the force of ordinary moral duties like truth telling?

Obligations set the boundaries of personal and political interests. Students need to think about the place of their own needs and desires in relation to public office and about how they should respond to superiors or subordinates who for personal advantage choose to violate the rules. Paying attention to ethical problems from the viewpoint of the individual policymaker leads easily into questions of character, of virtue, of temptation and corruption.[29]

The Ethics of Analysis

The skills of policy analysis are useful to bureaucrats, to legislators and their staffs, to those in the world of law and business who are concerned with policy. Some of the people trained in policy analysis, however, actually end up doing it full time. Those who accept official positions have the usual obligations of public officials, but they, and those who work outside the government, may have some special additional duties that come with being analysts.

Obligations of this sort arise as they usually do, from explicit undertakings and implicit promises, and from principles to which one adheres for various reasons. For analysts, many of the conflicts are likely to come in relation to their clients. How much should information be shaped to further political, or organizational, or financial goals? The problems may be especially acute for analysts working in the bureaucracy. Should they strive to be neutral researchers? Or is it appropriate for them to become advocates, defending programs and choices they think best with partial arguments and selectively chosen evidence?[30]

Analysts face particular difficulties in forecasting costs and benefits. Underestimating costs is often effective in reducing opposition to programs. Because the practice is common, the pressure to do it may be all

[29]Bruce L. Payne, "Devices and Desires: Corruption and Ethical Seriousness," in *Public Duties: The Moral Obligations of Government Officials*, ed. Joel L. Fleishman, Lance Liebman, and Mark H. Moore (Cambridge, MA: Harvard, 1981).
[30]Arnold J. Meltsner, *Policy Analysts in the Bureaucracy* (Berkeley, CA: University of California Press, 1976), pp. 282–285.

the greater—legislators, or bureaucrats at a higher level, may routinely reinflate the estimates they receive.[31]

The problems are important not only to those who will be full-time analysts, but to anyone involved in public policy who plays from time to time an expert's role, and to anyone who hires or counts on experts (and that is almost everyone). The central insights we can hope to give our students have to do with doubting and somewhat circumscribing the authority of expertise, recognizing that expert "knowledge" is likely to be mixed with guesses and assumptions and shaped by biases and desires. Since deception is the constant temptation of analysis, I also favor an initiation into straightforward question asking about immediate and long-term consequences of lies, along the lines that Sissela Bok urges and exemplifies in her clear-headed study, *Lying*.[32]

All the Issues?

Ethics is about what we ought to do, as individuals and in groups, and it is rare to find anything at issue in the political order that is purely technical, lacking entirely in any ethical content. That does not mean that ethics professionals have something revealing to say about every issue, especially not when the values at stake are clear in the debate. But pedagogically it is a good idea to pick an issue every now and then that seems at first not to be very interesting from an ethical point of view and then spend time elucidating hidden and incompletely formulated values.

The Clean Air Act and its amendments, for example, are chiefly about environmental values and economic efficiency. Sometimes the debates emphasize the questions of equity—who gains? who pays?— and more rarely the environmental values are clearly sorted out: physical and psychic health, aesthetic values having to do with recreation or with beauty. On reflection, however, other values are at stake as well: principles about how the government should relate to business; the trust of citizens in the authority of government or in the honesty of business; the sense of political efficacy of citizens involved in the debates. Recent plans for a partial shift from government regulations to economic incentives in this area are likely to have consequences in relation to all these values and more.[33] Were the officials who proposed the changes thinking with anything like this breadth?

[31]Martin Wachs, "Ethical Dilemmas in Forecasting for Public Policy," *Public Administration Review* 42, no. 6 (November/December 1982), pp. 562–567.
[32]Sissela Bok, *Lying: Moral Choice in Public Life* (New York: Pantheon Books, 1978).
[33]For a related view of omitted values in relation to the Clean Air Act, see John Forester, "Public Policy and Respect," *Democracy* 2, no. 4 (Fall 1982), pp. 93–101.

It would be fair to answer that we do not need ethical analysis to find these values. If they are indeed important, they will surely arise in the public debate. So they will, as long as the groups who share them are aware of what is happening and not excluded from the process of public argument. But careful value analysis in advance still appears to be the wisest course. Public and legislative debates are loose processes at best, with no guarantee that the path chosen will not needlessly or unfairly override important values. We cannot, and should not, hope to envisage every consequence of policy, nor is it reasonable or democratically sound to ask decision makers to act always in the service of some preplanned hierarchy of values. But speculation about the impact of policy on a broad range of values can produce especially helpful forethought. Such thinking is probably all the more valuable to those decision makers who have a special interest in improving the quality of public debate.[34]

It is worth noting that ethical issues are most likely to come up in a serious way in those courses—uncommon in some policy programs— that look at particular issues in some considerable depth. To the extent that policy programs follow Wildavsky's advice to emphasize analysis over subject matter, they will reduce the possibility of serious ethical inquiry.[35]

The Moral Issues

There are issues like abortion, the rights of homosexuals, and the prohibition of alcohol in which sharply different views about policy are based on deeply divergent fundamental moral views. On these issues the usual pattern of public debate may be reversed. Ordinarily talk gradually reduces the range of disagreement, specifying the differences more precisely and searching out the possible areas of compromise. With the moral issues, more debate may only lead to sharper differences.

In such circumstances it is fair to ask whether ethics has anything to contribute beyond the elaboration of one or the other side's case in the dispute (a task which can of course be useful). The parties involved are after all not likely to be moved; they hope, rather, to maintain or to

---

[34]A good example of just how much work by philosophers, historians, and political theorists might have to contribute to improving public debate is evident from a recent project of the National Humanities Center, *Energy and American Values*, by Ian Barbour, Harvey Brooks, Sanford Lakoff, and John Opie (Research Triangle Park, NC: National Humanities Center and Praeger, 1982).

[35]Wildavsky, p. 414. This advice strikes me as dubious on other grounds as well. It can lead to overconfidence in the ability of analysts, and to underestimating the value of bureaucratic experience.

strengthen their public support, to win or to defeat a change in the laws through working in the political process. It seems to me that in such circumstances ethics is nevertheless likely to make a special contribution.

That contribution is to attempt to make the arguments of one side clearer to the partisans of the other. This does not require remaining aloof from the conflict, but it does ask that partisans trained in ethics have a certain measure of detachment. Listening to the opposing arguments, explaining to one's own side the logic of those arguments and how they might be held sincerely by decent people, may moderate some of the powerful extraneous effects that fierce moral disagreements tend to have. Civility is a value that makes many things possible, and it is always threatened by the judgment that our opponents are not only wrong but evil, not only opponents but enemies.

We may have enemies of course. We may want to have them. My view here is only that listening carefully may help us to hesitate before making a judgment so difficult to change and so fraught with danger for the polity.

With my students I have often found the abortion problem particularly valuable in this regard. Assigning essays about it after half a semester in which students have been analyzing arguments with increasing skill and thoughtfulness can produce an unsettling response. Fairmindedness is suddenly forgotten. Papers from both sides—and here there usually are just two—sound like nothing so much as inadequate lawyer's briefs. The arguments of the opposing side are hardly heard. Talking over this result is where the teaching really begins.

The advantage of dealing with these issues is the effect they have in showing students something of the power of their own moral feelings and the coherence or confusions of their moral judgments. Why do they believe that cruelty to animals is wrong? What makes them sure that alcohol is not a moral but rather a practical question? Ethics may have much to offer in policymaking, but with the moral issues policy questions became superb instruments for teaching fundamental issues of ethics.

Hard Choices

Joseph Califano's memoir of his service as HEW secretary covers a broad variety of ethical issues about which he faced difficult decisions. In it he notes:

> Questions people once sought to have answered by prayer, issues once left for scientists to resolve in their laboratories, are now debated on the floor of Congress, by the brethren on the Supreme Court, thrown into the executive branch regulatory process, or demonstrated about. . . . In another age, these kinds of questions would have been fodder for Talmudic scholars, Jesuit

priests, family doctors, and medical school students and professors. The peculiar and inescapable fact of the eighties is that these questions are intensely political as well.[36]

Sterilization, kidney dialysis, laetrile—the issues Califano describes may not always be intensely political. But the shift of moral responsibility to government in many areas of health and welfare is documented throughout his book. The government will probably make an increasing number of choices as time goes by, choices about life and death and about the quality of life for the sick, the old, and the dependent.

Economic analysis has done much to clarify the debate about some of these choices. We need to know the costs of life-saving technology and to be able to compare the relative risks and benefits of the technological and treatment alternatives we face. But economics has no ready answers to questions of intergenerational equity, or any way to quantify the value of respect for age. The traditions of ethical argument have some real sophistication in relation to at least some of these issues, enabling us to go beyond the simple comparisons of cost to the fears and preoccupations of our citizens, and to questions of dignity and respect.

Courses in health policy would benefit from more attention to these concerns. Academics trained in medical ethics can play a valuable role in teaching here. So, too, can others teaching ethics in policy programs, if they are willing to spend the necessary time studying the substantive issues on which these courses turn.[37]

Issues in Political and Legal Theory

Many important policy issues are primarily and essentially questions of political theory or constitutional law. Questions of civil rights, policies about racial discrimination or affirmative action, for example, demand of analysts skill in fashioning and understanding normative arguments, as well as some knowledge of constitutional doctrine and democratic theory. Some of the issues surrounding the problem of illegal aliens are similarly philosophical questions at their core—what are the responsibilities of a country to the strangers living amongst us? What do we owe to others elsewhere?[38]

[36]Joseph A. Califano, Jr., *Governing America: An Insider's Report from the White House and the Cabinet* (New York: Simon and Schuster, 1981), p. 209.
[37]In this connection, see Marc D. Hiller, *Medical Ethics and the Law: Implications for Policy* (Cambridge, MA: Ballinger, 1981).
[38]Peter G. Brown and Henry Shue, *Boundaries: National Autonomy and Its Limits* (Totowa, NJ: Rowman and Littlefield, 1981).

Even with these issues, the values at stake must be seen in relation to the likely factual consequences of policy alternatives. On a matter like human rights policy in relation to countries violating the human rights of their own citizens, the important normative problems may be even more tightly bound up with complicated facts, as well as with competing values.

Many teachers and practitioners of policy analysis are well prepared to contribute thoughtfully to debates about such largely or partly normative problems, but I am worried that we may be teaching less well than we know. Even in political science, the tendency in recent years has been to squeeze the time available for political philosophy and constitutional law, in favor of giving graduate students more sophistication with varieties of technical analysis. In policy curricula the space for normative and theoretical concern is even less.

The Challenge of Political Philosophy

If political theory is needed for the resolution of various policy problems about competing values, it also has another more searching, more disturbing role. We value the great political theorists of the past in proportion to their capacity to surprise us. When these "epic theorists" confirm our ideas, they are probably not needed; when what they have to say is strange and troubling, we might do well to pay attention.[39]

The long perspective of political philosophy and its sensitivity to the possibility of large-scale change set it at odds with the incrementalist ethos of most work in public policy. The tension seems to me precious, worth building into the study of policy in some more visible way.

Because political philosophy reflects on the deepest questions—legitimacy and power, the distribution of wealth and property, liberty, law—it is a kind of preparation for crisis, for times when the most important values are threatened, when deep conflicts unexpectedly emerge.

We risk training analysts and policymakers who can cope effectively with everyday problems and midrange crises but who entirely miss the rare chance for large-scale progress and never see in time the overhanging doom. Political theorists predict not as scientists but as prophets; and, like Amos, they hope that their visions will not come true, that the nation will overcome its failings soon enough to avert the catastrophes they discern. We might do well to find some ways to listen.[40]

[39]Wolin, p. 1077.
[40]Charles E. Lindblom's 1981 presidential address to the American Political Science Association argues similarly: "Another State of Mind," *The American Political Science Review* 76 (1982), pp. 9–21.

The History of Policies

As a consumer of history, using it in the analysis of policy and in teaching about ethics and policymaking, I am more than ready to defend its usefulness to policymakers. But I remain an outsider to the profession, more than a bit shy of expressing many critical conclusions about work in the field. Readers interested in considering more fully the manifold connections between history and policy analysis would do well to begin with the wise counsels of Gordon Craig[41] and Ernest May[42] for foreign policy, and of Peter Stearns[43] for domestic policy. What I can appropriately do here is to urge my colleagues to bring historical concerns more directly into their research and teaching in policy analysis—an argument with examples.

Few policy problems are new, and most choices by decision makers turn out to be revisions of earlier decisions. Understanding the problem is inseparable from knowing at least the recent history of policy in relation to it. But how far back must one go? Is not the history of the early nineteenth century so far from the social and governmental realities of our day as to be essentially irrelevant? Or if not irrelevant, is it not at the very least much less important than more recent history?

The answers necessarily depend on the policy in question. Sometimes early history is important—the history of the decisions that determine present policy, or the history most present in the minds of those who will be subject to it. It would be foolish to make policies affecting the Sioux without knowing about Crazy Horse and Wounded Knee, and similarly unwise to make foreign policy decisions about Nicaragua without reference to earlier American military intervention there.

Anyone interested in prison reform needs to take into account the material on early nineteenth-century reforms offered by David Rothman in his widely praised study *The Discovery of the Asylum*.[44] The good intentions of the founders of the penitentiary system are in their way as astonishing as the terrible results of the system they established. Like

---

[41]Gordon Craig, "The Historian and the Study of International Relations," *The American Historical Review* 88, no. 1 (February 1983), pp. 1–11. See also his "On the Nature of Diplomatic History: The Relevance of Some Old Books," in *Diplomacy: New Approaches in History, Theory, and Policy*, ed. Paul Gordon Lauren (New York: The Free Press, 1979), pp. 21–42.

[42]Ernest R. May, *"Lessons" of the Past: The Use and Misuse of History in American Foreign Policy* (New York: Oxford University Press, 1973).

[43]Peter N. Stearns, "History and Policy Analysis: Toward Maturity," *The Public Historian* 4, no. 3 (Summer 1982), pp. 5–29.

[44]David J. Rothman, *The Discovery of the Asylum: Social Order and Disorder in the New Republic* (Boston: Little, Brown, 1971).

much good social history, his tale is a cautionary one. Reforms are often more difficult to win and less effective in practice than reformers hope and claim.[45]

Proposals to change policy in any area are likely to fail if they have been fashioned without a clear analysis of the circumstances and the political forces that led to the existing policy. Here history is likely to be the best available guide. Surely the long story of resistance by the U.S. Forest Service to a more preservationist wilderness law or to the recurrent proposals that it be moved from the Agriculture Department to the Department of Interior could have been anticipated by anyone who knew the facts Samuel Hays recounts in his *Conservation and the Gospel of Efficiency*.[46] Similarly, anyone interested in changing the pattern of economic regulation in American business would do well to understand how much cooperation and nongovernmental action was necessary for the successful establishment of the Securities and Exchange Commission.[47]

The history of policy includes the history of policymaking, and in this latter area some quite interesting work has recently appeared. Samuel Williamson's study of decision making in the Habsburg monarchy during 1914 confirms and extends essential features of the organizational process model that has been a principal tool of policy analysis.[48] That paradigm is itself a historically derived conception, and like the other tools of analysis, it can probably be made both more convincing and more subtle by continued testing in the light of historical experience.

Writing about the history of policy and policymaking is clearly on the rise, but the community of people working in this area is still quite small. Creating full-time history positions in policy schools and programs would improve our teaching and enrich ongoing conversations about policy; it would also encourage substantially more research of direct relevance to policymaking. Without continuing high-quality historical research, we risk making too much of too few cases, endlessly recycling the history we know, whatever its real value for our analytic purposes.

[45]David J. Rothman and Stanton Wheeler, "Introduction," in *Social History and Social Policy*, ed. David J. Rothman and Stanton Wheeler (New York: Academic Press, 1981), pp. 1–18.

[46]Samuel P. Hays, *Conservation and the Gospel of Efficiency: The Progressive Conservation Movement, 1890–1920*, 2nd ed. (New York: Atheneum, 1969).

[47]Thomas K. McCraw, "With Consent of the Governed: SEC's Formative Years," *Journal of Policy Analysis and Management* 1, no. 3 (1982), pp. 346–370.

[48]Samuel R. Williamson, Jr., "Theories of Organizational Process and Foreign Policy Outcomes," in *Diplomacy: New Approaches in History, Theory and Policy*, ed. Paul Gordon Lauren (New York: The Free Press, 1979), pp. 137–161.

Documentary Studies

Whereas careful observation of individuals and groups plays a major role in anthropology and sociology, the transformation of observation into documentary literature and art requires qualities of skill and judgment characteristic of work within the humanities. For public policy students the journalistic documentaries of film and television often provide useful alternative ways of looking at social problems and at official efforts to solve them. More contemplative or demanding documentary work (Fred Wiseman's video documentary, *Welfare*, for example) has a different sort of impact. For policy students, the rich tradition of documentary photography seems especially likely to affect the ways in which students perceive public policy and the people and communities that are subject to it.

Good documentary work in photography or literature or films is always evidence, testimony. Whether it begins in art, in empathy or ideology, or in curiosity about how things work or who gets what, it is necessarily and relentlessly particular: this city, those fields, these faces, are worth picturing in our minds.

The seriousness of the claim owes much to the aesthetic conviction that attentiveness can change us, can make us more alive to the people and the objects that surround us, more attuned to our own inner life, readier for the world's beauty, stronger against its terrors. These were the goals, and for many readers the achievements, of the passionately precise descriptions of James Agee and James Joyce, as they were the evident informing aim of Walker Evans' photographs of American Life.

The writers, photographers, and filmmakers who staked out the original territories of documentary had other hopes as well, more social and less individual. They believed the testimony of "human actuality" could prompt sympathy and imaginative identification, that it would provoke conscience and then action, that misery and injustice would not long be tolerated if only they were clearly seen. Their hopes for social transformation, somewhat tempered but also partly fulfilled, remain after five decades central to the documentary tradition.[49]

Often dramatic and inescapably subjective, documentary risks becoming propaganda. At its best, however, careful study of the particulars of human life undermines the simplicities of ordinary political argument and brings into question the confident syntheses of social science and political ideology. The great strength of documentary work is in fact its ability to show what others neglect: the unintended and ironic consequences of policy, the qualities of life in public institutions, the liveliness

[49]William Stott, *Documentary Expression and Thirties America* (New York: Oxford University Press, 1973).

of a community's streets or the depth of its memory; sometimes aspiration and generosity, or contrariness or downright meanness; often sadness and demoralization, or energy and joy.[50]

For those involved with the making of significant public choices, especially about social problems like crime or poverty or health but also in areas such as the environment or foreign aid, documentary offers abundant material for reflection and persuasion. Because so much government decision making is insensitive to the diversities of persons and communities, the role of careful social observation is often critical, even adversarial, pointing to factors ignored by economic and statistical analysis, or to costs and benefits overlooked or underestimated because the people who are to be hurt or helped have not been imagined in any lively way.

Reflective, personally committed, critical thinking is needed for policymaking, and indeed for any work of serious intent. Such thinking, uncommon in our schools and in our society, will not be made less rare through more training and greater technical skills. It may, however, be advanced by an education that shows the excitement and the worth of deeper understanding.

Documentary studies have a special potential here. They cut across the academic boundaries of literature, art, and social science, and they offer opportunities for thoughtful independent student work. Even more important, they are likely to engage the imagination of students, to rouse their curiosity and sometimes touch their hearts.

Studying and doing documentary work are not alternatives to an education in history and literature, nor are they any substitute for the methods and techniques of political and economic analysis. But for a present-minded and narrowly educated generation, documentary work offers an accessible opening into larger concerns and unexpected encounters with facts that may make analysis more worth doing.

Writing

In his study of policy analysts in the bureaucracy, Arnold Meltsner emphasizes that an analyst spends much of his time writing: "His ability to write is an essential ingredient of his bureaucratic success."[51] In politics and policymaking few pieces of writing have an automatic audience. Memoranda and reports, speeches and articles, all will fail of effect

---

[50]See, for example, two books by Robert Coles, with photographs by Alex Harris: *The Last and First Eskimos* (Boston: Little, Brown, 1978); *The Old Ones of New Mexico* (Albuquerque: University of New Mexico Press, 1973).
[51]Meltsner, p. 63.

if they are boring and unpersuasive. Policy students need to learn the art of rhetoric.

René Dubos is one example of an effective advocate whose writing can be genuinely persuasive. Consider his case against the purely preservationist environmentalism of Aldo Leopold and others. After contrasting Benedictine and Franciscan attitudes toward nature, he urges that Saint Benedict

> be regarded as a patron saint of those who believe that true conservation means not only protecting nature against human misbehavior but also developing human activities which favor a creative, harmonious relationship between man and nature.[52]

Dubos wants to praise those who have created "ecologically viable and culturally desirable" new environments. By using the evocative images of Dominican monasteries and farming practices, he establishes a position that seems as far from the Forest Service's rhetoric of multiple use as it is from the Sierra Club's save-the-wilderness campaigns. To help us see what he has in mind and to persuade us of the rightness or at least the decency and attractiveness of his view, he offers an image of "the Benedictine way of life"—"its wisdom in managing the land, in fitting architecture to worship and landscape, in adapting rituals and work to the cosmic rhythms."[53]

Policy students need models of writing. We ought to search, more carefully than most of us now do, for articles and books that make significant substantive and analytic points in prose of high quality. Beyond that, we need to demand of our students papers that are interesting, reflective, and clear.

PARTICULARS

When we praise someone as thoughtful, we are not just saying that he or she thinks a lot. We mean rather that this person has a sense of what it is important to think about, that the thinking comes soon enough, that it has effects on action. Thoughtfulness is a virtue, and like honor, courage, or constancy, it requires cultivation. This is to say that although thoughtfulness can hardly be directly taught, it seems to grow from certain kinds of experience and knowledge, and more especially in discussion or dialogue with others.

The virtues were said by the ancients to be forms of self-knowledge, and those people we call thoughtful do seem to know themselves es-

---

[52]René Dubos, *A God Within* (New York: Scribner's 1972), p. 168.
[53]Ibid., p. 174.

pecially well. They have some place to stand, to be and think from, some sense of who they are that lets their minds range unusually far.

The culture that supports and nourishes such qualities is not likely to be the cool, objective, calculating world of scientific or social-scientific training, because that education rarely asks people to look inside, or to connect up what they are studying with the things they feel, the particular and individual experiences they have had. In the several fields we call humanities, the older, opposing emphasis is more often present.

Allow me, if you will, to close this essay with a few examples that reflect this aspect of my subject. They are brief accounts of matters that I have talked about with undergraduates in my policy courses, the subjects having in common only my interest in words and the fact that each has been the occasion of interesting class discussion.

Philology

A piece of intellectual history that I do not believe is common knowledge emerged for me a couple of years ago in the course of some quick research the night before a class. I had been responding to a vocal partisan of some particularly reductionist point of view (a kind of psychological egoism, as I remember) and was putting together a sort of chart of the many forms and degrees of fellow-feeling our language has to offer.

In such circumstances the charms of the *Oxford English Dictionary* are almost irresistible, and in the turn of time I happened on the first use of *philanthropy* in English, Sir Francis Bacon's essay "Of Goodness and Goodness of Nature" (1595).[54]

Bacon writes that goodness, "what the Grecians called *philanthropia*," is called the greatest virtue, and at the beginning of his essay he says it is the same as Christian charity. A few sentences later, however, he begins to move away from this orthodox position, citing Machiavelli on the tendency of Christianity "to give up good men in prey to those that are tyrannical and unjust." Although Bacon hesitates to endorse such a heretical view, the middle ground he chooses is remarkable.

"Sell all thou hast, and give it to the poor, and follow me" Bacon quotes from scripture, and then he adds pregnantly, "but sell not all thou hast, except . . . thou have a vocation." Do not give away your goods unless you become a priest, "for otherwise in feeding the streams thou driest the fountain." This warning not to spend one's principal is, as Bacon knew, a long way from the accepted Christian moral teaching.

[54]Sir Francis Bacon, *Essays* (London: J. M. Dent, 1905), pp. 37–38.

The philanthropy he recommends is instead a classical notion, taken from the tradition that reaches back to Socrates.

A look at late Elizabethan England can shed some light on Bacon's moral innovation. The society was one in which the social pyramid sloped steeply, with wealth and political power concentrated at the top. And Bacon knew that among those at the top some were liberal and kind, others cruel and selfish. His problem was that the Christian moral vocabulary of late Elizabethan England was not quite adequate for making this essential distinction. Bacon needed the Greek word because he needed an alternative ethical position. The Christian demand for absolute altruism was simply unlikely to be honored by those Bacon most desired to affect.

Because their situation is in a way analogous, my students find the story interesting. Many arrive in my ethics class expecting exhortations to self-denial, and when I suggest that the less heroic, classical ideal of magnanimity might be a reasonable and ethical aim, more than a few are troubled. They have no plans to give away their money, but in some odd way they want to hear me tell them that they should.

In principle, Christian ethical ideals were as realizable by the poorest, meekest soul, as by the greatest. According to the values of Periclean Athens, the widow's mite would seem less large (though the story of Socrates shows that one did not have to be wealthy to be brave and generous even there). In any case, compared to Elizabethans or Athenians, or most of the present inhabitants of the world, Americans are quite rich. Why, I ask my students, do we not show the kind of natural generosity the Greeks expected and often found in those with such security and strength? The question sometimes elicits surprising answers.

Irony

More and more in teaching ethics over the last ten years—teaching about the values and the virtues that we set against self-interest and the urgent drive for power—I have found myself thinking of irony, trying to understand its impact and how it helps to see the world.

That the first World War, the War to End Wars, made the definitive case for irony is widely recognized. All the great abstractions—courage, honor, comradeship and glory—in those four years lost something of their grip: millions of men turned into meat, and the rhetoric of the statesmen getting emptier by the hour. The soldiers found the ironies in the ruinous, impossible strategies, in the abridgement of hope by death, in the contrast of military formality with the chaos of war.[55]

---

[55]Paul Fussell, *The Great War and Modern Memory* (New York: Oxford University Press, 1975), pp. 3–35 and *passim*.

Some have by now learned the lessons of the ironists: no praise of valor without a body count; no wars to extend democracy without at least some lively picture of the petty tyrants and the political gangsters with whom we are in league. Irony will not save us—but it helps us see some other truths more sharply. It also calls attention to the roles we play in the human comedy, adding laughter to our indignation at the hollow-sounding words of quite unironic leaders.

It may seem that irony is only for writers, for observers with no power, and it is true that statesmen rarely seem to catch the tone. One who did was Lord Melbourne, the governor of Ireland 130 years ago. Facing the problem of Catholic civil rights he sought advice, and the wisest people he turned to, Melbourne said, counseled concessions, liberalization, magnanimity. "The damned fools" on the other hand, urged rigid and unbending opposition. Melbourne followed his conscience and the counsels of the wise. You will not be surprised by the result. "What all the wise men said would happen has not happened," Melbourne tells us, "and what all the damned fools said would happen, has come to pass." Though they may have been right, Melbourne knew they were still damned fools.[56]

The irony catches the predicament precisely, and it demands an effort from the reader. It poses a problem, a puzzle that needs some resolution. For me, and I think for Melbourne, the principal effect is to call attention to the folly of believing that the effects of 200 years or more of fiercely resented injustice could be dispelled by a possibly temporary turn toward a more rational and generous course.

Irony has been an important teaching method at least since Socrates, and it has generally aimed at mental provocation. Whereas the language of moral exhortation often seems to suggest the mental work is over, those who use irony leave to their readers the main tasks of reasoning and learning.

The Boundaries of Time

For nineteen years a moment in *Cry, the Beloved Country* has reverberated in my memory:

> It was Msimangu who said, Msimangu who had no hate for any man, I have one great fear in my heart, that one day when they turn to loving they will find we are turned to hating.[57]

I had only vaguely remembered reading the words, and they did not strike me powerfully until Allard Lowenstein quoted them to me in

---

[56]Lord David Cecil, *Melbourne* (Indianapolis: Bobbs-Merrill, 1966), pp. 259.
[57]Alan Paton, *Cry, the Beloved Country* (New York: Scribner's, 1948), pp. 272.

Mississippi in the fall of 1963. You may rightly say that almost anything would be remembered in those circumstances. But when I went back to read it the whole book seemed to me as poignant as these lines, the sad beauty of the gorgeous land, the sad poverty of the people who had nothing but worn-out dirt. Now it seems sadder still, because the hatred is surely well advanced, and the turn toward love never really managed to begin.

The students who take my courses have learned, eagerly or reluctantly in other courses, how to think about comparing costs and benefits; there is another sense, however, in which they are reluctant to count the costs. The results of earlier choices, or earlier failures or defeats, are called "sunk costs" and do not count in weighing present options. Although the logic here is formally correct, there is among many policy analysts and students not only a willingness to set aside from the analysis the costs already paid, but also a desire to forget.

The alternative is to remember, to register the pain and anger of past catastrophes, to feel the guilt of earlier misjudgments. Such memories sharpen the appetite for better choices, impel a search for more decent alternatives. Some decisions get lots of time and care and others less—feeling the weight of tragedy and disaster may shift priorities. The essential thing to learn, after all, is what is trivial and what significant.

Does history sometimes occur in moments? Are there opportunities that unfold, are seized or vanish? Larry Goodwyn intends something like this in his phrase "the Populist moment in America," which serves as the subtitle to his *Democratic Promise*[58], and the case can be made that there were similar, largely unrealized possibilities in American politics during the period from 1963 to 1966.

However this may be, students and policymakers need to learn that time goes by. Lyndon B. Johnson lost a year in postponing Vietnam decisions until after the election of 1964, and the price was high. Time ran out for John F. Kennedy in Dallas, with no second term in which to take the promised bold initiatives. The armies move; the workers strike; the bridge collapses. Prediction depends upon the assumption that everything remains equal, but in politics nothing stays the same for long. And it is usually the irregularities, the unpredicted, unexpected happenings, that have the most dramatic consequences.

The poet Cavafy portrays Zeus as regretting his gift of immortal horses to Achilles when he saw them weeping for the dead Patroclus: "Men have caught you up in their misery." And so they had. "But," says the poet, "it was the eternal disaster of death that those two gallant

---

[58]Larry Goodwyn, *Democratic Promise: The Populist Moment in America* (New York: Oxford University Press, 1976).

horses shed their tears."[59] We need sometimes to mourn the irretrievable possibilities, to feel the pain, if only to build the fact of irretrievability, and the awesome responsibility of time, more firmly into mind and conscience.

The Task of the Novelist

A notion that always puzzles and disturbs my students may carry us a little further. In a late preface to *Wise Blood*, Flannery O'Connor speaks of her main character's choices and the problem of free will. It is an old subject in fiction—characters' lives and choices must be determined sufficiently so that they appear believable, consistent, "in character"; but only when they face real choices, authentic dilemmas, do they engage our deeper interest or excite our sympathy. O'Connor says about freedom of the will that it "is a mystery and one which a novel, even a comic novel, can only be asked to deepen."[60]

My policy students want mysteries to be solved, or at least to be in principle resolvable. That a novelist's task might be to deepen the mystery they find troubling. Yet at the heart of most literature and art, as well as much history, philosophy, and religion, there is a sense of the radically unknowable. What is made by men and women, what depends on choice and will, cannot be fully known. Our words, dependent as they are on context and connotation, usually capture only bits and shards of individual and social life. They can do more, of course, with care for sense and sounds and stories, and with the powers of persuasion. For good or ill.

[59]C. P. Cavafy, *Collected Poems*, trans. Edmund Keeley and Philip Sherrard, ed. George Savidis (Princeton, NJ: Princeton University Press, 1975), p. 5.
[60]Flannery O'Connor, *Mystery and Manners* (New York: Farrar, Straus and Giroux, 1969), p. 115.

PART V

Goals and Standards for Applied Studies in the Humanities

CHAPTER 12

Applied History
Policy Roles and Standards for Historians

PETER N. STEARNS

Many historians have been casting about for new or enhanced non-academic roles during the past several years. The Public History Association, one symptom of this new concern, is now six years old. The proliferation of graduate programs in historic perservation, archival training, and policy history also dates from about six years ago, although some specific programs have existed longer. At the same time, the new currents have hardly overwhelmed established professional operations in the discipline. Many academic historians are literally unaware of the surge. Some, dimly aware, are rather confused about what nonacademic history involves. They may see it as a new statement of history's relevance, recalling curricular battles of the 1960s, and therefore may claim participation without altering established habits. Or they may exaggerate the novelty of the effort and so oppose it as a threat to cherished disciplinary canons. There is continued need, then, to attempt a precise definition of what the new-wave, nonacademic history consists of, and where specifically policy-relevant history fits within this broader rubric.

Need also exists for a discussion of the standards that can be applied to public and policy history. The obvious cause of the public history surge—the growing cramp within academic ranks—raises equally obvious questions about the legitimacy of the effort. Is public history much more than a repackaging of familiar goods? Can it attract topflight historical thinking? There is obvious danger that new, somewhat gimmicky programs will draw only second-rate practitioners, with the choice positions, however reduced in number, still reserved for the standard ac-

PETER N. STEARNS • Department of History, Carnegie-Mellon University, Pittsburgh, Pennsylvania 15213.

ademic mode. The perceived decline in the quality as well as the number of history graduate students in recent years raises problems of standards even for historical research conventionally defined; these problems may be exacerbated by the simultaneous creation of new, seemingly job-relevant training outlets. Furthermore, even if these initial issues of quality can be handled, some elements of the public history approach, including the kind of research that claims new applicability to policy, raise intrinsic questions about evaluation according to established disciplinary canons. Nonacademic historians will be working for new clients and will perhaps be more directly constrained by their clients than conventional historians have been. They will be writing, if successful, not primarily for other academics or in publications in the history discipline—and as a result conventional historians will have problems of access to their work; the interaction between public and academic historians may prove difficult. In addition, then, to the attempt to improve a definition of historians' policy roles, there is need to stimulate discussion of the criteria for evaluating good and bad work in this newer genre.

The discussion of what applied history is and what its standards should be comes at a somewhat awkward time amid the new surge of interest in history's policy applications. A well-defined movement exists in policy-relevant history. Its practitioners agree on a number of key approaches and on the justification for their endeavor. Further basic definition risks redundancy for this group; this is where the discussion of standards, once certain conventions are briefly repeated, can be of particular interest, for such discussion works toward the next step in the field's theoretical development. At the same time, applied history is just beginning to catch the attention of other historians and humanists. Their new awareness leads to some confusion about how applied history differs from the relevance they quite rightly claim for themselves; it leads to criticisms, both valid and less valid, about applied history's intentions. For this group, some basic definition must be added to the discussion of standards. But the differential awareness of the committed and vaguely aware logically produces a final topic, of concern to anyone assessing a new application of the historical discipline: is the novelty both justified and necessary, in articulating valid uses of history that are not accomplished through conventional research? We are entering the stage, rather predictably, in which we reach a dialogue of the deaf, between specialists and generalists, partisans and skeptics; there are ways not to avoid controversy but to improve the focus of debate. As conventional historians increasingly come to grips with what has been a rather isolated current, questions about basic justification will multiply, and properly handled, they can help the applied historian advance his own conceptual structure as well.

DEFINITIONS: GOALS OF HISTORY AND POLICY USAGE

For all the recent flurry, historians have been slower than those in several kindred disciplines to define their nonacademic roles. Individual historians have long been employed in policy research areas, and various historians, academic and otherwise, have dealt successfully with other nonacademic publics. But a sense of identity, and a corresponding effort to define standards, has been lacking. Policy researchers have been hangers-on, at best, in the major associations in the discipline, their status a matter of individual commitment. Historians contrast, in this respect, with groups such as the applied anthropologists, who have taken a major role in areas such as health policy and who have their own association and professional standards.[1]

The reasons for history's lag, even aside from public perceptions of irrelevance, are not far to seek. Teachers so dominate history, in terms of sheer numbers, that other outlets or potential outlets have been downplayed until recently, even amid an employment crisis. Far more trained historians already work in the policy field than is commonly recognized, for professional historical associations are only now waking up to the desirability of counting and courting nonacademic professionals. Further, the fact that every member of our society has some expectations about what history is, based on school experience, adds to the constraints on the discipline's escaping a purely academic definition. History is the past, and we are not as yet a society attuned to recognizing explicitly that the past is particularly useful. Even many nonacademic history buffs, enjoying the antiquarian products of the discipline, curtail historians' assertions of utility beyond entertainment.

General Relevance

History has various claims, however, to wide public relevance. The largest claim, pervading history teaching as well as nonacademic activities, involves history as a basic ingredient of a liberal education, a key discipline in explaining how the world works. Academic history merits an important role in training policy makers. It instills careful research

[1]Willis F. Sibley, "Applied History and Applied Anthropology," unpublished paper, Cleveland State University (April, 1982).

habits, a sense of change over time, sensitivity to situations different from our own. Many historians could improve upon their utility in training future policy makers. For example, more explicit exploration of quite contemporary history, with careful analysis of how the present links to the past, might well be built into history surveys.[2] Too often, now, recent history is least well covered, and the present is not placed in context but rather ignored as something social scientists can best come to grips with. In research training, similarly, insufficient articulation is given to generalizable and distinctive skills, of utility outside the history classroom. Nevertheless, although historians are not always as thoughtful as they might be in preparing students to use history in the world's work, and although admittedly the relevance of historical training still needs defense in American curricular life, there should be little question about the basic issue. Policymakers who lack a historical sense and an understanding of how the past informs the present will function less well, have less grasp of how both they and the problems with which they deal fit into broader processes of change, than policymakers whose education did include a serious historical component. Similarly, good conventional historical research, and not only on the recent period, provides vital background information about present policy institutions and problems and examples of relevant policy functions in the past.

Academic history shades off into three other policy-relevant functions. History can be fruitfully used as part of direct training for policy work, not simply as part of a liberal educational background for such training. Practice in the use of analogy and an understanding of recent historical situations which will be part of the living memory of older colleagues with whom a fledgling policymaker will work can be built into the curriculum of business schools and public policy schools. Several models of such historical training have recently been developed, at a number of institutions.[3] This usage can be extended still further. It would be highly desirable for professionals such as doctors or engineers to be exposed to a serious, focused, and analytical history of their profession—and not the antiquarian glory trail that too often passes for medical or engineering history. Such exposure would place current practices in a temporal perspective, thus helping the recipients to view professional behavior as something more than a response to absolute dictates of science.

A second use for academic history is in dispelling policy-relevant assumptions about the past that are proved erroneous by orthodox his-

[2]Peter N. Stearns and Joel A. Tarr, "Applied History: A New-Old Departure," *The History Teacher* (August, 1981), pp. 517–531.
[3]Ernest May, "The Uses of History," grant proposal to the National Endowment for the Humanities, June 28, 1979.

torical research. The recent rise of social history has greatly extended historians' effective range in providing realistic understanding of a variety of social institutions in the past. When policymakers echo simplistic assumptions about the evolution of the family that help justify, possibly even help motivate current policy options, historians need to be able to correct the historical picture. Thus, to take a specific case, an understanding of the modern history of teenage sexuality—its major increase in the Western world from about 1780 onward—might modify shocked reactions of legislators suddenly concerned about present-day pregnancy statistics presented without any baseline from the past. The result of this kind of context need not prevent major new efforts at dealing with teenage pregnancy as a problem, but it warns against hasty reactions based on assumptions that some recent sexual revolution is alone responsible.[4] Another example: Many advocates of changes in current retirement policy point to a presumed golden age for old people when the elderly could work as long as they wished. Their image of the past is in error, and therefore some of their policy arguments are in error. We may need to modify current retirement policy, but we should not idealize the past as a justification for or guide to change in this area.[5] Historians need to develop as much outreach as possible, in adult programs and perhaps in direct policy consultation, in order to bring the most accurate picture of the past to bear on the issues of the day.

For historians do not need to urge that historical assumptions be used in approaching policy issues. Such assumptions are used whether historians intervene or not. There is simply no way to give full meaning to current data, whether on teenage pregnancy or the impact of retirement on the elderly, without some sense of how it compares to the past—some sense, therefore, of the nature and quality of trends that have led from a situation prior to present behavior, to the present behavior itself. At present we are poorly equipped to deal with assumptions about the past that prove false, because of historians' confinement to a youth-education role. The slowness of the dissemination of social history findings, as in the area of family evolution, suggests the need for a more aggressive and imaginative educational posture.

The third way that history inevitably intertwines with policy—not specific policy, but its orientation—is in its reflection of society's values. For good or ill, American society—and many other modern national societies—want to use history to reflect values; we find a presentation

---

[4]Maris Vinovskis, "An 'Epidemic' of Adolescent Pregnancy?" *Journal of Family History* 6 (1981): pp. 205–30.
[5]Lawrence Stone, "Walking Over Grandma," *New York Review of Books* 24 (1977): pp. 10–16; Andrew Achenbaum, *Old Age in the New Land* (Baltimore: Johns Hopkins, 1979).

of values through history more persuasive and textured than an abstract statement.[6] Thus, the values about America conveyed through textbooks clearly affect policy; and the values of smaller groups, reflected in feminist history for example, affect policy formulations of these groups. For good or ill also, but again surely inevitably, historians themselves use history to promote values, including their evaluation of their own times. Classic cases of the policy impact of such usage are the successive nineteenth-century French revolutionary invocations of interpretations of the great French revolution, as part of the intellectual buildup for another effort: first Guizot's interpretation, for 1830, then Lamartine's and Blanc's, for 1848, then (without the ensuing revolution) that of Jaurès. But another case in point, also interesting and more recent, was President Carter's fascination with Christopher Lasch's historical interpretation of the contemporary American personality.[7] Historians, in their wide evaluative function, inevitably impinge on the way policy is made and justified.

These aspects of history's policy relevance—its liberal educational role including key skills the discipline imparts, its insertion into policy training, its role in dispelling myths, and its related role in conveying values—are all part of history as conventionally performed, by academics. They can profit by some improved articulation, as part of the ongoing defense of relevance, and in the case of a policy-training role they demand some clever curricular manipulation, but they do not demand a recasting of the ways in which historians are accustomed to proceed. And the roles of conventional history are important; indeed, while arguing now for a more explicit policy function in addition, I would regard them as fundamental. One of the questions about an applied or policy history genre is the extent to which it might conflict with these more general, contextual functions, particularly that of critical evaluation.[8]

Recently, a number of historians, working at first in partial independence from each other, have revived a more explicit claim toward application: that historians should be directly involved in policy research and formulation. Their claim relates to the broader relevance of history; it certainly in no way disputes the desire of conventional academic historians to serve the training of policymakers in various ways. But applied history is not simply a restatement of the larger relevance argument. It seeks an expanded policy role for history, beyond the indirect role of education, even when that education is part of a policy-training process.

[6]Carl Degler, "Presidential Address," *Journal of American History* 67 (1980) pp. 7–25.
[7]Christopher Lasch, *The Culture of Narcissism* (New York: Norton, 1979).
[8]Degler, "Address," pp. 23–5.

Public History

Because it targets a nonacademic audience, applied history comes under the broader rubric of the current public history movement. Definitions here have become muddied of late, because of historians' new-found enthusiasm for novel roles. Hence, in addition to differentiating applied history from relevant history in general, the fit of applied history within public history requires comment.

Public history basically involves the use of history outside the academic context, for clients different from teenagers and conventional scholarly publishers.[9] Thus, public history includes the entertainment and edification of adults through museums and preservation efforts, media presentations, and group or institutional memorial histories that contribute to a sense of identity. This first aspect of public history, which focuses on methods of presentation to a nonconventional audience, may of course have policy implications. Group or neighborhood histories may spur or contribute to a new sense of dignity, thus feeding demands for new rights and possibly influencing the nature of the demands. History in this sense, though mainly of the academic variety, has recently served black and feminist movements. It has contributed to the labor movement as well, although more clearly in Europe than in this country; the current success of the *History Workshop* in England, uniting professional and amateur historians around shared political as well as scholarly goals, is a case in point. Public history presentations may also help historians grapple with misconceptions of the past that have policy implications. Thus, as professional historians aid and build on the current interest in family roots, they may teach not only research methods but a broader, conceptual understanding of the family as an institution over time. This in turn can contribute greater accuracy to the invocation of history in family-policy matters.

The first aspect of public history is vast, with many facets. It entails various kinds of nonacademic training, in media, museum work, and the like. With the exceptions noted, however, it is not directed at policy goals. And applied history, which does aim at such goals, is therefore a distinctive subset of public history, coexisting in fact somewhat uncomfortably with public history's other purposes.

History and Policy

Two kinds of history have direct and exclusive policy usage. The first is designed to provide a usable memory for corporations, branches

[9]See the journal *The Public Historian.*

of government, and private groups. This function begins at an archival base but includes far more than record keeping.[10] It involves making intelligible and accessible institutional actions of the past that help explain institutional dilemmas in the present. It involves providing instances of successful behavior in the past that has seemingly been forgotten but which might provide useful examples in present circumstances. According to report, the Polaroid Corporation recently sought historical explanation for decade-long difficulties with its labor force. It correctly perceived that one way to explain these difficulties and therefore to deal with them was to trace their origin, for the difficulties contrasted with an earlier pattern of labor relations within the corporation. According to report again, during the later phases of the Carter administration, an effort was mounted to recall the bases of success of the Marshall Plan, on grounds that this example of efficient action contrasted with the limper results of policy implementation in more recent decades. These two cases illustrate what may prove to be a growing use for analytical historical research. The size of modern bureaucracies and their fluctuations in personnel prevent any automatic memory of past policies. A new kind of record keeping is needed to match the changes in our institutional framework. The chronicler of kings can give way to the historian directly charged with handling masses of data and applying it selectively to current concerns.

This kind of policy history has yet to be fully analyzed. Press notices have dealt interestingly with individual cases in the corporate sphere, but no overall statement of goals and methods has emerged. The bureaucratic memory function almost surely expresses some tension between historian as memorialist—the traditional business-commissioned role—and more direct policy involvement, including critical analysis. One historian for a major corporation, for example, frequently performs quickie research on the company's glories, as ballast for public presentations by executives, along with some serious social impact research. There is tension also between a largely descriptive, record-keeping role— surely part of the usable memory function—and an analytical, policy-relevant use of these data. Despite these tensions, and the fledgling

---

[10]Michael C. Robinson, "Retrospective Management Analysis: A Test Case," *Public Works Historical Society* (1981), pp. 4–6; Thomas W. Riley and John G. Adorjan, "Company History: A By-Product of Good Records Management," *ARMA Quarterly* (October, 1981), pp. 5–8; Dan J. Forrestal, "Playing It Straight with Company Histories," *Public Relations Journal*, (February, 1978), pp. 27–8; Alexander Barrie, "Why Sponsor a Company History?" *Business World* (December, 1977), pp. 15–6; G. D. Smith and Laurence E. Steadman, "Present Value of Corporate History," *Harvard Business Review* (November–December, 1981); Margaret Price, "Corporate Historians: A Rare But Growing Breed," *Industry Week*, March 23, 1981, pp. 87–90.

status of the "new" corporate historians, I am increasingly persuaded of the opportunity and need for a serious historical research function as part of the continued development of bureaucratic operations.[11] Growing use of historical analysis in military policy evaluation, building from but going beyond the traditional training in strategic analogies, suggests a relevant pattern here.

Applied history *per se* involves more than providing a usable bureaucratic memory. It seeks to employ historical data and analysis in ways that will improve the definition of policy problems, aid in assessment of policy options, and directly suggest best options. Applied history could be called policy history, to help avoid the current confusions of *public, applied,* and *relevant,* save that policy history narrowly connotes a background statement on the development of past policies. Applied historians invoke their label both in tandem with other applied movements in kindred disciplines and because of prior usage of the term in a previous foray of historians into the policy field, during the late stages of the Progressive Era.[12]

Applied historians claim the utility of a number of conceptual approaches to historical data, singly or in tandem, as their approach to policy research and formulation. These approaches are elaborately defined in existing literature and need be only briefly summarized here.[13]

1. *Analogy.* Historians have clearly demonstrated that policymakers use analogy whether historians like it or not, both in framing policy responses and in justifying such responses after the fact.[14] Thus it is important to allow trained historians to assess the adequacy and germaneness of the analogies evoked in a policy situation, important also to allow historians to develop improved criteria, including multiple examples, in identifying and assessing possible analogies.

[11]Historical Evaluation and Research Organization, *Use of Historical Data in Evaluating Military Effectiveness* (Dunn Loring, VA: Hero, 1980) and *Historical Trends Related to Weapon Lethality* (Dunn Loring, VA: Hero, 1977); Henry Eccles, *Military Concepts and Philosophy* (New Brunswick, NJ: Rutgers, 1965); Julian Critchley, *Warning and Response: A Study of Surprise Attack in the Twentieth Century and an Analysis of Its Lessons for the Future* (New York: Crane-Russak, 1978); Stetson Conn, "The Pursuit of Military History," *Military Affairs* 30 (1966), pp. 1–8; Harry Yoshpe, *Our Missing Shield: The U.S. Civil Defense Program in Historical Perspective* (Washington, D.C.: Government Printing Office, 1981).

[12]Alan M. Schroder, "Applied History, and Early Form of Public History," *Public Works Historical Society Newsletter* #17 (1980), pp. 3–4; Benjamin Shambaugh, "Editor's Introduction," *Applied History* I (Iowa City: 1912), viii–xiii.

[13]Ernest May, *"Lessons" of the Past: The Use and Misuse of History in American Foreign Policy* (New York: Oxford, 1973); Seymour Mandelbaum, "The Past in Service to the Future,"*Journal of Social History* 11 (1977), pp. 193–205; Peter N. Stearns, "History and Policy Analysis: Toward Maturity," *The Public Historian* 4 (1982), pp. 5–29.

[14]May, "Lessons"; Mandelbaum, "Past"; David F. Trask, "Historians and Teamwork: The Case of Crisis Management," *American Historical Association Newsletter* 19 (1981), pp. 6–7.

Analogy has a special role in foreign policy and defense. Large numbers of historians are already employed in the military sector, training strategists and using historical analogies as a direct means of suggesting and testing possible strategies for the future.[15]

Analogy is also involved in the newer, less widely known field of retrospective assessments. Retrospective technology, the best-developed case, uses careful study of the impacts of past technologies to guide forecasts about the installation and particularly the impact of technologies in the future.[16] Here, as in analogical usage more generally, the essential argument is that history is the only available laboratory for many large social phenomena; that a purely narrative, beginning-to-end kind of descriptive history does not provide sufficiently usable or focused conclusions; that a carefully developed analogical approach produces some usable guidelines and caveats in the many situations wherein accurate prediction is impossible.

After the first flush of recent, explicit discussion of the use of analogy in politics—the basic approach, of course, goes back to Thucydides with a new lease on life gained in the Renaissance—some applied historians have become discouraged about analogy's potential for much save error. It is probable that analogy is sufficiently inescapable and that sufficient tools can be developed to improve its usage, that the analogical approach will continue to be a staple in the applied historian's contribution to policy.

Thus Ernest May and others urge improvements in the use of analogy by means of (a) increased explicitness about analogy's role in policy thinking and historians' role in providing analogies whether they mean to or not; (b) use of a wide range of analogies rather than a single particularly compelling case, often drawn from policymakers' political memory; and (c) analysis of the range of analogies in terms of key ingredients, toward improving the tests of applicability, rather than across-the-board comparisons.

Other applied history strategies are less ingrained than the habits of analogy, but they are in fact more promising. They include:

2. *Evaluation.* Policymakers are becoming increasingly aware that a host of policies are adopted without subsequent assessment. Essentially historical tools of data accumulation and interpretation aid in providing, say, ten-year impact statements. Evaluations of this sort—persuasively

[15]Conn, "Pursuit"; Critchley, *Warning.*

[16]Joel A. Tarr, ed., *Retrospective Technology Assessment* (San Francisco: Jossey-Bass, 1977); James McCurley, "The Historians' Role in the Making of Public Policy," *Social Science History* 3 (1979), pp. 202–7; Joel A. Tarr, "Changing Fuel Use Behavior and Energy Transitions: The Pittsburgh Smoke Control Movement: A Case Study in Historical Analogy," *Journal of Social History* 14 (1981), pp. 561–88.

suggested in a recent article on health care programs[17]—can contribute directly to reassessment of policies on the books or can be used analogically in subsequent policy situations.

3. *Paradigms.* Historians have had considerable recent success, at least in justifying policies adopted for economic reasons, by advancing a paradigmatic approach. This conceptual framework involves identifying the beginning point of a powerful new institutional or legislative approach to an endemic social issue, like what to do with the criminal or the insane, and showing the hidden agenda behind initial justifications of this approach. By proving (or, perhaps too commonly, assuming) that the institutional paradigm still obtains and is fraudulent as ever, historians can contribute to its reassessment. The paradigmatic approach involves both social and institutional factors and builds on the historian's sense of the importance of origins.[18]

Thus social control historians, pointing to the illiberal motives as well as results of apparently liberal reforms, launched early in the nineteenth century in public schooling and medical care, have had a serious impact at least in justifying measures such as deinstitutionalization in mental illness. They contend that exploding the myths surrounding the origins of key policies argues strongly for reversing the policies in question; thus, if asylum reform was not in fact liberal when first begun, the ongoing institutions it bequeathed probably harbor hidden and reprehensible control features. Similar paradigmatic efforts may be at work in the area of family and child care policy, here focusing on late nineteenth and early twentieth-century reform.[19] Even aside from social control paradigms, historians are well suited to deal with the inertia of key institutions as factors in realistic policy analysis.

4. *Trend assessment.* Applied historians are also interested in improving the definition of policy problems, and not just in evaluating or in finding analogies for policy response. Trend assessment here is a vital tool. Policy issues can be situated in time, to determine the power, constancy, and to some extent the predictability of their ingredients.

[17]R. C. Lippincott and J. W. Begum, "Competition in the Health Sector: A Historical Perspective," *Journal of Health, Politics, Policy and Law* 17 (1982), pp. 460–87; see also Phillip Smith and Peter Keen, "Historical Perspectives on School Financing," paper presented to the Second Annual Conference on Public History, Pittsburgh, PA, April 20, 1980.

[18]David J. Rothman, *The Discovery of the Asylum: Social Order and Disorder in the New Republic* (Boston: Little Brown, 1971); Rothman and Stanton Wheeler, eds., *Social History and Social Policy* (New York: Academic, 1981); John Conley, "Prisons, Production and Profit: Reconsidering the Importance of Prison Industries," *Journal of Social History* 14 (1980), pp. 257–75.

[19]Christopher Lasch, *Haven in a Heartless World: The Family Beseiged* (New York: Basic Books, 1977); Anthony Platt, *The Child Savers* (Chicago: University of Chicago Press, 1969).

Historians are more comfortable than most social scientists in dealing with breaks in trends or alterations in the factors supporting trends. They are also willing to deal with qualitative trends as well as behaviors that can be numerically represented. They can, for example, discuss social security policy in terms of trends in the quality of the retirement experience as well as demographic and fiscal trends.[20]

5. *Context.* Historians differ from most other policy experts in being trained to approach, fallibly to be sure, the whole human experience, and not just its economic, or political, or social facets. They thus can see linkages among aspects of a policy problem and assess probable consequences of a policy once adopted that may well escape other policy experts. Again, to use the social security example, the failure of most policy assessment to consider more than the juxtaposition of demographic and economic trends—to include not only an assessment of the retirement phenomenon in its historical dimensions but also an evaluation of political trends—represents a glaring example of the incompleteness of characteristic social science research.[21] This research rarely escapes its inherent tendency to segment the social experience according to disciplinary specialization. In this case, the failure to consider the kind of full context that most historians would automatically embrace had direct result in 1982 when President Reagan offered an economically and demographically justifiable, but politically disastrous, proposal in this area.

Applied historians thus have an arsenal of conceptual approaches through which they can organize historical data in ways directly relevant to policy formulation. They are genuine historians in that they seek to understand the role of change and continuity in explaining the human condition. At the same time, however, applied historians suggest the need for some distinctive training, in order to bridge the gap between conventional academic history and consistent policy roles.

APPLIED HISTORY AND CONVENTIONAL HISTORY

Training and Orientation

The distinctions sought through some special training and labeling include emphasis on the conceptual approaches outlined above, high-

---

[20]William Graebner, *The History of Retirement* (New Haven: Yale University Press, 1980); Gail B. King and Peter N. Stearns, "The Retirement Experience as a Policy Factor," *Journal of Social History* 14 (1981), pp. 589–626; an organizational inertia as a policy-relevant trend, see Anne Karalekas, "History of the CIA," U. S. Senate, Select Committee to Study Governmental Operations with Respect to Intelligence Activities, *Book III, Final Report* (Washington, D.C.: Government Printing Office, 1978).
[21]Felicity Skidmore, ed., *Social Security Financing* (Cambridge: M.I.T. Press, 1981), *passim.*

lighted explicitly as a set of analytical styles to be tested for applicability to any policy problem. Applied history as a distinctive genre is also intended to convey an unusual readiness to accommodate to the needs of public or private policy clients, much as applied branches of other disciplines are identified in order to avoid the impression of eager but unfocused job seeking—we are historians and it would be nice if some nonacademics gave us employment—or a purely academic style. Thus applied historians are urged to adopt suitable schedules for research, in order to meet the timing needs of real-world users. This on-demand timing ability is a key concern of actual employers, a point worth mentioning even to undergraduates in history—if not to one's own colleagues. Applied historians should seek appropriate brevity in presentation and experiment with a variety of presentation modes according to the usages not of academic history but of the policy area. They must be prepared to take topics from real policy needs, not from the dictates of a broader scholarly agenda. They must be willing to consider—usually—a fairly short and highly contemporary timespan and be able to treat this historically. In this they differ from the *de facto* reluctance of most academic historians to address the very contemporary with the same seriousness and analytical depth with which earlier time periods are approached.

Perhaps most important, applied historians must be more sensitive than academic historians to the need to cull out major conclusions and analytical generalizations, in lieu of a detailed narrative story. They may need to develop the narrative approach as part of their own preparation, but they can rarely hope to indulge this in a policy paper. To do so would be to court the kind of history-as-background usage that has bedeviled many historians' policy efforts in the past—the chapter that sets a problem chronologically but has no ongoing interaction with the subsequent policy research.[22] Finally, the applied historian must at least partially wean himself from the pure observer stance which the discipline normally inculcates. The degree of weaning will depend on circumstances, and it should never be complete. But applied historians must be prepared to make or at least assess policy recommendations. They must deal with the forecasting needs of many clients by offering predictions—and applied historians argue with some plausibility that through intelligent trend analysis, in context of broader forces, historians can deal effectively with a predictive approach. Or applied historians must offer alternatives to outright prediction and convince clients that these

---

[22]See, for example, Richard M. Brown, "Historical Patterns of American Violence," in H. D. Graham and T. R. Gurr, *Violence in America*, rev. ed. (Beverly Hills: Sage, 1979), pp. 19–48; Skidmore, *Financing*, ch. 1.

orientations to the future serve as a usable basis for forming policy. In the area of collective violence, for example, historians must note firmly the impossibility of predicting outbreaks but the necessity of using history to understand protest when it occurs and to grasp those factors that maximize the likelihood of protest.[23]

Distinction of Approach

The differences between applied history and conventional history permit graphic illustration. In 1968 the federal government, investigating collective violence, commissioned a number of historians to report on traditions of violence in the United States. Of necessity, the historians appealed to were academics. They produced some very fine essays, drawing on, among other things, the then-new current of social history which had already focused on protest as an index to the history of the lower classes. Of slightly less necessity, most of the historians appealed to offered either existing essays or quickly wrote descriptive summaries of incidents of violence in their major fields—resulting in comments on labor violence over time, vigilante movements, and so on. The result was a volume that has proved highly effective as a teaching instrument and which had some public impact, providing needed context for what was then an anguish-laden public concern.[24] And the volume had policy relevance: it taught that violence, however surprising amid the promises of the Great Society, was normal rather than novel and should not therefore be met with measures of desperation; that protesters were usually fairly solid citizens and that the protest movement of yesterday was often the respectable political current of today—which suggested restraint in dealing with current manifestations; and that the American tradition encouraged patterns of accommodation rather than thorough repression. These were useful messages, particularly in a chaotic period and after the misleading preachments of consensus historians who had distracted the American public from the extent to which violence and bitter disagreement had marked our past already.

But the volume was not applied history. The only essays that directly accomplished one of the topics an applied historian would first seize upon—what was new and what not new about current patterns of violence—was written by a sociologist. Historians blithely wrote about labor unrest with no attempt to juxtapose these patterns closely with current patterns. (They thus, in my view, failed to note the most important probable analogies between labor unrest and the urban violence of the

---

[23]Charles Tilly, *From Mobilization to Revolution* (Reading, MA: Addison-Wesley, 1978); Graham and Gurr, *Violence*.
[24]Graham and Gurr, *Violence*.

1960s, the early, unorganized manifestations of workers' agitation.) No historians provided a trend assessment of groups involved in the 1960s protest—young blacks, students—although this topic was clearly indicated by available knowledge. No historians, in other words, seized on the existing situation and used it as the basis for analysis. No historian ventured to offer an analogical shopping list of tactics that work or do not work in protest situations, although an alert reader can draw some analogies with Civil War draft riots and the response they elicited and with later nineteenth-century police strategies. Few historians even ventured into the second half of the twentieth century, leaving this for other social scientists and a single historian who had himself participated in the peace movement. And so the volume, interesting and useful as it was, produced only the vaguest policy guidelines and only the vaguest understanding of how current protest groups and tactics fit or failed to fit established patterns. Applied historians, in other words, could hopefully have contributed the genuine perspective that historians did provide (or have had the wit to call upon conventional historians to do so); but they could have addressed current concerns more directly, providing perspective and analogy explicitly relevant to policy options; and—so I fondly imagine—they could have done so quickly enough, as against historians' notorious work habits, to have met commission deadlines.

In defining applied history, then, we speak of some differences of orientation in research approach—not total differences, leading to some quantum leap in policy relevance, but differences nonetheless, and some even clearer differences in work styles and client sensitivity.

The applied historian, in sum, means to be a somewhat distinct version of the disciplinary genus. He not only seeks a nonacademic policy role but also develops some specific training and habits to qualify for this role. This does not, of course, prevent certain historians from operating effectively in both applied and academic spheres. Nor should there be any new inhibition regarding conventionally trained historians' policy career options; the transference has worked well in the past and should continue. Nor, finally, is there any assertion of applied history as a novel discipline. Applied historians are arguing that some new training ingredients can usefully increase historians' participation in policy research. They are aiming for kinds of topical focus different from those that have interested even most contemporary historians, and certainly for different kinds of patrons. Applied history may at times have to move against some of the currents in the mainstream discipline. If, for example, academic historical research returns to a more familiar narrative mode, as Lawrence Stone and others have suggested,[25] I think

---

[25]Lawrence Stone, *The Past and the Present* (London: Longmans, 1981), pp. 74–98.

applied historians will have to hold out for a more analytical approach, on grounds of the limited efficacy of narrative information in actual policy research.

Standards

The real and potential differences between applied and conventional history raise some obvious questions about appropriate standards for historians' policy work. Applied historians will normally be publishing in specialty journals rather than in mainstream historical outlets. This process has already begun, as historians peddle their wares to journals in educational testing, gerontology, and the like. This pattern is obviously different in kind from more familiar topical specializations, like the history of medicine or the history of public works, that produce journals read by nonhistorians as well as historians but which are controlled by conventional canons of the discipline. Applied and conventional historians will not always be talking to each other. Indeed, the separateness of the largest group of current applied history practitioners (*de facto*, though not so labeled), those doing military history for policy usage, provides a model for what can become a major problem of communication. And this means, as the military example may also suggest, problems of maintaining standards acceptable to the mother discipline.

For applied history raises several questions about standards, even aside from the tricky issue of relationships with academic history. It may attract relatively less able historians, who are lured by the prospect of jobs rather than devotion to the discipline itself. Many problems that applied historians will be called to work upon will hardly command immense intellectual respect. Chasing around legal records for evidence at land use hearings, combing corporate files for information about a single company's labor relations in the past decade, correlating Pittsburgh crime records and personnel allocations over two decades to produce recommendations on future staffing policy—these are hardly topics to rival the conceptual sweep of a Genovese or even the narrative elegance of a Mattingly. Thus, putting the most obvious problems together, one admits a distinct possibility that applied history may disproportionately attract the attention of second-rate people who possess third-rate skills because they are rather hastily trained in conventional history and who work on fourth-rate problems. But the charge can go deeper still. Applied history may threaten some of the virtues of history in its policy perspective role. Applied historians, hired by specific clients to work on definable policy issues, are not likely to be encouraged to roam widely into discussions of values, to serve thus as moral critics of their society or even some policy-relevant segment thereof. Their dependence on interested parties as patrons may jeopardize, even obscure any claim to objectivity. Fundamentally, their temptation to make recommendations, to be useful, may rob them of the detachment that is so vital to history as the classic evaluative discipline. Historians may offer more policy benefit by their promise or threat to measure each president after the fact, with the consciousness of working for a potentially hostile record that this prospect visibly induces, than if they actually worked for presidents on specific policy issues. The involvement of applied historians in the canons of whatever institution they normally work for may lead to bias the more dangerous because it is not clearly felt. This is a charge already leveled at military historians, accused even in their more critical work of furthering a larger militarist mentality in the American public.[26] After all, we have long harbored a suspicion that most historians of the contemporary period, even when superbly academic, have been little more than journalists, lacking the access to data and, even more serious, the perspective necessary to write good history. All the more we may suspect applied historians who work the same time period (for the most part), have even less time to gather data, and may not be allowed to wear tweeds.

How can an applied historian react to these charges? The movement is too novel for a coherent body of standards and criteria to exist. Some applied historians find aspects of the concern about standards premature—wait until we have had a chance to be corrupted and then we can talk about it. But many of the issues relating to standards have been discussed, if not resolved; ongoing concern is part of the standard-maintenance process itself.

A first large reaction to some of the charges adopts the "look who's talking" approach, and although this reaction cannot be the final word on the subject, it does have some merit.

Thus, are most academic historians in fact live-wire types, producing work that commands high conceptual interest, or indeed producing any work at all? One aspect of the discussion of second-ratism is that it tends to stem from first-rate (or aspirant) historians who forget about their own colleagues. I believe that the real problem of applied history, in this area, is not that it will attract many second-raters working on small problems—for history and all disciplines do this already—but whether it will attract some first-rate minds, capable of leavening the process, monitoring a good bit of specific research and making larger theoretical statements. And here, frankly, the evidence is not yet in.

Thus, let us be a bit cautious about throwing around charges of

[26]Peter Carsten, "Demilitarizing Military History: Servants of Power or Agents of Understanding?" *Military Affairs* 38 (1972), pp. 88–92.

client-induced bias. Surely a conventional discipline that regularly produces myopically patriotic school texts can hardly claim that its present clients induce no distortions in results. In fact, the largest case of existing applied historical work, that of military policy history, suggests substantial critical latitude. It is true that few Defense Department-employed analysts have condemned the whole military establishment, but many have vigorously criticized strategic decisions and previous military policy options. Indeed, historical work on the Korean war and on the Philippine insurgency helped produce the military's reluctance to become involved in Vietnam—for the military, we now know, had the most accurate historical analogies available. So, conventional history, even in academic sanctuaries, is not free from client pressure, and applied history need not be overwhelmed by such pressure. A good client, in fact, will want to allow some latitude in retrospective assessment, lest nothing be learned from the past at all. The remarks do not remove the issue of special bias and lack of perspective, but they do somewhat narrow the charge.

One angle of the bias problem merits separate attention, for it promises considerable confusion if and when applied historians take recognizable roles in government and corporate policy research. Many historians are likely to worry about applied history's service to the established order. Historians have a significant record of partisanship, sometimes of quite effective partisanship. They have used history to help rally and to add substance to partisan arguments of the day. In some cases, they have actually helped shape issues of the day. Surely one of the most telling examples of policy-effective history in recent decades is the corpus of revisionist diplomatic history, which contributed so heavily to policy reassessments and to changes in public perceptions of policy in the later 1960s. A large body of what Carl Degler calls instrumentalist history was developed in the past two decades also.[27] Feminist historians, for example, have used history effectively to illustrate present wrongs to be righted. Instrumentalist history supports current advocacies by reviving past examples of effective action and by giving historical depth to statements of inequities. Applied history, as outlined above, can be part of an instrumentalist approach. That is, applied historians can contribute to policy analysis by radical groups and in favor of the underdog.[28] But applied history is in principle neutral—it is not called to serve radical causes alone, or even primarily. In fact, successful applied history will often be found in service to established institutions. And this may rouse comments from other kinds of partisan historians that go beyond quar-

---

[27]Degler, "Address."

[28]Lee Benson, "Doing History As Moral Philosophy and Public Advocacy: A Practical Strategy to Lessen the Crisis in American History," paper presented to the Organization of American Historians, April 1, 1981.

rels of viewpoint to statements that peculiar faults inhere in the applied history approach. There is a tendency among instrumentalist historians to cover partisan quarrels with broader claims of conceptual inadequacy—at an extreme, as if historians lose objectivity when they stop serving the left.[29] Instrumentalist historians have every reason to monitor applied history to make sure that it is good history, and indeed to shift their own work to some extent from an instrumentalist to an applied mode in service of their cause. But it is important not to allow issues of partisanship to confuse or artificially to heighten the problems inherent in service to policy clients. Applied historians, whatever their client, can argue that their concern for human values, as part of the relevant historical record, can conduce to wiser, more sensitive policy than that produced by, say, economists and lawyers alone.

Even aside from any partisan confusions, ethical concerns must bedevil the elaboration of an applied history approach. Applied historians already debate among themselves the extent to which their research should confine itself to presentation and assessment of policy options, as opposed to shading over into actual advocacy.

In addition to what should be an ongoing internal debate, applied historians must benefit from regular interaction with conventional, academic historians. Applied history, if successful, is destined to become a subfield, not a separate discipline and not an approach that overshadows conventional historical research. Conventional historians, properly involved, can help keep applied historians honest, reducing undue client pressure for manipulation of results. As important, they can help applied historians, often devoted to a series of small research projects, link to wider conceptual concerns. Interaction begins, of course, with training programs which overlap applied historical and conventional historical work. The current interest of professional associations in reengaging historians already in policy positions with the wider discipline should aid the necessary interaction process. Interaction should include journals to which both types of historians contribute. Periodic opportunity to present applied history findings to an academic audience should encourage both generalization and linkage to broader problems of interpretation, otherwise easily forgotten by a practitioner accustomed to writing for policy specialists alone. Interaction must include a regular

---

[29]Tony Judt, "A Clown in Regal Purple: Social History and the Historians," *History Workshop*, 3 (1979), pp. 66–94. The radical critique has indeed begun already, and in its comments on policy-relevant history it reflects precisely the confusion between political and professional standards suggested here: Howard Green, "A Critique of the Professional Public History Movement," *Radical History Review*, 9 (1981), pp. 164–73. Other articles in this issue make considerably more useful remarks about other aspects of public history.

reviewing of applied history work, as produced for clients or at least as generalized from client-sponsored work. This procedure, which will require new flexibility and outreach on the part of academic journals, is essential not only to protect applied historians from the narrowest pressures of client sponsorship but also to encourage the kind of context, derived ultimately from orthodox historical research, that applied historians justly tout as one of their chief selling points. Interaction is important, finally, as a means of bringing into historians' range some excellent, essentially applied historical research that is not done by professionally trained historians but that bears both on policy concerns and on the standard research concerns of contemporary historians.[30]

Along with some careful and innovative procedures for interaction, applied history will benefit from some serious reconsideration of the place of contemporary history in historical research. Applied history provides opportunity to supplement and possibly to improve the analytical level of contemporary historical work. Here is the best response to the problem of the quality of researchers and issues which applied history will involve. Too much contemporary history has been purely fact-finding and narrative, reluctant to raise broader problems of interpretation. Revealingly, the most compelling histories of the United States since 1920—the histories that have an interpretive slant—have been written by nonhistorians.[31] Revealingly, also, the best work in social history, itself the most exciting addition to conventional historical research over the past twenty years, stops well short of 1920. Outside of diplomatic history, even leading work on the development of key institutions since the New Deal has often flowed from nonhistorians—or it is not available. There is, in other words, vital need for a revivification of contemporary history even from the standpoint of conventional academic research. We have too little sense of basic periodization, too little sense of the interrelationship among trends. And although some of this reflects the undeniable problems of contemporary history—the issues of data availability and perspective—some reflects an unfortunate unwillingness to take the same kinds of conceptual risks that the better practitioners routinely attempt with earlier periods. Applied history, in other words, will depend on a particular interaction with a breed of conventional historians willing to take on the service economy or post-immigrant ethnicity as serious historical issues. Applied history does run the risk of acquiring the journalistic, ho-hum taint of much contem-

---

[30]For example, Martha Derthick, *Policymaking for Social Security* (Washington, D.C.: Brookings Institution, 1979), unfortunately unreviewed in historical journals.
[31]Morris Janowitz, *The Last Half-Century: Societal Change and Politics in America* (Chicago: University of Chicago, 1978).

porary history—but it may also provide some incentive for a new approach.[32]

Interaction between applied and academic historians, through reviewing, shared journals, workshops, must serve one final feature of applied history itself. Applied historians are specially trained or at least distinctively oriented, to serve clients, cooperate with policy experts from other fields, participate rather than merely observe. But they are historians, and they are seeking to redirect certain aspects of policy research because of their fundamentally historical approach. They are not, in other words, meant to abandon some basic elements of their craft in their eagerness to please new masters. And they will need support from and regular contact with academic historians, including academic historians skeptical of the legitimacy of a direct policy role, in order to fulfill their mission.

Thus applied historians must be prepared to quarrel with some characteristic social science approaches to policy research. Concern for qualitative factors, including the role of human values in shaping policy problems and political realities, may frequently lead historians to broaden the evidence base that social scientists prefer.[33] Sensitivity to change may lead to disputes over the appropriateness of static modeling procedures, in adequately characterizing policy actors.[34] Applied historians will frequently be dealing with some rooted historical assumptions of policymakers themselves, which must be handled tactfully, without displays of academic bravado, but very definitely addressed. They may also have occasion to quarrel with conclusions reached in undue haste or with unduly facile predictions as the basis for policy decisions.

Applied historians essentially argue not only that history has relevant data and concepts that can be fruitfully employed in policy work. They argue also that policy research cannot avoid history, which therefore should be done well, and that policy research devoid of participation by trained historians is often bad research. They do not accept all the existing parameters in policy research and formation, humbly hoping for a few crumbs for themselves. To varying degrees, depending on the type of issue or policy area, they argue for some substantial changes in

[32]Edward Berkowitz and Kim McQuade, *Creating the Welfare State* (New York: Praeger, 1980).

[33]"Special Issue on Applied History," *Journal of Social History* 14 (1981), pp. 533–738; Stearns, "History and Policy Analysis," pp. 22–3.

[34]Baruch Fischoff, "For Those Condemned to Study the Past: Reflections on Historical Judgment," in R. A. Sheden and D. W. Fiske, eds., *New Directions for Methodology of Behavioral Science* (San Francisco: Jossey-Bass, 1980); Oran Young, "The Perils of Odysseus," in R. H. Ullman and Raymond Tanter, eds., *Theory and Policy in International Relations* (Princeton: Princeton University Press, 1972).

approach; and their contact with orthodox academic historians will support their stance.

Interaction and Differentiation: Reprise

The central thrust of applied history, vis-à-vis much existing policy research, is its focus on a grasp of complex processes of change as a key to many policy issues. Current applied history stems in fact from improvements in historians' grasp of change, particularly their new understanding of processes as well as events.[35] Applied historians thus differ from many social scientists who, true to their Enlightenment heritage, prefer static models of rational behavior or at best change proceeding in set directions or measurable by a small cluster of quantifiable indicators in their standard research approach. Like all good historians, applied historians are attuned to differential rates of change in a policy situation and are open to possible shifts in direction, or periodization, in key institutional or behavioral trends. This concern for change, in an area that does not conceptualize change well, is basic to the intellectual spice that applied history can offer its practitioners along with pragmatic appeal.

The standard historical interest in categorizing and explaining change returns us to a final definitional problem, already evoked but usefully confronted in summary. Since applied history is history, why bother with distinctive definitions or training? Many historians sympathetic to applied history's general goals will seek to subsume them under existing claims of relevance. Even some historians currently working in policy areas resist the idea of specialized training, on grounds that conventional history served them well and that an applied movement might demean their credentials.

Applied historians stake their claim to partial distinction from conventional history on two basic points. First, existing policy errors and omissions, based on neglect or incomprehension of historical findings or failure to seek historical analysis, suggest a definite need for more explicit policy approaches than history as a discipline has ventured in recent decades. Applied historians in this sense claim little basic novelty save in their explicit approach to the policy world. If conventional history had regularly attracted policy interest and use, the need for a discrete applied movement might well not exist. But the facts are otherwise. Hence new labels and some specialized training become essential.

[35]On applied history's relation to advances in conventional history, see Michael Kammen, ed., *The Past Before Us* (Ithaca, NY: Cornell University Press, 1980), and Peter N. Stearns, "History and Public Policy," George McCall, ed., *Social Science and Public Policy* (Port Washington, NY: Faculty Press, 1984), 91–128.

Second, applied historians note some characteristic habits among conventional historians that limit their policy effectiveness: difficulty in producing on demand; tendency to prefer chronological statements that locate a problem in time, over more focused conceptual work; reluctance to approach contemporary history and so—particularly in domestic policy matters—an undue temptation to spin a paradigmatic approach based on analysis of earlier periods even when called upon to talk about current policy;[36] and sheer inexperience in nonacademic modes. Anyone who has tried to reorient a student from a soup-to-nuts background approach—gun control from the Bill of Rights onward, for example—in favor of a history dynamically integrated with a grasp of a current policy issue, or anyone who has seen history used not only to locate a policy problem in time but to explicate it and to suggest options toward its solution can hardly doubt that applied historians must minimize some common impulses of the basic discipline.

These claims against conventional history are made carefully, without intent to displace or demean conventional research and with full realization of the need for continuous interaction between applied and mainstream history in order to guard standards of objectivity, maintain interpretive sophistication, and develop a new appreciation of the nature of social change as against existing policy research modes. Applied historians, in other words, seek a genuine identity that includes but is not confined to the tactical advantages to be gained from some distinctions from mainstream history—a genuine identity, but not a completely independent one.

This partial distinction dictates an overlapping but not entirely uniform set of standards in evaluating the quality of research results in applied history. Some humanists make a good case for a simple identity of standards: good philosophy thus is good philosophy, whether applied or not. To a point, this judgment should define the evaluation of applied history. Research methods and accurate rendering of sources, including an imaginative quest for relevant sources, do not distinguish the applied from the conventional. Careful handling of conceptual tools, such as periodization, should mark both branches, for the basic interest in the intelligible presentation of change must describe historians of all types. And these shared methodological and analytical values are the most important evaluative standards a historian has. But to go from this to the blanket assertion of unity risks some excessive academic contraints on applied historians. Thus applied historians cannot be measured by conventional canons in their choice of topic; they cannot be made to

---

[36]This tendency to redo conventional history when asked to apply to policy is a key fault of the rather disappointing Rothman and Wheeler volume (*Social History and Social Policy*).

play the game of filling academic research gaps or playing off against existing interpretations (although sometimes they will in fact contribute in both areas). Client-induced adjustments in form of presentation will also require some separate evaluation. Because applied historians will in fact be assessed by clients for their policy utility, it will become essential to build this criterion into the field itself lest it be misused by the narrowest client interest. It is this test, fundamentally, that conventional history cannot supply and might indeed distort through "normal" measurements of interest and originality. And it is in this respect that applied history must spin off from conventional evaluation. Applied historians must be able to judge a work to be good history but not good applied history—as in the case of *Violence in America;* and a study that because of topic choice is not recognized as interesting conventional history may still be ratable as good applied history even though it must pass strict tests in terms of use of sources and conceptualization.

Finally, applied history standards, including as they do an awareness of analytical approach, may usefully inform conventional criteria; even in overlap, the relationship involves more than the authority of the mother discipline imposed over her newest child. The explicitness with which applied historians can discuss their conceptual approach, as in use of analogy or trend assessment, may at times usefully fertilize the evaluations of conventional history itself, which are often unduly self-contained, often insufficiently articulate about how a particular piece of research contributes to the understanding of change. Even where evaluative standards overlap, in other words, applied historians need not always be docile handmaidens to superior academic brethren.

Prospects

The chances of applied history's success in gaining recognition as a serious contributor to policy are difficult to estimate at present. Thus far, of necessity, the clearest enthusiasm has come from an academically based sector, and some of their efforts have in fact replicated conventional historical approaches. In a society legitimately perceived as insensitive to history, with social scientists asserting primacy in the policy arena, applied history's claims, even if accepted in principle, might seem rather hollow. The confusion of existing definitions, among public history's more general efforts, may augur badly for the future. History may succeed in other public efforts, related more clearly to academic teaching roles, by simply seeking nonacademic "students" among amateurs of family history or of restored villages and still fail to gain increased voice in policy.

Yet there are some more encouraging signs. Social scientists concerned about a poor track record in forecasting or about modeling approaches that move too far from empirical data are open to at least some of the analytical thrusts of applied history.[37] The real need for an intelligible bureaucratic memory, shown in a number of recent corporate moves to sponsor historical work, opens the way to additional historical contributions. In the public sector, researchers working as historians and not as people who happen to have been trained in history, are regularly called upon in fields ranging from technology impacts—oceanic pollution is a recent case in point—to police retirement systems.[38] The existing impact of applied history is by definition hard to calculate, because most practitioners write in specialty journals that are not historical. The genre has sufficient achievement to date and sufficient promise to warrant renewed emphasis on the central tensions in the field: to serve those who shape policy, without yielding to existing notions of what policy research should cover: to use real history, but with new principles of selectivity. Ongoing concern about standards of evaluation raises real, but on the whole manageable issues; the field is not damned to mediocrity or mindless venality. The basic proposition is simple: history is not only needed in policy but is already inescapable; but this fact has not led to systematic intelligent use of trained historians in policy work; applied history seeks to develop the special methods needed to close the gap. Whether the field will mature or not is impossible to predict, but the effort is long overdue.

[37]Seymour Martin Lipset, "Predicting the Future of Post-Industrial Society: Can We Do It?," in S. M. Lipset, ed., *The Third Century: America as a Post-Industrial Society* (Stanford: Hoover Institute Press, 1979), pp. 1–35; Giandomenico Majone, "Anatomy of Pitfalls," in Giandomenico Majone and E. S. Quade, eds., *Pitfalls of Analysis* (New York: Academic, 1980), pp. 7–22; G. Morgan and L. Smircien, "The Case for Qualitative Research," *The Academy of Management Review* 5 (1980), pp. 491–500.

[38]See Peter Temin, *Taking Your Medicine: Drug Regulation in the U.S.* (Cambridge, MA: Harvard University Press, 1980); James Jones, *Bad Blood: The Tuskegee Syphilis Experiment* (New York: Macmillan, 1981); Richard Neustadt and H. V. Fineberg, *The Swine-Flu Affair* (Washington, D.C.: Department of Health, Education and Welfare, 1978); Samuel F. Wells, "Sounding the Tocsin: NSL 68 and the Soviet Threat," *International Security* 4 (1979), pp. 116–48; H. B. Yoshpe, *Stemming Inflation: The Office of Emergency Preparedness* (Washington, D.C.: Government Printing Office, 1972).

CHAPTER 13

Applied Humanities Inside and Outside the Academy
A Personal Case of Applied History

FRED NICKLASON

In recent years historians increasingly find themselves outside the class-room and inside law offices, corporations, and government bureaus. Although no satisfactory label applies to these "nonacademic histori-ans"—the term they dislike the most—they generally accept "applied historian" or "public historian," despite the fact that some of them work for private firms. "Independent historian" might develop but it too has questionable implications. Terminology aside, a growing organization of public or applied historians does exist, they meet in an annual con-vention, just as academic historians do, and they support a journal, *The Public Historian*, devoted to their interests.

The brutal question is, so what? What difference does it make that some historians write history and teach, whereas other historians write history and do not teach? They both do history. Then why the need for a distinction? As usual, it is more complex than first appears.

Academic historians criticize public historians in several ways. First, the motivation of the two historians differs. That difference in motivation is essential because it leads to differences in the subjects they write about and to differences in the questions they ask of their evidence. Second, academic historians claim disinterested reasons for writing history and they observe that public historians work for clients whose "outcome-oriented" needs necessarily determine the final product. Third, academic historians believe that there exist no adequate means of accountability, specifically peer review, for public historians, and therefore standards

FRED NICKLASON • Department of History, University of Maryland, College Park, Maryland 20742.

for admitting evidence in public history fall below the rules of evidence to which academic historians adhere.

Public historians fail to accept the criticisms. They come out of the same academic environment as their counterparts. They have the same academic mentors and they defer to these same authorities for acceptable dissertation topics. In short, both species of historians follow the same academic training rules. Moreover, they read the same history and share the same awareness of frequently shoddy research and substandard application of the rules of evidence. They may even know established historians who base their reputations on fudged evidence and ideologically determined questions of the best evidence. And they universally know too that no culture-bound historian, academic or not, is free of implicit assumptions inherent in all value systems. As for peer review, no one who lives in the world is unaware of the classic cases over the years of abuses of the review process that either unnecessarily denigrate or elevate the (typically) young scholar's effort. What is more—to make the strongest argument—public historians who write expert witness reports for testimony in court always face the ultimate standard in peer review because historians on the other side of the legal case potentially use the same evidence and moreover produce it for public view. In that context little chance of unethical shading of historical reality arises. In fact, no greater assurance against miscreant research exists.

Still, the academic historian presumably is the keeper of the keys to the kingdom of history. He sets the rules and the standards of ethics. If he says to the public historian, in dour tones, "It's not done," then that settles it, it should not be done. The vested interests of the client who requests history written for compensation tips the scales against it. That is the paramount criticism. Consequently, the public historian runs the risk of violating the historical profession's unwritten law that says that history shall not be client-oriented. Simply put, it is based on the widespread assumption that what the public historian concludes as historical fact differs from what he might conclude were that tainting element, the client, not lurking in the background.

All vested interests, of course, need not be economic. There exist both economic and noneconomic vested interests, and it is specious to believe that only the public historian retains his explicit, corrupt version as he pours over the documents while the untainted academic historian objectively analyzes his documents, all the while dodging his implicit values.

Still, a problem arises with historians working as consultants in legal cases because the attorney for whom he works is indeed an advocate and not disinterested. That view differs markedly from the needs of the able attorney, however, who seeks the best and most accurate historical information available. Exceptions of course exist, but in those cases, when historians allow the attorneys to push them beyond the evidence, there occurs not only a violation of historical ethics but a disservice to the client's case as well. Then the opposing attorney or historian, or both, has every right to take advantage of it, which is the beginning of peer review.

What is to be done? The easiest approach is to chide the public historian and to try to shun him into isolation. Sometimes that is all that is tried. After all, should that not be enough? It is not. The public historian will not go away. That approach is also a source of uncomfortable ambivalance to the academic historian. Given the low number of academic jobs available to recent history Ph.D.'s the academic historian is caught in a vexed web that entails inviting into classrooms the students who pay the university tuition money that then gets laundered into compensation to the professor who finds himself teaching some potential public historians.

The basic question remains: what difference does doing public history make? William James, an obstinately honest man, said it must make a difference for there to be a difference. So what is the difference? First we must get over the idea that as soon as the historian leaves the genteel groves of academe he automatically cuts a deal with the devil. The public historian, no more than the academic historian, does not say "my ethics for a job." If he does, then so be it, but if we assume he does then we must encompass in our assumption the unethical academic historian who cuts corners in his escape from the dire fate of public history. First, then, with a charitable spirit, we must clear the air of hidden values that include the academic's self-serving attitude that the public historian cannot keep the set of historical standards that his academic mentor had the good sense to impart to him. (Again, at some level the nonacademic client defeats his own purpose if he allows the applied historian to employ a "contented cow" approach that bases conclusions only on what the client wants to hear. Internal checks do exist.)

Another hurdle then arises. If the academic historian gets over his sense of wonderment that he ever questioned the public historian's ethics, then he must confront the occasionally baffling fact that the public historian works in a historical vineyard where the topics chosen for study and standards for relevance appear foreign. Even though functionally the basic questions may be the same, the evidence used may not. In partial explanation one can only observe that as political science is what political scientists do, so public history is what public historians do. Since they do a wide range of things, I cannot speak for them all. My personal and peculiar experiences as a public historian, however, contain some relevant illustrations.

I am a hybrid historian, part public, part nonpublic. The happy circumstance is that what I do as a public historian contributes to what I do as an academic historian, though public historical research is not as quickly publishable as academic research. There are reasons for that, some unique to the legal circumstances in which I work as a litigation historian, some peculiar to the academic world I have never left.

My dual identity began in the early 1970s. In the late 1960s I completed a doctoral dissertation that involved the first half of a biography of a late nineteenth-century politician who had served in the United States Congress for thirty-six years. I then began teaching at a university and continued my research on the biography, which involved considerable work in the history of federal Indian policy in the late nineteenth century. I performed that work in the acceptable primary sources diligently, mastered the secondary literature professionally, and used all the care that the craft of history entails. I was at the cutting edge of my field, totally absorbed in the subject, and happy that I would make that substantial historical contribution to which academic historians aspire.

Then, in the early 1970s, a request came from an attorney representing an American Indian tribe. He asked me to write the history of the relationship between his client, an Apache tribe, and the federal government. I was delighted at the opportunity to do a case study at the local level of the Indian policy I knew so well at the national level. No ethical questions arose. Indeed, the attorney taught me how to curb my adverserial tendencies. And with that lengthy study completed, and a negotiated award of $7,000,000 for the tribe to enhance my self-esteem, my department chairman asked me to design an entire course on federal Indian policy. That was a major undertaking. With that course under way, other tribal attorneys requested my services, and the experience as a public historian began. To this date I have worked for numerous tribes and contributed to attaining millions of dollars in legal settlements, including over $100,000,000 in the Black Hills case. So much for circumstances. Return to the main question. What difference has public history made for me?

Public history made a difference in my case because it provided a historical perspective that my conception of academic history did not. My accepted academic history experience served me well at one level, admittedly, and promised to pave the way for an established position in the field of late nineteenth-century history as a time period and federal Indian policy as a topical specialty. My public history experience, however, introduced me to an entirely different level of research and prompted the consideration of an entirely different kind of historical evidence, especially in the individual tribal record of the Bureau of Indian Affairs.

The new public history, however, did not fit with the old academic history, and therein lay the rub—the new so completely contradicted the old I had to rethink the latter entirely. My conclusion: my public history experience made such a profound difference in my perception of historical reality that I hesitated not at all in pursuing it.

What did not change is equally important. The new perspective required no change in the methods and rules for admitting historical evidence. I applied them, I hope, in a way that will ultimately have a greater historical impact than otherwise possible. It also caused no change in my basic interest in getting closer to the core of basic American racial and cultural values. A principal interest of mine lies in the analysis of how nineteenth-century white Americans explained themselves to themselves, especially with regard to race. The statement of that interest seems easy, the task difficult.

My concern with the subject of values is grounded in personal experiences that preceded any formal education. Although in the short term my personal experiences as a historical consultant to American Indian tribes conditioned the outward shape of my thinking, in the long run the inward memory of growing up in northern Minnesota among the impoverished Chippewa Indians in the 1930s and 1940s defined the more enduring measure of how I approach any study of American values. With the eyes of a child I could then see that Indians were different. The Chippewa's unacceptable social and economic status differed dramatically from even the minimum ground-level standards of the surrounding white population. If adults spoke of Indians in terms of derision but never in terms that might explain the origins of their condition, then the law provided the most elucidation available. While adults clearly drew the racial color line at the threshold of every home, then the legal color line, drawn at the front door of every beer tavern, also contained an unambiguous answer: Indians went crazy when they drank firewater. Consequently, whites could not legally sell alcohol to Indians. It followed, in a child's mind, that reds differed from whites because reds could not hold their liquor. Simple and childish reasoning attributed economic and social poverty to that one cause.

At the same time, every weekend, I now remember local white men who worked as loggers came into town from the woods, caroused drunkenly all night, and slept it off in the local flophouse. The Indians, for their part, hired the town drunk to deliver beer to them as they gathered in family circles in the high weeds alongside the railroad tracks. The lesson was clear. If the law could not prohibit whites from drinking alcohol, it could bar reds from its consumption. I do not remember when that distinction first became jarring. It continues to roll around like a hard pebble in my memory. It serves to sharpen my sense of how power works in history. From this instance I now see more clearly how ideology, vested interests of all sorts, and general cultural values are imposed and how they implicitly affect our daily lives and history. And from that process I have come to see how history too often is shaped by shortsighted views of the past in the light of American proclaimed values, and too seldom by analysis of those values as they are acted out in the pursuit of racially and culturally conditioned material needs. In that context my experience as a public historian focused my long-groomed personal values. Starting as a compulsive and eclectic reader, and developing into an obsessive researcher, I have gradually but surely developed a focus on an interest in American white–red relations as a means of understanding American white values.

Consequently, on the way from childhood to adulthood perceptions, the case of Indian prohibition came to be seen as but a symptom. From firewater to firearms, from the far-reaching control of their land to the broad exploitation of their water, timber, and grazing resources, the Indians have stood before the white-made law far short of their full rights. The examples are well known. For instance, while in the early nineteenth century the Supreme Court ruled in favor of the Cherokees, white Americans wanted their land, so with the approval of President Andrew Jackson the Cherokees went packing to Indian Territory with what they could carry. Again, in the late nineteenth century, the Gila River Pimas in Arizona Territory used their natural resource, the Gila River, to irrigate their lands as they had done from time immemorial, but avaricious white Americans violated their own water laws, deprived the Pimas of water to which they still possess the legal rights, and impoverished them where they stood. No removal was required. Every tribe has its own tale, unique to itself and often still to be told.

What needs emphasis is the common skein—that the American white dominant culture held its own law in contempt. When white-imposed law should have applied favorably to the American Indians, but did not, then the dominant white culture violated its own laws. The reds possessed no rights the whites felt bound to respect. That was the American Indians' "white problem," the "red man's burden." That should all be familiar to us, yet it is not, at least in the sense that it is not integrated into our interpretations of American history. Instead we tend to disguise it, to compartmentalize it, and indeed in some cases not to give it a compartment at all. In the process, in covering the experience of white-red relations, we tend to distort American history.

In the late nineteenth century, for instance, American Indians became the subject of the white rhetoric of benevolence, yet we seldom question the genuineness of those verbal proclamations. While downplaying the racism involved, white Americans of the time unabashedly imposed on Indians a virulent form of ethnocentrism—that is, prompted by the belief that they lived in a superior culture, white Americans in benevolent terms advocated the destruction of the red cultures. In turn, the white culture announced that it would replace the Indian cultures with the best of itself: Americanization-Christianization-Civilization. Down with tribalism and Indianness, up with individualism and private property. "Kill the Indian, save the man." All in the name of justice and love. That would make the individual Indian self-reliant or self-sustaining. If the Indians could be made to be self-sustaining (which at one time, of course, they were), then white society would no longer feel the guilty need to supply annuities to replace the Indians' traditional means of support, of which whites had deprived them. Therein lay the problem: How to convert culturally the red to white, to diminish the large Indian land base to a small Indian land base, and to enjoy the peace of the vanishing Indian and disappearance, too, of the cultural abrasion he caused. Within the context of ethnocentrism, white American humanitarians of the time considered the best of all the alternatives. Accordingly, they decided unilaterally to impose upon American Indians the ownership of 160 acres of land each, to sell off the "surplus" red aboriginal and treaty land to pioneering and enterprising whites on the frontier, and to use the proceeds to pay for the educational conversion of reds into whites. So legislation came to pass. In 1887 Congress approved the General Allotment Act, otherwise known as the Dawes Act, named after Henry L. Dawes, the subject of my early biographical effort in the study of federal Indian policy.

For an understanding of federal Indian policy, at least as late nineteenth-century white Americans announced it and most twentieth-century historians write it, the above policy description contains the boundaries of historical analysis. It defines the historical sources: congressional documents and debates, political speeches and humanitarian pleas, private manuscripts of relevant participants, published articles and books of the period and later, and occasionally some records of the office of Indian Affairs.

Yet when I undertook as a public historian the history of a single Indian tribe's experience under that benevolently designed nineteenth-century federal Indian policy, I found the historical terrain strikingly alien. No secondary literature existed. The primary documentation for that public history broadened my prospective because it forced the study of Indian policy from the bottom up, not from the top down. There emerged a growing recognition of the discontinuity between the avowed Indian policy of making the tribes self-sustaining and the practical effect at the tribal level of making them economically dependent. What is more, traditional studies of Indian policy left out the Indian. In short, actual policy received its shape not from congressional legislation but from white land hunger. Rather than follow the rhetoric of Indian policy that sought self-reliance for American Indians, the actual effect of the policy included, beyond cultural repression, the economic loss of land, water, and minerals, and the placement of the Indians on land that neither whites nor Indians wanted. For example, in my first case individual Indians received their Dawes Act land allotments—for farming—on the inhospitable and often steep continental divide while white squatters retained the accessible irrigable land and the water to make it productive. The effect of actual Indian policy belied its announced goals. Unable to support themselves, as a result of the effect of Indian policy, the Indians acquired a dependence upon the federal government rather than reliance upon themselves. Indian reservations entered the twentieth century with many of the same problems that third-world nations have today, that is, underdevelopment and dependence.

I am not certain that such policy duality would have been revealed by my historical efforts within the traditional academic mold, but public historical work clearly revealed it to me. Few tribal histories existed at the time. More exist now, but still too few academic historians link stated Indian policy at the higher echelons of government with actual Indian policy at the local level, although the two are hardly unrelated. More is involved than the discrepancy between ideals and reality. Policy is what policy does. Yet too often the announced Indian policy is taken as the reality, as the truest reflection of American white values, while scant attention is directed toward the crucial identification of values as actual people acted them out in concrete terms.

Perhaps the difference can be seen as a difference between legislative history and administrative history, where the stated purpose of legislation before passage receives historical analysis but the administration of legislation after passage receives little attention, even if historians could locate in that later context a truer expression of American values through the actions of real people going about their lives, however loathsome. That is my historical hobby horse: stated Indian policy is just that, a statement of abstract Indian policy, whereas actual Indian policy is something else because it is judged against results. The latter, I argue, is a better source for the examination of society's values. Academic historians have paid more attention to the former, public historians more to the latter. And therein lies one crucial difference between much of academic and public history—the difference between the nature of the documentation and the level of historical evidence allowed in the consideration of federal Indian policy. And so, again, what difference does that difference make?

The broader consequences of that difference reflect upon American history. If in black history we now look behind the contemporary rhetoric for a closer examination of American racial values, then why not in red history? If the experiences of blacks are crucial to understanding the period following the Civil War that historians call Reconstruction, then why not increase the historical evidence that contributes to an analysis of American values and include the experiences of reds? If we seriously want to allow into mainstream American values all the relevant historical evidence that affect them, even if it jars our self-image, then the implications are expandable. For instance, if we accept into our understanding of the Reconstruction years after the Civil War that some need existed for the racial control of blacks to keep them attached to the land in the South (to replace the control that slavery provided), then how about considering in the same period a comparable need to control the Indians while whites wrested the land from them in the West? This changes the context in which we view the white pioneer hero. Seen that way, the visible hand of the government accompanied that pioneer with military and civil policies that protected the interests of the westering white, while, first, collapsing the red's traditional means of livelihood and, second, diminishing the remaining resources that whites traditionally considered essential for self-support. Such a policy required transferring military troops out of the South, where they had just protected the originally unintended effect of freeing the black race, and deploying those troops in the West, where they would have the intended effect of subduing the red race. Was there a "Red Reconstruction"?

This need not be an exercise in racial self-hatred. On the contrary, it holds out the highest hope for attaining a greater degree of understanding American values. Placing limits on the historical evidence limits that self-perception, both historic and contemporary.

Take the experience of the American Indians more directly. Ask the question: What has been the price of omitting the white American's treatment of the red Americans as a reflection of American values? Admittedly, all Americans know about the battle massacres such as Wounded Knee, but most Americans attribute that event to a military aberration and as not typical. What is not within our society's memory are the more numerous nonmilitary instances in which the westering pioneers participated in illegal and unconscionable acts against the Indians. Historical evidence abounds for that conclusion. But back to the "price." My argument is that omitting the experiences of the American Indians not only omits the Indians, it as importantly distorts the image that whites have of their own history. Further, leaving out the Indians from white history has led Americans to accept historical theses about themselves that the inclusion of reds would otherwise cause them to reject. The most notable example is the case of Frederick Jackson Turner and his well-known frontier hypothesis that for so long influenced American historians. In the late nineteenth century and well into the twentieth, Turner argued that as the population of this country moved westward, the process and environment of the frontier stripped the people of their preconceived values, forced them back to a more primitive stage of society, and eventually produced the American democrat. In essence, the process and environment produced a unique American character.

The longevity and the impact of Turner's idea now often embarrasses many American historians, but it is even more disconcerting that when historians did begin their criticism of Turner they tended to accept him on his own terms. Some of the more sophisticated efforts might use comparative methods and provide a control group, as in observing the experience of Australians. The one obvious control group, however, that no one to my knowledge has used, perhaps because too obvious, was the American Indian. The Indian also moved westward. Confronted with hostile white Americans in what has to be the longest undeclared war in our history (and certainly one of the largest real estate transfers), various northeastern Indian tribes gradually migrated westward, from one frontier to another, in successive stages, all the while changing their environment and their cultures, even in some cases converting from a sedentary to a nomadic life. Indeed, the western-moving northeastern tribes, everlastingly on the cutting edge of their frontier, first introduced their western brothers to the values of the western European-American. It makes little difference to say that the red man's reasons for migrating differed from those of the white man. The fact is that he went and the process of doing so, in the environment he found himself, should have produced, according to Turner, the same effect as it did on the white American. It did not.

The point is that the difference in the values that whites and reds brought with them contributed to how they responded to their frontier experience. The eastern Indian in the West also stripped himself of more civilized modes and converted from a sedentary to a more flexible primitive nomadic life. Both white and red men shared the experience of uniting against a common enemy. Yet their different responses to comparable experiences indicates that preestablished values, whether European or American aboriginal, affected the outcome. Turner said in effect that the white American, with a European background, became the American democrat in the West. He led his readers to believe, however, that all people who underwent the frontier experience would come out in the same mold. With his thesis applying only to Euro-Americans, Turner should have said that the frontier produced the American democrat, provided he brought the right *European* values with him. Omitting the experience of the Indians therefore allowed Turner to leave out some essential ingredients in the American character. In effect, omitting the Indians allowed him, as well as his critics, to distort the values of the mainstream American.

This observation also becomes important later in the twentieth century when considering the "consensus" interpretation of the 1950s, especially Louis Hartz, who in *The Liberal Tradition in America* (1955) so impressively explained the consensus of American values. Following the idea of Alexis de Tocqueville, Hartz stressed the American uniqueness that evolved from the omission of a feudal past and that allegedly accounted for the absence of class and ideological conflict in this country. For Hartz, the United States emerged as the embodiment of the liberal tradition its people shared. When applying this interpretation to the late nineteenth century, however, a flaw in Hartz's analysis appears in that he omitted the ethnic and racial conflict of the period. Perhaps more than any other industrial nation of the world, the United States has struggled with the problem of ethnic and racial minorities. Indeed, in the light of the evidence that exists from the 1622 Indian massacre of whites at Jamestown to the 1890 white massacre of Indians at Wounded Knee, it might be suggested that in place of the European class conflict Americans substituted an abrasive ethnic and bloody racial struggle. For Hartz to omit this reality again distorts the history of this nation and the white American's image of it. If early twentieth-century progressive historians (Turner among them) saw economic conflict everywhere, and mid-century consensus historians saw no conflict anywhere, they both shared a blindness to the history of the Indian as a vehicle to explain American values. The evidence of ethnocentrism and racism directed against the Indian fits neither the progressive nor the consensus interpretation of American history. The answers to our "so what?" more clearly emerge.

To perceive more closely what happened in our past, it is suggested, we need a change, or expansion, in our view of American history to include racism and ethnocentrism in it. Understandably, we generally allow ourselves to see only the fulfillment of the ideals we intensify and hold aloft for others to see. This is natural, but it also implies the reverse, that we unconsciously blind ourselves from observing the actual suffering and destruction wrought by the fulfillment of those ideals. Put another way, we see the positive product of our efforts but repress the negative effects. Yet our products are also things destroyed, such as nature, of which we originally thought the Indian was a part. If we do wish to face historical reality, positive idealisms should share the stage with their negative counterparts. If, in expanding the western American area of freedom, white Americans take pride in the unrestricted competitive capitalism of the settler who aggressively carved out a living for his family on the land in the West, and if whites elevate those actions to the pantheon of liberalism, then in all candor they will also have to admit that in the process of achieving those high liberal values, that same settler, in response to the Indian, committed some of the most illiberal acts of our history. In short, white virtues were connected to white vice. To ignore that is to ignore historical reality.

To include ethnocentrism and racism in our interpretations of American history, therefore, also requires a reconsideration of the liberal tradition as Hartz expounds it. As with a restriction on the Turner thesis, one approach might be to change the term from "liberal tradition" to "white liberal tradition" and thereby recognize its limited applicability. To say that the achievement of America's highest ideals included the lowest American shame is to recognize an important ingredient of universal history. Specifically, to say that the liberal tradition applied to whites and whites alone is also to recognize it as a racist and ethnocentric tradition and one that therefore violates its very equalitarian characteristics. That is essentially what is involved when we acknowledge that Americans fought the American Revolution in search of freedom while paying for that search with the produce of slave labor of another race. Although it is not seriously proposed that we completely scrap the liberal tradition as an interpretation, the realization of the necessity for its revision can help give us the vision to incorporate racism and ethnocentrism into our recognizable history, and to incorporate it not as a paradox or as an exception but as an integrated and organically related part of American historical values.

The least one can say about American Indian policy in the late nineteenth century is that it was based on the same principles and motivations of acquisitiveness that propelled the white man across the continent and beyond. Whites responded to reds the way they did, not by recanting their white ideals but by reiterating them. The result was always the same—either physical or cultural destruction of the Indian. And either form of destruction rewarded whites with more land. They seldom recognized that each gain in power over the land threatened their own avowed values of justice. More often they used the term *justice* as an explanation for their actions. Anti-Indian racism and ethnocentrism, it is suggested, provided the rationale. In order for western Americans to purge themselves of the guilt that followed from the inhumane and illiberal treatment that Indians received at their hands, they needed a belief in the innate biological and cultural inferiority—or even nonperson status—of the American Indian. Without that belief in the Indian's inferiority, the treatment of Indians would have been considered a direct violation of liberal values. In effect, therefore, racism and ethnocentrism justified illiberalism. Put another way, liberalism had racism and ethnocentrism built in, even if still uncomfortably and yet unrecognized.

Finally, the question arises: What if Americans were able fully to allow evidence of an illiberal past into their societal memory? What good would it do, what would it accomplish? Quite aside from whether it can be accomplished, my judgment is that the attempt should be made to a greater degree than in the past. The reason for at least initiating that process lies in our knowledge of what effect the suppression of personal experiences can have on individuals. And, extrapolating from individual memories to societal memories, a case can be made for the need to deal with our uncomfortable national past in the interest of preparing us better to prevent a repetition of future guilt-provoking experiences. It is not now historically far-fetched to see part of the midtwentieth century as a second reconstruction for blacks. And even if the racial analogy cannot be made with close precision, I think it also not historically inaccurate to interpret the 1972 Indian trashing of the Bureau of Indian Affairs as the price mainstream Americans had to pay for their previously complacent belief that American Indians somehow did not resent their version of having to go the back of the historical bus. Indeed, we have to acknowledge our experience of a "dark and bloody ground" of American Indian policy that still limits a confrontation with race, ethnocentrism, and the brutal effects of power in relation to both.

Persistent dominance, one hopes, has its breaking point. As historians now generally recognize, all relationships contain the potential for dominance. Whether sexual (men over women), racial (whites over blacks, reds and yellows), regional (North over South), economic (rich over poor), professional (doctors over patients), the pattern of dominance-dependence emerges at some point in a confrontation that neither party finds comfortable. I do not go so far as to claim that one breed of historian is now exclusively contributing to these fields of history. I do claim that public historians in my field are making their substantial contribution to an essential process that all hope will find our society of many races and ethnic groups more at peace with itself.

My own academic historian-public historian niche includes the experience of American Indians. Never have so proportionally few had such an effect on so many. It was not necessarily of their own doing. To paraphrase Arthur Schlesinger, Jr., from *The Crisis of Confidence*, appropriately subtitled *Ideas, Power and Violence in American Today* (1969),[1] Americans began as a people who killed reds and enslaved blacks and, however righteous our professions, no nation could act as we did with-

---

[1]Arthur M. Schlesinger, Jr., *The Crisis of Confidence: Ideas Power and Violence in America* (Boston: Houghton Mifflin, 1967), p. 10.

out burying deep in ourselves, our customs, our institutions, our conditioned reflexes, and our psyche, a propensity toward violence. It is
almost, Schlesinger concluded, as if that experience fixed a primal curse
on our nation that still affects us. That curse was self-inflicted. It will
not disappear with the histories of federal Indian policy that most traditional academic historians write. And it will not disappear with attempts to disguise it in smooth words or suppress it with omission. As
Robert Penn Warren writes toward the end of his recent poem, "Chief
Joseph of the Nez Percé" (1983), no ironies exist in history:

> For those of sound
> Of heart there is no ultimate
> Irony. There is only
> Process, which is one name for history. Often
> Pitiful. But, sometimes, under
> The scrutinizing prism of Time,
> Triumphant. [2]

An explication of Warren's passage is that in the long run irony
(and paradox) is not an explanation for history; process is. And although
"often pitiful" (and painful), "sometimes" it ultimately triumphs. Also,
my interpretation is that public historians in the "ultimate" sense will
have their day. In the classic tragedy the hero's original strong point is
the source of his ultimate downfall. In the American story, although the
white's initial technological strength subdued the American Indian, in-
dications are that chinks now exist in that strength. And signs are too
that what weakness the American Indian originally possessed, especially
in his relation to the environment, contains the enduring value that
some whites now desire to imitate. Perhaps public historians will follow
that pattern.

---

[2]Robert Penn Warren, "Chief Joseph of the Nez Percé" (New York: Random House, 1983),
   p. 63.

CHAPTER 14

Intellectual Standards in the Humanities

OTIS L. GRAHAM, JR.

Peter Stearns addresses a range of issues, none of them trivial, some large enough for an entire conference. The central concern is with the relation of the new public history,[1] especially in its application to policymaking, with the established realm of academic history. He is uneasy about their relationship because of what he hears and sees on both sides of the newly emerging encounter. Campus-based historians are training many or most of the new breed for the other world they will enter, but many academics are disdainful of the enterprise and neither seek nor

---

[1] I am not convinced that "applied history" is to be distinguished from "public history" as Stearns argues. He appears to see public history as set apart by its methods of presentation "the entertainment and edification of adults" (p. 227, this volume). Applied history aims at more serious work, i.e., policy. I do not think the distinction holds. Progressive era historians, a handful of them, used the term *applied* history for all forms of nonteaching, off-campus history. Perhaps the term should have been repeated when, in the early 1970s, the impulse stirred again. It was not. Bob Kelley used the term *public history*, which he has defended on several occasions. It is widely used. It refers to all historical work purchased or subsidized by the nonacademic community and conducted and enjoyed away from campuses. Historical work affecting public policy may be done by some academics, but if one "works for," as consultant or employee, the entity making the policy and it is not an institution of education, one is not an academic but a public historian. I see no grounds for preferring either label, public or applied, except that the former is in general usage. Until otherwise persuaded, I distinguish between academic and public history. Applied history is not a subfield of anything, but a label that has lost out in the recent struggle to establish terminology.

OTIS L. GRAHAM, JR. • Department of History, University of North Carolina, Chapel Hill, North Carolina 27514.

accept sustained contact with off-campus history. The absence of inter-change injures both parties. Public historians are deprived of access to theoretical invigoration and the realm of professional practice where the highest standards are established. Academic historians, especially if they work in the contemporary period, have much to gain from the applied historians, many of whom work almost entirely in that too little travelled zone between history and journalism.

No one of us from the campuses, least of all those who are close to the public history movement, could deny that these problems exist. They deserve the careful attention that Stearns and all of us may give it. I trust it will not be misunderstood if I express the hope, indeed the expectation, that his concern will in not too many years seem dated. Something of the same set of concerns agitated the early academic econ-omists, then political scientists, then sociologists, anthropologists, and others, now even some philosophers along with the historians, as one by one the social sciences with their secure university base have found their degree holders taking jobs off the campuses and thus shifting the center of gravity and the very nature of the profession itself. We are quite late in the game, and our colleagues at the faculty club will be happy to tell us how long they, too, have struggled to bridge the aca-demic-public gap within their disciplines. We have been slow to produce individuals and to encounter the social setting which combined to take history off the campus, for all the reasons that Stearns recognizes. He is right to emphasize attitude as much as job markets. We see ourselves, and the public stubbornly sees us, as teachers, or fiddlers with unread monographs. Now we must deal with the problems which come with the new opportunities. These problems the other social sciences, and the natural sciences before them, have long faced. It does not make them the less difficult to recognize because they are familiar and have histories elsewhere. The profession whose internal history I know best, planning, offers an example. Stearns reports the debate among some public his-torians over whether they should offer only scenarios or take the step to advocacy; the planners have been tangled around that issue for two decades or more. *Politicization* it is called, the "attractive nuisance" of disciplines thought to have something useful to sell.

The universe of professional history, of course, will face different configurations of both problems and opportunities as it becomes sig-nificantly split between those who teach teenagers, as Stearns bluntly puts it at one point, and those who sell their wares to adults who pay money directly and with a much more serious interest in the product. If the interchange between the two remains as intermittent and the relationship as wary as today (and it will not, in part because people like Stearns and those at this gathering are addressing the matter), he sees the costs to academics as much lower than to those historians who are moving into the larger society. In this he is probably correct, and I intend in a moment to turn to his account of those costs to the innovators and how they might be minimized and the gains secured. But my own observation is that academic historians have even more to gain from training and professionally interacting with the new practicioners than he sets out. He is right to stress, perhaps to be excused for overstressing, the unsatisfactory quality of much contemporary history, for example. A flourishing off-campus set of professionals, working necessarily upon contemporary and future themes, should encourage more academics to do their work in these zones, ignoring the shallow remarks of colleagues about "journalism" or "instant history." There may also be for them, as he argues, "a revivification of contemporary history," although I am not quite sure what he has in mind when he speaks of "a new approach."

For me, the advantage of working with public historians and of my own ventures at addressing contemporary policy issues, has been chiefly the necessity to educate myself in the literature of economics, political science, demography, and urban sociology. There is much benefit in the intellectual encounter with more theoretically inclined disciplines than my own, and beyond this there is the constant necessity to contend with the arguments of those who come at problems from other (and usually nonlinear) perspectives. One must learn the other languages in use among social scientists and bureaucrats, assimilate their point of view, explain succinctly and clearly the corrective influence that historical knowledge offers.

I do not suggest that only policy engagement leads one to reach out to other disciplines for a working knowledge of what they are about. There has been much of this among historians in recent years. But historians of the twentieth century tend to lag behind in this endeavor and thus to benefit especially much from the necessity to work on policy problems with the attendant swarm of bureaucrats and social scientists. It is not that we who work the recent past are peculiarly uncurious about the other disciplines, by contrast with the social historians, for example. The medieval historian interested in a French village, the student of colonial America, are not literally crushed by their evidence. They may more easily find the time and the adequate incentive for indispensable cross-disciplinary borrowing in order to probe their limited evidence in fresh ways. Breakthroughs there are more often conceptual than a matter of new evidence, though the two are often combined. The historian of recent societies, by contrast, is buried under an avalanche of paper, much of it never before analyzed. One lacks the time for, and does not often sense the need of, keeping in close touch with the secondary literature in the main social science fields. But once engage oneself in policy deliberations upon a complex matter such as immigration policy or urban policy, as I have done in a small way, and one is simply forced to understand the concepts and language of the other players. Policy engagement, for the contemporary historian, rescues him from document suffocation by compelling an engagement with other social science literature.

Another set of benefits may be mentioned, more moral than intellectual. History is on the defensive on the campuses, bureaucratically but also psychologically. Yet each of us will say, if asked, that the world needs more and better history, not less. "Going public," as it were, brings a chance to take the offensive, to expand the influence of the human record and its analysis. This is bracing to all of us, even if we watch it from the ivied towers. When we trek to the business school or medical school to offer lectures or courses on their past and use of the past, when we discard our reservations and counsel some legislative committee or city government or courtroom, when we hear our returning public history graduates tell of communities electrified by displays of their own histories or of cultural or natural resources protected from the bulldozer by a skillfully written report, we are improved and newly inspired people.

But Stearns is rightly more concerned with the costs to public historians of the degree of separation from the academy that characterizes the early stage we are in. These costs appear to him to be intellectual and also political, if that is the right word to designate the erosion of objectivity and scholarly standards which is to be expected in the more direct client relationship out in a world where an historian is unprotected by tenure, the AAUP, and the general assumption that he is irrelevant. I have not seen a more constructuve discussion of what might be done to address these problems than Stearns offers. Academics must write in "their" journals, they in ours; the same regular interaction must be pursued in professional meetings, conferences. Campus historians will benefit from more frequent tours of duty in government and industry, and replacements ought to be recruited from the ranks of professionals practicing public history who desire a tour in the academy. Access to public historians' work is a major problem which Stearns has not missed. Bob Kelley launched *The Public Historian* to bring small remedy for several of the foregoing problems, but more must be done. The publication of the work of public historians and their wide review in journals of all constituencies is of crucial importance. A prize structure as diverse as our own must grow up for those who produce company histories, family and community histories for clients, environmental impact reports, public presentations for audiences at national parks or historic sites. Professional recognition of superior work keeps the dogs at bay to some extent, reminds paying clients that an intimidated historian is not a great asset, that others are watching. Other professions have established periodic accreditation, and this deserves consideration in the larger discussion of professional standards.

From quality control issues, the Stearns essay then turns to how historical inquiry ought or might influence policymaking. His points of entry for history are: the provision of institutional memory; historical analysis in the policymaking cycle, as in the definition of problems and the offering of options; retrospective evaluation; "paradigms," a line of thought which I did not entirely understand; trend assessment; attention to context. I have no serious quarrel with this, though my colleagues and I within the course we have developed at the University of North Carolina Business School have reduced this list to institutional memory, which we see outside the policy process, and on the analytical side where policy is engaged, a special concern with time and context.

The idea suggested by the word *time* holds that an executive or executive group making policy, public or private, will benefit from a trained sensitivity to our profession's central preoccupation, change and continuity over time. As Lawrence Veysey put it recently, "an overriding concern for temporality distinguishes the historian from academics of all other persuasions—except astronomers, earth scientists, and some biologists, who might be called the historians of nature."[2] Where are we in the stream of time? Historians push that question to the front of discussion and then proceed to disaggregate the confluence of flowing matter which constitutes any present. If we develop skill at anything, it is in the discernment of what parts of the received heritage of any contemporary moment retain or even gain in force and momentum and which are tending toward debility. Every moment, and of course the future, is composed of strands from the past, but these are never of equal vitality. Reasoning by simple analogy confers on every part of the inherited past—all institutions, practices, ideas, organizations, memories—the same force and effect as possessed when last they meshed. Historical nihilism regards them all as depleted, the world as made new. Historians do not agree on many things, but we all know that time enervates *and* initiates as it moves, that it undermines many a fighting faith before that is fully known, and launches new forces of unsuspected power. The trick, it might be said, is to know when the hand of heritage is heavy or light, and where. This discernment assists us in accounting for uneven rates of change, perceiving when situations are open for movement and innovation, or stabilized and stalemated against change.

---

[2]John Higham and Paul Conkin, eds., *Intellectual History and the Social Sciences* (Baltimore: John Hopkins University Press, 1979), p. 7.

The second idea restates history's credentials as an integrative discipline and stresses the insistence of the historical imagination upon seeing matters whole. Sister disciplines would not readily concede such a claim, but which of the social sciences possesses the inclination to blend economic, political, intellectual, cultural, climatic, geographic, demographic, scientific, technological, organizational, psychological factors and concepts? Most, in fact, confine their energies within the boxes of ideas, organizations, marketplace, politics. Historians have, of course, been so confined, as every year's crop of monographs attests. But at its best the historian's grasp is eclectic. We thirst for the social whole, the relevant if not the entire context.

Policymakers who develop such an appetite for the impinging variables of social context will have reaped a second sort of benefit from the craft of historical reconstruction. Whether this be called synchronic analysis, or attention to setting or context or the horizontal dimension, its neglect is the primary occupational hazard of each social science in its turn, but also of each trade, each corporation marketing a product, each segmented part of complex institutions. Policy error comes often in the form of a surprise from some impinging factor or factors whose bearing upon one's own narrower plans, indeed whose very existence was often screened out of the analysis. "Exogeny forever!" suggested Arthur Schlesinger, Jr., when asked for the historians' motto. We honor our assignment at contextual reconstruction most often in the breach, perhaps, but our discipline is inherently holistic and better nurtures that contextual perspective which is so often defeated by the training of the economist or psychologist, the organizational confines of bureaucrat or executive. This seems to me a promising intellectual framework for training in how history may enlighten policy choice. It does not address the form of the historians' input, which Stearns sees, if I read him correctly, as post-decision evaluation, writing about paradigmatic shifts currently underway or looming ahead, writing memos to identify trends. He mentions at some point the creation also of scenarios of the future, and I would have stressed more affirmatively the historian's inherent strengths in constructing probable futures. As specialists in change, with what Sir Lewis Namier once called an understanding of how things *do not* happen as well as how they might, historians possess special capacities for disciplined scenario building. We are hesitant, but the study of the future is congenial terrain and we should plunge in. Policymakers will construct models of the future whether we assist or not, often just extrapolating what they think they remember. Historians could be of considerable help in this.

Now let me register some doubts, not dogmatic ones I hope, about Stearns's handling of the usage of analogy. He is certainly correct to state that "policymakers use analogy whether historians like it or not," and that the past is the only laboratory we have, in most cases, to examine how events might come together in the future. I confess myself among those whom he finds "discouraged about analogy's potential for much save error." What we know of the misuse of the "lessons of the past" by public policymakers in an almost unrelieved story of misapplication of the presumed teachings from some early disaster or success. Analogy enters decision making mostly as a prop for some view adopted for ideological or interest-group reasons, and it is a mischievous influence. Stearns finds it "probable . . . that sufficient tools can be developed to improve its usage," and I hope that he is right. But until that work is done my own handling of analogy (in the course we teach at the UNC Business School) has been to attempt to neutralize it. It is not difficult to discredit the uses to which analogies have been put, to display the corrupting influence of past examples, to expose its influence in limiting options and closing off debate. As in the case of "forced" busing, I may be talking only of facile analogies, and there may be sophisticated analogies or analogizing with which to replace it. The few suggestions to which Stearns calls our attention in May's book do not go far enough, I fear, toward the carefully controlled use of this mischievous part of the historical heritage. My own entirely skeptical view of analogies is surely not the best we can do, but skepticism will be a significant part of our approach to analogies even in that bye-and-bye when we have developed methods to use them as well as defuse them—or, in the words of a recent song allowing me to complete this metaphorical excess, know when to hold 'em and know when to fold 'em.

From this wide-ranging paper I select one other discussion to join and extend. This is the matter of standards among those who work for other than teenage clients. Stearns seems to me here astutely to anticipate some of the pressures and to understand that high standards in any line of work derive not from guidelines or officially adopted codes but from the widest access to finished product, routinized peer review, multiple forums for discussion, talk, criticism, praise. Standards come mostly from institutional interactions, and his paper is helpful in sketching some of these. Innovation will surely be required here. Academic historians do not routinely look back to make a systematic assessment of who was right and who was wrong about slavery or New England town family structure or electoral realignment, and why. But public historians who are involved with policy will be continually guessing about the present and future and going on record about it. Like economists who dabble in prediction, and most of them do, these historians will find reinforcement for high standards of performance in an institutionalized and professional review of how their work held up. There ought someday to be a journal called, *Policy Analysis and Recommendations by Historians: A Look Back After Twenty Years, with Prizes.* It is a terrible title, but an intriguing idea for those like Peter Stearns who know full well that the new field of off-campus history contains special hazards and requires compensatory innovations.

Finally, I am most enthusiastic in this paper about the candid and penetrating confession that "we" have clients too, that pressures upon the profession's vaunted freedom of inquiry and objectivity are quite heavy in our ivied institutions, and that our record in rising above them is blemished. We are not without extensive experience in how to be corrupted. How right Stearns is that client pressure is not a new thing among historians, who have faced it in their academic situation from the beginning. Only in degree and in type, but not in kind, does the academic historian experience a different set of corrupting pressures than the friends of Clio who work outside. Within just the last year or so I have been involved in tenure reviews or professional advancement decisions concerning individuals in labor history and women's history. These are flourishing subfields, where professionalism is strong. In each case it is hard to imagine a historian employed by a town, a bank, a neighborhood, or a federal agency encountering more pressure from involved interests who wished to keep the bad news suppressed and the good news up front, to close out the discussion or constrain it. Stearns knows full well that we do our work in a steady crossfire of pressures from consumers and other interested parties. We will make more headway in meeting the problem of maintaining standards in the off-campus setting if academics come to the discussion not as judges but as scholars who in their own way have experienced client and audience pressure to modify the product.

There are those humanists who worry that the role of moral critic to society may be lost as history moves into close contact with contemporary social concerns and secures new paymasters. Of course, there were always constraints. Boards of trustees and state legislatures who so largely fund academic history have a qualified affection for the First Amendment. Yet, taken in all, our campuses are places of remarkable freedom—more, surely, than we effectively use. Now, many of our young colleagues are leaving the compromised detachment of the campus for a more fully engaged life as historians out in society. How, some ask, can this be but a major setback in our long struggle to act as humanistic critics, to tell society the bad as well as the good news and remind it of truths that it will not often pay to hear? Such thoughts represent a healthy reflex, but, as Stearns wisely says, this is another of those manageable problems which have come with the rise of public history. The academic historians' record as moral critics is not terribly strong, but it is vital. Nothing in the expansion of history off campus much alters the confluence of pressures within which we as humanists move in a commercial society. New roles bring slightly more seductive temptations, slightly more formidable constraints upon critical thought—perhaps. I am at one with Stearns in finding the hazards significant, manageable, and decidedly offset by the potential gains.

In any event, there is nothing new about these hazards but their configuration and the relative absence of countervailing pressures and safeguards. A profession that has always struggled for objectivity amid the conflicting expectations of those who paid the bills and both near and distant consumers, we should be capable of finding new ways to reinforce and advance our dedication to truth, to high professional standards. Camus reminded us that art always advances between two chasms, frivolity and propaganda. We may say the same for history, and although the chasms are a given of our circumstances, so also is the possibility of finding high ground between them.

CHAPTER 15

Standards in Philosophy
Pure and Impure? Or Applied and Unapplied?

RUTH MACKLIN

PHILOSOPHY: APPLIED AND UNAPPLIED

There are limits to what can be said about applied humanities, just as it is of questionable validity to generalize about the humanities in their purer form. In this essay, I will confine my observations and analysis to philosophy. Most of the examples and illustrations will be drawn from the applied field known as bioethics, since that is the area with which I am best acquainted. But my conclusions should extend to other fields within applied ethics—engineering ethics, business ethics, legal ethics—as well as to areas of philosophy outside the domain of ethics. The fact that bioethics is probably the most highly developed of these areas makes it a rich field for analysis of the subject of intellectual standards.

A preliminary remark about the term *applied ethics* is in order before I state the main thesis of this account. I find the word *applied* somewhat tendentious, since the contrast it invites is with pure philosophy, or humanities, or ethics. Now the word *pure* is almost always used as a term of praise; it has a positive connotation, especially when contrasted with its opposite, *impure*. In an equally tendentious fashion, then, I will turn the phrase around and contrast applied philosophy with unapplied. The term *bioethics* already encompasses the notion of being applied, so in contrast to applied ethics, I shall speak of unapplied ethics.

What makes applied ethics applied? Three possible candidates come to mind: (a) the *topics* addressed by writings in applied ethics, (b) the

RUTH MACKLIN • Department of Epidemiology and Social Medicine, Albert Einstein College of Medicine, New York, New York 10461.

contributions to the literature in applied ethics by scholars and professionals outside the academic discipline of philosophy, (c) the relevance
of these writings to policy concerns and decision making in the public
arena. The correct answer seems to be that the term *applied ethics* is used
to refer to a bit of each—sometimes to one or the other of these three,
and occasionally to all three. In the interest of avoiding a prescriptive
definition, I will use the term loosely to refer to all three candidates for
the *applied*. Yet, as I shall argue, not everything that fits the description
applied ethics should be considered works of applied philosophy.

My main thesis can be stated in two versions, one descriptive, the
other normative. The thesis, put generally, is that the same intellectual
standards accepted and used in unapplied philosophy pertain to applied
philosophy. More precisely, the two versions are: (1) intellectual standards in applied philosophy are or can be the same as those in unapplied
philosophy; (2) intellectual standards in applied philosophy should be
the same as those in unapplied philosophy.

There are several subordinate theses for which it is necessary to
argue in the course of supporting the main theses just noted. Evidence
brought forward in support of these subordinate theses will serve eventually to back up the main theses. Here, then, are two subordinate claims:
(a) the distinction between applied and unapplied philosophy is not as
clear as some people apparently take it to be; and (b) when the *philosophical* elements of applied and unapplied philosophy are the same,
then the intellectual standards are and should be the same. In the next
section, those elements will be spelled out in some detail. In support of
the thesis that the distinction between applied and unapplied philosophy
is not as clear as some people apparently take it to be, I cite two lines
of evidence: one historical, the other contemporary. Let us look at the
historical evidence first.

HISTORICAL EXAMPLES

In a situation similar to that regarding the distinction invented in
the twentieth century by the analytic school of philosophy between
metaethics and normative ethics, writers in the history of philosophy
made no formal or explicit distinction between pure and applied philosophy. As exemplary and broad-ranging a philosopher as John Stuart
Mill wrote *A System of Logic, Utilitarianism, Principles of Political Economy*,
and *On Liberty*, among numerous other works. Which are pure and
which applied? Of the writings on ethics, which are normative and which
metaethical? *A System of Logic* seems quite pure, but that may be more

a function of the discipline of logic than any feature intrinsic to Mill's work. Logic is a pure discipline, if any discipline is.

Utilitarianism is a thoroughgoing blend of normative ethics and metaethics, often difficult to separate in this poorly understood classic. There does not seem to be much we can identify as applied in *Utilitarianism*, even in advance of proposing a precise definition of applied and unapplied ethics (or philosophy). But *On Liberty* is notoriously difficult to classify and truly seems to be a thoroughgoing blend of applied and unapplied philosophy. Does Mill offer general principles regarding the conduct of government toward individuals and the relationships between individuals? Yes. Does Mill argue for those principles or seek to provide evidence in support of them (as opposed to merely assuming them)? Yes. Does Mill anticipate objections and offer counterexamples— genuine and alleged—to his own general principles? Yes. These features of *On Liberty* qualify it, at least provisionally, as a work of unapplied philosophy, falling within political and social philosophy as well as ethics. At the same time, *On Liberty* discourses at considerable length on topics that fall squarely in the domain of what is today considered applied philosophy: "First Amendment" freedoms—freedom of speech, freedom to publish, etc.; the opium trade (Mill countenanced the almost unrestricted sale of drugs); and other areas. If *On Liberty* were written today, it would be classified (if not dismissed) as applied by the purists in philosophy. Yet the intellectual standards embodied in that work and the standards by which it is still discussed and evaluated are identical with those works inhabiting purer realms of political, social, and moral philosophy. It is hard to classify *On Liberty* neatly into applied or unapplied philosophy.

A second, perhaps more surprising historical candidate is Plato's *Republic*. Who can deny the applied thrust of the *Republic:* a blueprint for an ideal society; prescriptions regarding censorship of art, music, and literature; a detailed plan for the education of various classes of society; proposals for regulating marriage and the family; and a rigid social classification of roles, duties, and functions of social classes. Yet Plato does not draw up this blueprint out of thin air or weave it out of whole cloth. The entire scheme rests on some epistemological and metaphysical assumptions—assumptions about how knowledge is acquired—moral knowledge, as well as other Forms; assumptions about the nature of expertise, about the ontological status of ideal types and how we come to know them; assumptions about the relation between knowledge (cognition) and behavior (action), and about motivation to act. That Plato's psychology was primitive or wrongheaded is less significant than the fact that his work rested on those assumptions. That his ideal society was authoritarian and paternalistic is less important than that he addressed topics debated today under the heading of applied philosophy: censorship, genetic engineering, withholding the truth from citizens for their own good ("noble lies" or "convenient fictions"). Plato could not have made the distinction between applied and unapplied philosophy.

A final historical example: Immanuel Kant. Although the vast body of Kant's writings is as pure as one finds in philosophy, his *Lectures on Ethics* stand out in stark contrast. Here, it could well be argued, the intellectual *standards* are indeed different—lower, one might suggest. Kant's essays "Suicide," "Duties Towards the Body in Regard to Life," and "Ethical Duties Towards Others: Truthfulness" lack the epistemological underpinnings of his other works. He makes the same points but merely assumes or presupposes in these applied writings what he takes infinite pains to lay out in his *Critiques* and other systematic works. This is, I think, because the *Lectures on Ethics* are popular works of philosophy and not because the subject matter is applied. As in any popular philosophy—or science or social science, for that matter—the intellectual standards are different. But we must not make the mistake of confusing popular philosophy with applied philosophy, as I believe the purists are wont to do.

CONTEMPORARY EXAMPLE

For the contemporary illustrations, I need only cite the writings of continental philosophers—in particular, existentialists—to note that the distinction between applied and unapplied philosophy is hardly recognized, whether in ethics or in social and political philosophy. If Anglo-American philosophers look down their noses at the continental school, it is not because the distinction between pure and applied is not made sharply. I suspect the reason lies in less clarity and precision of language, in more obscure and abstruse prose style, and a certain quality of vagueness that pervades philosophy outside the Anglo-American and positivist and neopositivist traditions. But here I tread on dangerous turf and no doubt reveal my own biases in favor of analytic writings and those in philosophy of science whatever the country of origin. Sartre, however, would not have thought much of the alleged distinction between applied and unapplied philosophy.

The preceding observations were made in support of the claim that the distinction between applied and unapplied philosophy is by no means as clear as some apparently take it to be. The next section focuses on the similarities between applied and unapplied philosophy. Put very generally, the similarities are those that serve to characterize the discipline of philosophy itself, at least in its analytic or Anglo-American mode. To the extent that the elements discussed below are realized in the same manner, with clarity, precision, and soundness of reasoning, to that extent are the intellectual standards the same in applied and unapplied philosophy. To the extent that works fail to meet these standards, they are bad philosophy—whether applied or unapplied. But if these elements are largely absent, then the work in question, even if it falls in the category of applied ethics, is probably not philosophy at all.

A comparison with the distinction between pure and applied work in scientific fields is instructive. In another paper in this volume, Edward Layton describes the development and status of engineering as an applied scientific field. Although it appeared at first as though engineering would have to adhere to the standards governing scientific inquiry in, say, theoretical physics, it later emerged that engineering could develop legitimate standards and methods of its own. The situation in humanities generally and in philosophy in particular has both a parallel and a disanalogy with that of science and engineering. The parallel lies in the fuzzy boundary between the unapplied and the applied. Just as Layton describes the difficulty of distinguishing science from applied science, so too, as I have suggested, it is hard to draw that sharp line in many traditional and contemporary writings in social, political, and moral philosophy.

Yet a major difference lies in the multidisciplinary nature of an applied field such as bioethics. Not practiced solely by philosophers, bioethics has contributors from medicine, law, theology, the social sciences, and even journalism. To insist on adherence to the methodology and standards of any single academic or professional discipline would be dogmatic and contrary to the very enterprise of multidisciplinary scholarship. It would be unwise, if not impossible, to impose any particular set of intradisciplinary standards on a multidisciplinary activity; but it is surely possible to strive to attain the rigorous standards of accuracy, clarity, and reasoning common to many fields of inquiry. If applied ethics, like bioethics, is such a multidisciplinary effort, it may be a mistake to use the standards employed within philosophy, standards that may be termed *internal*. But applied philosophy, including writings in bioethics by philosophers, can and should meet the same standards adhered to in the best philosophical traditions.

THE PHILOSOPHICAL ENTERPRISE

The following elements are features of philosophical works. The categories in the classification schemes below are not mutually exclusive;

many books and essays incorporate one or more and occasionally all of these elements. Perhaps these categories do not exhaust the features of philosophical writings, but I offer them as paradigmatic characteristics of the philosophical enterprise. I propose these features in a hierarchy that moves from the seemingly most pure to the allegedly most applied.

A. Defining terms and analyzing concepts
B. Attending to the logic of arguments, detecting fallacies, and uncovering assumptions
C. Analyzing and interpreting other writings—within or without philosophy
D. Constructing hypothetical arguments for or against positions (whether or not one accepts the underlying assumptions or the conclusions of the arguments)
E. Offering sustained normative arguments in favor of a substantive position held by thinkers outside philosophy

Rather than try to explicate these characteristics of philosophy writings in terms of further description, I will use the method of paradigms to illustrate these categories. No examples from unapplied philosophy are used, since they will come readily to mind among philosophers, while the categories above should ring true for nonphilosophers. As for the examples selected for applied philosophy, all are taken from bioethics. Either the titles, a quotation from the work, or a brief description of the content should suffice to make the point for anyone unfamiliar with the articles or books themselves.

Defining Terms and Analyzing Concepts

Much maligned by many outside of philosophy, the activity of defining terms and analyzing concepts has been central to philosophical inquiry since Plato. It is no doubt the peculiar style and perseveration of linguistic analysts from the so-called Oxford school that has occasioned the abuse heaped upon contemporary philosophy by its detractors. Yet even in the field of bioethics we find this feature of philosophical inquiry in abundance, whether it stands alone as the purpose of an article or is embedded in works having a larger purpose. The following are illustrations of articles the main aim of which is to explore definitions or analyze concepts or phrases having currency in the domain of bioethics.

1. Tom Beauchamp and Arnold Davidson, "The Definition of Euthanasia."[1]

[1]Tom L. Beauchamp and Arnold I. Davidson, "The Definition of Euthanasia," *The Journal of Medicine and Philosophy* 4 (1979), pp. 294–312.

2. Albert Jonsen, "Do No Harm."[2]
3. A number of articles in the collection entitled *Concepts of Health and Disease,* edited by Arthur Caplan, H. T. Engelhardt, Jr., and James McCartney;[3] in particular: Christopher Boorse, "On the Distinction between Disease and Illness"; Joseph Margolis, "The Concept of Disease"; Caplan's "The 'Unnaturalness' of Aging. . ."; and my own "Mental Health and Mental Illness: Some Problems of Definition and Concept Formation" (originally published in *Philosophy of Science,* as the title might suggest).
4. The "paternalism" group. Most of these articles by philosophers go well beyond the activity of definition and conceptual analysis, but they contain at least that and devote some time to commenting on each others' proposed definitions and the adequacy of one another's conceptual analysis: Gerald Dworkin, "Paternalism" (originally published in *The Monist*);[4] Tom Beauchamp, "Paternalism and Biobehavioral Control" (also from the *Monist*);[5] two by Charles Culver and Bernard Gert (Culver is a psychiatrist, Gert a philosopher): "Paternalistic Behavior," originally published in *Philosophy and Public Affairs,*[6] and "The Justification of Paternalism," originally published in *Ethics;*[7] and Allen Buchanan, "Medical Paternalism," from *Philosophy and Public Affairs.*[8]

My reason for mentioning the journals in which a number of these articles originally appeared relates directly to the question of standards, at least as perceived by the mainstream of the profession. Journals such as *Philosophy and Public Affairs, Ethics, Philosophy of Science,* and *The Monist* are mainstream philosophical journals, whose editorial boards and reviewers are among the standard setters and perpetrators of intellectual fashion within the discipline. The fact that *Philosophy and Public Affairs* is devoted to applied topics in philosophy is less important for this point than that its contents are accessible almost exclusively to philosophers. In an early meeting of the project for which the essays in this volume

[2]Albert R. Jonsen, "Do No Harm," eds. Samuel Gorovitz and Ruth Macklin *et al., Moral Problems in Medicine,* 2nd ed. (Englewood Cliffs, N.J.: Prentice-Hall, 1983), pp. 99–107.
[3]Arthur L. Caplan, H. Tristram Engelhardt, Jr., and James J. McCartney, eds., *Concepts of Health and Disease* (Reading, Mass.: Addison-Wesley Publishing Co., 1981).
[4]Gerald Dworkin, "Paternalism," *The Monist* 56 (1972), pp. 64–84.
[5]Tom L. Beauchamp, "Paternalism and Bio-Behavioral Control," *The Monist* 60 (1977), pp. 62–80.
[6]Bernard Gert and Charles M. Culver, "Paternalistic Behavior," *Philosophy and Public Affairs* 6 (1976), pp. 45–57.
[7]Bernard Gert and Charles M. Culver, "The Justification of Paternalism," *Ethics* 89 (1979), pp. 199–210.
[8]Allen Buchanan, "Medical Paternalism," *Philosophy and Public Affairs* 7 (1978). Reprinted in Gorovitz and Macklin, pp. 49–60.

were written, Daniel Callahan referred to this journal and its contents as falling within the category of "philosophers writing for one another," in contrast with philosophers who do applied philosophy aimed at practitioners in another discipline, say, medicine; and Arthur Caplan pointed out that the references in *P&PA* in footnotes and to other writings are largely to other articles that appeared in this same journal. When one looks at the editorial board and the authors represented in the pages of *P&PA*, one finds the intellectual standard bearers in the discipline, people with faculty appointments in philosophy departments at the most prestigious institutions or, at least, in departments recognized as highly prestigious regardless of the institution. The journal *Ethics* has recently become somewhat more interdisciplinary, under the editorship of a political scientist, Brian Barry; but still the contributors are primarily philosophers, political theorists, and theoretical economists, who typically meet high intellectual standards in their own fields. The areas they represent are ones that cross disciplinary boundaries (political philosophy and political theory, for example). The standards adhered to in these journals are those I referred to as internal, ones that are used in evaluating philosophical writings of the more traditional, unapplied sort.

Attending to the Logic of Arguments, Detecting and Uncovering Assumptions

This second feature of philosophical writing is likely to cut across all other categories, so it would be hard to find books or articles having exclusively these elements. An example is Allen Buchanan's article "Medical Paternalism," already mentioned above. In addition to analyzing the concept of paternalism and offering correctives to the definitions proposed by others (Dworkin, Beauchamp), Buchanan spends considerable time uncovering assumptions physicians make when they invoke paternalistic arguments in support of their behavior. For instance, Buchanan explores the assumption—sometimes implicit, at other times explicit—that disclosing bad news to patients about their diagnosis or prognosis will result in foreseeable harm to that patient; or that disclosing risks of treatment will eventuate in patients' refusal of the recommended treatment. Buchanan thus goes beyond the mere activity of defining and analyzing concepts and encompasses the further features of uncovering assumptions and assessing the soundness of paternalistic arguments offered by physicians. This article also falls in one of the subsequent categories, as well: offering sustained normative arguments in favor of a position. Buchanan includes in his essay arguments of his own intended to show that medical paternalism is unjustified in a large number of instances typically occurring in medical contexts.

Another well-known group of articles falls under this heading—the "killing and letting die" group. These divide into two categories: the narrowly philosophical, applied only by virtue of the topic; and the others, likely to be both accessible to nonphilosophers and also of interest to them. In the first, narrow, grouping are the following: Timothy Goodrich, "The Morality of Killing";[9] Jonathan Bennett, "Whatever the Consequences";[10] Daniel Dinello, "On Killing and Letting Die";[11] and P. J. Fitzgerald, "Acting and Refraining."[12]

What characterizes this group as narrowly philosophical, applied by virtue of their topic alone? First of all, at least the last three in this group are parasitic on one another, the second two discussing the first article. All three originally appeared in the British philosophical journal *Analysis*, renowned, as its title implies, for short, highly analytic, tightly argued little pieces. They all also contain another feature, guaranteed to deter readers unaccustomed to analytic philosophical style, however otherwise interesting the topic or the article might be. That feature is the use of x's and y's, a's and b's, and numbering systems that use primes. Some examples follow. From Bennett:

> The difference between "X killed Y" and "X let Y die" is the sum-total of a vast number of differences such as that between "X killed Y in one of the only n possible ways" and "X killed Y in one of the only $n+1$ possible ways." If the difference between "$\ldots n \ldots$" and "$\ldots n+1 \ldots$" were morally insignificant only because it was *too small* for any moral discrimination to be based upon it, then the sum-total of millions of such differences might still have moral significance.[13]

And from Dinello:

> (A) x killed y if x caused y's death by performing movements which affect y's body such that y dies as a result of these movements.
> (B) x let y die if
>   (a) there are conditions affecting y, such that if they are not altered, y will die.
>   (b) x has reason to believe that the performance of certain movements will alter conditions affecting y, such that y will not die.
>   (c) x is in a position to perform such movements.
>   (d) x fails to perform these movements.[14]

---

[9]Timothy Goodrich, "The Morality of Killing," *Philosophy* 44 (1969), pp. 127–39.

[10]Jonathan Bennett, "Whatever the Consequences," *Analysis* 26 (1966), pp. 83–97. Reprinted in Gorovitz *et al.* (eds.), *Moral Problems in Medicine*, 1st ed., (1976), pp. 276–281.

[11]Daniel Dinello, "On Killing and Letting Die," *Analysis* 31 (1971), pp. 83–86. Reprinted in Gorovitz *et al.*, ibid., pp. 281–284.

[12]P. J. Fitzgerald, "Acting and Refraining," *Analysis* 27 (1973), pp. 133–39. Reprinted in Gorovitz et al., ibid., pp. 284–289.

[13]Bennett, ed. Gorovitz *et al.*, pp. 279–280.

[14]Dinello, ibid., p. 283.

And with the reader's indulgence, one from Fitzgerald:

> At one end of the scale is (a) the case where *all* alternatives would have avoided death. X kills Y in the only way possible. At the other is the case (b) where all alternatives but one would not have avoided death: X does not do the only thing that would save Y. In between are:
> (a') X kills Y in one of the five ways possible.
> (a") X kills Y in one of the fifty ways possible.
> (a"') X kills Y in one of the five hundred ways possible; etc.[15]

Now perhaps there are still some philosophers around who believe that writing in this manner is a necessary condition for maintaining intellectual standards in the discipline. I do not know. But I hazard the guess that if articles like these were submitted to *The New England Journal of Medicine* they would be rejected out of hand (and rightly so). I can visualize reviewers for that prestigious journal rolling their eyes at these samples. Yet that journal did publish an article on the topic of killing and letting die, written by a philosopher, James Rachels.[16] Rachels mounts the argument that there is no morally significant difference between killing and letting die, contrary to what many physicians appear to think. Moreover, he argues, a case can be made for claiming that some instances of letting die are morally worse than some cases of killing, namely, those in which greater suffering occurs when the patient is allowed to die (say, by slow starvation) rather than by a humane act of direct killing. Whatever one thinks of Rachels' conclusions, or of some of the particular arguments he offers, there is little doubt that his article meets the internal standards set by philosophers in journals such as *P&PA* and *Ethics*. The fact that Rachels wrote his article in a manner wholly accessible to physicians, the vast majority of readers of *NEJM*, and further that it also has philosophical merit serves to support the descriptive part of my thesis: that applied ethics not only can but does in many cases meet the intellectual standards of unapplied philosophy.

The style of philosophical writing exhibited in the examples from Dinello, Bennett, and Fitzgerald offers a clue about the transmission of standards within an academic discipline. The norms of intradisciplinary scholarship are learned by students as early as their undergraduate years, and more typically, they are acquired in graduate school as part of the socialization into the profession. Thus it should come as no surprise to find those norms reflected in articles submitted for publication in professional journals edited and reviewed by the same faculty members who supervise graduate work at the leading schools and whose contributions to these same journals aid in establishing a set of standards. This is not

---

[15]Fitzgerald, ibid., p. 287.
[16]James Rachels, "Active and Passive Euthanasia," *The New England Journal of Medicine* 292 (1975), pp. 78–80.

to confuse intellectual standards with norms or even fads in the style and content of scholarly writing. The intellectual standards in pure and applied philosophy have endured since the ancients, but stylistic modes such as that displayed above in the articles from *Analysis* come and go.

Another article in this category is by Philippa Foot, entitled "The Problem of Abortion and the Doctrine of the Double Effect."[17] This article is very clearly written, in plain English, with no x's, y's, a's, b's, primes, or double primes. It originally appeared in the *Oxford Review*. Foot's article is an exemplary piece of philosophical reasoning. It is also quite telling in another respect: not only does the author not take a clear stance on the abortion controversy, but she confines her discussion of the moral principles to the Roman Catholic "doctrine of double effect." She concludes the article by acknowledging: "I have not been arguing for or against these points of view but only trying to discern some of the currents that are pulling us back and forth." That is surely a respectable aim for a philosophical article, but one not likely to interest those concerned about the moral status of abortion, be they philosophers or nonphilosophers.

Finally, there are two articles by the same author, the philosopher John Ladd, that may be classified as applied metaethics. In the best tradition of philosophical ethics, Ladd attends to the logic of arguments, detects fallacies, and uncovers assumptions. He also engages in some conceptual analysis and offers a few prescriptive definitions. One article, entitled "Legalism and Medical Ethics,"[18] explores what Ladd calls "legalism," the tendency to conceptualize issues and moral solutions in terms of rules and their attendant duties and obligations. He contrasts this approach with another, which he prefers and argues for, focusing on roles and responsibilities to others deriving from those roles. Because the subject matter is the doctor–patient relationship, there is little question that this article must be classified as applied ethics. Yet because Ladd's philosophical approach is clearly recognizable as an instance of metaethical analysis, it can be judged by the same standards used to evaluate philosophical writings of a more traditional sort in contemporary ethics. His other article, "Some Reflections on Authority and the Nurse,"[19] is also a metaanalysis, in this case more political and social than narrowly ethical. Although Ladd's conclusions in these articles have implications for normative ethics, the articles themselves are not, strictly

---

[17]Philippa Foot, "The Problem of Abortion and the Doctrine of the Double Effect," *Oxford Review* 5 (1967), pp. 5–15.

[18]John Ladd, "Legalism and Medical Ethics," *The Journal of Medicine and Philosophy* 4 (1979), pp. 70–80.

[19]John Ladd, "Some Reflections on Authority and the Nurse," Gorovitz and Macklin, pp. 138–146.

speaking, essays in normative ethics. The same could be said for much philosophical writing classified as metaethics, and those that succeed in meeting high philosophical standards often blend metaethical and normative concerns, in much the same way as the historical examples cited at the outset.

Analyzing and Interpreting Other Writings—within or without Philosophy

I will not provide examples of this well-known philosophical category, since they are easy to detect. Here again, whether a particular book or article on an applied topic meets the intellectual standards of unapplied writings in philosophy is a matter that needs to be determined in each instance. As a paradigm, I offer Alan Donagan's "Informed Consent in Therapy and Experimentation," which appeared in *The Journal of Medicine and Philosophy*.[20] Donagan's article is largely a review article, in the best scholarly tradition of exploring the roots in the history of philosophy of some current principles and practices in an applied area—in this case, the doctrine of informed consent. It is accessible to the nonphilosopher with a scholarly bent, and the journal in which it appears is evidence for that fact. *The Journal of Medicine and Philosophy* is much more philosophical than medical. The average reader of typical medical journals, for example *The Journal of the American Medical Association*, could barely comprehend or maintain an interest in its lengthy, rather scholarly articles. The intellectual standards of *The Journal of Medicine and Philosophy* are not those I have called internal to philosophy. Articles written by nonphilosophers for this publication would not meet the intellectual standards of mainstream philosophy. The same is true, I fear, for many of the articles written by philosophers. It is impossible to back up these general statements sufficiently by citing only a few examples, so I will not even try. But let me note with some dismay that I believe this is a failed effort—an attempt to blend philosophy and medicine in a scholarly journal straddling both fields, but an attempt that sadly does not succeed. Although the subject matter is applied philosophy, most of the contributions fail to meet the standards adhered to in mainstream philosophy.

Constructing Hypothetical Arguments for or against Positions

I will cite only one example in this category, one notable for its philosophical cleverness and at the same time for its negative reception

---

[20]Alan Donagan, "Informed Consent in Therapy and Experimentation," *The Journal of Medicine and Philosophy* 2 (1977), pp. 310–327.

outside the narrow philosophical community. It is the much-discussed article by Judith Jarvis Thomson, "A Defense of Abortion," which also appeared in the Princeton in-house publication, *Philosophy and Public Affairs*.[21] I cite the article here for two reasons. The first is to note how it falls squarely within the category under discussion—a category likely to be dismissed as irrelevant by nonphilosophers. In Thomson's own words:

> Most opposition to abortion relies on the premise that the fetus is a human being, a person, from the moment of conception. . . . I am inclined to agree . . . that the prospects for "drawing a line" in the development of the fetus look dim. I am inclined to think also that we shall probably have to agree that the fetus has already become a human person well before birth. . . . On the other hand, I think that the premise is false, that the fetus is not a person from the moment of conception. . . . But I shall not discuss any of this. For it seems to me to be of great interest to ask what happens if, for the sake of argument, we allow the premise . . . I propose, then, that we grant that the fetus is a person from the moment of conception.[22]

Whereas many writers on the abortion controversy devote their main efforts to arguing for or against the "personhood" of the fetus, and still others argue for the irrelevance of the personhood of the fetus to the question of the moral permissibility of abortion, Thomson proceeds with an analysis based on a hypothetical premise she herself rejects. That tactic sits very well with philosophers and probably aided in the article's acceptance in the first number of the first volume of *P&PA*. But it is not this feature of Thomson's article that has incurred the disdain of writers outside of philosophy. Instead, it is her fanciful example of the violinist. I shall now repeat that example, for readers unfamiliar with it, along with a different example by another writer on abortion that illustrates a point about philosophers' use of analogical reasoning. But first, here are the examples.

In Thomson's illustration, a famous violinist is hooked up to your kidneys, which he needs to sustain his own life for a period of nine months, after which he will have recovered. The violinist is a person, and so he has a right to life. Your life is not endangered, only your freedom to move about for nine months. We are supposed to consider the violinist an appropriate analogue to a fetus, and you and your kidneys as analogous to a pregnant woman and her life supports for the fetus. If your right to disconnect yourself from the violinist overrides his right to life, the argument goes, should it not follow that a woman's

---

[21]Judith Jarvis Thomson, "A Defense of Abortion," *Philosophy and Public Affairs* 1 (1971), pp. 47–66. Reprinted in eds. Tom L. Beauchamp and LeRoy Walters, *Contemporary Issues in Bioethics* (Encino, CA: Dickenson Publishing Co., 1978), pp. 199–209.
[22]Ibid., p. 199.

right to terminate her pregnancy overrides the fetus's right to life? One can admire Thomson's philosophical imagination, yet reject the soundness of the analogy on a number of different counts. Arguing in general against the use of artificial cases, John T. Noonan (a law professor and foe of abortion) writes about this one:

> The similitude to pregnancy is grotesque. It is difficult to think of another age or society in which a caricature of this sort could be seriously put forward as a paradigm illustrating the moral choice to be made by the mother.[23]

And Mary Anne Warren, whose stance on abortion is at the opposite pole from that of Noonan, criticizes Thomson's analogy on the grounds that it is too weak to do the work required in the abortion argument:

> The Thomson analogy can provide a clear and persuasive defense of an abortion only with respect to those cases in which the woman is in no way responsible for her pregnancy, e.g., where it is due to rape.[24]

The second example is that of a kitten hypothesized by Michael Tooley in his attack on the potentiality principle as used in the abortion argument. Imagine we have a chemical that, if injected into a kitten, would enable it to develop into an adult cat having the intellectual and psychological abilities of a human adult. Tooley relies on the reader's intuition that it would not be wrong to kill a kitten injected with this chemical, and reasoning by analogy he rejects the potentiality principle as applied to the human fetus.[25] Noonan responds to this artificial case in a similar fashion to his reaction to Thomson's example. A problem with the use of artificial cases as a strategy for arguing a moral point is that the debate shifts to a discussion of the preposterousness of the example, and hence to the adequacy of the analogy, leaving the real issue aside.

Offering Sustained Normative Arguments for or against a Substantive Position

For this final category, I will list only a few examples. They include: Daniel Wikler's "Ought We to Try to Save Aborted Fetuses?" which appeared in *Ethics*,[26] and his "Persuasion and Coercion for Health," from the *Milbank Memorial Quarterly*.[27] The latter is not a philosophy journal but a highly regarded publication in the interdisciplinary field

---

[23]John T. Noonan, "How to Argue About Abortion," Beauchamp and Walters, p. 210.

[24]Mary Anne Warren, "On the Moral and Legal Status of Abortion," Beauchamp and Walters, p. 221.

[25]Michael Tooley, "Abortion and Infanticide," *Philosophy and Public Affairs* 2 (1972), pp. 37–65.

[26]Daniel I. Wikler, "Ought We to Try to Save Aborted Fetuses?" *Ethics* 90 (1979), pp. 58–65.

[27]Daniel I. Wikler, "Persuasion and Coercion for Health," *Milbank Memorial Fund Quarterly/Health and Society* 56 (1978).

of health policy which enjoys an excellent reputation among scholars from different academic specialties. Other examples in this category include Sissela Bok's article "Placebos," which appeared as a section of her book *Lying*,[28] and Kai Nielsen's "Radical Egalitarian Justice: Justice and Equality,"[29] an article on health policy and justice that meets high standards of philosophical scholarship while at the same time being accessible to those whose discipline or background lies outside philosophy.

These articles, along with many others that could be cited, serve to show that applied philosophy need not be a mere technical exercise, exhibiting little else than flashy argumentive skills of logicians. Sound, persuasive arguments that take a decisive viewpoint on ethical issues of wide social and political importance are a good deal more than sophisticated linguistic games. At its best, applied philosophy illustrates the inextricable blend of reason and moral commitment, devoted to the task of providing insight and understanding.

APPLIED PHILOSOPHY AND APPLIED ETHICS

The foregoing discussion suggests a few conclusions about the nature of applied philosophy and the standards it embodies. The chief difference between applied and unapplied philosophy appears to lie in the topics addressed by these two fields of inquiry. Yet that is only a superficial difference, since, as we have seen, some articles written by philosophers on topics such as killing and letting die display little beyond technical virtuosity.

More importantly, that an article addresses a topic in applied ethics—say, bioethics—offers no guarantee that it proceeds in a philosophical manner. Compare, for example, an article that appeared in the *Hastings Center Report* on the ethics of fetal therapy and an article on roughly the same topic that was published in *Ms.* magazine. The former article, by William Ruddick and William Wilcox[30]—both philosophers— is a careful examination of a range of issues surrounding the emerging techniques of *in utero* therapy: consideration of the fetus as a patient, pitting the rights of the pregnant woman against the rights of the fetus, the implications of this new therapeutic development for the long-standing abortion debate. Regardless of whether one agrees with the conclu-

---

[28]Sissela Bok, *Lying: Moral Choice in Public and Private Life* (New York: Pantheon Books, 1978).

[29]Kai Nielsen, "Radical Egalitarian Justice: Justice as Equality," Gorovitz and Macklin, pp. 519–527.

[30]William Ruddick and William Wilcox, "Operating on the Fetus," *Hastings Center Report* 12 (1982).

sions drawn by Ruddick and Wilcox, there is no question about the intellectual standards they adhere to in undertaking their analysis. In contrast, the article in *Ms.* magazine, written by a nonphilosopher,[31] consists largely of rhetorical flourishes and tendentious claims, although it includes an accurate descriptive account of the therapeutic techniques themselves (the author is a biologist on the faculty at Harvard). Topic alone, then, is not sufficient to characterize a work in applied ethics as philosophy. Whether the intellectual standards I have referred to as internal to philosophy should govern nonphilosophical writings in applied ethics may be a matter of some dispute. A reasonable conclusion is that high intellectual standards are not limited to use by philosophers who edit or review journals within the field and that those high general standards should govern interdisciplinary work.

A feature of philosophical writings mentioned briefly at the end of the preceding section is that of providing *insight* and *understanding* into a problem or a subject of inquiry. Although only the best philosophical works succeed in providing genuine insight or deep understanding of the issues they explore, those are the features that philosophers have traditionally striven to attain. Works by the greatest philosophers, those who have succeeded in providing genuine, recognized insights, have been hailed for their contributions to human understanding. (Such contributions are not, of course, limited to philosophical writings.) The authors of those works possess wisdom, as well as the analytic skills of argumentation and reasoning that minimally qualify many mere technicians who contribute to the philosophical literature.

A look at the background papers prepared by philosophers at the request of the National Commission for the Protection of Human Subjects during its tenure and the more recent President's Commission on Ethics in Medicine is instructive. Addressed primarily to nonphilosophers, these papers contain a minimum of the technical jargon and terminology accessible to other philosophers but not to other professionals or to the lay public. Yet they use the tools of philosophical analysis and in the best instances provide insight and understanding into the social and moral concerns they grapple with.

Lest the conclusions in this paper be dismissed as the biased observations of one who works in the field of applied philosophy, let me close by quoting the words of Lee Hamilton, a member of the United States House of Representatives from Indiana, who has had three philosophers, including an APA Congressional Fellow, working on his staff. It could not simply be the dazzling logic and analytic techniques of those

[31]Ruth Hubbard, "The Fetus as Patient," *Ms.* (October 1982).

philosophers that prompted him to write these remarks in a letter to the Executive Secretary of the American Philosophical Association:

> It seems to me that philosophers have acquired skills which are very valuable to a member of Congress. The ability to analyze a problem carefully and consider it from many points of view is one. Another is the ability to communicate ideas clearly in a logically compelling form. A third is the ability to handle the many different kinds of problems which occupy the congressional agenda at any given time.
>
> I do not mean to imply that philosophers are the only ones who possess such skills. Of course, they are not. What I find especially useful in philosophers, however, is that their skills are refined and concentrated by training in such a way that the exercise of those skills is second nature. I am not obliged to tell them that careful analysis and clear presentation is needed. I am not uneasy when I set them to work in new areas of inquiry. I am confident that the methods they follow will yield sound results.[32]

---

[32]Lee Hamilton, letter, *Proceedings of the American Philosophical Association* 55 (1982).

CHAPTER 16

Literature and Medicine
Standards for Applied Literature

KATHRYN MONTGOMERY HUNTER

There is an inescapable difficulty in describing the standards for intellectual work in a field that is only just now coming into existence. Applied history, or history in the service of public policy, has at least informally its own history, which, as Peter Stearns has demonstrated,[1] sustains the current debate over its proper conduct. Bioethics has a substantial past, however brief. It is possible to say what constitutes good work in an applied field that has flourished so abundantly, particularly when its criteria and its relations with its parent discipline have been the subject of so much internal strife and justification. Applied literature is different. The study of a poem or a play, a novel or a short story as a critique of the social reality it claims to mirror is in one sense as old as literature itself. But its late twentieth-century manifestation in literature and medicine, like the comparable undertaking in women's studies, is recent enough and still thin enough that a discussion of standards must be somewhat speculative. This essay, then, is written quite near the beginning of a necessary debate.

Is literature and medicine a field? The singular verb *is* demands an affirmative answer. Is literature and medicine to be understood like ham and eggs or like apples and oranges? Denial is awkward—"No, literature and medicine are not a field." But, in fact, the question has not been answered satisfactorily. The current status might be expressed by a dis-

---

[1]Peter Stearns, Chapter 12 of this volume.

KATHRYN MONTGOMERY HUNTER ● Department of Preventive, Family, and Rehabilitation Medicine, University of Rochester School of Medicine, Rochester, New York 14642.

289

junction of grammar and logic: literature and medicine is not a field, not quite yet.

This is so because it is not yet entirely clear how the study of poetry, drama, and fiction concerned with such universal matters as birth, growth, illness, age, and death differs from the study of literature in general. The use of that literature in the education of physicians has proved valuable wherever it has been attempted, and it is to this enterprise and its attendant literary scholarship that the current assumption of literature and medicine's status as an intellectual field refers. There is now a journal, *Literature and Medicine*,[2] the first volume of which bore the modestly assertive subtitle, "Toward a New Discipline," and there have been collections of literature having to do with doctors[3] and essays on that literature.[4] The question here, and it is paralleled by a similar question only lately beginning to be answered in women's studies,[5] is how this enterprise differs except in the specificity of its topics from business as usual in literary scholarship and criticism. What is lacking in the "field"— and in a theory of the field—is interactivity, some demonstration of the inextricable nature of the alliance between literature and medicine that will assert its inevitability and value as an intellectual as well as a pedagogical enterprise.

Joanne Trautmann's report of the 1975–76 symposium that inaugurated the topic, *Healing Arts in Dialogue: Medicine and Literature*, struggles with the problem of interactivity. Her title suggests that dialogue is a criterion of disciplinary relatedness or union, and perhaps even an assumption upon which the symposium was based. Yet the meetings, five of them held over the course of a year and a half, were most fascinating even as they foundered on just this issue. The book is an inventive potpourri of papers read, responses transcribed, summaries of discussion, and letters and poems and stories exchanged between meetings; it renders ordinary proceedings dull by comparison in their failure to create or capture dialogue. But the book took five years to produce, and it is haunted by Trautmann's refusal to forget or ignore the Tenth Dialogist, a "shadowy presence" named only in the index, who quit after the first session saying, "*And* is a neutral word. You can link

---

[2]*Literature and Medicine: Toward a New Discipline* (Albany, NY: State University of New York Press, 1, 1981).

[3]Joseph Ceccio, ed., *Medicine in Literature* (English and Humanities series) (New York: Longman, 1978); and Norman Cousins, ed. *The Physician in Literature* (Philadelphia: W. B. Saunders, 1982).

[4]Enid Rhodes Peschel, ed., *Medicine and Literature* (New York: Neale Watson Academic Publications, 1980).

[5]*Feminist Literary Criticism* (Working Paper #3) (Research Triangle Park, N.C.: National Humanities Center, 1981); see particularly Lydia Blanchard, "Feminist Literary Criticism: The Feminist Criticism of Literary Criticism," pp. 31–56.

anything and anything else, and pretend for awhile that you have a subject, but do you really have one?"[6]

That remains the question for literature and medicine, and upon its answer depends the discussion of standards. For if applied literature pursues the engineering model, a model Edwin Layton has shown does not obtain in engineering,[7] then the standards will consist of medicine's view of literature's utility, its relevance to diagnosis and treatment. This, of course, has been the grounds for literature's exclusion from medical education and even from undergraduate premedical curricula. If, on the other hand, literature and medicine is construed by an enlightenment model, the customary standards of literary study will prevail; enlightenment is what literature and literary criticism traditionally have claimed to be and do. But both these models are unsatisfactory, limiting literature and medicine to an adjunct and subsidiary status in one of the parent disciplines. Neither alternative would constitute an independent discipline. With Joanne Trautmann and with G. S. Rousseau, who calls for a reciprocity between medicine and literature (that he does not entirely demonstrate) in his recent assessment of the territory for *Isis*,[8] I hope for an interactive relationship, which will constitute literature and medicine as a field. Only such interactivity will enable literature and medicine to withstand criticism from its constituent disciplines and to contribute both to literary study and to the understanding of medicine. This essay describes the "protofield" that now exists, outlines the interactivity requisite to its status as a separate intellectual endeavor, and, finally, describes the standards that may obtain and the relationship with its related, parent disciplines that will result.

THE ENLIGHTENMENT MODEL

What literature offers medical education is well established, and this pedagogical movement,[9] together with medicine's contributions first of plot and character to literature and then of pathology to creative psychology and literary biography,[10] up till now have constituted the claims

---

[6]Joanne Trautmann, ed., *Healing Arts in Dialogue: Medicine and Literature* (Carbondale, Ill.: Southern Illinois University Press, 1981). The conference was sponsored by the Institute on Human Values in Medicine.

[7]Edwin T. Layton, Chapter 4 of this volume.

[8]G. S. Rousseau, "Literature and Medicine: The State of the Field," *Isis*, 72 (September 1981), 406–424.

[9]Thomas K. McElhinney, ed., *Human Values Teaching Programs for Health Professionals*, Institute on Human Values in Medicine, Report 14 (Ardmore, Pa.: Whitmore Publishing Co., 1981).

[10]William Ober, *Boswell's Clap and Other Essays* (Carbondale, Ill.: Southern Illinois University Press, 1979).

to interactivity between the disciplines. But this is little different from the use of literature in regional, ethnic, or women's studies: there is mutual illumination both in teaching and its attendant scholarship but little shaping interaction.

Much of this similarity is due to the character of literary study itself. For applicability and application are traditionally the normal state of literature and literary study. Using the criteria for applicability cited by Robert Bellah that the study be practical, ethical, and relevant,[11] there is, before the turn of the twentieth century, no "unapplied literature." Horace asserted that literature was meant to teach and to delight, and although one or the other of this dyad has predominated at different times down to our own century, this view has prevailed. That is not to say that literature is a fund of moral lessons waiting to be drawn like teeth from impacting language and form. The reduction of literature to extractable "morals" in the preceding century led in the twentieth to a violent rejection of the instrumental model of literature and an over-reaction against the Horatian, rhetorical conception of literature—both in the works themselves and in literacy criticism. The example of social socialist realism only reinforced this response. Whereas Ruth Macklin can point out there is no unapplied philosophy, in particular no ethics not addressed to an audience and not concerned with human conduct,[12] postmodern literature has attempted to evade applicability; and much contemporary literary criticism, like contemporary historiography, has made nonapplication its fundamental assumption. But the pendulum shows signs of returning. John Gardner's 1978 manifesto, *On Moral Fiction*,[13] argues for the traditional view of literature's rhetorical function, and the limits of the objectivist study of literature have been widely observed. Bellah in this volume describes

> how difficult it is for the humanities, seen as disciplines in a university, itself seen as a place for the production of objective knowledge, to communicate genuine narrative. . . . Narratives become objects, along with all other objects, to be decontaminated, mounted, and hung as specimens in a museum. If, in spite of everything, students insist on identifying with them and living them we are more apt to be baffled than pleased.[14]

Literature, as this passage implies, is particularly well suited to such application. Like history and philosophy, literary study was not a part of the medieval scholastic curriculum. Instead they were worldly pursuits that unlocked storehouses of practical knowledge about how to conduct oneself and how to regard the vicissitudes of individual and

[11]Robert Bellah, Chapter 7 of this volume.
[12]Ruth Macklin, Chapter 15 of this volume.
[13]John Gardner. *On Moral Fiction* (Boston: Basic Books, 1978).
[14]Robert Bellah, p. 119.

political life. Literature offers its readers an imaginative grasp of other lives, other experiences, a shared look at another view of human existence. This is the traditional function of storytelling. Although it is unfashionable to assert literature's moral nature—literature professors are rightly wary of becoming preachers—stories and poems and plays are always, however subtly, normative. Literature is present to the mind so much more vividly than much of our everyday experience. It is whole, rounded, fleshed out with meaning (even when that meaning is the unavailability of meaning), whereas our own lives and the lives that we touch are unfinished, fragmentedly perceived, and often laden with meaning that we would rather forget. Instead of extrapolated lessons, then, we are given a sense of the variety, possibility, and unpredictability of the human universe. Texts are the occasion for interpretation and thereby engage and encourage our practical wisdom and our useful knowledge of the world. We envision how life ought to be lived, how it almost falls short, and how we might muddle through in spite of it all. Narrative presents human experience in its social context, raising questions of character and motive, conflict and choice. Poetry engages concepts of the self, with its ways of apprehending human interaction and of creating meaning. These are moral concerns. There are no answers here; instead we become aware that the individual life is lived on a common stage, but one larger and older than we may have thought.

The use of literature in medical education is only a more particular instance of literature's applicability. Its inherent applied nature is simply more evident in a highly pragmatic setting with the consequent need to justify literature's presence there. Literature has a special relevance to medicine. It is concerned with life and death and with the meaning of choices, both everyday ones and those faced in crisis. Literature focuses on the individual in relation to others—in the family, in health care encounters—and in relation to the self in its consciousness, in growth and learning, and in the acceptance of death. It places these matters in a larger context as forces such as war, epidemics, economic fluctuation, and social change make themselves felt in the individual life. Edmund Pellegrino has observed that the two disciplines share a need for committed distance and a concern with close observation, a "simultaneous detachment from and attachment to life."[15]

Because medicine attends the crises that are the stuff of literature, there is little that is written that could not in some way be an illustrative case for medicine, broadly conceived. In its turn, literature may prepare

[15]Edmund D. Pellegrino, "Foreword" to Trautmann, ed., *Healing Arts in Dialogue*, p. ix. See also his "Introduction: To Look Feelingly—The Affinities of Medicine and Literature," in Peschel, ed., *Medicine and Literature*, pp. xv–xix.

doctors to understand better the subjective reality of the doctor–patient relationship; certainly it gives resonance to both individual patient-care dilemmas and to the consideration of abstract ethical principles. Doctors need a curiosity about the human condition to see them through the frustration and frequent boredom of a professional life that is less heroic than expected. Literature can provide a sense of how lives are lived which may alleviate the distancing and alienation that come of seeing patients intimately but briefly, often without knowing "what happens next."

For students there are two bonuses: they have the chance to experience an imaginative confrontation of situations that they will witness often in their future, and, because medical school is not only long and arduous but often stultifying as well, literature may also have a therapeutic use when applied to the wounds of professional education.[16] Beyond the working knowledge of the human condition it offers, literature can also stimulate an analysis of the profession they are about to enter. How doctors have used their lives in their writing is useful for its insights into the nature of doctoring. Expanded to a consideration of the image of the doctor in literature and viewed diachronically, reading results in some instructive observations on social history: for example, it was only in the first sixty years of the twentieth century that doctors were depicted as cultural heroes. Before that and after, they have been the ripe targets of literary satire.

Stories and poems and plays also provide splendid case studies for ethical reflection. William May has used recent drama for this purpose— *Whose Life Is It Anyway?* and *The Elephant Man*—and the *Hastings Center Report* pretended it was a theatre review.[17] Anne Hudson Jones and Edward Erde have collaborated lately on an essay in ethics that examines friendship as an ideal to which the doctor–patient relationship should aspire.[18] Their examples are drawn from two recent novels by Marge Piercy and William Nolen that are case studies in this relationship of a depth unavailable to social science. Not facts, perhaps; but truth nevertheless, since the meaning of fiction is subject to experiential confirmation by each reader. These applications of literature are closely related to the teaching of literature and medicine in medical schools, and not

---

[16]Henry Silver, "Medical Students and Medical School," *Journal of the American Medical Association,* 247 (1982), 309–10, is most striking among the recent spate of essays both for its brevity and for its central analogy: medical students exhibit the symptoms of battered children.

[17]William F. May, "From Obscurity to Center Stage: Three Plays," *The Hastings Center Report,* 11 (December, 1981), 24–30.

[18]Anne Hudson Jones and Edward Erde, "Diminished Capacity, Friendship, and Medical Paternalism: Two Case Studies from Fiction," *Theoretical Medicine,* 4 (Fall 1983), 303–322.

surprisingly theologians were familiar with the strategy long before the founding dean at Pennsylvania State Medical School at Hershey, George Harrell, ever thought of creating a department of humanities in a medical school and allowing that department to hire a professor of literature.

It has been objected that the teaching of literature and medicine to medical students reverses the customary order of education. While the undergraduate curriculum has become more specialized and preprofessional, graduate education has been asked to become broader and more nearly liberal. There seem to be good arguments in favor of this. Students in medical school are older and surer of their roles and of the value of "soft," nonfactual knowledge than they were as premeds. Furthermore, literature and medicine integrates the consideration of values issues into professional life: novel reading, for example, is not something that must be put away with childish things. And not only is the hunger for meaning assuaged, a need largely unaddressed in professional education, but in addition a traditional way of meeting that need is relearned or reinforced.

Other objections are more serious. Most physicians, no matter how much they may like to read, regard literature as irrelevant to their professional concerns: the diagnosis and treatment of illness. Enlightenment is all very well, but will it help take care of patients? Robert Coles's 1979 essay on the value of novels for the practicing physician, "Medical Ethics and Living a Life,"[19] was the first and is still the most accessible defense of literature and medicine. He maintains that the moral reflection engendered by novels is actually indispensible, if not quite useful, in everyday clinical practice. It is this conjunction of enlightenment and indirect utility, which Martha Nussbaum's essay traces from the classical tradition,[20] that is the source of literature and medicine's strength as a pedagogical enterprise. Physicians do feel its usefulness; Eric Cassell has offered instances: literature, he says, teaches a sense of process in time, provides a vision of life's ordinary wholeness often unavailable to the clinician, and encourages language skills useful for describing patients as well as for understanding them.[21] In addition, literature's apparent irrelevance is an advantage in a clinical situation. Unlike philosophy, it can never be perceived as a value-neutral system, ready-made to solve clinical problems. Those who apply literature in such a setting are in no danger of being mistaken for moral engineers or experts, rivals even, in possession of an answer machine. Instead, for a literary consultant it is relatively easy to mark situations as moral problems, place them in a long line of similar situations, and to acknowledge that there are likely

[19]Robert Coles, "Medical Ethics and Living a Life," *New England Journal of Medicine*, 301 (August 23, 1979), 444–6.
[20]Martha C. Nussbaum, Chapter 1 of this volume.
[21]Eric J. Cassell, Chapter 10 of this volume.

to be no clear solutions. For clinicians as for the rest of humanity, literature is a defamiliarization of the everyday, a source of clinical (and aesthetic) distance.

In contrast, the objections of mainstream literary scholars to literature and medicine have to do with what they see as literature's slide into excessive relevance in the medical setting: cooptation and a skewing of the literary canon. Those of us who teach literature in medical schools use short pieces and excerpts; we read minor works and neglect masterpieces; and we indulge in simplistic critical approaches. Like Holden Caulfield's brother, we have moved to Hollywood and become prostitutes. It is true that John Stone and Richard Selzer, both doctors, may be taught more often than comparably good contemporary writers. William Carlos Williams is read first as a short story writer and then as a poet. Tolstoy becomes the author of the "The Death of Ivan Ilych," and *War and Peace* is forgotten; *Middlemarch* is returned to a first-draft state in which it was Lydgate's story. A thorough rereading of Gwendolyn Brooks's *Children of the Poor* awaits an invitation to speak to the Adolescent Maternity Unit, while "The Mother," her poem about abortion, is used over and over again. Minor works, like Samuel Shem's satire, *The House of God*, are discussed with a seriousness out of proportion to their merit. Theme is often more important to interpretation than critical methodology, and authors' lives and their relation to the texts, especially if they are doctors, may be discussed heretically often. A literature professor in a medical school might even offer students only stories of doctors as heroes or pander to the soap-opera assumptions about medicine that even the most realistic students must work to shed. But there are built-in defenses both in literature and in medical education against the worst of these heresies. Literary quality is high because time is short and good works are more easily read and discussed than poor ones. Poetry is particularly useful: students admire its difficulty and it is short. In a day that may include five hours of class time, two or more hours in lab and more than 100 pages of reading, a poem gives a lot for its length. And literature's own polysemousness guarantees that, even if a topic has determined the choice of a work, in a class of more than four bright students the discussion and, above all, the learning will soon turn to questions of interpretation. If there is little time in medical education for careful, extended discussion of critical matters, there is in exchange a rerooting of literary criticism in ongoing moral life.

The criticism of the materialist assumption inherent in literature and medicine's enlightenment model is more difficult to answer. By this account, literature and medicine is so taken up with the discussion of social reality in its lectures and courses and essays on "the images of

. . ." and "the doctor as . . ." that it falls into the trap of assuming that literature only holds a mirror up to nature, is nothing but an unfailing representation of the way things are. Might postmodern criticism—particularly phenomenology, hermeneutics, and deconstructionist criticism—offer new understanding of this literature or of medicine itself? Indeed, this could well be the source of a genuine union of medicine and literature, a union that would render the word *applied* quite meaningless.

Such an objection to the enlightenment model may have motivated the denial by Trautmann's Tenth Dialogist that literature and medicine is or ever could be a discipline. Is the topic a defensible intellectual field in the absence of reciprocity, interactivity? Medicine contributes a great deal to literature, but this is little different from the comparable contributions to literature of history or psychology. And what does literature contribute to medicine, as distinguished from its contributions to medical education? These are serious questions which those of us wading around in what we hope is a field must attempt to answer.

The final criticism made of literature and medicine is the more superficial protest against the enlightenment model, mentioned near the beginning of this essay: that we are not prostitutes but missionaries who in our zeal to convert that strange tribe in white coats have betrayed our formalist critical heritage in favor of Victorian moralizing. In our hands, criticism, which might have been approaching scientific objectivity, has been muddied by considerations of author and intention, audience and social context, all of which are inherently imprecise and value-laden. But just as Stephen Toulmin has recently described "How Medicine Saved the Life of Philosophy,"[22] ten years from now it ought to be possible to write a comparable essay about the new work in literature and medicine which will have helped revivify the mainstream criticism and teaching of literature.

LITERATURE AND PUBLIC LIFE

With literature and medicine as a paradigm, it may also be possible again to assert, first, literature's usefulness, however indirect, to the professions, which, William Frankena has argued, supply the foundations of modern moral principles,[23] and, second, its relevance to public life. Can a literary education lead to better people, socially responsible

[22]Stephen Toulmin, "How Medicine Saved the Life of Philosophy," *Perspectives in Biology and Medicine*, 24 (1982), 736–50.
[23]William Frankena, "The Philosophy of Vocation," *Thought*, 51 (December 1976), 395–408.

professionals, better public policy?[24] This is precisely *not* what humanists, mindful of what might be called the Jeb Stuart Magruder Rule,[25]
would want to assert. Still, literature is value-laden and normative, and
it offers not only patterns for individual action that may be followed or
shunned but fictive situational analogs suitable for contemporary application. In fifth-century Athens, rhetors recited passages from *The Iliad*,
then explicated and interpreted them, applying them to contemporary
public policy. In Nixon's Washington, Elliott Richardson and William
Ruckleshaus resigned as attorney general and deputy attorney general
rather than fire Archibald Cox, the special Watergate prosecutor whose
independence they had guaranteed before Congress; without denying
the existence of personal and political components of their decisions, it
is nevertheless possible to see the pattern of their action in the tradition
of Greek tragedy. As the most public of literary genres, drama has always
been used politically. The Earl of Essex was charged with treason by
Elizabeth I, who regarded his revival of Shakespeare's *Richard II* as a
part of the evidence. Bertoldt Brecht's *Threepenny Opera* is an adaptation
of John Gay's *The Beggar's Opera*, which in 1728 had satirized the corruption of Robert Walpole's government; when Brecht's play opened in
Hitler's Berlin, it was quickly banned. *Antigone* has recently been staged
in Warsaw.

In his elegy on the death of William Butler Yeats, W. H. Auden
wrote that upon the evidence "poetry makes nothing happen"; yet "it
survives, / A way of happening, a mouth."[26] We read the *New Yorker*
short stories to see who we are now. We read stories and autobiographies
about heroic defiance of mortal illness or about equally heroic accommodation to it. Martha Weinman Lear's *Heartsounds*, Helen Yglesias's
"Semi-Private," even Robin Cook's paranoid mystery novels reexamine
the relationship between patients and doctors in a highly technological
medical system. Rational suicide is undergoing revaluation in a society
that reads Lael Wertenbaker's *Death of a Man*, regards the lives and deaths
of Virginia Woolf, Sylvia Plath, and Anne Sexton as a part of their poetic
statement, and flocks to see Marsha Norman's *'Night, Mother*. If the
paradigm of literature and medicine is generalized to other professions
and to public decision making, the use of literature as a critique of social
reality will be subject to the same criticism: irrelevance, cooptation, crit-

---

[24]Bruce Payne suggests that literature might enlighten policy analysis in Chapter 11 of
this volume.

[25]Jeb Stuart Magruder, convicted of Watergate-related crimes, spoke glowingly of his
education in the humanities at Williams College, particularly the ethics course he took
from William Sloane Coffin. Mr. Magruder has recently completed his studies at the
Princeton Theological Seminary.

[26]W. H. Auden, "In Memory of W. B. Yeats," lines 34–41.

ical heresy, naive materialism, and missionary moralizing. But the defense of literature as an element of education for citizenship sounds very like a good description of the goals of a liberal education—and that is no more than the proper concern of traditional, mainstream literary study.

THE INTERACTIVE MODEL

Given the inherent applicability of literature and literary study, then, how can literature and medicine constitute itself as an independent intellectual endeavor, a discipline that will engage both physicians and literary scholars? What can literature offer medicine, beyond enlightenment, that might clarify our understanding of the nature of medicine or shape its practice? The answer seems to lie in the application of literary criticism and literary theory to the discourse and rituals of medicine.

Looking at medicine with eyes trained in the study of literary texts, the observer soon finds several topics that might be regarded as proper to a discipline of literature and medicine: the military metaphors of clinical language, the prevalence of narrative despite the profession's distrust of anecdotal evidence, and a reliance upon ritual, which is implicit even in the word *rounds*. Medical phenomena yield new meaning when asked questions usually reserved for texts. Ideas of heroism in medicine deserve scrutiny, for example, in a surgical residency at a time when cost constraints call for Aeneas or Jimmy Stewart rather than Achilles or John Wayne. The parallel between therapeutic distance and aesthetic distance, alluded to above, has implications for the primary care specialties, which regularly lose some of their most promising and sensitive students and residents to the clearer, more cerebral subspecialties. To a literary eye, the syndrome letters in the *New England Journal of Medicine*—accounts of nonce events of unusual, even comic etiology like "Space Invader's Epilepsy," "French Vanilla Frostbite," or "Urban Cowboy Paraesthesia"—become a quasi-literary genre with interesting implications for the philosophy of medicine and medical education. And a grand rounds on limiting the medical treatment of a patient without family and now in a chronic vegetative state suddenly seems very like a Greek chorus, chronicling the past, weighing the future, supplying a moral resonance which had been lacking for both the patient and the staff.[27] Above all, there are the stories. The profession that scorns the anecdotal is in fact up to its ears in stories, using them to educate, to

[27]Kathryn Montgomery Hunter, "Limiting Treatment in a Social Vacuum: A Greek Chorus for William T.," *Archives of Internal Medicine*, 145 (1985), 716–719.

suggest the uncertainty of today's fact, using them to bridge the gap between book learning, abstract principles on the one hand and clinical practice on the other, the need to act and explain action in spite of uncertainty.[28]

These interests constitute something like a literary criticism of the text that is medicine. Without denying that medicine is "about" patients and illness, such an approach enables us to grasp the meaning and value inherent in its practice, its education, and its writing. Medicine cannot of itself address questions of its meaning. That is not its task, but rather the task of philosophy, literature, history—all the humanities. It requires a language, an attention to the details of discourse and custom which constitute the text, and a grounding in the theories of meaning.

If this sounds like what a number of cultural anthropologists do, there is good reason. They have proceeded as if the cultural life of a people were a text to be recorded and each of its details to be read and understood in relation to each of the others and to the whole. The facts are not enough. There can be no objective reporting of observed detail outside physical and most biological science. How, then, is a social science to describe its knowledge—particularly when it concerns another culture, which entails an unresolvable tension between an insider's knowledge and an outsider's judgment? What Clifford Geertz calls "thick description" answers the fact–value question with an unfolding, narrative, organic wholeness; his account of a Balinese cockfight,[29] for instance, bears a strong resemblance to a brilliant, thorough work of literary interpretation. The cockfight, explicated, is an image, a metaphor, which unravels the meaning of the whole.

This scrutiny of medicine as text which I am proposing has an instructive parallel in the activities of everyday clinical life. There, too, is an epistemological problem, for how is a physician to apply general pathophysiological principles to the individual patient? There are rules of thumb, of course, and the long residency training is meant to inculcate them. There is also the elusive skill or personal quality[30] called clinical

[28]Harold Bursztajn, Richard I. Feinbloom, Robert M. Hann, and Archie Brodsky, *Medical Choices, Medical Chances: How Patients, Families, and Physicians Can Cope with Uncertainty.* (New York: Delacorte Press/Seymour Lawrence, 1981).

[29]Clifford Geertz. *Interpretation of Culture* (Boston: Basic Books, 1973).

[30]The 1981–83 Project on the Professional Education of the Physician conducted by the Association of American Medical Colleges debated whether "clinical judgment" was properly a fundamental skill or a personal quality and therefore to which "working group" it belonged. Both groups reported on the matter, implying that although it may be in part an innate quality, it nevertheless can be educated and encouraged—or neglected. Alvan R. Feinstein has long maintained that it can be regularized and studied rigorously; see *Clinical Judgment* (Baltimore: Williams and Wilkins, 1967); and his series on clinimetrics "An Additional Basic Science for Clinical Medicine: I–IV," *Annals of Internal Medicine,* 99 (1983), 393–7, 544–50, 705–12, 843–8.

judgment, which a resident of my acquaintance has described as "what's left when the facts are forgotten." But even in full possession of the facts, the scientific information, there is no absolute certainty in its application.

Clinical medicine is a rational, science-using enterprise that requires both the knowledge of a body of scientific fact and theory and the clinical skill that guides the application of knowledge to the treatment of the individual sick person. The knowledge is essential, hence the medical school phrase for human biology, "the basic sciences." The clinical skill is also essential. If it were not, well-programmed computers, given complete data, would rapidly make doctors obsolete. But in fact, no matter how sophisticated the technology may be, diagnosis and treatment cannot be left to a computer analysis. In part this is because artificial intelligence can only replicate the already known. But in addition human variables and their concatenation approach the infinite. This is not surprising to the literary observer; on the contrary, certainty and invariance in human detail suggest that a story has been abridged, as in the customary medical case history.[31] This abridgement is useful and necessary but, of course, not the whole human truth of an illness. According to Sir William Osler, the legendary diagnostician who insisted on pragmatic bedside teaching that applied book knowledge to the individual case, "there is no teaching without a patient as text, and the best teaching is that taught by the patient himself."[32] The doctor stands in the same relationship to the patient as the literary critic to the poem. The task is the same: to read and interpret the signs, whether they are words or physical findings. As scientific information, pathophysiology is very like etymology: once we know what the dictionary says, we must discern which of the several definitions applies here. We will not have seen the sign in just this text before.

Thus the idea of the patient as text makes room for an acknowledgment of uncertainty in what often has been regarded as a science rather than a scientific, rational, human discipline. It also admits the social and emotional factors that, more often than we once suspected, create the human variability of the single medical case. Here, for comprehensive knowledge, we must know more than the initially useful case history. In addition to its flattening of subjective detail which allowed the testable, scientifically knowable state of the body to stand out in relief, we need also a narrative, a life history; for meaning and value are embodied in narrative's account of cause and effect, change and potential, in its account of subjective experience over the course of a

[31]Larry R. Churchill and Sandra W. Churchill, "Storytelling in Medical Arenas: The Art of Self-Determination," *Literature and Medicine,* 1 (1981), 73–79.

[32]Sir William Osler, "On the Need of a Radical Reform in Our Methods of Teaching Medical Students," *Medical News,* 82 (1903), 49–53.

lifetime of interaction with others. It is the individual life story in which questions of moral choice are always embedded.

Just as literature and medicine encourages practical wisdom and a sense of the larger social world in which medicine is practiced, offering at a safe distance experience of illness, age, dying, otherness, so the application of literary theory to medicine informs our understanding of the nature of medicine as a human enterprise and thus, perhaps, may shape its practice. Interpretive theory concerns itself with questions of meaning and value, which medicine, in order to get on with its work, must often take for granted. Borrowed from the humanities, originally from the study of sacred texts and then from its extension into textual study generally, hermeneutics addresses the predicament of the human sciences, the impossibility of separating human fact from human meaning either in the observer or in the observed.[33] Insofar as medicine differs from human biology, requiring additional knowledge for action in the world, it shares the predicament of the human sciences. An interpretation of medicine, then, may be a means of intellectually justifying medicine's assessment of human data, which are inaccessible to technology and not easily or convincingly quantifiable. Interpretive theory is capable not only of interpreting medicine to itself but of reconciling it to its inexactitude and uncertainty, whereas literature itself can constitute a way of bearing the assault to the physician's sense of control that is a consequence. Literature thus simultaneously provides a materialist critique of medicine's social reality and provokes a more profound examination of its fundamental assumptions. If literature and medicine is capable of revivifying the present-day study of literature, so the application of literary theory may restore medicine to its status as a human science.

STANDARDS

The intellectual standards for these applications of literary study are no less rigorous than those of the mainstream academic humanities, yet the interactivity itself requires that the two enterprises will differ in their focus, differentiating literature and medicine from traditional literary study. Comparable developments in history and engineering, in history and public policy, and in bioethics suggest that there will be more new journals, a disciplinary association of increasing strength and peculiarity within the Association for Faculty in the Medical Humanities (itself a

---

[33]Mary B. Hesse has described a hermeneutics of science in *The Structure of Scientific Inference* (London: Macmillan, 1974). Richard Rorty denies the epistemiological "predicament" in *Philosophy and the Mirror of Nature* (Princeton: Princeton University Press, 1979).

splinter of the Society for Health and Human Values), and some pressure for new training programs or postdoctoral fellowships.

This last seems at first glance misguided. There is no need to encourage professional study of the humanities in the absence of jobs, particularly when teaching and writing about literature is what, at their best, traditional graduate programs already prepare their students to do. What is needed for a scholarly career in literature and medicine is a good, undogmatic version of the traditional program that will encourage students of literature to consider texts in several ways, including their social and political contexts. Knowing how to teach well, no small matter, and an acquaintance with epistemology, the history and philosophy of science and of medicine, and the workings of society would be helpful, but it is difficult to imagine a graduate education that could provide or guarantee all this. After a good traditional education in literary history and theory, broadly conceived so as to prepare its students for citizenship in the intellectual world, a postdoctoral fellowship in a medical school with a flourishing program in the medical humanities should suffice.[34]

Scholars in literature and medicine, whether Ph.D.'s in literature or M.D.'s, will pursue a variety of topics in their essays and lectures: they will write and speak about poems and plays and stories and about literary theory, about medical matters illuminated by works of literature, and about literary theory applied to the interpretation of medicine. The first two are properly mainstream literary activities informed by knowledge from medicine, and, whether the author is an M.D. or a Ph.D., the old standards of literary study will apply. Essays will be published in mainstream journals or, on the evidence of the first two volumes, in *Literature and Medicine*, a mainstream sort of journal concerned with a focused body of literature. The third and fourth activities belong more precisely to literature and medicine: the application of literature and literary theory to medicine, its issues and its meaning. These scholars will seek a more general audience of readers: in medical school classrooms and general medical journals, at interdisciplinary conferences concerned with the broad education of physicians, and medical conferences including grand rounds, and in books and other publications that reach the educated public concerned with the crisis of confidence in technological medicine. Because the study of literature is inherently an enlightenment activity, many of the standards for these essays and lectures will differ little from

[34]The Institute on Human Values in Medicine provided postdoctoral fellowships of this sort from 1970 until 1980, supporting much of the first wave of applied humanities in medicine. Edmund D. Pellegrino and Thomas K. McElhinney, *Teaching Ethics, The Humanities, and Human Values in Medical Schools: A Ten-Year Overview* (Washington, D.C.: Institute on Human Values in Medicine, Society for Health and Human Values, 1982).

those for the mainstream study and teaching of literature. The pedagogical field of literature and medicine is all but indistinguishable from the teaching of nonmajors in an undergraduate college. The goals are a certain level of cultural literacy, a familiarity with traditional human responses to the human condition, a cultural citizenship. Individual scholars will be criticized, as for example Leslie Fiedler and Christopher Lasch have been, if they become better known for their broader, more public writing than for their earlier, more traditional, less generally applicable studies. A widened focus is academically suspect even when other standards are maintained: clarity of thought, attention to the text, a knowledge of the tradition and the literary canon, skill and critical self-consciousness in the use of literary theory. The question is: Is this still literary study? Or simply essays in social criticism? That there is a question suggests that literature and medicine is at this point a discipline *per se* and that this work must not be judged solely by mainstream literary scholars. Not that they should be excluded: their estimate of the critical soundness of intellectual work should be joined by assessments of its enlightenment value by medical educators and of its relevance (but not its utility) by doctors who see patients. Thus work in literature and medicine, although it must be judged by many of the criteria of academic literary study, should nevertheless be free of the constraints of literary criticism that cut literature and literary theory from its roots in the world of moral choice. New obligations have replaced the objectivist-critical ones: to speak clearly to readers educated in other disciplines, to abandon the dream of the 1960s (and of literary study as a quasi-science) of raising up a dynasty of disciples, and to address public issues responsibly and medical issues fairly and with a sense of their intimate connection to our cumulative history and our individual life stories. Then literature and literary theory may constitute a critique of medicine which will free its practitioners and its patients both from a mistaken understanding of its nature as a human endeavor and from the social and political forces that have alienated from medicine the traditional understanding of illness, suffering, and death as central to the human condition.

PART VI

On Applying the Humanities: A Response

CHAPTER 17

The Applicable Humanities

ROBERT L. BELKNAP

This chapter is a response to the experience of reading, listening to, and discussing the other papers in this volume. It draws on the information and considers the assumptions in the other papers, but it also tries to think in the most general terms about the position of the humanities today and about the different imaginable ways of applying the humanities. The seven basic points I outline here emerge from the collision between the practical social idealism which underlies most of these papers and an impractical individualistic perversity which I have acquired over a quarter-century of using texts in the humanities to help students at many levels of sophistication in many fields to explore the implications of positions and activities they take for granted.

THE HUMANITIES AS NOW UNDERSTOOD MAY BE APPLIED, ALTHOUGH EARLIER DEFINITIONS OF THE FIELD REJECTED APPLICATIONS

The phrase *applied humanities* provokes discussion not because our modern understanding of the field conflicts with the idea of application but because the word *humanities* drags a train of superseded meanings through its history; those early meanings influence our reactions long after they have ceased to influence our formal thinking. Two thousand years ago, when Cicero rejected an applied study, rhetoric, as the proper center of an education for public life, he advocated instead the humane values which a knowledge of the major texts would instill. Two centuries later, the more pedantic Aulus Gellius dissociated the word *humanities*

ROBERT L. BELKNAP • Department of Slavic Languages and Literatures, Columbia University, New York, New York 10027.

from even the level of practical involvement implicit in our modern words *humane* and *humanitarian* defining it simply as "study and training in the good arts," which he took to be a peculiarly human activity. Five hundred years ago, the Renaissance humanists rejected still another practical application, the highest of all in an age of faith, and for centuries, as Robert Bellah's paper phrases it, "divinity was a contrast term to humanity."

Today virtually any characterization of the humanities includes the study of rhetoric, of humane values, and of religion, but the long-superseded rejections of these applied studies still affect the ways people react to the humanities. Midwestern fundamentalists treat those of us who study the humanities as if we were still important pillars of worldly secularism and not, as Bellah shows, the last skeptical, shamefaced, perhaps doomed repository of religious and ethical thinking in a secularized academia. A scientist who had probably never read Aulus Gellius but had absorbed that early vision of the humanities once complained that he understood a literary scholar's work because he read lots of novels and enjoyed them, whereas the literary man was cut off from any appreciation of work in organic chemistry. The literary man asserted a more modern understanding of the humanities when he said, "I drink alcohol and enjoy it, whereas you have never analyzed a novel." And William Bennett, who certainly has read Cicero, attacked the idea of the applied humanities this year with the same arguments that Cicero had used in defending a very different version of the humanities against a very different applied study, rhetoric. A child resembles another child more closely than it resembles its adult self, and yet those who have loved or hated that child will react to the adult with startling inattention to the change they plainly see. The humanities in Cicero's day were closer to the natural science of that time than to the humanities today, yet those who love or hate the humanities will often react in ways appropriate to an earlier stage.

Today our definition of the humanities still rejects one great world of application, the creative and performing arts. We reject creation and performance, but not as unworthy or unimportant; in fact, they are logically prior to that study of the arts which constitutes a large part of the humanities; the arts simply have a different intellectual and social structure and in the practical world are supported by different state and national endowments. Yet, as Jerome Schneewind's paper makes clear, the central definition of the humanities in our time emerges not from old tradition, not from the structure of our intellectual world, and not even from government, but from the administrative division of our universities. In academia, the natural sciences have nature as their subject and approach it in the field or, increasingly, in clean laboratories. The social sciences take aggregated humans as their subject and approach them through questionnaires or censuses, and increasingly, through data banks in elegant computer memories. The humanities have texts made by differentiated human beings as their subject matter and approach them through libraries, museums, and other repositories, the dustier the better.

The humanities, therefore, are the study of texts, primarily in the field of philosophy, religion, music, literature, the visual arts, and the many branches of history. The boundaries of this definition need be no more sharp than those in the academic reality they describe. Mankind is a social animal, and no art or thought springs fully armed from the head of any lone creator. Insofar as we are social, social scientists can throw real light on our art and thought. Insofar as we are animals, biologists, psychologists, and physical anthropologists can do the same. Symmetrically, the study of physics may belong to the humanities because physics is man-made, although nature is not. Some universities place the history of science in the history department and others in the science departments. History itself is a social science in some universities and a part of the humanities in others, but these administrative ambiguities parallel the ambiguities in our definition. More anomalously, most universities place linguistics with the humanities and mathematics with the natural sciences, although language exists in society, and mathematics is man-made in much the same way as the arts. The anomaly emerges from the uses of these two fields. Since linguistics has served literary studies for generations, and mathematics has become the language of the sciences, the application of these fields has determined their academic home.

This paper undertakes to list the things that academics do with texts today and to sort out from that list the activities which the discussions in our seminar reveal as likely to have applications outside that world which generates our modern definition of the humanities.

THE BASIC STARTING POINTS FOR WORK IN THE HUMANITIES HAVE PRACTICAL APPLICATIONS WHICH ALREADY ENRICH THE WORK OF ACADEMIC SCHOLARS

Since the modern definition of the humanities locates them in academia, and academia relegates the mere acquaintance with texts to the realm of unprestigious pedagogy, it makes sense to list the operations which professors perform upon texts. Through history, the field has added more and more kinds of operations to that list but has rarely stopped an activity once begun.

The first sort of work includes the basic starting points for work in the humanities, which are also the starting points in the history of the field. The process begins with the collecting of man-made materials: stories, songs, dances, rituals, pictures, artifacts, arguments, and other texts. It goes on with the storage, preservation, arrangement, and restoration of these materials, the work of curators, librarians, conservators, cataloguers, archivists, and the like, and of those whose expertise rests on access to and control of such materials, papyrologists, numismatists, archival researchers, and so on. This basic kind of work with texts may offer an example of applicable humanities, but it may simply be an activity which we have always shared with fields like law and government. Fred Niklason's paper gives a clear example of the ways in which a trained historian can use his skills to serve the legal needs of Indian tribes whose lawyers lack the time and archival experience to document the positions they wish to take. Perhaps the most important lesson in Niklason's presentation is the value his research has for "pure" historians. Without such political, legal, and economic applications, much of Indian, black, immigrant, labor, business, professional, and woman's history might lie unexamined in the archives until it disintegrated. Many of our discussions considered the dangers of such departures from the ideal of disinterested research, and we kept recurring to two facts: much pure research in the humanities has a tendentiousness of which its authors may or may not be fully aware; and applied uses of our techniques operate in the presence of adversaries who make it impossible for an archivist or other specialist to ignore the evidence against his position.

Many of the basic activities of scholars in the humanities have no distinct boundary at all with the world of the applied. Many scholars establish texts, organize information, discover the biographies and bibliographies of creators and thinkers, or publish texts with information that makes them more accessible or useful. Our social system in its wisdom already regards such activities sometimes as a part of the humanities, residing in academia, and sometimes as an application of the humanities, residing in the worlds of publishing or the arts.

Connoisseurship, authentication, and attribution remain the most ambiguous activities in the humanities. The academic guarantee of belonging to a given author, painter, composer, saint, or philosopher may multiply the value of a piece of paper. In this area the humanities have long been applied for the highest and the lowest purposes. The worlds of art departments, curatorial staffs, auction houses, and art galleries were linked long before the phrase *applied humanities* existed, but in our time expertise has grown so arcane that university credentials seem to matter more than university expertise.

THE INTRINSIC, EXTRINSIC, AND IMPRESSIONISTIC CRITERIA FOR JUDGMENT IN THE HUMANITIES HAVE APPLICATIONS THAT DESERVE EXTENSIVE STUDY

A second area of activity in the humanities also involves judgment, but judgment of the importance or the value of a text, rather than its authenticity. In literary criticism, this judgment has little prestige right now; "book reviewery" is a term of abuse. Yet the judgment of texts and the protection of texts from judgment, from early times to the present, have constituted a large and diverse part of the work of the humanities. Evaluation takes three forms, intrinsic, extrinsic, and impressionistic. At the simplest level, intrinsic evaluation judges texts on such pedantic criteria as adherence to what are regarded as either natural rules or established conventions of genre, grammar, vocabulary, rhyme, scansion, anatomy, perspective, harmony in color or music, logical forms in argument, and so on. It may also involve the author's skill in practices which rest not on fixed rules but on techniques available: imagery, tropes, transitions, ordering of argument, or adherence to a particular style or cultural fashion. At a higher level, intrinsic judgment may regard the overall consistency of a text, either in the philosophical mode, "Page 11 contradicts page 6," or in the historical mode, "This literary character (or historical figure) dies in April and wins a battle the following May." These essentially intrinsic judgments claim to deal with the text as such, but of course they reflect the critic's assumptions. One generation will praise irony and ambiguity whereas another will reject them. Shakespeare's generation and our own use rhymed couplets sparingly, for special effects. Dr. Johnson's generation considered *Paradise Lost* very fine except that it was not in rhymed couplets.

In addition to these judgments which the humanities treat as belonging to the text itself, the field forms many judgments on criteria extrinsic to the text. In our generation, most of these criteria are moral, religious, political, or based on a curiously detached sense of magnitude. These criteria often work at cross purposes: "no style but great power," "It's a masterpiece of evil." The extrinsic judgment of a text will naturally vary with the moral, religious, or political position of the critic. The judgment of importance or magnitude would seem to be closer to the intrinsic evaluations, and it certainly has more staying power. This continuing importance of a certain canon of classics has many explanations. Some ascribe to a classic an intrinsic integrity of impact which comes from having all the techniques coordinated about a single goal. Others ascribe to it the possession of so many ambiguities that the criteria of every extrinsic approach seem viable. In Stalin's time, those Soviets who prospered claimed to believe that judgments about value or importance existed in the superstructure, or cultural world, and that everything in the superstructure reflected the situation in the base, or economic relation to the instruments of production. In Soviet hands, this explanation rationalizes a principled rejection of intrinsic judgment as insufficiently subject to political control, but today it is reemerging in a simpler form, reminiscent of Antonio Gramsci's theory which claims that certain texts receive the marker "great" from critics when those texts serve the needs of the class in power. Once having entered the canon of great works, they benefit from an elaborate system in the humanities for salvaging canonical texts from our better judgment.

Judgment may depend, however, not on the text itself and not on the relation between the text and the outer world, but on the impressions the text makes on the person who experiences it. At certain periods, and in the hands of certain critics, this impressionistic power is immense. At other periods, extrinsic or intrinsic criteria are more fashionable, and the reader's response often masquerades as an appeal to internal or external criteria. "What perfect craftmanship!" or "How true!" or "How new!" sometimes really mean "Gee whiz!" and tell far more about what the text actually did to a reader than about the ordering of the text in relation to the outer world or its departure from previous practice. Originality and realism may, of course, be operating criteria of the extrinsic kind, but critics who appeal to them often hedge their statements about with modifiers that take them out of the realm of cultural history and into that of personal judgment: "Never had any one spoken in *just* this voice before," or "This was the first *serious* expression of this question," or, in the realm of realism, "He had caught the *hidden* spirit of this historical moment."

Many outsiders to the humanities believe that we spend all our time on impressionistic judgments of texts, but the extrinsic and intrinsic criteria for judgment are more prevalent and more often applicable outside of the field. A skilled logician can occasionally see the flaw in a political, economic, or even a biological argument, although Ruth Macklin's chapter in this book confirms the rarity of real-life situations clear enough to admit the use of logic and difficult enough to need it. In marketing, in politics, and in much of the practical world, style and rhetoric matter rather more than logic. In these areas, the techniques of evaluation become prescriptive, and the criteria for good speeches in Homer and Sophocles may suggest ways of selling breakfast food or moving multitudes to mayhem. Evaluation may demystify and de-emotionalize the practical world: the critical examination of a commercial or an oration may protect us against its manipulations, as in the classic interchange between two girls: "Johnnie asked me to marry him!" "Doesn't he do it beautifully?" I once vented my righteous ire at a university administrator and received a telephone call the next day: "Bob, I've just read your nastygram. It's really beautifully done." This paper does not propose the application of genre designation to conflict resolution as a major example of the applied humanities, because scholarly language of many kinds replaces passion with what professors used to call "distance" and street people used to call "cool." Aeschylus's *Eumenides* illustrates this function of legal definition chopping to reduce blind rage to coherent dispute, and commissions of inquiry use the same technique when something horrible has occurred.

Evaluation, then, as practiced in the humanities, has many realized and many potential uses in other fields, as well as many applications which it long has shared with other fields. In the humanities, the tension between ostensible and real criteria for evaluation may be clearer than elsewhere. The clarity of our history shows how rules which seem like facts of nature turn out to be conventions, how political criteria pose as moral ones, or how a statement about truth or originality or artistic mastery may mask a judgment about political acceptability or a direct impression on a critic.

THE TECHNIQUES FOR PREVENTING JUDGMENT OF A TEXT HAVE A LONG HISTORY OF APPLICATION BEYOND THE HUMANITIES

The deceptive tendency of criteria for judgment makes it hard to explain the origins of a canon of classics, but it draws attention to the self-sustaining tendencies of such a canon once it exists. We use five chief techniques to save a classic or a sacred text from its internal errors or external implications: the linguistic, the allegorical, the Talmudic, the historical, and the textual. Those whose church asserts the literal truth of every word in the King James Bible and also the unqualified evilness of alcohol make Christ's turning water into wine acceptable by using a linguistic device: they simply say that in this case the word *wine* means unfermented grape juice. The allegorical salvation of a text has even greater power: the post-Pauline Christians could reconcile their distrust of sex with the magnificent erotic poetry of *The Song of Songs* by reading it as an allegory for the longing Christians feel for heaven, or the church, or the lord God. This approach demands an elaborate set of point-for-point correspondences between the plainest meaning of the text and the hidden matter that it stands for. The Talmudic way of saving a text protects it from internal contradictions and from its immoral or incorrect assertions by adding elements to the original account which make it acceptable. Lenin's theory of imperialism adds a codicil to the Marxian text which eliminates a conflict with the course of history. The historical way of saving a text is less creative but has a more modern look to it. St. Augustine, for example, accepts a rule of chastity but confronts the textual fact of David's hundreds of concubines. He reads the Bible as a document in history and accuses himself of having earlier applied the test of human minds and measured the conduct of the human race by the measure of his own customs. In his *Confessions* (as F. J. Sheed translates Book 3, Chapter 7) he says, "I failed to see that the justice obeyed by these good and holy men was all the more excellent and admirable because while it contained all its precepts in one and never varied; yet it did not order and decree all things alike, but to each age what was proper to each." Cultural relativism of this sort permits the salvation of many classics that would otherwise conflict with modern morals or mores. The final and the costliest way to save a classic or sacred text sacrifices some part of its literal infallibility for the sake of its greater integrity and authenticity as a document. When God told Noah to take the birds and clean beasts into the ark by sevens, and they went into the ark two and two, scholars in different traditions used verbal, allegorical, Talmudic, and historical techniques to salvage the holy text, but the textual scholars asserted that Genesis includes more than one early account and that the compilers' failure to edit out an anomaly as evident to them as to us proves that these proto-texts were already too sacred for tampering.

All of the techniques emerged in our Mediterranean tradition for the salvation of its great classical text, Homer, its great sacred text, the Bible, and its great intermediate text, Plato. The presumption of infallibility which mobilized the ingenuity of Hellenistic, patristic, and Talmudic scholarship has now expanded over virtually every text that certain modern critics study. It can lead to conclusions that test our credulity, but it deprives the humanities of the easy way to dismiss a problem: "It makes no sense." This presumption that nothing in a text is meaningless or purposeless operates in our field to produce the same intellectual restlessness that came from Einstein's rejection of a random universe. This search for sense in apparent aberrations has moved far beyond its position in the humanities as the defender of texts. It can lead to ingenuity in natural science, to paranoia in politics, and in general to the refusal to accept a rebuff to one's curiosity.

THE HUMANITIES USE IIMPRESSIONISM, DECONSTRUCTION, AND EXPLICATION TO MEDIATE BETWEEN TEXTS AND THOSE WHO EXPERIENCE THEM

When they are not involved with judging texts or making authentic texts available, most scholars in the humanities mediate between texts and those who experience them. At the level related to impressionistic judgments, such mediation aims to enhance the impact of the text on an ordinary person by presenting the experience of a particularly receptive one. At its worst, it used to use a breathless language to convey a message to the reader: Get in there and emote! Such highly personal criticism has returned to fashion in a form comparable to the ideal of Walter Pater, who felt a hundred years ago that the proper thing to do with a work of art was to make another work of art about it, bringing one's own imagination and one's store of associations to bear upon its material. Jacques Derrida has produced some of the more exciting of such personal mediations between art and those who experience it. His deconstructions in some sense are works of creative art and not fully a part of the humanities.

In another sense, all works of art comment on other works of art, and one of the greatest activities of the humanities is the annotation and explication of texts to let the reader see them in their linguistic, historical, and cultural context. The most fashionable form of this activity is the study of intertextuality, the examination of texts in the light of other texts that they imitate, answer, cite, allude to, or use in other ways. Critics who seriously use originality as a criterion for value sometimes charge that this mediation between the text and those who experience it interferes with the direct appreciation of the text. In many cases, however, explication contains cultural, historical, or linguistic background which is indispensible for any real encounter with the texts. More important, the inability to respond to *Oedipus* or *King Lear* most often has the same cause as much other emotional frigidity, terror before the unknown. Explication of texts provides the body of understanding which liberates a reader's normal capacity to react to a text designed to affect an audience strongly.

The impressionistic and the deconstructive effort to share one's own reaction to a text may look exportable to other fields but actually has been there right along, at least as prayers or battle cries have stirred an audience with a leader's reactions to some experience. With explication, the case is the reverse; at its best, it has that nineteenth-century positivistic spirit which treats art or thought as if it belonged to the natural world. It is a set of practices which entered the humanities in Hellenistic times, flourished in the Renaissance, but really came into its own in that third great period, the nineteenth century, with its glorious dream that the humanities might become a branch of natural science.

INTERPRETATION TODAY USES MODELS BORROWED FROM ORGANIC, SEMIOTIC, SOCIAL, AND PSYCHOLOGICAL THINKING AND SOMETIMES RETURNS THESE BORROWINGS WITH INTEREST

Beyond these realms of impressionism, deconstruction, and explication, the humanities mediate between texts and those who experience them in several ways which go by the name of interpretation, or (when we wish to be pretentious) hermeneutics. The four favorite models for interpretation come from outside the humanities, from biology, communication, sociology, and psychology.

Organic form has been a critical term for many generations now, almost always with implicit praise for the way great complexities are coordinated into a whole the integrity of which defies mechanical understanding. Organic imagery appeals particularly to those who describe how the creative process brings a work of art to life, or to those who show the birth, unfolding, maturity, senescence, and death of genres, movements, cultures, or much of history. In the humanities, we often justify the use of organic language metaphorically, saying that art or history or religion or philosophy resembles living things in their ontogeny or phylogeny. We sometimes feel that we are using another figure of speech, synecdoche, to justify such usage, saying that the humanities treat matters which are a part of life and therefore demand organic thinking. Most often, we use such imagery without realizing that it demands any justification at all. This model seems to have no application outside of the humanities, since it may well be man's oldest way of understanding inanimate things of any sort, to treat not only works of art and thought, but also storms and rivers and volcanoes as if they were alive.

A much more fashionable part of the humanities uses the semiotic model instead of the organic. Semiotic thinking emerges from the collision between two of the great intellectual achievements of recent times. The first was Saussure's nineteenth-century sense of speech as a structural arrangement of signs, or arbitrary associations between something signified, like a meaning, and some signifier, like a word or a part of a word. The second was Shannon's model for a telephone as a system that encodes a sender's message, transmits it through a channel, like a wire, and reconstitutes it at the receiver. In recent years, the semiotic model for interpretation has become far more subtle than the original outlines, studying systems of speech, gesture, and custom and exploring the differences between the code the sender uses and the code the receiver uses. This rich model for understanding the arts and thought comes from the field of linguistics and engineering, but it now offers promising ways of understanding negotiation and maneuver in the worlds of business, labor, politics, diplomacy, and every other area of intricate interaction.

The third great model used in interpretation has already entered into this discussion among the criteria for evaluation. This is the social reading of the work of art or thought. In different generations, different social interpretations have been popular. In some, the work of an individual embodies the overall social structure in which it emerged: Dante's Hell is arranged in layers because Dante's society was arranged in layers. In others, the practicalities of reception explain artistic fact: Dickens appeared with the emergence of a literate class to buy the periodical editions of his novels. In other generations the idea of membership in a group such as a family or a social class becomes more important than the culture as a whole or particular interactions: Pascal's god reflects the nature of the authority under which Pascal grew up. At present, power is the popular word, and social interpretations tend to see works of art and thought as purposeful creations augmenting the hegemony of a group in power. Some social interpretations have a rather charming simplicity in the practicality they ascribe to authors. Others elaborate wonderfully obscure connections between one's social position and one's works. The concept of social class complicates this sort of interpretation, with its fascinating problems of definition on different continents at different times, and its even more fascinating problem of discovering the mechanisms by which classes relate to the subject matter of the humanities, the work of individuals. The social interpretation of art and thought not only derives its awarenesses from the social sciences; it offers insights to the social sciences about other ways drama, novels, genre paintings and other works of art see class and social structure. The concept of the dialectic complicates social interpretation even more. If organic interpreters believe that art, history, and thought have the structure and career of a plant, and semiotic thinkers believe this subject matter has the structure and career of a language or a telephone, then Marxian thinkers believe that all thought and history and much of art have the structure and the career of an argument, in which thesis and antithesis collide to provide a synthesis. The intricacies of this process are legion, but the humanities can make one great contribution to that world of social thought from which the humanities drew the idea of the dialectic: it can remind those thinkers that the dialectic is a metaphor.

The fourth great model for interpretation today is the psychological. Here, the subject matter of the humanities has played a great part for generations. Hamlet and Oedipus lie at the heart of modern psychological thinking, and psychologists today read literary scholarship as well as literary texts for insights into psychic needs and problems. Over the past century psychological interpretations have taken three forms: interpretations of characters in the texts, interpretations of the texts as the expression of unconscious forces or configurations which the conscious minds of creators like Leonardo or Poe repress, or the interpretation of texts as forms and allusions which operate directly on the psyche of the person experiencing them. Most psychological studies within the humanities treat people not (as social interpreters often claim) as parts of a whole, but as wholes made up of parts whose identities and even intentions can be discerned. This vision of the components of a person as possessing certain of the qualities of a person has a rich past in medieval allegory and now shapes much of psycho-history and the psychological interpretation of art or thought. This vision of humanity has already been applied in somewhat tawdry ways, and with limited effect, in television programming and advertising, in politics, diplomacy, jury selection, and other areas that can draw on psychology unfiltered through the humanities. But psychology today lacks the unanimity that characterizes the harder sciences like physics and chemistry over broad areas of their domain, and those who apply its techniques to art and thought can be instrumental in discovering the subtleties and clarities that future generations will apply in nobler ways.

ALL THE FASHIONABLE MODELS FOR INTERPRETATION CAN LEAD TO HERMENEUTIC DESPAIR WHICH IS LITTLE MORE THAN A RESTATEMENT OF THE HUMAN CONDITION

These four models of interpretation lead to remarkably similar positions when driven to their extremes and applied to interpretation itself. Psychological interpretation sees a text as serving a creator's needs and repressing what a creator dares not face. But interpretations, explications, and the rest are texts, the meanings of which also demand interpretation, and so on into nihilism. The social reading also undermines other readings, including social ones, by explaining them away in the light of the interpreter's needs or purposes. In this way, the history of criticism ceases to be John Stuart Mill's gradual approach to truth about a text in the interchange of ideas. It becomes a series of statements responding more to the social needs of the interpreters than to the text itself. Such criticism is half-way back to the Nabokov hero or the pedants in the eighteenth-century plays who feel that reading texts may do no harm but that their interpretation of the text is all that really counts. Semiotics also rests on the assumption that a meaning exists before communication. Since no two human beings have exactly the same code, the meaning can never be properly reconstituted. Moreover, while a work of art does embody many elements from its creator's personal, vicarious, imaginative, cogitative, and literary experience, as an author is writing the second part or the second draft of a novel the most vivid element in his experience is the first part or the first draft. Tolstoy once announced with some surprise that his character was dying. In the same way, all works of art feed back into themselves so intricately as to preclude access to any original message. If the psychological, social, and semiotic models undermine themselves and one another, the organic model stands alone, and the end of all organic processes is death.

Since all four of the great modern models for interpretation in the humanities seem to be headed toward nihilism or despair, many scholars in the humanities disclaim the knowability of their subject matter; history becomes the study not of what happened but of what people say happened; philosophy despairs of making logical systems tight enough to avoid both contradictions and statements which can neither be proved nor be disproved; religious studies take the death of God for granted.

Many observers treat this current nihilism as the end of the humanities; I feel less apocalyptic. The limits now being set lie at the rarified fringes of our fields. Logical systems may always be flawed, but finding the flaw remains as hard as before, and moving it further toward the unknown is a noble pursuit. Our readings may always be tainted by our hangups, our class loyalties, or the inadequacies of our linguistic and other codes, but being mortal is no reason to abandon our doctors or commit suicide. Of course our biases deceive us; of course our problems and our texts extend beyond our ken. At last, the most elegantly fashionable masters of the humanities are thunderstruck by the discovery that we are human. If it did not make me sound like a New Yorker, I would say, "So what else is new?" Instead, I shall simply say that since Socrates, and probably long before, humanity has found it healthy every few generations to remind itself of its limits.

This new humility promises to be the great field for the applied humanities in the future. We can ask the scientist, the businessman, the demagogue, the demagogue's constituency, and, always, ourselves, "Are you the master or the captive of your metaphors?" As our discussions here made clear, we will rarely show poeple how to use history in their decision making, but we will constantly be challenging the analogies and the facts upon which people may be relying for their decisions. We will reassert the superiority of fiction over fact as a place to pursue the truth. We can never know for certain whether the historical Richard III was a nice man, but there can be little doubt about the blackguard in Shakespeare's play.

We have special possibilities that center in that broad part of the subject matter of the humanities which claims not to be true. In this area we can take a text and have far more of the relevant data as to whether page 11 contradicts page 6 than scientists or social scientists can have for answering serious questions about their subject matter. This ease of access to the real issues makes the humanities far less sequential than other fields. We can learn things from good undergraduates. Natural science professors can learn only from undergraduates who are geniuses. Our main function in academia may well continue to be as a repository of demonstrability to the students who come to us persuaded that anything they say sincerely is true, or worse, that only experts have the gimmick that entitles them to an opinion. A beautifully run laboratory may occasionally give undergraduates a chance to define a problem, make a formulation, design an experiment to test it, and carry out that experiment; but many third-year graduate students in the natural sciences are shocked at their first encounter with this whole sequence. The making and testing of formulations in the humanities requires no equipment but a text and an objectionable teacher.

One curious fact emerges from the nonsequential nature of the humanities as a field. Geometry evolved from that measurement of the earth's surface which its name implies into more and more abstraction, culminating in the study of relationships which cannot exist on earth at all but are really a mapping of what the human mind can conceive, a branch of psychology. Economics seems to be following the same route, from the household management which its name implies, through greater and greater abstraction, until now the matrices plot not only alternative future economic patterns and paleoeconomic trade relationships, but also economies which cannot exist on earth but are maps of the conceivable. Physics seem to be following a similar route from the physical world through greater and greater abstraction into something that traces the boundaries of the conceivable.

Biology, with the design of genes, and chemistry, with the design of molecules, may be starting down the same road. The humanities have been at all points on this road from the very start, dealing sometimes with the concrete world in sharp detail, sometimes with high abstraction in the realms of philosophy, theology, and artistic theory, and always turning toward those departures from what claims to be true which set the mind free to outline its own identity. Here all the sciences and all the social sciences can turn to the humanities to see their future and their past.

Index